HOSTILE
SKIES

HOSTILE SKIES

*A Combat History of
the American Air Service
in World War I*

JAMES J. HUDSON

SYRACUSE UNIVERSITY PRESS

First Paperback Edition 1996
98 99 00 01   6 5 4 3

Library of Congress Catalog Card Number: 68-15913
ISBN 0-8156-0061-5 (cloth)
ISBN 0-8156-0465-3 (pbk.: alk. paper)

Manufactured in the United States of America

To
Mabel Elizabeth
Karen
AND *Deborah*

James J. Hudson enlisted in the U.S. Army Air Corps during World War II, and was stationed at various bases, including North Africa and Italy while participating in the Sicilian, Naples-Foggia, and Southern France campaigns. His aerial combat experience as a fighter pilot included 191 missions of the strafing, dive-bombing, escort, interception, and convoy-patrol type in P-39, P-38, and P-47 aircraft. He received his B.A. and M.A. from the University of Arkansas and his Ph.D. in history from the University of California at Berkeley.

Over Flanders and its chill seas mist-hung,
Or over France, through hostile wind-swept skies—
They sought the fateful bullet made for them,
Their bullets destined how no man can tell . . .

from *The Conquerors*, Frederick M. Clapp

FOREWORD

IT IS NOW a half century since the young men wearing the
American uniform first flew into Europe's hostile windswept skies
to battle the enemy. During those five decades numerous books
have been published on the organization, leadership, and aircraft
procurement aspects of the American Air Service. In addition, several monographs have been written by or about various American
aces. A few authors have told the history of World War I in broad
outline while tracing the larger Air Force story from its beginning
in 1907. But the actual combat story of the men who flew the
Nieuports, the DH-4's, the Camels, the Spads, the Breguets, the
Salmsons, and the Capronis has not yet been told. I have attempted
to tell the story in some detail in the present volume.

In order to give adequate background to the history of those
young warriors who fought without parachutes and in the bitter
cold from open cockpits high over Toul, Chateau-Thierry, St.
Mihiel, the Somme, the Piave Valley, and the Meuse-Argonne, I
have found it necessary to examine the training, organization, and
problems of the infant United States air arm. This study comprises
the first four chapters. The real meat of the chronicle, however, is
the battle experiences of the boys who made up the service squadrons at the front.

Except for the story of a few volunteers, the history of actual
combat of the American Air Service covered only seven short
months. Yet, as a combat force, the Air Service came a long way
from its cautious beginning in April of 1918, when a single observation squadron equipped with obsolescent aircraft and two pursuit
outfits flying unarmed Nieuports ventured into the skies over Toul.
Their three-month's stay in the relatively quiet Toul sector proved
all too short. In the savage battles around Chateau-Thierry in July

and August, the little American force, then numbering seven squadrons, was thrown against some of the best *Jagdstaffeln* in the German Air Force. The experience was bloody, but the young Americans learned their lessons well. The Air Service built around the survivors of the Marne inferno for the autumn campaigns coming up. At St. Mihiel, American squadrons fighting alongside their French, Italian, and British Allies began to look like an effective force. Several of the twenty-six American squadrons involved were still raw and inexperienced, but the presence of the veterans of the Toul and Marne fighting gave the force stability. In the rain and mud of the Meuse-Argonne offensive the Americans proved worthy of their opponents in every way.

Had the war lasted a few more months, the Air Service, without a doubt, would have reached the awesome potential so optimistically predicted by its advocates in the spring of 1917. Although the American Air Service never had more than forty-five squadrons in combat—and that many only in the last few weeks of the conflict—it did establish a tradition of courage and persistence which was carried on into the Second World War, Korea, and Vietnam.

ACKNOWLEDGMENTS

THIS book could not have been written without the help of a great number of individuals. Grateful acknowledgment is made to the scores of World War I fliers and ground personnel who contributed letters, diaries, pictures, flight logbooks, and accounts of personal experiences. I am especially indebted to the following men: Leland Carver, Elliott White Springs (deceased), Charles R. D'Olive, General Carl A. Spaatz, General Joseph T. McNarney, Neil Goen, Leighton Brewer, Edward V. Rickenbacker, William D. Frayne, Daniel P. Morse, Fred A. Tillman, General Bradley J. Saunders, Samuel B. Eckert, Senator Spessard L. Holland, Professor W. Stull Holt, Louis Rabe, A. Raymond Brooks, Ralph I. Coryell, Thomas G. Cassady, James A. Dinwiddie, Floyd E. Evans, General Bradley Gaylord, Charles L. Heater, David W. Howe, Francis L. Irvin, Clinton Jones, W. Watson LaForce, Professor Lawrence Kinnaird, Percival G. Hart, General Ralph Royce, Frederick M. Clapp, General Clayton Bissell, Henry C. Bogle, Clarence M. Young, General Errol H. Zistel, Gilbert P. Bogert, F. K. Weyerhaeuser, Walter R. Avery, William P. Taylor, and J. J. Smith, who provided me with the names and addresses of hundreds of World War Air Service personnel. Without that list the writing of this book would have been delayed by many months.

For endless courtesies and much valuable assistance, I thank the staffs of the University of Arkansas Library, the United States Air Force Historical Division Archives, the Air University Library, the Library of Congress, the National Archives, the New York Public Library, the Air Force Museum, and the Smithsonian Institution. Especially do I wish to thank Miss Grace Upchurch, Mrs. Helen Jo Adkisson, and Joseph C. Borden, of the University of Arkansas; Miss Marguerite K. Kennedy, chief of the Archives Branch, USAF

Historical Division; John Taylor, of the National Archives; and Marvin W. McFarland, of the Library of Congress.

To my colleagues at the University of Arkansas I owe a great debt. Dr. Robert E. Reeser, chairman of the History Department, was kind enough to read the entire manuscript and make valuable suggestions. Dr. Orland Maxfield, of the Geography Department, performed the cartographic work for the book, and Dr. Walter Lee Brown, of the History Department, provided valuable aid in locating research materials. Dr. Virgil W. Adkisson, dean of the Graduate School, secured competent secretarial assistance for me and tolerated my sometimes less-than-efficient work for his office during the final stages of the project.

Mrs. Hazel Kirkpatrick typed the manuscript and made helpful suggestions about its format. Her careful proofreading caught many errors before the manuscript was forwarded to the publisher.

My greatest debt is to my wife, Mabel Elizabeth, who accompanied me on several research tours and copied many long documents with speed and accuracy. In addition, she typed the original draft of the manuscript and made significant and valuable suggestions on clarity and style. Most of all she offered constant encouragement—without that faithful support the work would never have been completed.

Finally, my thanks are extended to the United States Air Force for teaching me to fly and for having enough confidence in me to allow me to carry the American insignia into the hostile skies of World War II. I learned there to appreciate some of the thrills, terrors, and problems of air combat. Perhaps that high adventure has enabled me to come a little closer to understanding the Lukes, Rickenbackers, Kindleys, Littauers, Carvers, and Hoppers of 1918.

JAMES J. HUDSON

Fayetteville, Arkansas
Fall, 1967

CONTENTS

ILLUSTRATIONS

MAPS

TABLES

HOSTILE
SKIES

I

The Eagle Struggles to Take Wing: From Aviation Section to Air Service

SUNDAY 14 April 1918 would be a day long remembered in American Air Service history. At Gengault airdrome, a short distance from the old French town of Toul, low heavy clouds, driven by a strong southwest wind, scurried across the dreary morning sky, and a fine mist obscured the tree-lined airdrome boundary a few hundred yards away. A half-dozen tiny Nieuport single-seater fighters, each bearing the "Hat-in-the-Ring" markings of the 94th Aero Squadron, stood in front of the open mouth of a large shedlike hangar.

Inside the low stone structure which served as the 94th Squadron headquarters, three warmly dressed young pilots waited on stand-by alert. At a table in the center of the little alert room two of them, Lieutenants Alan Winslow, of Chicago, Illinois, and Douglas Campbell, of Mt. Hamilton, California, half-heartedly played casino to pass the time. The third, Lieutenant James Meissner, a tall New Yorker, sat a few feet away idly turning the pages of a book. The three were somewhat disappointed at not being chosen to fly the squadron's first official war patrol which had taken off earlier that morning. Led by Captain David McK. Peterson and consisting of Lieutenants Reed Chambers and Edward V. Rickenbacker, the patrol had broken up in the foul weather and had already returned to the field.[1]

Winslow, Campbell, and Meissner had begun their scheduled three-hour alert duty at 6:00 A.M. Because of the cloudy, misty

1

weather they did not expect anything to happen, and as the slow minutes ticked by nothing did happen. The marathon casino game continued. Then, at 8:45—just as Winslow built eights and Campbell prepared to take the build—the alert signal sounded. Balloon observers nearby reported two enemy aircraft in the vicinity at 3,000 feet. Books and cards were tossed aside, and the alert pilots sprinted across the wet sod to their waiting Nieuports. Within a matter of seconds each of the three pilots was safely buckled in his tiny cockpit and the contact signal was given. Meissner's Gnome rotary refused to start, but Campbell and Winslow took off with a roar into the heavy mist. As they cleared the trees at the edge of the airfield, the pair almost collided with two fast scout biplanes dropping down out of the low-hanging clouds. The planes carried black crosses, and it was apparent that the German pilots, lost in the miserable weather, had ducked below the clouds to find a familiar checkpoint.

The ensuing air battle was short and deadly. Both Americans opened fire immediately; Winslow's opponent sideslipped to return the fire, sending a machine gun burst through the Nieuport's wing. Winslow made a hard turn, almost brushing the treetops, and fired a long burst into the German's engine and fuselage. A moment later the enemy aircraft, a Pfalz D-3, crashed on the edge of the airdrome, marking the first air victory scored by an American-trained unit. Only seconds after Winslow's victim smashed to the ground, Campbell sent an Albatros D-5 down in flames a few hundred yards away. The whole affair had required four and one-half minutes. Nothing could have done more for the morale of the inexperienced 94th Aero Squadron than this sensational success within the sight of hundreds of officers and men at the home airdrome.[2]

Although the American Air Service was hardly out of its romper stage by April, 1918, it was, nevertheless, a far cry from the tiny and inept Aviation Section of the Signal Corps on the opening day of America's "war to end wars." On 6 April 1917 not a single air unit had been trained for warfare.[3] The two flying fields operated by the Army had only 55 trainers, of which General John J. Pershing later said, "51 were obsolete and the other 4 were obsolescent."[4] Not a single combat-type plane was owned by the United States Army, and no American then serving in the American military forces had had actual combat flying experience. One army flier asserted that not a single air officer in Washington had ever seen a fighting plane. This amazing lack of preparedness is all the more difficult to understand when considering the fact that the European war had been raging for almost three years. Certainly, many political and military leaders in the United States must have anticipated the possibility of war, yet the entire Aviation Section contained only 131 officers, mainly pilots and student pilots, and 1,087 enlisted men in April, 1917.[5] Only 26 officers were considered fully trained, bearing the rating of Junior Military Aviator.

Perhaps more incredible than the almost complete absence of any tangible air strength was the absence of plans and programs for building an air service that could fight in Europe. Indeed, there was an almost complete lack of knowledge on which to base the program to fill the skies with a "cloud of planes." In the years of American neutrality the Army had failed to send trained observers abroad to gather technical and operational information from the battle front. The U.S. aircraft industry was not prepared to make up its deficiency quickly: Because of the rapid changes in combat models and exaggerated ideas of security, the Allies had not turned to America's aircraft industry for airplanes as they had for other arms and munitions. About a dozen aircraft companies were considered capable of producing military planes, but their output was pitifully small. In the year before America entered the European war, nine factories had delivered only 64 of the 366 planes ordered by the government. Like the air officers in Washington, few, if any, of the builders had seen a modern tactical aircraft. "Fewer still knew what went into its construction other than the airframe and engine."[6]

The responsibility for the lack of realistic plans in 1917 must rest primarily on the shoulders of the military establishment, but the lack of planes and manpower can be blamed largely on the repeated failures of Congress to appropriate money for military aeronautics. Even in the field of military planning, Congress did little to make the situation easier. Efforts to provide a General Staff that could pull together and coordinate the often conflicting agencies of the War Department had been none too successful in the decade preceding America's "crusade to make the world safe for democracy." Congress was deeply suspicious of what it termed a "foreign innovation" and limited the number of General Staff officers stationed in Washington. In the spring of 1917 there were only twenty. It is not surprising that there was a lack of sensible planning and that it took the War Department many months to put its house in order. As one historian put it recently: "If the Aviation Section did not know what it needed to fight the war, neither did the Army or Navy —nor the country as a whole—have any notion of what was required."[7]

Aviation was relegated to a comparatively insignificant role in the Army's original mobilization plan. An initial Aviation Section appropriation of $10.8 million made in May and a second one for $43.4 million voted in June merely confirmed this minor role. The press and the public in general were enthusiastic about expanding the air arm, but many army generals still looked upon the airplane as a noisy toy. On 1 May Brigadier General George O. Squier, chief Signal Corps officer, recommended the addition of six aero squadrons and two balloon squadrons to the seven aero squadrons already in existence.[8] But this modest increase would have to await congressional action, and to the advocates of air power the prospect of achieving an effective air weapon was indeed dim.

Fortunately the young air officers in the national capital received a boost from across the Atlantic. Within three weeks, large and well-staffed missions from both Britain and France arrived in Washington to appeal for full participation of the United States on the battle front. Under the able leadership of England's Lord Balfour and France's former Premier Viviani and Marshal Joffre, these delegations argued, among other things, that the United States could most effectively help the struggling Allies by sending a powerful air force to the Western front in time to take part in the 1918 campaign.[9] Perhaps the clincher came on 24 May 1917, when President Wilson received a cablegram from French Premier Alexandre F. Ribot proposing a program that became the basis of army aviation expansion. Ribot asked that the United States plan to send to the front, by the spring of 1918, 4,500 airplanes, 5,000 pilots, and 50,000 mechanics with the necessary accompaniment of personnel and material to "enable the Allies to win supremacy of the air."*

As Colonel Edgar S. Gorrell, official historian of American Expeditionary Force, Air Service, wrote after the war: "From that cablegram [Ribot's] grew America's world war aeronautical program."[11] Forwarded from the White House to the Joint Army and Navy Technical Board, the French proposal received the approval of that body on 27 May. The War and Navy Departments gave their stamp of approval on the same day, and Major Benjamin D. Foulois, the senior flying officer then in Washington, was put in charge of a team to work out the details. Young Henry H. Arnold, then a major and one of the first army officers to win his wings, caught the thrill and the challenge of the hour:

We were told to prepare a Bill for Congress. Our understaffed Airplane Division in the War Department received the news with great interest. It was our first program. . . . At this time we ranked fourteenth among the nations of the world in aviation. Actually it was worse than that. Statistics aside, we had no air power at all. In the raw, the country's manpower, industrial strength, and the national know-how in general assured the building of any kind of military force we wanted—*if* there was a realistic organization of energy and material, and *if* there was time. Was there time?[12]

Foulois's group, aware of the "supreme opportunity" and working under great pressure, drafted the program in a few days. As elaborated by the officers of the Aviation Section, the program called for 22,625 airplanes, including 12,000 of the latest service models, and a training establishment equipped to graduate 6,210 pilots from primary schools.[13] In addition, approximately 45,000 aircraft engines and a large number of spare parts would have to be produced.[14]

The size of the proposed aviation program was breathtaking. Ribot was asking the newest member of the Allied team to produce more aircraft in one year than France had manufactured in three years of war. Undoubtedly, the formidable request was more than a tribute to America's industrial capacity because it was not yet known in Paris whether the American people would be prepared

* There is considerable evidence that Lt. Col. William "Billy" Mitchell, then in France as an air officer, contrived to have the French government put pressure on the United States to increase its air program.[10]

and willing to send a large expeditionary force of millions of men to the battle front. Perhaps the French, shrewdly gauging American public opinion, thought it would be easier to sell a war of machines.[15]

Any serious doubts about America's ability to implement the gigantic program in the scheduled time was submerged in a wave of public enthusiasm. Secretary of War Newton Baker approved the plan in June and submitted it to Congress with the comment that "The aircraft program seems by all means the most effective way in which to exert America's force at once in telling fashion." The bill calling for an appropriation of $64 million was passed without a roll call vote on 24 July 1917—just two months after the Ribot cablegram.[16] This was the largest sum ever appropriated by Congress for a single purpose up to that time. However, in order to secure support for unprecedented appropriations, those in charge of military aviation, civilian and military officers alike, made rash predictions. As James Lea Cate wrote in 1948: "Perhaps their claims were inspired by inexperience rather than by outright lack of candor, but they were wholly unwarranted; and when the failure of the program became a matter of common knowledge, reaction was bitter."[17]

With the appropriation fight won, the Aviation Section faced the problem of converting money into trained manpower, squadrons, planes, and equipment during the early summer of 1917. In August, aviation leaders received approval to raise 345 combat squadrons, 81 supply squadrons, 11 repair squadrons, 45 construction companies, and 26 balloon companies. Of these, 263 combat squadrons were scheduled for use in Europe by 30 June 1918. These plans may have looked good on the Aviation Section's wall charts, but it was soon discovered that no amount of money would buy time. As Dr. C. D. Walcott, of the National Advisory Committee for Aviation, put it: "Even the most generous preparations do not open up the years that have passed and enable us to carefully lay the foundations of a great industry and a great aerial army."[18] It must be remembered that there was no appreciable civil aviation activity in the United States before 1917. There were no airlines upon whose experience and facilities the country could draw to compensate for its military deficiency. America had no civil pilots; nor did it have civil airports and other aviation services—in short, none of the great reservoir of civilian aviation which in more recent wars has become the very backbone of national defense.

By December, 1917, aircraft production had lagged so far behind schedule that both civilian and military officials were forced to make more realistic proposals. After consulting with the American Expeditionary Force Commander in France early in 1918, the War Department approved a new program of 120 combat squadrons to be in operation at the front by 1 January 1919. In August of 1918, General Pershing and the War Department agreed on a final plan calling for 202 squadrons to be in the combat area by 1 July 1919. Of these squadrons, 60 would be pursuit, 49 corps observation, 52 army observation, 27 night bombardment, and 14 day bombardment. In addition to the combat squadrons, the plan provided for 133 balloon companies.[19] Although only 45 combat squadrons were at the front on 11 November 1918, it seems likely that the 202 squadron program would have been achieved had the war lasted until the middle of 1919.

The organization of military aeronautics in the United States was wholly inadequate for fighting a full-scale war. Not only was there a shortage of personnel at the command level, but there was also a confusion of organizational responsibility. In seeking the answer to this problem, several organizational changes were made in the twenty months of war. These rather profound changes "decidedly improved" army aviation and "pointed the way to future greatness."[20] The first Army Aviation Office had been set up as the Aeronautical Division of the Signal Corps in the summer of 1907, and after 1914 it had been moved to the Aviation Section of the corps. When the war came, the Aviation Section, with so small an officer corps, was unable to provide adequate direction for the expansion program or commanders for the combat units. Consequently, it turned to civilian sources for leadership, and "while many of the industrial and professional men who were recruited were able enough, few had knowledge of aviation requirements or military procedure."[21]

From the opening months of the war a ready source of technical advice was available in the National Advisory Committee for Aeronautics (NACA), and early in the conflict several joint army-navy aeronautical committees were formed. Perhaps most important of these was the Aircraft Production Board, a subsidiary of the Council of National Defense, established in May of 1917. Congress gave this organization legal status as the Aircraft Board on 1 October 1917.[22] Under the leadership of Howard E. Coffin, one of the founders of the Hudson Motor Car Company, the Aircraft Board advised the military services on quantity production and all related material problems. Although patterned somewhat after the famed Cowdray Air Board in England, this committee lacked the authority of its English prototype. Since the Board operated under the Secretaries of War and Navy, it tended to advise rather than "supervise and direct" as the law required. Nevertheless, this Board "did the basic planning of the aircraft production effort and saw it through the first year of the war."*

To further complicate the air story, the organization and training of air units was a responsibility of the chief signal officer, who did not have a controlling voice in the production of aircraft and materials. The General Staff operating within the War Department had no real experience in air matters and was busy with other and more familiar problems. As a result of the high command's neglect, the air program, in effect, "assumed a position of semidetachment from the rest of the war effort with a shaky organization and no precedents to serve as a guide."[24]

The Signal Corps, under pressure from Congress and the people to produce results, created several new divisions in the Aviation Section and made each division directly responsible to General Squier, who was already overworked. In his book *Global Mission,* published some thirty years after the war, General Henry H. Arnold caught much of the atmosphere of confusion in noting that Air Division personnel were scattered all over Washington. Indeed, the air arm could not even settle down to a single name; it was known variously as the "Aviation Section," the "Aeronautical Division," the "Airplane Division," the "Air Division," the "Air Service Division," and so on. Each of these divisions referred to "the same old 'Aviation Section of the Signal Corps,' which typical of the confusion was renamed a half dozen times, but was the same suboffice

---

* In addition to Coffin, the Aircraft Production Board consisted of Edward A. Deeds, Sidney D. Waldon, and Robert L. Montgomery, all civilians, as well as Gen. George O. Squier, chief signal officer, and Admiral D. W. Taylor, chief of the Bureau of Construction and Repair of the Navy.[23]

until we were finally pulled out of the Signal Corps as a separate 'Air Service' of the 'National Army' in May, 1918."*

Despite the confusion and chaos in Washington, many able individuals served valiantly to achieve some degree of success. In July, 1917, the aeronautical organization, then known as the Airplane Division, was headed by Lieutenant Colonel John B. Bennett and included Lieutenant Colonel Charles de Forrest Chandler, Majors Henry H. Arnold and Hiram Bingham, Captains T. DeWitt Milling, L. H. Brereton, Aubrey Lippincott, and Howard Marmon. In one of the numerous changes in nomenclature the Airplane Division became the Air Division on 1 October 1917. In the meantime, Benjamin D. Foulois, recently promoted to brigadier general, had replaced Colonel Bennett as chief. Foulois did not remain in this position long, however, for in November he joined the American Expeditionary Force overseas as its chief of Air Service, and Brigadier General Alexander L. Dade succeeded him as head of the Air Division in Washington.[26]

Personal dedication and hard work on the part of individual Aviation Section and Aircraft Board staff members was not enough to compensate for organizational confusion. By the spring of 1918, production had lagged to such a degree that the public's optimism of the previous year had given way to painful disillusionment. From this disappointment came investigations and charges that the agencies handling the aircraft production program were inefficiently organized and administered. Findings revealed some inefficiency but no graft or corruption.† Actually, America had a much better record in the production of airplanes than in the manufacture of heavy artillery and tanks, but because of the early boastful claims of the air advocates, failures in the aircraft program seemed more stunning.

The outcome of the relative failure of the air program was a "sweeping reorganization of the whole aeronautical structure of the War Department."[28] On 21 May 1918, President Wilson transferred

* Most of the Henry H. Arnold papers are now housed in the manuscript division of the Library of Congress in Washington, D.C. Letters, notes, and reports contained in this collection reflect Arnold's general disgust at the flying officers' lack of voice in air matters in the early months of the war.[25]

† Perhaps the principal investigation was conducted by a committee headed by Charles Evans Hughes in the summer of 1918. Hughes's report was placed in the hands of the Attorney General of the United States on 25 October 1918.[27]

military aeronautics from the Signal Corps, where General Squier already had his hands full with signal operations, to two new agencies under the Secretary of War: the Bureau of Aircraft Production and the Division of Military Aeronautics. The latter, under Major General William L. Kenly, just returned from a tour of duty in France as Pershing's chief of Air Service, was responsible for training and operations. The Bureau of Aircraft Production, formed from the old Equipment Division of the Signal Corps, was given complete jurisdiction and control over production of planes, engines, and aircraft equipment. Since its head, John D. Ryan, former president of Anaconda Copper Company, was also chairman of the civilian Aircraft Board, "a close and helpful connection existed between the two agencies."[29] On 29 May 1918 the two new agencies were made a part of the Air Service, but no one person was chosen to coordinate their efforts. There still was a gap between the builders and the fliers, and, as will be seen in a later chapter, sharp differences of opinion over aircraft types, engines, and equipment could and did develop. It is amazing that the government did not bridge this gap at once. President Wilson, on 27 August, some three months after the creation of the Air Service, solved this problem by appointing Ryan director of the Air Service and Second Assistant Secretary of War. The latter position gave Ryan enough prestige and authority to control and coordinate the two agencies adequately, and had the war continued until the end of 1919, the original claims on behalf of aviation might have been vindicated.[30]

NOTES

1. "History of the First Pursuit Group," History of the Air Service (American Expeditionary Forces, Series N, IV), 4. This typewritten manuscript is part of the Gorrell Histories presently housed in the National Archives, Washington, D.C. Although a hodgepodge of unit histories, combat reports, rosters, letters, cablegrams, statistical studies, pictures, and charts with little organization, this collection is one of the most valuable resources for the study of the Air Service in World War I. The collection of these items began in late 1918 and continued into 1920. Project officer in the program was Col. Edgar S. Gorrell, one of the "boy colonels" of the Air Service (he was only twenty-seven at the end of the war); consequently, the reports are commonly called the "Gorrell Histories." The author has seen the original reports, but all citations in the present work refer to the microfilm copy of the Gorrell Histories.

2. "Two Boche Planes Felled by Yankees," *Stars and Stripes,* 19 April 1918,

quoted in *Cross and Cockade Journal,* Spring, 1960, 54–55; William Mitchell, *Memoirs of World War I,* 191–92; William E. Barrett, *The First War Planes,* 110.

3. "The Men and the Machines," *Air Power Historian,* October, 1957, 192.

4. John J. Pershing, *My Experiences in the World War,* I, 17. See also Henry H. Arnold, *Global Mission,* 50.

5. Alfred Goldberg, ed., *A History of the United States Air Force, 1907–1957,* 13.

6. Wesley Frank Craven and James Lea Cate, *The Army Air Forces in World War II,* I, 7.

7. Goldberg, *History of USAF,* 13–14.

8. Sam Hager Frank, "Organizing the U.S. Air Service—Developments in the United States," *Cross and Cockade Journal,* Summer, 1965, 145.

9. Russell M. McFarland, "The Foreign Missions to the United States," unpublished manuscript in the National Archives, Washington, D.C.

10. Craven and Cate, *AAF in WW II,* I, 5. See also Edgar S. Gorrell, *The Measure of America's World War Aeronautical Effort,* 1; and "The Early Activities of the Air Service, A.E.F." (Gorrell Histories, AS AEF, 1918, A, I), 3.

11. Isaac D. Levine, *Mitchell: Pioneer of Air Power,* 98.

12. Arnold, *Global Mission,* 50–51.

13. Craven and Cate, *AAF in WW II,* I, 5.

14. Gorrell, *America's War Effort,* 1; Goldberg, *History of USAF,* 14.

15. Craven and Cate, *AAF in WW II,* I, 6.

16. *Ibid.*

17. *Ibid.,* 5.

18. Arthur W. Sweetser, *The American Air Service,* 45.

19. *United States Army in the World War, 1917–1919: Reports of Commander-in-Chief, A.E.F. Staff Sections and Services,* XV, 245. This is a collection of extracts from the reports of the various sections to the Commander-in-Chief as compiled by the Historical Division of the Department of the Army. The section entitled "Final Report of Chief of Air Service, American Expeditionary Forces" was written by Maj. Gen. Mason M. Patrick, and will henceforth be cited as Patrick, *Report to Commander-in-Chief.*

20. Goldberg, *History of USAF,* 15.

21. Craven and Cate, *AAF in WW II,* 7; "Preliminary Inventory of Records of the Army Air Forces," unpublished manuscript in Records Group No. 18, National Archives, Washington, D.C., 2.

22. "Preliminary Inventory," 2.

23. Goldberg, *History of USAF,* 15; see also Sweetser, *Air Service,* 93; Theodore M. Knappen, *Wings of War,* 23.

24. Craven and Cate, *AAF in WW II,* 8.

25. Arnold, *Global Mission,* 56–57.

26. "The Men and the Machines," *loc. cit.,* 193.

27. See U.S. Dept. of Justice, *Report of the Aircraft Inquiry.*

28. Goldberg, *History of USAF,* 15.

29. *Ibid.;* "Early History and Headquarters" (Gorrell Histories, AS AEF, A, I). See also "Preliminary Inventory," 2. Col. Henry H. Arnold was made assistant director, Military Aeronautics.

30. Goldberg, *History of USAF,* 15.

II

"Gas Driven Flying Horses":
Aircraft and Equipment

IN THE first burst of enthusiasm for air power during the late spring of 1917, General George Squier, then head of the Army Signal Corps, appealed to the American people to "put the Yankee punch in the war by building an army in the air, regiments and brigades of winged cavalry on gas driven flying horses."* Congress answered this call with a more than adequate appropriation of dollars, but it was soon discovered that dollars alone do not make an air force. The rose-colored and overly optimistic early program seemed, at least temporarily, to cloud the vision of those individuals responsible for its execution. Few realized that the twelve American companies then capable of producing military aircraft could not reach the 22,000-plane goal planned for the first year.

Not only was the infant American aircraft industry inadequate for the actual manufacture of the needed aircraft, but sufficient raw materials were often difficult to secure. For example, drastic governmental action had to be taken to insure an adequate supply of spruce—the tough, resilient wood used so extensively in the construction of World War I airplanes. In effect, the federal government took over and operated the spruce industry of Washington and Oregon. No less than 27,000 Air Service officers and men were

* Gen. Squier, one of the few army officers to earn the Ph.D. degree after graduating from West Point, was a distinguished scientist and air enthusiast. Early in World War I he served as military attaché with the British Army and returned to the United States full of enthusiasm for employing airplanes in combat. He was appointed chief signal officer on 14 February 1917.[1]

12

assigned to the Spruce Division of the Aircraft Production Board. Working in forests, mills, and railroads, "they helped the industry increase production by 2,500 per cent."*

What kind of aircraft should be produced for use on the Western front? From the very beginning it was recognized that the greatest single problem would be the production of combat aircraft fit for use in Europe. With no precise knowledge of their aviation requirements, American aviation leaders turned to their European allies for advice. To gather the vital technical information, the Army sent a large mission, headed by Major Raynal C. Bolling, to Europe in June of 1917. The Bolling Commission, specially selected by the Aircraft Production Board, was armed with broad authority from the Secretary of War to study aircraft design and production facilities in France, England, and Italy. Its principal objectives were: (1) to establish free exchange of rights to manufacture all classes of aviation material; (2) to send sample airplanes, engines, and accessories to the United States; (3) to prepare for the purchase of aircraft in Europe; (4) to prepare for the training of personnel in Europe; and (5) to assist the Air Service of the Allies by allocation of raw materials.[3]

Although only recently commissioned in the Army, Major Bolling was an excellent choice to head the European mission. In addition to having served as general counsel to the United States Steel Corporation, where he had demonstrated outstanding business and administrative ability, he had long been prominent in aviation circles. He had taken an active and significant part in the establishment of the Aero Club of America, an organization which did much to advertise and promote aviation during the last years before America's entry into the war. Bolling had also induced several affluent New Yorkers to establish, organize, and promote the Air Reserve for New York and build the air station at Mineola. This site, the home of the 1st Aero Company, served as a training base for many reservists from all over the United States in the troubled days just prior to the outbreak of the war.†

---

* The Spruce Production Squadrons were under the command of Col. (later Gen.) Bryce P. Disque.[2]

† Gen. Foulois made Bolling chairman of the Joint Army and Navy Aircraft Committee in the fall of 1917, but relieved him of the job on 19 January 1918, when Bolling recommended that the committee be abolished because it served no useful purpose. Shortly thereafter, Bolling, then a colonel, requested permission to

The mission landed in Liverpool on 26 June, and in the next thirty days it visited and studied the aviation facilities of England, Italy, and France. Despite the speed of this strenuous tour, much valuable information was gathered, and combat-type planes as well as other aviation items were collected and sent to the United States for testing and possible reproduction.[5] After the first grand fact finding tour, the Bolling Commission was divided according to new instructions and duties. Acting on General Pershing's orders, Bolling remained in Paris to take command of aviation matters in the Zone of the Interior.[6]

As a result of the mission's findings it was decided to forego, at least for the present, the development of purely American designs and the manufacture of pursuit planes, whose models changed too rapidly for standardization in factories so far removed from the battle front.* To fulfil the goals set for July, 1918, it was decided that the United States should concentrate on the building of trainers, the production of the English-designed De Havilland-4, a two-placed reconnaissance bomber, and the manufacture of the newly developed Liberty engine. Other combat types, including pursuits in large numbers, were to be purchased from the Allies.[8]

The Bolling Commission actually played one of the most important roles in the war. Not only had it selected the planes to be produced in the United States and made arrangements for the purchases abroad, but it had also made decisions, even if implicit, incidental, or unintentional, which in the long run were to influence air doctrine as well. Indeed, one historian wrote recently that "the Bolling Mission had a remarkable opportunity to shape and give direction to the doctrine of air power in the United States."[9] Unquestionably, the influence of this mission, together with the recommendations and plans of Billy Mitchell, fashioned the frame and

---

prepare himself for work at the front with one of the fighting air units; he was given a roving commission. In order to make a first-hand study of the combat situation, Col. Bolling drove from one unit to another. In March, 1918, he and his driver inadvertently approached too near the German lines at Amiens and were ambushed. Bolling was killed in the exchange of shots. The memory of Col. R. C. Bolling was honored by the establishment of Bolling Field, now called Bolling Air Force Base, in Washington, D.C.[4]

* The airplane, especially the pursuit type, is one of the most short-lived of all the implements of war. For example, during World War I, the British put twenty-seven different types of single-seater aircraft into service, the French thirty-one types, the Italians thirteen types, and the Germans twelve types, seven of which appeared on the Western front in the last six months of the war.[7]

fiber of the Air Service in the AEF. The formal report of the Bolling Commission held a middle-of-the-road course between the extreme views of the exponents of long-range bombardment—such as Mitchell and British General Hugh M. Trenchard—and the French advocates of tactical aviation. Even though Bolling and his chief assistant, Captain Edgar S. Gorrell, were impressed with the doctrine of strategic aviation, especially as propounded by the Italians Giulio Douhet and Gianni Caproni, it must be remembered that representatives of Allied armies and General Pershing's staff sat in with the mission during its deliberations. Most of the army commanders favored close tactical support. Consequently, first priority in the American production program went to training aircraft and planes for use in close support of ground armies. Bolling, however, did recommend the creation of a force of fighting planes and bombers as soon as the needs of tactical support had been met. In other words, an independent strategic air force was visualized.[10] Although this hope did not become actual fact at the time, during the last six weeks of the war General Mitchell had begun to use a small portion of his air strength strategically.

Perhaps the outstanding American contribution to the air war was the development and mass production of a truly fine high-horsepower aircraft power plant—the Liberty engine. During May of 1917 it was learned that Great Britain was manufacturing or experimenting with thirty-seven different service engines, and France with forty-six more. Air leaders in Washington concerned with the problem, such as Colonel Edward A. Deeds, a newly commissioned industrialist, discussed the possibility of copying one or more of the Allied engines. Finally, the decision was made late in May to develop an original engine. According to the plans, this engine should lend itself to rapid mass production and should have enough power to remain serviceable for at least two years. According to one story, two recently commissioned engine experts—Lieutenant Colonels E. J. Hall, of Hall-Scott Company, and J. E. Vincent, of Packard Motor Company—were locked in a suite in the Willard Hotel in Washington on 29 May, and within forty-eight hours had designed the Liberty engine. This is only partly true, as engineers from a number of motor companies and the Bureau of Standards contributed their efforts to the project. Whatever the truth may be, the speed with which the engine was conceived was breathtaking. On

4 June, only one week after the project was undertaken, the engine design was approved by the Aircraft Production Board and the Joint Army and Navy Technical Board.[11] The first Liberty engines were hurried to completion in the latter part of June, 1917, by distributing orders for parts to eleven automobile plants and foundries. The first 8-cylinder Liberty was tested by the Bureau of Standards on 4 July and the first 12-cylinder model on 25 August 1917. All features of the newly designed engine were based on well-proved aeronautical and automotive engine practices. Americans might have been behind in airframe production in 1917, but they had no superiors in the manufacture of engines. Within a short time the 12-cylinder Liberty was stepped up from 330 horsepower to 440 horsepower and was being produced by Packard, Ford, Lincoln, Nordyke & Marmon, Willys-Overland, Olds, and General Motors companies.[12]

In September, 1917, the Army contracted to buy the Liberty; the following month the Navy, after testing the engines on a flying boat, also arranged to purchase a sizeable number. Although factories had to be enlarged, personnel trained, and other difficulties solved —such as coal and alloy steel shortages, railroad tie-ups, and sabotage—production was well under way by December. When the firing stopped the following November, no less than 13,574 Liberties had been produced and American factories were turning out 150 engines per day. Furthermore, some 60,000 others were on order by the United States and the Allies, and plans were being made to put the 12-cylinder Liberty in every reconnaissance and bombing aircraft. In addition to the highly successful Liberty engine, American factories during the war built over 10,000 Curtiss OX-5 and Hall-Scott A7A engines to be used in training airplanes.[13]

It was fortunate indeed that the United States was able to produce the Liberty in such volume, for the effort to copy the engines of the other countries was a comparative failure. American factories required thirteen months to reproduce a Hispano-Suiza pursuit engine and some nine months to turn out a British Gnome rotary engine, despite the constant assistance of foreign experts. Although the Wright-Martin Company built 3,912 Hispano-Suiza engines by the end of the war, most of these were of the 150-horsepower type, already obsolete on the Western front, and none were actually delivered to the AEF. Every Hispano-Suiza used by American Air

Service combat units during the conflict was built in France. Approximately one thousand French-designed 80-horsepower Le-Rhone rotary engines were built by Union Switch and Signal Company for use in training aircraft.[14]

Unfortunately, the United States aircraft industry was unable to match the Liberty engine success story. Early in the summer of 1917 the Bolling Commission had recommended, among other things, that American industry concentrate its prime effort on the building of the British DH-4, a relatively fast and effective single-engine biplane. A service model of the plane plus the necessary engineering blueprints and plans were shipped to the United States during July, 1917.

Despite the enthusiasm and desire of Americans to get started on their ambitious program "to darken German skies with planes," the project got off to a slow start. Existing aircraft companies expanded their capacity many times over, and new companies came into the industry. But the narrow base of this expansion, the lack of centralized control, and the intricacies of the technical problems involved in putting new and foreign airplane designs into production sapped the wholehearted effort of most companies.

It was obvious to realistic men that there would be a lag, perhaps a long lag, between the beginning of construction of the DH-4 in America and its arrival in Europe. Allied experience had shown that after completion of design, construction, and complete testing of a type of aircraft, it took about ten months to get quantity production started. As Colonel Gorrell summed it up years later: "Because of our intervening ocean we had to add another three months for shipment, a total of 13 months." On 18 October 1917 the De Havilland was ordered into production in the United States, and the first DH-4 equipped with a Liberty engine was shipped from Hoboken on 15 March 1918. It made its maiden flight over France on 17 May, and by July the American-built reconnaissance bomber began to arrive in France in quantity. On 2 August 1918 the 135th Aero Squadron went into combat operations on the Western front equipped with DH-4's. Over 1,200 of these planes had been turned over to the American Expeditionary Force by the time of the Armistice.[15] Yet the American public, whose hopes were based on reports more enthusiastic than accurate, expected more.

There was not only criticism of the speed of the DH-4 production program but also a growing doubt concerning the quality of the plane itself. Although the first DH-4 produced in the United States had been flown in November, 1917, until late spring of 1918 it had not been officially tested for performance. Colonel Arnold later wrote, "No pilot who would be required to fly the plane in France had been allowed to fly it. The Division of Military Aeronautics which was required to train pilots to use this plane had not only not been furnished any for use, but had not been allowed to use one in a test flight." Thus, and understandably, "there was considerable dissatisfaction and lack of confidence in the ability of the DH-4 to equal the performance of Allied and enemy aircraft." After much agitation on the part of the flying officers in Washington, a board was finally appointed to meet in Dayton, Ohio, during the week of 24 April–2 May 1918 for purposes of testing a plane already being sent overseas as an operational aircraft.

The ensuing test of the Liberty-powered DH-4 was a long chain of disasters which did much to confirm the "lack of confidence" felt by many pilots in the plane. Arnold, then assistant director of Military Aeronautics, described the woes of the testing team in the following words:

On April 24th a full throttle test for endurance was made but due to the auxiliary gravity tank failing to function, the plane was forced down after one hour and fifty-two minutes in the air. During this test the radiator shutters broke due to vibration; shock absorber rubbers on the landing gear were stretched too tight, were not large enough, and had to be changed. The radiator shutters would not remain open in the air. The main gasoline tank was leaking badly. On April 25th a half throttle test was made. It was found necessary to descend at the end of the two hours due to the fact that five spark plugs had been broken.[16]

Difficulties with the aircraft and its engine continued through the next several days. On 2 May the test plane went into a spin from 300 feet and killed Lieutenant Colonel Henry J. Damm and Major Oscar Brindley. Since Brindley, who was flying the plane at the time of the accident, had had over 2,000 hours of flying experience and was considered one of the most skilled pilots in America, most observers were convinced that the crash was a result of the failure of the aircraft. The tests were completed later in the month by other test pilots. Fortunately, most of the bugs in the aircraft were worked out by the time of its assignment to a combat squadron in August of 1918.[17]

Although there was some difference of opinion on the performance of the American De Havilland, most combat fliers believed that it was poorly suited for observation and even less desirable for bombardment. Incendiary bullets were particularly effective against this type of airplane, according to one AEF flying officer, who was later a major general in World War II, because the gasoline, under pressure, was carried in a tank without a protective covering. The blind angles, areas in which the enemy could approach without coming within range of the guns, were very wide.[18] Many would have preferred the French Salmson or Breguet, but the American air industry was committed to the large-scale production of the DH-4. By the end of the war 3,431 of these planes had been delivered to the American Army.[19]

The DH-4 was not the only combat type of aircraft produced in the United States during the war. As early as August of 1917 the possibility of building a night bomber was discussed. Several types were considered, and two were finally accepted for production— the English Handley-Page and the Italian Caproni. The big Handley-Page was chosen because it was easy to obtain blueprints and drawings for it, and the instructions were in English; the Caproni was selected because it was considered superior in performance. Captain Gabriele D'Annunzio, the famous Italian soldier-sailor-poet-aviator, and a team of fourteen men arrived during the fall of 1917 to start guiding the production of the Caproni triplane with three Liberty engines. Difficulties with the Italian language and the fact that American engineers could not read the Italian blueprints caused postponements, however. Consequently, only one Caproni was built in the United States prior to the Armistice.[20]

Although general drawings of the Handley-Page were available in August of 1917, the detailed blueprints did not arrive for several months. Since the English machine was too large to ship intact, it was decided to fabricate the small parts and sub-assemblies in American factories and ship them to England for final assembly.

Late that fall the so-called Handley-Page Agreement was signed by Air Minister Rothermere, of Great Britain, and General Benjamin Foulois, of the United States. This rather prophetic document called for "the shipment to England of the parts for 300 Handley-Page airplanes, during the months of May, June, and July 1918, and thereafter 40 sets of parts to be sent each week." In addition, the agreement stated that thirty American Handley-Page squadrons should be ready for operation by 1 September 1918. Three thousand carpenters, bricklayers, and general laborers were to be dispatched to England at the earliest possible moment to prepare the fields. Further, a revolving pool of 15,000 American mechanics would be kept training in Great Britain at all times. This balanced plan required a highly integrated kind of teamwork which was not possible at the time, and parts for only 101 Handley-Page bombers were shipped. None were assembled before the end of the war.[21]

In addition to their efforts with the DH-4, the Handley-Page, and the Caproni, American aircraft companies built a few British SE-5 pursuits and Le Pere and DH-9 reconnaissance planes. One DH-9 and two Le Pere experimental aircraft had been delivered to the AEF when the Meuse-Argonne drive was halted in November, 1918. The Le Pere, a plywood machine designed by a French aeronautical engineer around the Liberty engine, had a speed of 136 mph, and was potentially a much better plane than the DH-4 or the more up-to-date DH-9.[22] The Bolling Commission had originally recommended that the United States build French Spads and British Bristol pursuits. The Curtiss Company contracted to build the Spad, but a later cablegram from Bolling advised that the pursuit production be left to the Allies, and the project was dropped. Neither of these planes was actually built in America. In the fall of 1918 the American airplane builder Glenn Martin had his Martin twin-engine bomber ready to go into production. This machine was considered superior to both the Handley-Page and the Caproni, but the war ended too soon to get it into combat.

Perhaps the greatest American success in airplane production came in the manufacture of training planes. As a result of the early Bolling recommendations, American authorities had lunged full speed into this area of production. In the early months of the war most available resources were concentrated on the construction of primary trainers, beginning the three-stage pilot training program adopted in May, 1917.[23] Some early difficulty was encountered when it was discovered that production orders could not be widely distributed because of a squabble over patent rights held by the

Wright and Curtiss companies. This problem was quickly solved, however, by the creation of the Aircraft Manufacturers Association, which took over the patents on a $200 per plane royalty basis.[24]

After some investigation and study, the Curtiss JN4-D, powered by a 90-horsepower Curtiss OX-5 engine, was approved as the standard primary trainer for all flying schools. In May, 1917, the Aircraft Production Board recommended the construction of 1,500 of these planes—popularly called "Jennies."[25] As early delivery of the Jenny proved to be slow, the Standard Aero J-1 primary trainer, equipped with a Hall-Scott A7A engine, was also approved, even though it was considered decidedly inferior.[26] Some 1,600 of these Standard Aero J-1's were produced before the JN4 production caught up with the demand for primary trainers in June of 1918. At that time the J-1 was withdrawn from service. A total of 5,280 Jennies were ordered by the Army, and 3,746 were completed before the Armistice.[27]

Advanced trainers, in considerable demand at flying schools in the United States after July, 1917, were not in production during the first several months of the war. This delay caused a serious breakdown in the advanced training program and forced the sending of many cadets overseas before the French schools were equipped to train them. As a substitute for specially designed advanced trainers, the Curtiss JN was equipped with 150-h.p. Hispano-Suiza engine, available machine guns, photographic, radio, and bombing equipment; it was put into service during 1918 as the JN4-H and JN6-H. More realistic advanced training airplanes, planned in 1917 but not delivered until 1918, were the Thomas-Morse S4-B and S4-C, equipped with Gnome and LeRhone engines, and the DH-4, powered by the Liberty 8-cylinder engine.[28]

In addition to planes manufactured in the United States, the Air Service obtained several thousand machines from the Allies. Early studies made by the Bolling mission indicated that, no matter how optimistic the promises of production, no completed aviation equipment made in America could be shipped to the battle front in time for the campaign in the spring of 1918. Consequently, Bolling recommended substantial purchases of equipment in France. A contract with the French, known as the Agreement of August 30, 1917, was prepared and signed by the French Air Ministry and the Commander-in-Chief, AEF—General John J. Pershing. Under this contract the French promised to deliver 875 training planes and 5,000 service-type aircraft to American forces in France by 1 June 1918.* They also agreed to provide an additional 8,500 aircraft engines. For its part the United States was to furnish, by 1 November 1917, certain specific tools and raw materials needed for the fulfilment of the French obligation. Because of a shortage of shipping space, the United States only partially fulfilled her side of the agreement. France, too, found it difficult to meet her own aviation needs and supply the American requirements. Less than one-quarter had been delivered to the AEF by June, 1918, and only 4,791 had been turned over to the Americans by the end of the war.[29]

An agreement was also made with the Italian government during the summer of 1917. Under this proposal the United States would buy 500 S.I.A.-7B's and from 250 to 300 Capronis with the appropriate engines.[30] Only 19 Italian-built aircraft were ever delivered. In addition to the French and Italian purchases, the United States bought planes from England; approximately 260 British-built planes, mostly Sopwith Camels and SE-5 pursuit types, had been delivered to the AEF by the time of the Armistice.†

In spite of the failure to approach the originally planned figure, American industry produced 11,760 planes of all types. Of these, 3,500 were service aircraft, mainly DH-4's. Although only 1,200 American-built combat aircraft actually reached France by 11 November, they were then being constructed at the rate of 13,500 per year.[32] Six more months of war might have seen the "regiments and brigades of winged cavalry mounted on gas driven horses" in sufficient numbers to have driven the Germans from the sky, as promised in June, 1917.

* The service aircraft included 1,500 Breguets, 1,500 Nieuports, and 2,000 Spads. Most of the trainers were the 23-meter, 18-meter, and 15-meter Nieuports.

† The 17th and 148th Aero Squadrons, attached to the British until late October, 1918, were equipped with Sopwith Camels as was the 185th Squadron (night pursuit) stationed in the St. Mihiel area. The 25th Squadron was equipped with SE-5's.[31]

NOTES

1. Quoted in Goldberg, *History of USAF*, 14.
2. *Ibid.*, 15; Arnold, *Global Mission*, 63.
3. Patrick, *Report to Commander-in-Chief*, 23. See also Harford W. H. Powel,

"Brief History of Army Air Forces," unpublished manuscript in USAF Historical Division Archives, Maxwell AFB, Montgomery, Ala., 63.

4. "The Men and the Machines," *Air Power Historian,* October, 1957, 197. See also Gorrell, *America's War Effort,* 3.

5. A large number of cablegrams from Maj. Bolling to Washington concerning recommendations of the Commission can be found in "Cables Exchanged with USA" (Gorrell Histories, AS AEF, A, XXI). See also Gorrell, *America's War Effort,* 4; and same author, "Brief History of the Air Service, AEF" (A, I), 20–68.

6. "Report of Aeronautical Commission, 15 August 1917," reproduced in *Air Power Historian,* October, 1960, 223–32.

7. See Gorrell, *America's War Effort,* 5–6.

8. Sweetser, *Air Service,* 190.

9. I. B. Holley, Jr., *Ideas and Weapons,* 57–58.

10. *Ibid.,* 58; "Report of Aeronautical Commission, 15 August 1917," *loc. cit.,* 225–26.

11. Arnold, *Global Mission,* 62; Knappen, *Wings of War,* 63–75.

12. Knappen, *ibid.,* 85–131; Powel, "Brief History of AAF," 62.

13. Gorrell, *America's War Effort,* 69–71; Clayton L. Bissell, *Brief History of the Air Corps and Its Late Development,* 28–29.

14. Gorrell, *ibid.,* 69–72.

15. *Ibid.,* 2, 35.

16. Henry H. Arnold, "History of the Aviation Section (Signal Corps) and Division of Military Aeronautics, from April 1917 to October 1918," unpublished manuscript in Arnold Papers, Manuscript Division, Library of Congress, Washington, D.C., 115–17.

17. *Ibid.*

18. Bissell, *Brief History,* 61. See also Lt. John G. Winant, "Report on the DH-4" (Gorrell Histories, AS AEF, E, I).

19. Gorrell, *America's War Effort,* 34.

20. Arnold, *Global Mission,* 69–70.

21. *Ibid.*

22. *Ibid.*

23. G. W. Mixter and H. H. Emmons, *United States Army Aircraft Production Facts,* 45.

24. Bissell, *Brief History,* 29; "The Cross License Agreement," Bureau of Aircraft Production File, Box 11, National Archives, Washington, D.C.

25. Mixter and Emmons, *Production Facts,* 12, 42.

26. Bissell, *Brief History,* 29.

27. Powel, "Brief History of AAF," 60.

28. *Ibid.*

29. Gorrell, *America's War Effort,* 35.

30. "Report of the Aeronautical Commission, 15 August 1917," *loc. cit.,* 232.

31. Gorrell, *America's War Effort,* 35.

32. Sweetser, *Air Service,* 247–48.

III

Putting Wings on Men:
Training for the Air War

A STURDY JN-4 training plane settled gently to the ground and rolled to a stop in the middle of the big grass-covered landing field. Then, while the 90-horsepower OX-5 engine continued to idle, a tall, blond Canadian instructor pilot unbuckled his safety belt, calmly climbed out of the front cockpit, and, taking his seat cushion with him, announced casually to the cadet in the back seat: "You are ready to take it up alone, mister."* With scarcely a backward glance the veteran pilot strolled toward a small group of men standing in front of a nearby hangar.

The perspiring cadet, William P. Taylor, a twenty-three-year-old Plainfield, New Jersey, youth, reflected briefly on his three and a half hours of flying experience as he waited for his instructor to move away from the biplane. Most of those 210 minutes had been spent in learning the feel of the rudder, elevator, and aileron controls and in making a score or more takeoffs and landings—some good, many bad. Now was the moment of truth! Yet if he had any misgivings, they were pushed away by the instructor's casual wave. After all, the instructor, whom he idolized, was a veteran RAF combat pilot† just back from the fighting in Europe, and he should

---

* Letter from William P. Taylor to author, 29 July 1964. This item contains a wealth of excellent material on early pilot training in both America and England.

† Some of the early cadets took their primary flight training in Canada or at RAF-operated fields in Texas. In these schools many of the instructors were combat veterans back from the fighting front. One was Vernon Castle, the famous dancer, who had shot down two Huns before being assigned to instruct in America. Early in 1918 Castle was killed in a mid-air collision with a cadet at Taliaferro Field in Texas. Castle was Taylor's flight commander but not his instructor.

know when his cadet was ready to take wing. Taylor felt no special fear, only a nervous excitement as he taxied to the end of the field and turned the nose of the little Jenny into the wind. A final scrutiny of the cockpit indicated that all was in order. Remembering the advice hammered into him so often by his instructor, the cadet carefully looked to both sides and the rear to see that no other aircraft was in the area. With this routine out of the way, Taylor then adjusted his goggles and slowly advanced the throttle. Almost immediately he realized he had not accounted for the change in the Jenny's flight behavior caused by the removal of the 185-pound instructor from the front seat. The little machine bounced two or three times and practically leaped into the air. Before he could adjust to the new flight attitude, the hangars and other buildings along the flight line had dropped away to the rear. Shortly after passing over the boundary of the field, the fledgling was in sufficient control to attempt a gentle turn to the left—a maneuver achieved with only a slight skid. A minute later a second left turn was executed, and Taylor started the downwind leg parallel to the landing field. For the first time since the takeoff he had time to congratulate himself on getting the plane into the air in a creditable manner. His elation, however, faded somewhat as his thoughts turned to landing the "spirited bit of canvas and metal." A short distance beyond the upwind boundary of the field Taylor banked left into the base leg of his first solo landing approach. A final turn into the wind was accomplished in a reasonably smooth fashion, and the cadet retarded the throttle to lose altitude for the landing.[1]

It was at this stage in his solo flight that Bill Taylor's troubles really began. "It seemed," he wrote later, "that the plane would never come down as it had when I made such nice landings with the instructor on board. I finally decided that I couldn't keep on across even a big airdrome at a height of fifteen feet, so I nosed it over and I hit the ground and bounced back up to my original worrisome fifteen feet. By that time the big landing space was coming to an end and I gave it the gun and around I went thinking it over."[2]

In front of the hangar, instructors, mechanics, and cadets alike groaned and shouted encouragement to the unhearing novice. Minor crashes had been commonplace during the past several days at Benbrook Field, and all eyes followed young Taylor in his second circuit around the airdrome. This time, however, the young New Jersey man gave himself plenty of room and set the Jenny down smoothly in the first few hundred feet of the grassy field. Moments later he taxied the trainer up to the big hangar and proudly accepted the congratulations of the onlookers. He had taken the first step which would lead him to the skies over France as a pursuit pilot. Taylor's solo experience was typical of the hundreds of cadets who went through primary flight training in the United States during the latter half of 1917 and the first half of 1918.*

Although planes and equipment were difficult to obtain during the opening months of America's war, men were not only available but willing. Stories of the air war in Europe and its "knights of the blue" such as George Guynemer, René Fonck, Baron Manfred von Richthofen, Oswald Boelcke, Albert Ball, Mick Mannock, James McCudden, and Billy Bishop had fired the imagination of American youth. By the summer of 1918 at least 38,000 of America's finest young men had volunteered for flight training in the Army. Hundreds more were to cast their lot with the naval aviation program.

Despite the large reservoir of manpower available, the Air Service had serious training problems. Not only were there few training aircraft, but in April of 1917 there were only three pilot training schools in the country.† Furthermore, on the day the United States declared war, the Army had only 65 flying officers, many of whom held administrative positions and were unavailable for any kind of training program. Of the small crop of pilots, a few had seen active service with Pershing's punitive expedition in Mexico, and the rest were either recent graduates of the flying school at San Diego or were still under instruction. None of them had ever flown a modern service-type aircraft, and the majority had trained on a system of controls differing sharply from those then in use on the war front. No observers or bombardiers had been trained.[4] Transforming the

---

* Taylor served with the crack 148th Aero Squadron on the British front during September and October, 1918. In November he moved with the squadron to the Toul area of the American sector. The 148th Aero flew Clerget-powered Sopwith Camels while on the British front.

† Of these, Hazelhurst and Rockwell Fields were in operation as primary flying schools for the Regular Army. Essington Field, Pa., was established to train national guard units.[3]

eager thousands of youths into pilots, observers, bombardiers, and ground crews was indeed a staggering task.

It was evident from the beginning that most of the enormous training program would have to be carried out in the United States. With its tiny force of 1,200 officers and enlisted men and its three flying fields—at San Diego, California; Mineola, Long Island; and Essington, Pennsylvania—the Army's air arm began an ambitious expansion program in April, 1917. In the next nineteen months the Air Service was to increase 150-fold.[5]

It was decided early that training would be standardized; the old highly personalized prewar methods would not serve to train rapidly the thousands of pilots needed. Plans called for a three-phase program—ground, primary, and advanced.*

To coordinate the air training program, Dr. Hiram Bingham, a Yale University history professor, was commissioned a major in the Signal Corps and placed in charge of all United States Schools of Aeronautics. Because of his varied background the forty-two-year-old Bingham was eminently qualified for the post. After winning his Ph.D. degree from Harvard University in 1905, he had taught at Princeton, Johns Hopkins, and Yale and had written several books. The son of a prominent missionary, he had traveled widely and explored many of the remote areas of the world. His exploration of the little-known Simon Bolivar route across Venezuela and Colombia in 1906–1907 won him national attention, and he quickly became one of the most popular lecturers in the country. With war clouds threatening, Bingham had joined the Connecticut National Guard as a captain in 1916. Anticipating the coming importance of aviation, the dynamic young professor learned to fly in the early months of 1917; thus, by the time America was thrust into the inferno, Bingham was capable of accepting the burden placed on his shoulders.[6]

It was believed that the quickest and best method of handling the ground-school phase of the air training program was to work through the nation's colleges and universities. By the end of May, Major Bingham had established ground schools for cadets at six leading educational institutions—at the universities of California,

* Shortly after the war opened, the team of Col. John B. Bennett, Maj. Benjamin D. Foulois, and a small staff traveled to Canada to study the Canadian training program. The American plan was based on their report.

Texas, Illinois, at Ohio State and Cornell Universities, and at the Massachusetts Institute of Technology. Until the end of the program, a few weeks after the Armistice, these six schools plus two others—Princeton and Georgia Tech—received 22,689 cadets and graduated 17,540. The civilian schools had met the challenge.[7]

Upon acceptance into the service, the prospective pilot became a flying cadet. He held that status throughout his course of training until he passed his Reserve Military Aviator (RMA) test and received his commission. He was enlisted, technically, in the Signal Enlisted Reserve Corps at a salary of $30 per month with quarters, uniform, and food allowance of 60 cents daily provided by the government. At any time, of course, the cadet was subject to discharge if it became "obvious that he [was] mentally or morally unqualified to become an aviator."[8]

During the eight- to twelve-week assignment to ground school the cadet was subjected to a strenuous program. He received basic instruction in the principles and theory of flight, radio, codes, and photography, in the operation and maintenance of aircraft engines and machine guns, and in the care of the airframe itself. Here he also learned the theories of cooperation among the Air Service, the infantry, and the artillery. In addition, he was given primary instruction in meteorology and astronomy; he devoted considerable time to learning discipline, military law, and some idea of officer behavior. He also participated in drill and calisthenics. From reveille at 5:30 A.M. until taps at 9:30 P.M. the cadet was busy.[9]

Because most of the necessary flying fields had yet to be built, the Army's primary flight training program was unable to keep pace with the ground-school expansion. As it would take weeks, perhaps even months, to select sites* and construct adequate training bases in the United States, Canada agreed to provide flying facilities during the summer months of 1917. In return, Canada would be given the use of American fields in the south during the winter. Because of this arrangement several hundred American cadets were able to start their training before air fields at home were completed. Meanwhile the construction program went ahead

---

* An airfield selection board, headed by Maj. Henry H. Arnold, was appointed on 5 August 1917, and within one month sites for most of the airfields to be constructed during the war had been chosen.[10]

at a furious pace, and by Christmas some fifteen United States training bases were in use, including several that were to become landmarks in the history of the air arm. Among the more famous fields opened during the war were Kelly Field and Brooks Field at San Antonio; Taliaferro Field near Fort Worth; Love Field, Dallas; Call Field, Wichita Falls; Rich Field, Waco; and Ellington Field, Houston, all in Texas; Scott Field, Belleville, Illinois; Chanute Field, Rantoul, Illinois; Selfridge Field, Mt. Clemens, Michigan; Wilbur Wright Field, Dayton, Ohio; Langley Field, Virginia; March Field, Riverside, California; Mather Field, Sacramento, California; and Post Field, Fort Sill, Oklahoma. Wisely, the Army built most of the fields in the southern or southwestern states where flying conditions were good throughout the year. At the close of the war there were twenty-seven flying fields in the United States plus another sixteen in Europe.*

During his six- to eight-week stay at a primary flight school the cadet received some 40 to 50 hours of flying training, usually in Curtiss JN-4's.† At the end of that time the cadet was given the Reserve Military Aviator's test, and if successful he was awarded his RMA wings. The typical RMA test consisted of the following:

(1) Climb out of a field 2,000 feet square and attain 500 feet altitude, keeping all parts of the machine inside the square during climb.

(2) Glides at normal angle, with motor throttled. Spirals to right and left. Change of direction in gliding.

(3) At 1,000 feet cut off motor and land within 200 feet of a previously designated point.

(4) Land over an assumed obstacle 10 feet high and come to a rest within 1,500 feet of the same.

(5) Cross-country triangular flight of 30 miles, passing over two previously designated points. Minimum altitude 2,500 feet.

---

* Although most of the airfield sites had an obvious advantage from the point of view of weather, the aero construction squadrons charged with the task of actually building the airfield frequently found other difficulties. One such squadron reporting for duty at Eberts Field, Lonoke, Ark., in February, 1918, found "a partly constructed camp built in what was later discovered to be a rice field. At Morrison, Virginia (the squadron's previous location), it was thought all the mud in the world had been collected but at Lonoke we decided that they didn't have any at Morrison except the little that was left after filling Arkansas."[11]

† Due to an acute shortage of these aircraft in the early months of the war, some Standard Aero J-1's were used.[12]

(6) Straight-away cross-country flight of 30 miles. Landing to be made at a designated destination. Both outward and return flights at minimum altitude of 2,500 feet.

(7) Fly for 45 minutes at an altitude of 4,000 feet.[13]

On receiving his wings, the cadet was commissioned a lieutenant and awarded an extra 25 per cent wage as flight pay. Of the approximately 15,000 cadets who entered primary flying schools in the United States, 8,688 received their RMA ratings. About 2,000 others were trained at overseas schools, making a total of more than 10,000 pilots trained during the war.[14]

Even before the Bolling mission returned from its tour of the European Allies in the early summer of 1917, it was generally realized that most of the advanced flying would have to be carried out in France, England, and Italy. Since there were no planes in the United States suitable for advanced training and "no pilots qualified to give advanced instruction,"[15] the necessity of schools and training centers in Europe for advanced and specialized flying was obvious. Therefore, arrangements were made in June, 1917, for the construction of a large American school about seven miles from the city of Issoudun in central France. Since a railway to the site had to be built and the arrival of the material was delayed, construction was not actually started until 18 August 1917.

Meanwhile, it had become apparent that a sufficient number of pilots with preliminary training could not be expected from the United States in time to meet the program then being contemplated. For that reason the government had to call upon Allied schools in Europe for help in primary as well as advanced training until American facilities were ready. After discussing the matter with the Allies, General Pershing requested that 100 cadets per month be sent to Europe beginning on 1 July. Several eligible Americans already in France, serving mainly with the Ambulance Corps, quickly took advantage of the opportunity and enlisted for flight training. Cadets from the United States, however, did not arrive in any sizable number until October, November, and December, and by that time the weather was unfavorable for training. The loss of favorable flying weather, the increase in the Allied Air Service's programs, making it necessary for them to utilize their schools to capacity, and the precarious situation at Caporetto on the Italian front combined to defeat, in large measure, the plan for early preliminary training. Consequently, most of the cadets then in France were thrown back on American schools for this elementary training. In the fall of 1917 the only American school where primary flying could be taught was the base at Tours,* which had been taken over from the French on 1 November. This school, soon to be known as the 2nd Aviation Instruction Center, could handle only a fraction of the American cadets then arriving in considerable numbers.[16] Most of these cadets were honor graduates of American ground schools and had been sent abroad as a "reward for good work and high qualities." When they could not be placed in a primary flying school they were sent to Issoudun, where the advanced flying school was being built, to wait their turn. Since Issoudun was not equipped with the type of machine being used in primary flight training, they were called upon to perform construction duties and a variety of other menial tasks. There were approximately 1,000 cadets so occupied in January, 1918, and they became known as the "Million Dollar Guard" since they each were paid $100 per month. At the rate at which the training was then proceeding it would have required at least ten months to place them all in primary flying schools.[17] At times there was near mutiny.[18] In the words of General Mason M. Patrick, chief of Air Service, AEF: "Only the high caliber of the men themselves prevented a complete loss of morale under these conditions."[19] Most of the cadets were eventually moved to the Air Service Concentration Camp, at St. Maixent, from which they were funneled into schools as vacancies occurred.

As cadets in the "Million Dollar Guard" slaved in the mud of Issoudun and St. Maixent awaiting their chance to climb into the cockpit, their morale received still another blow. Cadets who had remained in the States were now arriving as officers, having received their commissions upon completion of preliminary training there. In many cases these newly commissioned officers had entered the service months after those awaiting training in France. In order to correct this injustice, the War Department, on the advice of the AEF, decided to commission all cadets in Europe with the rank

* This school was originally intended for observation training, but the necessity of giving preliminary instruction to cadets required that it be devoted to that use. The school was poorly equipped and had a capacity of not more than 100 students per month.

they would have held had they been commissioned at the time of their graduation from ground school. Should any cadet not successfully complete his flying training in Europe, his commission would lapse, and he would be returned to enlisted status. The plan went into effect in February and March of 1918.[20]

Even though hard pressed to keep abreast of their own training needs, the French provided much valuable assistance to the Americans. Many of the instructors in both the preliminary and advanced phases of the American program, especially in the early months, were veteran French fliers just back from combat tours at the front. These men were to have a profound influence on the pilot-training methods used by the American Air Service in France. The French system was based on a "gradual absorption of the knowledge of the art of flying by the pupil by his being transferred from one machine to another until he finally reached the best of its particular type."[21] This meant that the cadet was started out on Penguins (or rouleurs) —planes with clipped wings. These machines, of course, could not fly but did give the beginner practice at taxiing in a straight line and the opportunity to accustom himself to controlling a two-piece throttle. From the Penguin the cadet usually passed on to the large-winged biplace, the 23-meter Nieuport. After soloing in the 23-meter Nieuport, the student was sent to another field where he practiced in the 18-meter Nieuport, a single-place biplane that was somewhat faster and more difficult to fly. Finally the cadet moved to yet another field for training on the 15-meter Nieuport—a still smaller winged, faster, single-seater, which had been used for pursuit work earlier in the war.[22] Although it usually required a long period of time to turn out a finished pilot by this method of gradual progression, the French were convinced that the number of lives saved more than compensated for the loss of time. Perhaps this method was wise, for in the words of Charles R. D'Olive, who later became an ace with an American squadron, handling the rotary engine Nieuport was like "trying to fly a gyroscope."[23]

In addition to serving as instructors in American flight schools, the French accepted a few Americans into their own schools as allowed by the exigencies of their training program. These men usually received 25 to 30 hours in Farmen or Caudron planes before moving on to advanced-instruction programs. In all, 444 U.S. students were graduated from primary flying in French schools.[24]

The troubles of preliminary flying training dealt with by the American Air Service in France during the fall of 1917 were duplicated to a lesser degree in Great Britain. The first group of fifty-three American cadets arrived at the British School of Military Aeronautics in Oxford early in September,[25] and by 1 October most of the more than 200 cadets to be immortalized later as the "war birds" had arrived in England to begin primary flight training. Due to the gifted pen of one of them, Elliott White Springs, of Lancaster, South Carolina, and a Princeton graduate, this detachment became one of the best-known groups of the war. His stories such as *Nocturne Militaire, Leave Me with a Smile, War Birds and Lady Birds,* and *Above the Bright Blue Sky,* along with John MacGavock Grider's *War Birds: Diary of an Unknown Aviator,* were to thrill air enthusiasts in the decades between the two world wars.[26]

Ground-school training for the war birds began soon after their arrival in England, but because of a shortage of planes and facilities most did not actually start their flight training until late fall.[27] For example, Field Kindley, who soon became one of the top U.S. aces in the war, did not start his flight training in the "Rumpty," the famous Farman primary trainer, until 16 November 1917. Nevertheless, training in England went forward at a fast clip once started.* Unlike the cautious Penguin methods of the French, the English concentrated on faster training even at the expense of greater casualties.† The Gosport method—a speaking tube connecting the instructor with the student—proved to be a valuable teaching device in the British system. American schools eventually tried to mold the best of all the Allied training systems into one of their own with a result leading one foreign observer to remark, "The British tell them to go North, the French tell them to go South, the Italians tell them to go West, so they usually do what they think best, and go East."[29] Altogether, approximately 500 Americans received all or part of their training in Great Britain. Of these, 216 pilots were sent to the Royal Air Force in the field, and served with the British or in the two American pursuit squadrons, the 17th and the 148th, which were completely trained and equipped by the RAF

---

* Kindley passed from the "Rumpty" after less than eight hour's flying. He completed the Avro phase in less than one month and was then moved to single-seater Sopwith Pups and Camels, the latter a first-line fighter.[28]

† Some thirty-four Americans were killed in England during flight training.

and operated on the British front. Ninety-six other completely trained pilots were sent directly to the American Air Service on the French front;[30] a majority of those trained in England went into pursuit aviation.

In addition to preliminary training in England and France, some instruction for Americans was provided in Italy. In the late summer of 1917 the Italian government offered to build a school for American fliers at Foggia, about 200 miles southeast of Rome. This offer was accepted, and on 28 September 1917, primary flight training at Foggia, soon known as the 8th Aviation Instruction Center, was started. Captain Fiorello H. LaGuardia, then a United States congressman and later mayor of New York City, headed the first large detachment of cadets assigned to the Foggia school. Because of the relatively good flying weather in southern Italy, training continued with few interruptions through the next several months. During the course of the war some 450 students were sent to this school for primary training, and 407 eventually graduated. On 19 January 1918 the Foggia school was expanded to include advanced pursuit training in the S.I.A. biplane and bombardment work in the Caproni.[31] In all, 121 students completed the bombardment training, and ninety-six served at the front in Italian squadrons.

Like the British and the French, the Italians had their own special training techniques. In the words of Claude Duncan, one of the American cadets who took his primary training in Farmans at Foggia during the fall and winter of 1917,

The Italians had a belief that you couldn't absorb more than ten minutes of flying in a day, so you would go out and get your ten-minute hop and that was all for the day. Of course, you stayed out on the line, observed, listened and picked up what you could. It took a long time, at ten minutes a day, to get any time in.

In fact, Duncan made his first flight on 10 October 1917, and was graduated on 22 February 1918, with only eighteen hours of flying time. There were many reasons, of course, other than the "ten minutes a day" philosophy for the slow pace of the training program. According to Duncan,

Flying took place out in the area around the line of hangars. We had positions along the hangar line just so far apart where each class would report with an instructor and fly from that same place every time. Well, if the wind was the wrong direction and too strong, we didn't fly because they couldn't change their position on the line. . . . Each training unit consisted of an airplane, a pilot instructor, a motor mechanic and an airplane mechanic, and the crew of students. Well, out of three Italians, there would be one of them, it might be the pilot, the motor mechanic or the airplane mechanic, who could talk a little bit of English; sometimes not very much. In our particular setup the motor mechanic, I think, was the one that spoke English. We would go up and fly around with the instructor and come down. He would tell the motor mechanic what he wanted to tell us and the motor mechanic would say it to us in English. If we had any questions, it went back through the same channel. I think we got as much information out of talking with each other as we did out of the actual instructors because the information that they gave quite often was not too clearly worded.[32]

In addition to the organization and language difficulties in Italian schools, there was not enough aircraft available for advanced training. The S.I.A., although exceedingly good as far as performance was concerned, was simply too fragile for heavy-handed cadet treatment and had to be withdrawn from school use. Training in Caproni bombers was greatly reduced because of a shortage of spare parts and labor.[33]

Training in Europe by Americans for Americans is best characterized by the Aviation Instruction Centers (AIC's), most of which were developed to handle advanced and specialized training. Each of the nine AIC's tended to specialize in some particular aspect of the instruction program though some, such as that at Issoudun, served a dual role.

The 3rd Aviation Instruction Center at Issoudun was intended primarily for advanced and pursuit instruction, and all pursuit training except aerial gunnery was carried on there. After a thorough course in advanced flying on 18-meter and 15-meter Nieuports, the pursuit student, usually by this time a commissioned officer, was carefully drilled in acrobatics, formation flying, and simulated combat with camera guns installed on the machines. Since the trainees were frequently challenged in mock dogfights by combat-hardened instructors, they got a rigorous wringing out which undoubtedly saved many lives on the front later. Because of the violent acrobatic action in the tiny high-powered fighters, the fatality rate in pursuit training was high—one fatality for each 9.2 graduations as compared with one in 50 for both observation and bombardment. Yet, it was the pursuit pilot who received the headlines and hogged most of the glory, deserved or not, and there was never any scarcity of young men to rise to the challenge.

Most of the 766 pursuit pilots who received their training at Issoudun were sent to the Zone of Advance and assigned to operational squadrons.[34] Several, however, were retained at 3rd AIC as instructors—in many cases to their own disgust and disappointment. One of these was First Lieutenant Edward V. Rickenbacker, the wealthy racing car driver from Columbus, Ohio, who eventually became America's ace of aces with twenty-six official victories. Rickenbacker on several occasions appealed to Major Carl "Tooey" Spaatz, the school's commander, only to be told that he was too valuable as an instructor to be spared for combat. Finally in desperation, Rickenbacker tried another approach—doing acrobatics over a football crowd at a very low altitude. This got him grounded until another instructor was assigned to replace him. On discovering Rickenbacker's plan, Spaatz called him into his office and angrily barked, "If you want to go so badly I don't want you anyhow."[35] Thus one unhappy instructor made his way to a combat squadron.

The Issoudun complex of air fields was well planned to handle the maximum air traffic with relative safety from mid-air collision. At the time of the Armistice, ten air fields were in operation. Of these fields, the first three, devoted to more elementary training, were clustered around the school headquarters. The seven additional fields were wholly separate and complete installations several miles from the main camp. Also, a landing strip was reserved for acrobatics class. "This system permitted indefinite expansion, established a high *esprit de corps* at different fields, and permitted ready comparison as to the respective merits of officers and engineers in charge of commands."*

Providing facilities for training in aerial gunnery proved one of the most difficult problems in the development of pursuit pilots. Because of the French government's reluctance to permit promis-

* Col. W. G. Kilner, head of the Training Division, was to have much to do with the planning and construction of the Issoudun facility. The main field was composed of hangars, headquarters, living quarters, shops, hospitals, stores, and recreation centers, with well-laid-out roads and communications facilities.[36]

cuous firing of machine guns from the air in populated areas, most advanced gunnery training was conducted at two schools on the coast of the Bay of Biscay. One of these was Cazaux, approximately forty miles southwest of Bordeaux; the other was at St. Jean de Mont, near the mouth of the Loire River. The latter school had to be built from scratch. "This wild, barren coast dotted with sand dunes 30 to 40 feet high and about as far apart," wrote one observer, "presented originally as uninviting a spot for flying as man ever looked upon." The engineers cleared it of the scrub vegetation and "neatly amputated the dunes, leaving a level sand floor for a field, separated from the ocean by a line of dunes to serve as a wind break and barrier."[37] The almost uninhabited location permitted uninterrupted firing in the area. The future aces of the American Air Service were given instructions in the intricacies of the rather crude gun sight of the day and practiced shooting at aircraft-towed sleeve targets as well as small fixed balloons. Frequently the student pilots released small balloons from the cockpit and then maneuvered to shoot them down. In addition, most managed to get some strafing practice on the ground targets.[38]

As the American training program picked up momentum, Cazaux and St. Jean de Mont were hard pressed to keep up with the gunnery instruction needs. All pursuit pilots trained in France, and almost all trained in the United States, had to be provided with gunnery instruction; observers and gunners from observation and bombardment squadrons had to be given firing practice. Eventually a small amount of closely regulated shooting was allowed in areas adjacent to the schools at Issoudun, Tours, Clermont-Ferrand, Chatillon, and Souge. Ground gunnery also was instituted at all principal schools.

In order to relieve some of the pressure on the two major aerial gunnery facilities, a school was opened at Furbara, Italy, in the spring of 1918. At Furbara, gunnery training was on the 13-meter Nieuport, with a Lewis gun mounted on the upper wing. Lieutenant Leland M. Carver, of Detroit, Michigan, later a top pilot with the 90th Aero Squadron, described some of the difficulties at Furbara: "Ground school lectures were given by Italian officers in French which I translated into English for the Americans."[39] A shortage of machines and the distance from other training centers further complicated matters, and the Furbara project was abandoned after only two classes (a total of fifty-two pilots) had completed their program.[40]

In addition to being trained at the pursuit schools at Issoudun and the 9th AIC in England, American fighter pilots were also trained at two other centers. The 4th AIC at Avord, the largest French flying school, was used for the training of surplus officers and cadets. The 6th AIC at Pau was probably the very first of all French training sites used by Americans, for unofficial training started there in the late summer of 1916—before the United States entered the war. Since many of the pilots produced at Pau became members of the LaFayette Escadrille, the school had a distinguished reputation.[41]

Although the observation pilot and his observer received far less publicity than the pursuit pilot, they actually served as important a part in the ultimate victory. In fact, in the view of General Mason M. Patrick, "the work of the observer and the observation pilot is the most important and far-reaching which an air service operating with an army is called upon to perform."[42] The duties of the observation team, especially the observer, were very complex. For example, it was the observer who had to familiarize himself with the sometimes featureless terrain over which he was flying, operate a camera, a radio and other signaling devices, direct the pilot, continually observe the tactical situation on the ground, jot down notes for his later reports, adjust artillery fire, and frequently to use a "pair of Lewis machine guns in a 100-mph wind stream against enemy pursuit planes." In the words of a recent writer, "It should not be forgotten that the men who wore the single wing were the successors of the Cavalry scouts of the past, and upon their judgment and powers of observation sometimes depend the conduct of battles involving many thousands of soldiers."[43]

Training of observers in the AEF commenced in the autumn of 1917 upon the arrival of the first brigades of field artillery in France. Observers were detailed from these brigades, and the first air work was given by a French observation squadron stationed at Le Valdahon. This training was soon supplemented by an observer school at Amanty and by qualified artillery observers sent to serve with French squadrons at the front. Some of these men received a severe initiation into combat. One of them, Lieutenant Fred A.

Tillman, was later awarded the American Distinguished Service Cross while working with Escadrille 260 in the Reims area on 26 June 1918. Young Tillman, son of John N. Tillman, U.S. congressman from Arkansas, was shot down in the shell-torn area between the lines and, "though himself wounded in the neck and knee, picked his badly wounded pilot up in his arms and carried him through heavy fire 200 meters to the French first lines."* Only a small number of observers, mostly transfers from the artillery, could be trained with French squadrons, and their instruction was limited generally to the use of observation with artillery. It was apparent very early that other facilities would be needed.

The 2nd Aviation Instruction Center at Tours was originally scheduled for observation training, but the base was not available for observation work until 16 January 1918 because of the great need for primary pilot training. On that date the first class of 200 students commenced their program; during the remaining months of the war Tours was to be the principal basic-training airfield for both observers and observation pilots. Since the more advanced work could not be given here, however, five small finishing schools were opened up at Chatillon, Souge, LeValdahon, Meudon, and Coetquidan. At all of these schools observation teams who had finished the course at Tours were given actual practice with either infantry or artillery or both. In all, 1,250 observers entered training schools in the AEF, and 831 graduated.[45]

Contrary to the hopes of such air leaders as General Billy Mitchell and Colonel Edgar S. Gorrell for a large strategic bombing force, comparatively few bombardment teams were developed before the end of the war. Bombardment training was started at Clermont-Ferrand, ten miles west of Lyon in south central France, on 1 December 1917. This installation, known generally as the 7th Aviation Instruction Center, had been used by the Michelon Airplane Company for a testing field. The facility for this work was very modest, only two squadrons of enlisted men, the 96th and 97th Aero Squadrons,✝ and twenty Breguet airplanes being available. The seventeen pilots who were first to arrive had received only primary training

---

* Writing forty-six years after the action, Tillman says nothing of the "heavy fire," stating, "By dragging him and carrying him [Lt. Brequet, his French pilot] we made it to the lines with the dull witted Germans staring over their trenches at us without firing a shot."[44]

✝ The 96th was to be the first day bombardment squadron to see action.

and had to be taught to fly the Breguet, as well as prepare to serve as instructors to train future classes in precision bombing. The first formal class arrived at the 7th AIC in February, 1918, but training was somewhat delayed by the fact that ten of the twenty Breguet airplanes had to be set aside for use at the front, and no other planes could be obtained at the time. It was not until September that the school received DH-4's; most of these machines, even then, were not equipped with bomb racks. Although the pace of bombardment training increased substantially after the arrival of the DH-4's, only 212 pilots and 262 bombardiers were turned out at Clermont-Ferrand by 1 December 1918.[46]

Due to the small capacity of the Clermont-Ferrand school and the location of the field in a valley surrounded by mountains—a terrain which did not lend itself to successful forced landings—no night bombardment training was attempted there. Consequently, the Air Service sought another site for this training. Since the Americans planned to use the giant, twin-engine, British-designed Handley-Page bomber for night operations, it was decided to locate the night bombardment school in England. In the latter part of September, 1918, such a base was opened at Ford Junction, near Chichester; delay in receipt of the airplanes, however, prevented any effective instruction up to 11 November, when the center was evacuated and the personnel returned to the United States. No American night bombardment squadron got into combat, but a few individuals did. During the summer and fall of 1918 some twenty pilots and six bombardiers were selected for training as instructors and sent to British schools and then to the British front for further experience. These were the only officers fully trained in night bombardment.[47]

Fliers alone did not make an air force. Thousands of mechanics, engineering officers, administrative officers, supply personnel, and a host of other specialists were needed if the air mission was to be properly fulfilled. Schools for various officer specialties were established at airfields and educational institutions scattered about the United States. The principal adjutant schools were located at Kelly Field, Texas, and Ohio State University, where over 1,200 officers were graduated. Seven hundred and twenty-six engineering officers were fully trained at the Massachusetts Institute of Technology, and approximately 850 supply officers completed their training at Georgia Tech.[48]

The remarkable development of aerial photography and radio communications created a demand for a large number of officers and enlisted men in these specialties. Most of the photography personnel were trained at the Rochester School of Aerial Photography and, according to General Patrick, were "highly satisfactory." The school's proximity to Rochester's vast photography industry undoubtedly helped the situation. Since there was a shortage of trained American instructors in the AEF, most of the actual combat photographic instruction was conducted by the French.[49] Schools for various other trades were established in the United States where, by the end of the summer of 1918, instructors had succeeded in converting many thousands of civilians into adequate soldiers.[50]

The training of mechanics began slowly. It was at first believed that a sufficient number of trained mechanics could be obtained from civilian ranks. But by the early fall of 1917 it was obvious that even a machine-oriented nation such as the United States would have to find other sources. Schools had to be opened to train enlisted men in airplane engines, propellers, ignitions, welding, instruments, vulcanizing, copperwork, sailmaking, and airframes. While more permanent instruction centers were being prepared, hundreds of men were sent to American factories for short courses in airplane and engine construction, armaments, and motor vehicles. Still others were given basic training at northern flying fields that had been closed down during the winter. Beginning in December, 1917, the Air Service placed heavy reliance on large technical institutions such as Pratt Institute, in Brooklyn, New York.[51] As of May, 1918, some 10,000 men had been trained in 17 courses in 34 different schools, more than half in the technical institutions. By the early summer of 1918 the Air Service had met its most pressing need for mechanics; thereafter all training in the United States was concentrated at two large schools: Kelly Field, Texas, and St. Paul, Minnesota. A total of 7,600 men were trained at these two schools before the end of the war.[52]

To expedite training and at the same time release British mechanics for duty with combat squadrons, an agreement was made on 5 December 1917 to train a large number of Americans in England. Under the agreement, the United States would maintain a pool of 15,000 trainee mechanics in British flying schools and factories at all times. As each group of Americans completed its training, it was to be replaced by a new class arriving from the United States and then would be sent to service squadrons in France. Because of the slowness of the arrival of new trainees and the increased need for mechanics by American schools and service squadrons in France this system proved something less than satisfactory. In an attempt to meet the urgent need in France, a new withdrawal procedure was worked out in the summer of 1918. By this arrangement, the British agreed to "release 5,000 of our personnel . . . and we agreed not to withdraw over one-fourth of our personnel from any one station and in so doing not to denude any one trade. This meant that either we would have to sacrifice our *esprit de corps* and make up the outgoing squadrons from sections of four different squadrons in training, or we would have to distribute our squadrons so that only one-fourth of any one squadron would train in one place." American air leaders eventually decided to use the latter method.[53]

Thousands of American mechanics also trained in French factories and American schools in France. During the military crisis of the fall of 1917 the French government made a formal request for 332 officers and 4,000 enlisted men to be put in their automobile factories in order to release the same number of French mechanics for service with squadrons and aircraft factory work. The United States willingly accepted this assignment and, under the leadership of such men as Lieutenant Colonel Henry Joy, former president of Packard Motor Company, Colonel C. G. Hall, and Major R. C. Kirtland, recruited and organized four mechanics regiments of 1,000 men each. After a brief stay at Camp Green, South Carolina, these men were sent overseas.[54] Still others were dispatched to the complex of mechanics schools in the Paris area, soon to be known as the 1st Aviation Instruction Center. A few Americans were trained at the mechanics' schools at Bron. This establishment, located near Lyon in central France, was known as the 5th Aviation Instruction Center. Still other mechanics received on-the-job training at such flying schools as Tours and Issoudun.[55]

In addition to pilots, the United States endeavored to train a sizeable number of balloon crews. Balloon training was given originally at Fort Omaha, Nebraska, where the program consisted of five weeks of basic military training and ground school and four weeks of practice at balloon maneuvering. With the approach of winter weather, the balloon school was moved to the warmer climate of Camp John Wise near San Antonio, Texas. It was soon ascertained that the single school could not meet the Army's plan for 69 balloon companies scheduled for the summer of 1918.[56] Consequently, three other balloon schools were established: at Camp Eustis, Virginia; Fort Sill, Oklahoma; and Ross Field, Arcadia, California. By the end of the war 751 balloon officers had been trained, and 89 balloon companies had been organized, of which 33 had been sent to Europe. Two others were organized and trained in France. On 11 November 1918 the balloon force had a strength of 17,000 officers and men in the United States or abroad.*

* The seven volumes of Series F of the Gorrell Histories are devoted to the balloon section of the Air Service. Although it was intended to give observers and maneuvering officers a full course of instruction in the U.S., it was not possible to do so at first without seriously delaying the arrival overseas of balloon troops. This condition made it imperative to establish a balloon school in the AEF. The school was first located at Cuperly in the Marne area, close to the French balloon school at Vadenay, from which valuable technical assistance was secured. The German advance in the latter part of March, 1918, made necessary a hasty move to Camp Souge near Bordeaux.[57]

NOTES

1. Letter from William P. Taylor to author, 29 July 1964.

2. *Ibid.*

3. Gorrell, *America's War Effort,* 12–13; "The Men and the Machines," *Air Power Historian,* October, 1957, 200. See also Bissell, *Brief History,* 21.

4. Patrick, *Report to Commander-in-Chief,* 257.

5. "The Men and the Machines," *loc. cit.,* 200.

6. For an excellent account of the first year of America's epic struggle to train her air force see Hiram Bingham, *An Explorer in the Air Service.*

7. Gorrell, *America's War Effort,* 14.

8. Hiram Bingham, "Building America's Air Army," *National Geographic Magazine,* January, 1918, 83.

9. *Ibid.* Contact, "Making a Pilot," *Blackwood's Magazine,* March, 1918, 290; Henry Woodhouse, *Textbook of Military Aeronautics,* 182–85.

10. See Arnold, *Global Mission.*

11. "History of the 500th Aero Construction Squadron" (Gorrell Histories, AS AEF, E, XXIII), 2. "The Men and the Machines," *loc. cit.,* 200; Goldberg, *History of USAF,* 19; Gorrell, *America's War Effort,* 14.

12. See letter from Lawrence Kinnaird to author, 26 April 1960; Powel, "Brief History of AAF," 60; Bissell, *Brief History,* 37.

13. Woodhouse, *Textbook of Military Aeronautics,* 189.

14. Gorrell, *America's War Effort,* 14–23.

15. Patrick, *Report to Commander-in-Chief,* 257.

16. *Ibid.,* 257–58. In all, approximately 2,300 cadets without preliminary flying training were sent to Europe or enlisted overseas.

17. *Ibid.*

18. Letter from Lawrence Kinnaird to author, 26 April, 1960.

19. Patrick, *Report to Commander-in-Chief,* 258.

20. *Ibid.*

21. Arnold, "History of the Aviation Section (Signal Corps) and Division of Military Aeronautics, from April 1917 to October 1918," Arnold Papers, Manuscript Division, Library of Congress, Washington, D.C., 17.

22. Vance Bourjaily, "Memoirs of an Ace," *Esquire,* August, 1954, 31. This article deals with the training and combat experiences of Lt. Charles R. D'Olive, who became an ace while flying with the 93rd Aero Squadron. Also see letter from Lawrence Kinnaird to author, 26 April 1960; George B. Richards, compiler, *War Diary and Letters of John Francisco Richards II, 1917–1918,* 43–73.

23. Bourjaily, *ibid.*

24. Patrick, *Report to Commander-in-Chief,* 261.

25. *Ibid.*

26. *War Birds: Diary of an Unknown Aviator* was prepared for publication by Springs in 1926 and is really the history of the 210 cadets who went to England in September of 1917. Although no author of the *Diary* is listed, Springs, in the foreword of the 1951 edition, revealed that Grider, who was shot down and killed in the summer of 1918, was the unknown author.

27. *Ibid.,* 35–45; James J. Hudson, "Captain Field E. Kindley: Arkansas' Air Ace of the First World War," *Arkansas Historical Quarterly,* Summer, 1959, 3–31.

28. Hudson, *ibid.,* 7–9.

29. Arnold, *Global Mission,* 65.

30. Patrick, *Report to Commander-in-Chief,* 262. For the most detailed study of pilot training see "Pilot Training in England" (Gorrell Histories, AS AEF, B, IV).

31. Patrick, *ibid.,* 260–61. For a detailed study of the American training experience in Italy see "History of Air Service Activities in Italy" (Gorrell Histories, AS AEF B, I), 54–80.

32. John Sloan and George Hocutt, "The Real Italian Detachment—Transcription of a Tape Recorded Interview with Brigadier General Claude E. Duncan, U.S.A.F. (Retired)," *Cross and Cockade Journal,* Summer, 1960, 45.

33. Patrick, *Report to Commander-in-Chief,* 261.

34. *Ibid.,* 263–65.

35. "Interview with Captain E. V. Rickenbacker by Donald Shaughnessy, 20 February 1960," unpublished transcription now in USAF HD Archives, Maxwell AFB, Montgomery, Ala.

36. Patrick, *Report to Commander-in-Chief,* 268; see also H. A. Toulmin, *Air Service, American Expeditionary Force, 1918,* 285.

37. Toulmin, *ibid.*

38. "Interview of Douglas Campbell by Ken Leish, June, 1960," unpublished transcription in USAF HD Archives, Maxwell AFB, Montgomery, Ala.; Bourjaily, "Memoirs of an Ace," 31.

39. Memorandum from Leland M. Carver to author, 26 January 1965.

40. Patrick, *Report to Commander-in-Chief,* 261.

41. "The Men and the Machines," *loc. cit.*, 203; Arch Whitehouse, *Legion of the Lafayette*, 16–28.

42. Patrick, *Report to Commander-in-Chief*, 262.

43. Thomas G. Miller, ed., "Eyes of the Army: The Observation Corps," *Cross and Cockade Journal*, Spring, 1962, 81.

44. See letter from Fred A. Tillman to author, 23 July 1964; Henry R. Stringer, *Heroes All!* 391. Many of the early observers were field artillery officers and merely attached to the Air Service. See questionnaire statement from Henry C. Bogle to author, 12 July 1964.

45. Patrick, *Report to Commander-in-Chief*, 263. For a detailed study see "History of 2nd Aviation Instruction Center" (Gorrell Histories, AS AEF, I, VII).

46. "History of 7th Aviation Instruction Center" (Gorrell Histories, AS AEF, J, VII); Patrick, *ibid.*, 264. The graduates of Ellington Field, the bombardment school in the U.S., never arrived in sufficient numbers to keep the Clermont-Ferrand school running at full capacity.

47. Patrick, *ibid.;* "Night Bombardment Training" (Gorrell Histories, AS AEF, J, V).

48. Gorrell, *America's War Effort*, 15; Powel, "Brief History," 51.

49. Patrick, *Report to Commander-in-Chief*, 285; "Photography Section" (Gorrell Histories, AS AEF, G, I).

50. See "Training Section" (Gorrell Histories, AS AEF, J, I).

51. Powel, "Brief History," 56; Goldberg, *History of USAF*, 21.

52. Bissell, *Brief History*, 35–36; Powel, *ibid.*

53. Capt. H. S. Alexander, "Critical Study of Training of American Mechanics in England" (Gorrell Histories, AS AEF, B, V), 3–16.

54. Arnold, *Global Mission*, 60. The complete story of these regiments is told in the Gorrell Histories, AS AEF, H, I–IV.

55. "The Men and the Machines," *loc. cit.*, 202–203.

56. Sweetser, *Air Service*, 294. A balloon company was made up of 170 officers and men and was equipped with two balloons under combat conditions. See also Bissell, *Brief History*, 37.

57. "The Men and the Machines," *loc. cit.*, 201. For an excellent account of balloon activities in the AEF, see Spaulding West Ovitt, *Balloon Section of the American Expeditionary Forces*.

IV

"A Lot of Good Men Running Around in Circles": Organization in the AEF

EVEN THOUGH war clouds had been gathering over America for some time, there were only five U.S. Army Aviation officers in Europe on that fateful day, 6 April 1917, when Congress voted a formal declaration of war. Three of these officers, Captains Joseph Carberry, Millard Harmon, and Davenport Johnson, had just arrived in France to begin flight training in combat-type aircraft. The fourth, Captain C. G. Chapman, was assistant military attaché in London; the fifth was an air observer then in Spain. But that air observer was the aggressive dynamo of energy, Major William Mitchell, who was to write his name large in the history of American air power.[1]

Upon hearing of the war vote, the ramrod straight, thirty-seven-year-old Mitchell caught the first train north to Paris to keep his date with destiny. Of a wealthy Milwaukee, Wisconsin family, Billy, as he was known by his friends, had had many cultural and educational advantages not available to most of his contemporaries. His paternal grandfather was Alexander Mitchell, a Scottish immigrant who had built a banking, railroad, and industrial empire in the Midwest. His father, John Lendrum Mitchell, for many years United States senator from Wisconsin, had implanted in his son a great interest in languages, literature, and world politics. Young Mitchell would have ample opportunity to use all three skills in his work with the Allies during the war years.

After graduation from Racine College preparatory school in

46

1895, Mitchell entered George Washington University, then known as Columbian College, where he was studying at the outbreak of the Spanish-American War. Somewhat to the consternation of his anti-imperialist father, Billy left college to join the 1st Wisconsin Infantry Regiment as a private. Within a matter of weeks he was commissioned a second lieutenant in the Signal Corps. With the "splendid little war" over, young Mitchell served with the occupation forces in both Cuba and the Philippines. It was during the struggle against the Filipino insurrection leader, Aguinaldo, that Mitchell came under the influence of that dashing soldier of fortune and maverick spirit, Colonel Frederick Funston. The latter's affinity for criticism of the military hierarchy and breaking of red tape seemed to rub off on the strong-willed lieutenant from Wisconsin.*

After a few months in General Arthur MacArthur's Philippine Command, Billy Mitchell asked for and received an assignment to a mission charged with the construction of an Alaskan telegraph system. During the two years (1901–1903) in Alaska, Mitchell spent much of his spare time devouring books on the subject of aeronautics and engineering. In this he was constantly encouraged by General A. W. Greeley, chief of the Signal Corps and a friend of the Mitchell family, who was even then inculcating into his subordinates, as Billy subsequently put it, "the feeling that some day we would navigate the air."[3]

On returning from Alaska, Mitchell, then a captain, served brilliantly in various Signal Corps jobs in the United States and Cuba. In 1906 he was assigned to duty in San Francisco after that city had been devastated by earthquake and fire.[4] By this time the young officer was firmly committed to a military career and took advantage of every opportunity to advance himself. In 1908 he graduated "with distinction" from the Army School of the Line and attended the Army Staff College the following year. After a second tour of duty in the Far East, Mitchell was assigned to duty on the General Staff, a post he held from 1913 until late 1916. Only thirty-two at the time of his assignment, Captain Mitchell was the youngest man ever to serve with that august body.[5]

---

* Funston was instrumental in capturing Aguinaldo, the Filipino rebel, and securing his pledge of allegiance to the U.S. In 1906 Funston, then a general, commanded army units in San Francisco during the earthquake and fire disaster.[2]

It was during the General Staff period of Billy Mitchell's life that the aeronautical seeds planted a decade before began to germinate. Henry H. Arnold, then a lieutenant conducting flying training at the Army Flying School at College Park, Maryland, remembered his first meeting with Mitchell shortly after the latter's return to Washington. "One day a sharp-faced, eager young captain of the General Staff came to see me. He was not a flyer himself, but was working on a paper to present to the Army War College. . . . His questions about the air were intelligent and to the point; in fact, it was he who did most of the talking, asking questions only to get concrete facts and accurate data. It seemed as far back as April, 1906, he had written in the *Cavalry Journal* that 'conflicts no doubt, will be carried out in the future in the air. . . .' "[6]

While still on the General Staff in 1916, Mitchell learned to fly. "This I had to do outside office hours," he wrote in his diary. "The only time I could get away was on Sunday; so I used to take a boat down the Potomac River from Washington to Newport News, Virginia, on Saturday night, fly all day Sunday, and be back in the office on Monday."[7] For a short time Mitchell, recently promoted to major, was in charge of the Signal Corps' tiny aviation arm. However, chafing at what he considered lack of vision in Washington and eager to gather information that would be valuable in preparing the infant American air arm for the war he believed to be inevitable, he asked to be sent overseas as an official observer. He had been in Spain less than a week when war came for the United States.[8]

Major Mitchell arrived in Paris on 10 April "amid the gloom that pervaded the whole country." General Joseph Joffre, hero of the Marne campaign of 1914, had been replaced by General Robert Nivelle because of Joffre's opposition to the planned spring offensive—an effort he was convinced had little chance of success. The new commander was firmly committed to the massive attack on the strongly held German position along the Hindenberg Line. It was apparent to almost every man in the street that the cost in French lives would be high, and even America's war entry had not dispelled the feeling of foreboding. Young Mitchell reflected on the futility of the land struggle as he rode the darkened streets of the French capital to the American Embassy. "It seemed to me," he wrote, "that the utility of ground armies was rapidly falling to zero, due to the great defensive power of modern firearms."[9] Even though his own concept of air power was still uncertain, he had already concluded that the war could not be won except by indirect pressure.

With characteristic energy and disregard for military protocol, Mitchell plunged into the task of setting up an American aviation program and learning first hand the true nature of the air war. Within a matter of hours after his arrival in Paris, he established an American aviation office at 49 Boulevard Hausemann. After consultation with the French Aeronautic Headquarters, Mitchell prepared plans for the coming American air effort in Europe. In his diary he wrote, "We made up a list of all equipment needed, showing the kinds of airplanes, types of engines and instruments, and an estimate of raw materials required for the make-up of such planes, including armament and radio, with notations on the probable time it would require to construct them."* This program was completed and sent to the United States on 20 April 1917, only ten days after Mitchell's arrival in France. Although hastily prepared, the report contained many worthwhile ideas. When nothing came of the suggestions, the intense young officer wrote bitterly, "It was the beginning of a series of blunders made by those directing aviation in Washington, which culminated later in that department being virtually removed from authority of the War Department and put in the hands of business men."†

Until Pershing's arrival in June of 1917, Billy Mitchell was something of a free-lancer, and his inspections took him to various headquarters, depots, and airfields. For ten days he visited with French combat units at the front, asked hundreds of questions, made notes, and even flew several reconnaissance flights over the battle area in a borrowed aircraft. During this period he deluged Washington with a steady flow of reports on every subject from bombs to German parachutes. Views which were later to stud his public statements began to appear in his diary: "The only defense against aircraft is

---

* Mitchell and his team of young air officers in Paris recommended that the Spad, Breguet, and Salmson be adopted as the standard operational aircraft for the U.S. service squadrons.

† Receiving no answer to his recommendations, Mitchell turned to the French government as an effective channel for his ideas and, by his own account, was largely responsible for the Ribot Cable of 24 May 1917.[10]

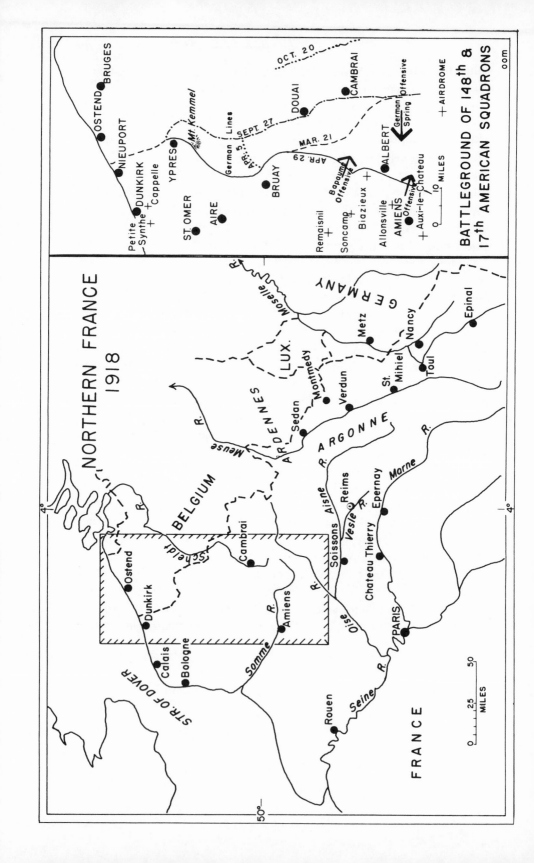

other aircraft." "It looked as though the war would keep up indefinitely until either the airplane brought an end to the war or the contending nations dropped from sheer exhaustion."[11]

In early May, the irrepressible Mitchell visited Major General Hugh M. Trenchard, then commander of the Royal Flying Corps, on the British front. During the few days with that disciple of strategic air power, the American was profoundly impressed. It was under Trenchard's influence that Mitchell's already vaguely held concepts of air power began to jell. He supported fully Trenchard's dictum that an airplane is an offensive, not a defensive, weapon and expressed enthusiasm over the latter's views on deep behind-the-line bombardment and unified air command.[12] Actually, at the time of America's entry into the war, there were no clearly defined theories or doctrines on the use of air power, though the major European powers had gradually evolved ideas and techniques applicable to their particular situations. The British and Italian theories were generally similar in that each tried to stress the importance of the strategic concept of aerial warfare. The French and the Germans, on the other hand, concentrated more on close support with the ground forces, artillery-fire adjustment, and air reconnaissance. Consequently, Billy Mitchell's respect for Trenchard, with his strategic concepts, was significant for it was to be British rather than French doctrines which guided his own development and, through him, American views on air warfare. Mitchell's position was supported in large measure by Colonel E. S. Gorrell and Major R. C. Bolling, who had picked up similar views from Caproni and Douhet in Italy.[13]

The organization of the Air Service AEF began in Washington on 26 May 1917, when Major Townsend F. Dodd, an experienced flier and veteran of the Mexican border crisis, was assigned to General Pershing's staff as Aviation Officer.[14] Major Dodd immediately appointed to his staff Lieutenant Birdseye B. Lewis, who had served with him on the Mexican border, and sent him to New York to engage clerks, interpreters, and chauffeurs. One of the chauffeurs picked by Lewis was Sergeant Edward V. Rickenbacker, a well-known racing car driver.

On 29 May 1917 Pershing and his staff sailed for Europe on the *Baltic,* arriving in England on 8 June. After a brief stay in London, the AEF Commander moved his headquarters to Paris, where by the middle of June he had established liaison with the French high command. Meanwhile, Dodd conferred with British air officials and visited a number of air stations. On arriving in the French capital on 20 June, he immediately set up headquarters in the building already occupied by Mitchell and his small free-lance staff. Dodd's incumbency was short lived for, on 30 June, Billy Mitchell, now a lieutenant colonel and the ranking American air officer in Europe, was made Aviation Officer, and Dodd became his assistant.[15]

Shortly after his arrival in Paris, Pershing appointed a board of officers, including Mitchell, to recommend the composition and organization of the Air Service in the AEF. The board began with the assumption that a decision in the air must be sought and obtained before reaching a decision on the ground. With this principle in mind, the Mitchell-dominated board recommended a strategic force of thirty bombardment groups and thirty fighter groups plus a second force of a size based on the strength of the ground forces to which it was attached. Pershing approved only the second category. Although later programs included both bombardment and pursuit squadrons, at no time was permission granted to establish an American strategic bombing force as such. Actually, "the composition of the American Air Service in France was probably determined more by nature of the aircraft obtainable than by programs of tactical doctrine."[16] The programs adopted by Pershing's staff did have some influence on aircraft production in the United States in 1918, but the hard fact remained that most American squadrons flew foreign aircraft in combat. The Americans had to take what the Allies could spare beyond their own needs.

The magnitude of the problems confronting the Air Service in France during the summer of 1917 required enlarging the organization. Colonel Mitchell, still with the title of Aviation Officer, AEF, was given jurisdiction and control over the front-line areas known as the Zone of Advance, while Major Bolling, who had remained in Europe after the completion of his work with the Aeronautical Mission, was given charge of the Zone of Interior. This arrangement led to divided responsibility and some confusion.[17] In order to solve this problem, Pershing, on 3 September 1917, appointed Brigadier General William L. Kenly, a field artillery officer, to be chief of Air Service, AEF, with authority over both.[18] Bolling, the production expert, became assistant chief of the Air Service in charge of supplies, while Mitchell was appointed air commander, Zone of Advance. Early in September, Kenly and Mitchell moved to Chaumont, the new location of the General Headquarters of the American Expeditionary Forces, while Bolling remained in Paris. Despite the new arrangement, there was something less than complete cooperation between Mitchell and Bolling.[19]

Still another reorganization of the Air Service in Europe occurred in the late fall of 1917, when Brigadier General Benjamin D. Foulois arrived in France with a ready-made headquarters staff of 112 officers and 300 enlisted men. After a careful inspection of American air activities, Foulois, one of the first flying officers in the U.S. Army, succeeded Kenly as chief of Air Service, AEF. Employing almost entirely officers from the large staff brought with him from the United States, General Foulois put the new organization into effect on 12 December. Eight new section heads, each with the title Assistant Chief of Air Service, were created. The sections and leaders established by this action included: Policy, Colonel W. B. Burtt; Administration, Colonel H. C. Whitehead; Technical, Colonel Ambrose Monell; Training and Organization, Colonel H. C. Smither; Operations, Colonel R. O. Van Horn; Balloons, Colonel Charles de Forrest Chandler; Personnel, Lieutenant Colonel T. A. Baldwin; and Supply, Lieutenant Colonel T. F. Dodd. Bolling, now a colonel, was relieved of his old post as assistant chief of Air Service, Line of Communication, and appointed chairman of the Joint Army and Navy Aircraft Committee, a position which he held for slightly over a month. He was relieved of his duties with this committee on 19 January 1918, when he asked that the committee be abolished because it served no useful purpose. Mitchell retained the position of air commander, Zone of Advance, but all Air Service projects not actually under the control of combat troops were placed under Colonel R. O. Van Horn, thus relieving Mitchell of location and construction responsibilities.* The new organization

* The construction of the 1st Air Depot at Colombey-les-Belles was begun in October, 1917. This depot served as a receiving and distributing point for personnel, material, and supplies in general and as a site for shops for engine, airplane, and motor-transport repairs not serious enough to require shipment farther to the rear. An airdrome would be needed at this place to accommodate several squadrons. By the time of the Armistice the depot contained 357,363 square feet of floor space.[20]

under General Foulois practically eliminated the Zone of Advance as an administrative office and by concentrating all sections in Paris made that city the principal seat of operations.

Foulois's reorganization was far from satisfactory to Mitchell. Although he remained the commander of the combat forces, only the 1st Aero Squadron, commanded by Major Ralph Royce, was then in the Zone of Advance, and even that unit would not be ready for battle for some weeks. Mitchell's resentment toward the new arrivals, almost none of whom, he vowed, had ever seen an airplane, was clearly brought out in his memoirs: "A more incompetent lot of warriors had never arrived in the zone of active military operations since the war began. . . . While Foulois meant well and had had some experience in aviation in the United States, he was not at all conversant with conditions in Europe. As rapidly as possible, the competent men, who had learned their duties in the face of the enemy, were displaced and their positions taken by these carpetbaggers."[21] That Mitchell had nothing but contempt for these newcomers is indicated by his description of one of the early staff conferences. "This conference," he wrote, "was one of the funniest military councils that I have ever attended. I said nothing but just listened. One of these officers after another would get up and talk about things that have practically nothing to do with aviation. It was like a spiritualist meeting in which each would get up and tell about the visions he had had the night before and then the one that repeated his vision would be given the job of either carrying it out or investigating it further."[22]

Developing an Air Service in France under the intense pressures of war presented tremendous difficulties. Jealousy and friction within the Air Service further complicated the situation, and in this matter Billy Mitchell was far from guiltless. He quarreled with Van Horn over responsibilities in the Zone of Advance and publicly criticized the Air Service organization in the AEF. In addition, he seemed reluctant to give the new section heads the benefit of his longer and wider experience in the war theater.[23] In January, 1918, when Foulois moved to Chaumont "with his staff of non-flyers," Mitchell scornfully wrote, "It was bad enough to have this crowd down in Paris but to bring them up near the line was worse. It reminded me of a story told of old Major Hunter of the cavalry, when General Otis, in command of the Philippines, had taken him to task for not accomplishing more. Major Hunter replied that he had two hundred men who had never seen a horse, two hundred horses that had never seen a man, and twenty-five officers who had never seen either. This was the state of the entourage with which General Foulois had surrounded himself."[24]

Actually, Mitchell was much too hard on Foulois and his staff. It is true that of the eight officers who were put in charge of sections in the reorganization in December, 1917, only two—Colonel Charles de Forrest Chandler (Balloons) and Lieutenant Colonel T. F. Dodd (Supply)—were flying officers, and only Dodd had been in France for any length of time. Nevertheless, the other officers in the top echelon were experienced administrators and had tackled the huge Air Service problems with energy. General Foulois, a veteran flier with operational experience with the 1st Aero Squadron in Mexico, might have preferred to use flying officers in top positions, but there simply were not enough capable aviators available for the gigantic task ahead. Since many of the jobs could be done by ground officers, as Foulois explained to Mitchell in a letter dated 19 March 1918, it would be unwise not to use them.[25] There is no evidence that he ever planned to put a nonflying officer over combat units.

In February, Secretary of War Newton Baker announced in Washington that the first American battle planes, nearly five months ahead of schedule, were en route to France. In reality, as ascertained later, not a single plane had left for the AEF. But Germany had already launched its *Amerikaprogram*—a great aircraft production program to counterbalance the anticipated American weight. On 21 March, some two weeks after the Communists took Russia out of the war, the Germans struck on the Western front with savage force. The surprise blow, mounted under cover of night to avoid aerial detection, virtually destroyed the British Fifth Army in the Amiens sector. Fortunately, General Foch, the chief of staff of the French armies, was able to plug the hole in the line by rushing troops from Italy, but the disaster exposed the crucial need for a unified command over all Allied forces. Within a short time Foch was elevated to the position of supreme allied commander.

During the crisis, Pershing, who had been holding out for an independent American force, offered to put any or all American troops then in France in the front lines. American airmen, too, were more than willing to do their part, but only the 1st, 12th, and 88th Observation Squadrons, then training at Amanty, and the 94th and 95th Pursuit Squadrons, at Villeneuve-les-Vertus, were in any way ready for combat. These squadrons were equipped with dangerously obsolescent aircraft, a fact which Mitchell perhaps unfairly blamed on General Foulois. When the latter, unable to obtain Salmsons for the observation units, accepted Spad 11 two-seaters, Mitchell angrily wrote, "He [Foulois] is no longer able to fly himself, consequently, does not know the danger of this aircraft."[26]

During the spring of 1918, internal jealousies continued to flame. There was mutual antipathy between air officers and ground officers, many of whom were newly commissioned civilians. The fliers were loath to take advice from men who resolutely refused to climb into an airplane; ground officers accused the aviators of being temperamental, of lacking discipline, and of substituting a "hodgepodge of independent personalities for an ordered administration."[27] Pershing spoke of the Air Service headquarters as "a lot of good men running around in circles."[28] The lack of progress in the AEF, aggravated to be sure by production failures at home and delays in French deliveries, could no longer be ignored. It was apparent that what the Air Service needed was a "square-jawed will and a strong hand able to apply discipline and see that the several units cooperated according to a given plan, on a given date, in a given way and no other way."[29]

On 29 May 1918, Pershing brought in as chief of Air Service a West Point classmate and senior Corps of Engineers officer, Brigadier General Mason M. Patrick.[30] The Commander of the AEF reasoned that Patrick would be able to stand above the strife of the ambitious young air officers, almost all of whom—including Foulois and Mitchell—were under forty. The appointment of Patrick may have dampened strategic air thinking, but it did bring order out of confusion.*

Under the reorganization of 29 May 1918, lines of authority were made more precise, and the whole administrative structure

* Being a ground officer, Patrick was inclined to think in terms of reconnaissance and close support. He was not rigid, however, and toward the end of the war he was listening with some sympathy to Mitchell's appeal for more bombardment aviation.

was revamped. Two weeks after taking the Air Service post, General Patrick announced the following staff positions:

Colonel W. B. Burtt, Chief of Air Service at Hdq. G.H.Q.
Colonel H. C. Whitehead, Asst. Chief of Air Service, Hdq. S.O.S.
Col. R. O. Van Horn, Asst. Chief of Air Service, Advance Section, S.O.S.
Colonel C. de F. Chandler, in Charge of Balloons, Radio, and Photography.
Lt. Colonel H. Dunwoody, Asst. D.A.S. at Paris, and Supply Officer, A.S.
Lt. Colonel W. G. Kilner, in Charge of Training.
Major W. C. Allen, in Charge of Assembly, Salvage, and Repair.
Major George A. Robertson, in Charge of Transportation.
Major H. A. Toulmin, Jr., in Charge of the Coordination Section.[31]

After a thorough study, a more modest objective of 202 combat squadrons was substituted for the previous AEF Aviation Project of 386.[32]

Air command changes were also brought about by the Patrick reorganization. Mitchell, as chief of Air Service, 1st Corps, remained subordinate to Foulois, who was placed in charge of aviation at the front with the title of chief of Air Service, First Army. Although command problems were eventually smoothed out, it was difficult for the two to work together. The colorful, dashing, and aggressive Mitchell, determined to cut red tape and get things done, was bound to clash with the more studious and orthodox Foulois. The clash came quickly on 2 June, when Foulois, accompanied by Lieutenant Colonel Frank P. Lahm, arrived at Toul to take over the office of chief of Air Service, First Army, a post temporarily held by Mitchell. Mitchell apparently believed that he was being shoved aside and that he would be denied his destiny—the role as commander of the combat squadrons. During the transfer of authority he was petulant and uncooperative—perhaps even insubordinate. The result of this bickering was a long letter from Foulois to General Pershing on 4 June 1918, in which the former requested that Mitchell "be immediately relieved from duty as Chief of Air Service, 1st Corps, and that he be sent to the United States."[33]

Pershing, in desperate need of high caliber officers with senior flying status, was reluctant to lose an officer of Mitchell's combat potential and, through General J. W. McAndrews, his chief of staff, urged Foulois to reconsider his request. McAndrews pointed out that Mitchell was capable of good work and expressed the view that the colonel did not intend to be insubordinate. Continuing, he stated: "The General wished me to say to you that he wants you to meet Colonel Mitchell even more than half way in this matter and accept from Colonel Mitchell the assurances that he knows the latter is ready to give you."[34] Two days later Foulois notified McAndrews that Colonel Mitchell had offered his full cooperation and that he would let the matter drop.[35]

Mitchell declined Foulois's offer to make him his chief assistant and, instead, requested that he be allowed to serve with a combat command. Foulois approved this request, and during the next several months relations between the two were greatly improved. In fact, Foulois backed his stubborn subordinate when the latter quarreled with the army corps commanders over control of observation squadrons in the Chateau-Thierry campaign.[36] This was crucial, for had General Foulois not sided with him in this case, Mitchell would undoubtedly have been sent home. Finally, in an unusual act of self-denial, Foulois recommended that Mitchell be given the command of the Air Service, First Army, and asked for himself the position of assistant chief of Air Service under Patrick. This change, completed in August, paved the way for Billy Mitchell to become what he most wanted—the top American air combat commander of the war.

From this point, operations proceeded smoothly and the combat forces expanded rapidly. General Foulois, on 27 August, was appointed chief of Air Service, Zone of Advance, with all tactical units not otherwise assigned under his command. In this position the dedicated Foulois worked feverishly to prepare American air units for the St. Mihiel and Meuse-Argonne campaigns. An indication of his success in this task is the fact that, from August until the end of the war, Air Service units operating on the front were kept at full strength, and morale was generally high.[37]

During the last months of the war the organization of Air Service, AEF, became much more sophisticated. The official headquarters in Paris was under the immediate supervision of Colonel Henry C. Whitehead, the chief of staff. General Patrick established all general policies, but for administrative matters not affecting general policy there were two assistant chiefs of staff—General Foulois and Colonel Halsey Dunwoody.[38] Foulois at Headquarters, Service

of Supply, Tours, had charge of all personnel records, the supervision of training, the administration of the Balloon Division and
the Air Service centers in the Service of Supply. Section heads
under his direction included such able officers as Colonel Walter
G. Kilner (Training), Colonel Charles de F. Chandler (Balloons,
Radio, and Photography), Lieutenant Colonel George W. De Ar-
mond (Personnel), Captain E. L. Jones (Information), and Major
James E. Chaney (Cables).*

Colonel Dunwoody, the assistant chief of Air Service, Paris, was
in command of all personnel in that city and, in addition, acted as
chief of Supply. This position was one of the most important in the
whole picture of the Air Service. Among other duties was his responsibility for providing material and equipment necessary for
carrying out the Air Service program. Making and supervising contracts with Allied and neutral governments and with individual con-
cerns were his responsibilities, as were receiving, assembling, and
dispatching airplanes, engines, and war equipment secured from all
sources, including the United States. Also under Dunwoody's direct
supervision were the Night Bombardment Section, headed by Colonel Ambrose Monell, and the Technical Section, headed by Lieutenant Colonel E. J. Hall. Monell handled the American night
bombardment program, in both France and England, and coordinated with other Air Service units concerned with this program. His
London office handled such problems as the assembly of Handley-
Page bombers then being built in the United States and the training
of American flying personnel and mechanics stationed in England.
Hall, the engine expert, "supplied advice on engineering questions,
provided data and estimates for proposed developments and was
charged with acceptance, inspection and testing of new aircraft and
engines."[39]

Although air officers such as Billy Mitchell frequently challenged
the arrangement, the ultimate control over air combat units rested
with the Army. In the words of General Patrick:

The Air Service was organized with the principle that at the front it is a
combat (not a staff) arm and is to be employed in combination with

* In addition to the two Assistant Chiefs of Staff, the Air Service maintained
liaison officers in both England and Italy. Col. Clarence R. Day was charged with
responsibility for Air Service matters in England, while Maj. Robert Glendinning
had similar duties in Italy.

other similar arms of the Service. The units of the Air Service are organized as integral parts of larger units, divisions, army corps, armies and the G.H.Q. Reserve. They are therefore commanded in the full sense of the word by the commanding generals of these larger units, whose decisions are executed by their General Staffs. Responsibility for the performance of the allotted task rests upon the Air Service officers commanding the unit or units involved.* The Air Service originates and suggests employment for its units but final decision is invested in the commanding general of the larger unit, of which the Air Service forms a part. . . . There is no separate chain of tactical command in the Air Service.[40]

In actuality, however, Mitchell, who commanded the combat squadrons during the last few weeks of the war, did exercise considerable independence in his choice of objectives.

The First Army, organized on 10 August 1918, grew so rapidly that it was soon expedient to create a second American Army. On 14 October, Colonel Lahm was assigned as chief of Air Service, Second Army. At the same time, Mitchell, then a brigadier general, became chief of Air Service, Army Group, and Colonel Thomas DeWitt Milling, another pioneer flier, was given command of air units of the First Army. Four days before the Armistice, Colonel T. F. Dodd, Pershing's first Air Officer, was assigned to command combat units in the newly created Third Army. What had started out as a long, rocky road had by the end become a turnpike to real air power.[41]

* To coordinate work between the combat groups and the corps headquarters, the position of chief of Air Service for each corps had been created during the summer of 1918. This organization was especially effective in handling the operations of observation units. Officers who served as chiefs of Air Service are listed in Table III of this volume.

NOTES

1. Gorrell, "The Early Activities of the Air Service, A.E.F." (Gorrell Histories, AS AEF, B, I), 1.

2. Levine, *Mitchell,* 52–53.

3. *Ibid.,* 62.

4. "Biographical Note," Gen. Wm. Mitchell Papers, Manuscript Division, Library of Congress, Washington, D.C. This collection contains some 19,200 items, including letters, telegrams, diaries, clippings, photographs, and a mass of manuscripts, largely unpublished. Of particular interest among the unpublished writings are the

transcripts of books on Alaska as a key to the air defense of the United States, the Pacific as a probable scene of World War II, and the history of aviation in World War I. These works, with illustrations, are accompanied by war and administrative diaries, inspection reports, and voluminous eyewitness notes on which they are based. In addition there is much material on testimony before various congressional committees, many portions of which do not appear in the printed record. Of course there is substantial coverage of the famous court-martial of 1925–26.

5. *Ibid.;* see also Levine, *Mitchell,* 81.

6. Arnold, *Global Mission,* 37–38.

7. William Mitchell, *Memoirs of World War I,* 10.

8. *Ibid.,* 9–14.

9. *Ibid.,* 14–15.

10. *Ibid.,* 16–17.

11. *Ibid.,* 59; Levine, *Mitchell,* 92–94. Also, see Mitchell, "Before Pershing in Europe," uncorrected draft of Mitchell's wartime diary, Mitchell Papers, Manuscript Division, Library of Congress, Washington, D.C.

12. Levine, *ibid.,* 95–97.

13. J. L. Boone Atkinson, "Italian Influence on the Origins of the American Concept of Strategic Bombardment," *Air Power Historian,* July, 1957, 141.

14. "General Order No. 1, Headquarters, American Expeditionary Forces, Washington, D.C., 26 May 1917," appearing in U.S. Department of the Army, Historical Division, *United States Army in the World War, 1917–1919,* XVI, 1. Gen. Pershing's orders appear in a number of document collections; all material cited from AEF Headquarters has been drawn from Vol. XVI of this set.

15. "General Order No. 3, Hdqrs., AEF, Paris, 30 June 1917," *ibid.;* see also Levine, *Mitchell,* 100; Mitchell, *Memoirs,* 134.

16. Goldberg, *History of USAF,* 21–22.

17. Patrick, *Report to Commander-in-Chief,* 238.

18. "General Order No. 31, Hdqrs., AEF, Paris, 3 September 1917," *loc. cit.*

19. Benjamin D. Foulois, "Air Service, American Expeditionary Forces, 1917–1919," unpublished manuscript in Gen. B. D. Foulois Collection, USAF HD Archives, Maxwell AFB, Montgomery, Ala., enclosure B.

20. *Ibid.,* 5–34; War Department, Office of Director of Air Service, "Brief History of the Air Service, AEF," 3–4.

21. Mitchell, *Memoirs,* 165–66.

22. Mitchell, "Before Pershing in Europe," *loc. cit.,* 130–31.

23. Foulois, "Air Service," enclosure D, entitled "Lack of Cooperation between Colonel [later Brigadier General] William Mitchell while Serving as Chief of 1st Corps Air Service and Brigadier General B. D. Foulois, Chief Air Service, AEF."

24. Mitchell, *Memoirs,* 177–78.

25. Foulois, "Air Service," enclosure D.

26. Mitchell, "Before Pershing in Europe," 188.

27. Toulmin, *Air Service, AEF,* 76.

28. Mason M. Patrick, *United States in the Air,* 16.

29. Toulmin, *Air Service, AEF,* 76.

30. "General Order No. 81, Hdqrs., AEF, France, 29 May 1918," *loc. cit.*

31. Toulmin, *Air Service, AEF,* 91.

32. Patrick, *U.S. in the Air,* 17, and *Report to Commander-in-Chief,* 245.

33. Letter from Chief of Air Service, First Army, to Commander-in-Chief, AEF, 4 June 1918, quoted in Foulois, "Air Service," enclosure D.

34. Letter from Gen. J. W. McAndrews (chief of staff to Pershing) to Gen. B. D. Foulois, 8 June 1918, quoted in Foulois, *ibid*.

35. Letter from Foulois to McAndrews, 10 June 1918, quoted in Foulois, *ibid*.

36. Letter from Maj. Gen. Malin Craig to Col. Mitchell, 1 July 1918, quoted in Foulois, *ibid.;* see also Mitchell, *Memoirs,* 215–23.

37. "The Men and the Machines," *Air Power Historian,* October, 1957, 199.

38. Sam H. Frank, "Organizing the U.S. Air Service: Developments in Europe," *Cross and Cockade Journal,* Autumn, 1965, 265–66.

39. *Ibid*.

40. Patrick, *Report to Commander-in-Chief,* 249–50.

41. "The Men and the Machines," *loc. cit.,* 199.

V

Combat in a Quiet Area: The Toul Sector

AMERICAN AIR SERVICE units began combat operations at the front in the spring of 1918.* For several reasons the Toul Sector was selected as the place for the untried Americans to gain experience that would bridge the gap between the training schools and actual war conditions. In this comparatively quiet area in Lorraine, bounded on the west by the Meuse River and on the east by the Metz-Nomeny-Nancy highway, opposing armies were facing each other in well-defined positions which had been established early in the war. Both the Germans and the Allies were using this sector as a rest area for tired troops as well as a training area for green units. In spite of the fact that these conditions might possibly give the young Americans a false idea of the realities of war, the sector had certain obvious advantages. American squadrons would have a chance to organize and perfect their flying techniques without committing suicide in a more active section of

---

* The AAS was first represented on the Western front by American pilots attached to a squadron of American mechanics on 19 February 1918, when the ground crews of the 103rd Pursuit Squadron arrived at LaNoblette, a small village six miles northeast of Chalons-sur-Marne, and assumed charge of the machines of French Squadron Spad 124, the famed Lafayette Escadrille. Seventeen other American pilots, only recently released from French service, reported to Maj. William Thaw, the new commanding officer of the 103rd, and continued their operations against the enemy without interruption. For the next five months, this squadron continued under the command of the French Army, first over the Champaigne sector from LaNoblette, then over the Aisne sector from Bonne Maison, near Fismes, and finally over the Ypres-Lys sector from near Dunkirk. Since the 103rd was not under American control and as it was not, in a real sense, a new outfit, it will not be discussed until mention of the 3rd Pursuit Group of which it became a part later in the summer.

the front. Also the rich coal and iron mines near Metz, the fortress itself, and railway systems at Sedan and the southwest made the region protected by the Lorraine front of vital importance to the Germans. This gave American air and ground units concentrated in that area a feeling of purpose. Finally, sufficient airdromes and facilities to handle American squadrons already existed in the Toul area.[1]

The American air build-up in the Toul sector began early in 1918. On 16 January the nucleus of the newly formed 1st Pursuit Organization and Training Center, under the command of Major Bert M. Atkinson, left Paris and proceeded to Villeneuve-les-Vertus in one seven-passenger Hudson touring car and three small Fiat trucks. This small cadre would eventually become the staff of the 1st Pursuit Group. Villeneuve, a short distance from Chalons, was then occupied by the famous French 12th *Group de Combat,* commanded by Commandant Menard, and was chosen because it "would provide a wonderful opportunity for the young American pilots to observe the work of the French aviators." During the next few days, Atkinson and his small staff, consisting of Captain Philip J. Roosevelt, Captain John G. Rankin, and six sergeants, were occupied in arranging for the barracks, machines, and hangars for the squadrons that would arrive soon. Construction of the barracks was started on 2 February by French and Italian laborers working under American officers. Thirty-six Nieuport pursuit planes were promised by the French, and by the middle of February, several flying officers, including First Lieutenants Seth Low and Hobart A. H. Baker and Captain J. J. Miller, had reported for duty.[2]

The 95th Aero Squadron arrived at Villeneuve on 18 February, and was placed under the command of Captain J. J. Miller. This squadron had been activated at Kelly Field, Texas, on 20 August 1917; it was trained, and it departed for overseas at the end of September. On 16 November the 95th arrived at Issoudun, where its men helped convert a sea of mud into a training base (the Third Aviation Instruction Center) that was to do much to prepare many later U.S. squadrons and pilots for combat.[3]

The thirty-six Nieuports promised by the French had not arrived on schedule. In fact, it was rumored that the planes were needed elsewhere on the front. At this, Major Atkinson, a tough-minded regular army officer, "burned" the telephone lines to Paris and to the Air Service General Staff at Chaumont only to learn that the Air Service Headquarters was moving to Tours. Information on the Nieuports was vague, but repeated inquiry brought results when, on 26 February, Atkinson was notified that thirty-six Nieuport 28's were waiting at Paris for use by the unit. Miller and nine other pilots immediately set out for Paris. The next day ten more pilots followed.[4]

The 94th Aero Squadron, consisting of 16 officers and 120 men, reported in at Villeneuve on 5 March, and were placed under the command of Major John F. Huffer, a veteran of nearly two years of service with various French escadrilles. Organized at Kelly Field on 20 August 1917, this outfit had trained in the United States and reached Issoudun early in 1918. It now became the second tactical squadron to join the 1st Pursuit Organization Center.[5]

Meanwhile the pilots who had hurried to Paris to pick up the new aircraft had been prevented from returning by heavy snow and sleet storms. For over a week the impatient young warriors waited. Finally, on 6 March, fifteen were able to take off for the Villeneuve airdrome; only Captain Miller and five others, however, were able to complete the journey that day. Several made forced landings along the way, and it was not until 8 March that all the planes were safely down on the sod of the Villeneuve airdrome. For the first time the American portion of the base reverberated with the angry sputter of 160-h.p. Gnome rotaries.[6]

The first combat casualty in the 1st Pursuit Organization Center came from an entirely unpredicted quarter. On the morning of 9 March Captain Miller, the personable commander of the 95th Aero Squadron, returned to Coincy to pick up one of the Nieuports which had been left behind in the mass transfer of aircraft to Villeneuve-les-Vertus. While waiting for the Nieuport to be made ready for the flight back to his home base, Miller borrowed a Spad fighter and, accompanied by Majors Davenport Johnson and Millard Harmon, flew a volunteer patrol over the Reims sector of the front. The flight had hardly reached the lines when Major Harmon was forced to turn back with engine trouble. A short time later the remaining pair was jumped by two German pursuit planes, and

Miller was seen to go down in a spin. Later reports indicated that he crashed behind enemy lines and died the next day in a German hospital.*

Although the two American pursuit squadrons at Villeneuve now had planes, they had been unsuccessful in obtaining machine guns to arm them. Despite this rather startling deficiency, the 95th Squadron flew its first patrol along the Marne from Epernay to Chalons on the morning of 15 March. A second patrol was carried out in the afternoon of the same day. On each of these patrols, three unarmed Nieuports were accompanied by one Spad from the French *Escadre* based at Villeneuve. Similar flights were carried out over the next several days. The purpose of these missions was to discourage German reconnaissance flights, and though conducted on the Allied side of the lines, they were audacious undertakings to say the least.[8]

In addition to the lack of machine guns, American pursuit aviation received still another setback when it was discovered that most of the pilots in the 95th Aero Squadron had not had gunnery training. Much to their chagrin, some sixteen of the fliers were ordered to Cazaux, on the southwest coast of France, to complete the gunnery course. The few pilots who had completed the program were transferred to the 94th Squadron.[9]

The situation took a turn for the better for the 94th Aero Squadron when machine guns began to arrive on 28 March. The next day Major Raoul Lufbery, a recent transfer from the Lafayette Escadrille, where he had been the top ace with seventeen victories, led two patrols over the lines. The first patrol was composed of Lieutenants Edward V. Rickenbacker and Douglas Campbell; the second was made up of Lieutenants Thorne C. Taylor and John Wentworth. These flights were more in the form of a training mission than a combat patrol, and Rickenbacker's plane was slightly damaged by antiaircraft fire.[10]

As a result of the German offensive beginning on 21 March 1918, it became necessary for the green American units to evacuate the Villeneuve airdrome to make room for French and British night bombardment squadrons. Consequently, Atkinson's staff, the 94th Aero Squadron, and the ground personnel of the 95th Aero

* Both Davenport Johnson and Millard Harmon held the rank of major general in the U.S. Army Air Force in World War II.[7]

Squadron were moved to Epiez (Meuse) on 31 March 1918.[11] The 1st Pursuit Group historian described the situation in the following terms: "The new camp at Epiez was a sea of mud and it rained incessantly. Little was done in the way of patrols, but the mechanics were kept busy on the machines, and guns were being mounted and synchronized." [12] Indeed, the squadron needed this short breather in order to prepare itself for the more active days ahead.

Huffer's 94th Aero Squadron hardly had time to unpack when still another was required. On 7 April the squadron was ordered to Gengault airdrome, approximately two miles northeast of Toul, to commence active operations under the Eighth French Army. Major Atkinson's staff and the ground personnel of the 95th remained at Epiez for the time being. With the experienced Lufbery leading most of the patrols, the squadron, soon to be known as the "Hat-in-the-Ring" squadron, now began its real war activities. On 12 April the dynamic little Lufbery claimed the destruction of an enemy plane, but no confirmation could be obtained. The green American outfit thus had to wait for its first official victory over the Boche.[13]

The American squadron was not long delayed in cutting its teeth against the Hun, for on Sunday morning, 14 April 1918, Lieutenants Alan Winslow and Douglas Campbell shot down a pair of German pursuit planes on the Gengault airdrome. Winslow sent his opponent plunging to earth a few seconds before Campbell's victim crashed and is generally considered to have scored the first American air victory of World War I.* Because these kills oc-

---

* Although Lt. Alan Winslow is generally credited with having scored the first American air victory of the war, there are several counterclaims. William E. Barrett has made some study of this subject. A young American, A. Whitten Brown, flying as an observer with No. 2 Squadron RFC, destroyed a German plane in 1915. Brown's claim, according to Barrett, is invalid because he had to renounce his American citizenship in joining the RFC. That point disqualifies all other Americans who had enlisted in the RFC. Bert Hall, serving in the French Air Force, where one did not have to take an oath of allegiance, shot down a German plane on 21 August 1915. He was wearing a French uniform, however, and the victory went to a French escadrille. In May, 1916, Kiffen Rockwell was the first to score for the Lafayette Escadrille which was eventually incorporated into the U.S. Air Service, but at the time of his victory the U.S. was neutral. Raoul Lufbery, while with the Lafayette Escadrille, scored a kill two days after America entered the war, but he was wearing a French uniform, and the Escadrille was still a part of the French Air Force. Perhaps a better claim can be made by Lt. Stephen W. Thompson, who volunteered for a flight as a gunner with a French squadron and destroyed

curred on the first official day of the 94th Squadron's war work, and because the sensational air battle took place over the home airfield, the victories served as a terrific morale builder.

Fired by this early success, the 94th rapidly picked up momentum. Within six weeks the squadron had been credited with seventeen official victories and several more unconfirmed kills. On 23 April, Major Lufbery and Lieutenant Douglas Campbell attacked an enemy plane and saw it catch fire but were unable to get a confirmation. Two days later Lieutenant Edward V. Rickenbacker sent a "Boche down out of control" but, like Lufbery and Campbell, was unable to find sufficient witnesses. Rickenbacker, who would end the war as the top American ace with twenty-six victories, scored his first official victory on 29 April, when he and Captain James Norman Hall intercepted a Pfalz fighter in the vicinity of Vigneulles-les-Hattonchatal and sent it down in flames.[15] Under the rules then prevailing on the French portion of the front, both pilots were given credit for one victory, though the squadron could be credited for only one plane destroyed. American pilots working with the British received only fractional credit if two or more contributed to the destruction of an enemy aircraft.

On 2 May 1918 Lieutenant James Meissner, one of the squadron's flight commanders, attacked three enemy planes over the Foret De La Rappe area and after a short fight brought down one of the machines in flames. "During the combat the entering wedge and the covering of the upper wings of his plane were torn away"; he was able to make a landing, however, inside the American lines. Meissner had inadvertently found the weakness of the maneuverable little Nieuport 28—its upper wings were prone to shred in a dive. For his destruction of an enemy aircraft and his skill in landing his own disabled machine, Meissner was awarded the Distinguished Service Cross.[16]

an enemy plane on 5 February 1918. He was wearing an American uniform and only the fact that he was flying as a volunteer with the French clouds his claim. Then there is the claim of Paul Baer, a member of the Lafayette Escadrille, which had been absorbed into the U.S. Air Service on 18 February 1918 as the 103rd Pursuit Squadron. On 11 March 1918 he destroyed a German plane for the Lafayette Escadrille's first victory after its members accepted American commissions. As some would point out, however, the 103rd Squadron did not count because it was still serving on the French front, where it had been known as the Lafayette Escadrille; all its pilots in March, 1918, were French trained. Even Alan Winslow's claim to be the first can be challenged by this reasoning as he, too, was French trained. Perhaps Douglas Campbell has a better claim.[14]

On the day following Meissner's narrow escape, Captain David McKelvey Peterson, the calm, steady transfer from the Lafayette Escadrille, scored his first victory with the 94th Squadron. The Honesdale, Pennsylvania, man had enlisted in the French Air Force in October of 1916, and was commissioned a captain in the U.S. forces in January, 1918. He had been credited with the destruction of one enemy plane while with the French. During May of 1918 he became an ace, his third and fourth victories coming on 15 May and his fifth on 17 May. The fifth victory was credited to the 95th Squadron, as Peterson had been assigned to that squadron to give it experienced leadership.[17] On 25 May he was made squadron commander, replacing Major Davenport Johnson. James Norman Hall and Charles B. Nordhoff, in *The Lafayette Flying Corps,* wrote of Peterson:

. . . it may be said without exaggeration that he was the only American who never had a thrill from his adventures as an airman. No event of the war ever stirred the tranquil depths of his nature. He simply couldn't be elated or depressed, frightened or overjoyed . . . as a patrol leader he was without equal.[18]

While Huffer's 94th Squadron was carrying on the war alone at Toul, two new units joined the 1st Pursuit Organization Center at Epiez. The 147th Aero Squadron arrived on 22 April, having been activated in the United States in November, 1917, trained, and sent overseas via Liverpool, LeHavre, and Tours. Two days later the 27th Aero Squadron made its appearance. This outfit, eventually to become one of the outstanding combat units of the war, was organized at Kelly Field as Company "K" of the 3rd Provisional Aero Squadron on 8 May 1917. On 15 June 1917 it was redesignated the 21st Provisional Aero Squadron, and on 23 June 1917 became the 27th Aero Squadron. It went overseas early in 1918, following the path to England, LeHavre, Tours, and Issoudun before coming to Epiez.[19]

Also during the last week in April, the flying officers of the 95th returned to the fold after completing their gunnery course at Cazaux. During the following week several reconnaissance and combat patrols were mounted from Epiez. Since this airdrome was somewhat distant from the battle area, the decision was made to move the 95th, along with the staff of the 1st Pursuit Organization

Center, to Toul, where the 94th was already playing an active role. The move was completed on 4 May, and on the next day the 1st Pursuit Organization Center became the 1st Pursuit Group with Major Bert M. Atkinson in command. The 27th and 147th Squadrons remained in training at Epiez until 1 June when they, too, joined the 1st Pursuit Group at Toul.[20]

Despite somewhat spotty weather, the 94th and 95th Squadrons continued to operate over the Toul–St. Mihiel–Pont-a-Mousson front with considerable success throughout the month of May, 1918. Fortunately, their chief opponents were the rather unaggressive 64th and 65th *Jagdstaffeln* based at Mars-la-Tour, a dozen miles east of the fortress town of Metz, plus several reconnaissance units located in the same general area. By the end of the month both Eddie Rickenbacker and Douglas Campbell, of the 94th, had achieved the status of ace. The twenty-two-year-old, Harvard-educated Campbell, whose father was at the time head of the Mount Wilson Observatory and who would later become president of the University of California, was the first American-trained pilot to become an ace. At least he was so considered in May of 1918. He had received his ground-school training at Cornell University, and in August, 1917, he had been one of the first cadets sent overseas. After completing his flight training at Issoudun, he was stymied temporarily in a training and administrative role at the big 3rd AIC complex. After much argument and diplomatic maneuvering, however, he won assignment to the 94th Aero Squadron on 1 March 1918. The quiet Californian was involved in a series of firsts. He participated, along with Lufbery and Rickenbacker, in the first familiarization patrol over the battle lines; on 14 April he scored one of the first, if not the first, victories won by an American squadron. In line with this pattern, Campbell became an ace on 31 May 1918 by destroying a Rumpler two-seater in a gruelling fifteen-minute duel over Lironville.* A week later he was wounded and returned to the United States.[21]

Actually, a good case could be made that Rickenbacker was the first American-trained pilot to reach acedom. By scoring kills on 7 May, 17 May, 22 May, 28 May, and 30 May, he ran his total

---

* In 1935 Douglas Campbell became associated with Pan-American Grace Airways and in 1939 was appointed vice-president. Since 1948 he has been vice-president and general manager of the airline.

to six victories on the Toul front. Failure to get immediate confirmations of Boche aircraft destroyed on 7 May and 30 May, however, lost for him, at least for the moment, the honor of being the first ace. That he retained no bitterness over this turn of events is indicated by the fact that, in his book *Fighting The Flying Circus,* Rickenbacker writes glowingly of Campbell as "America's first ace." Rickenbacker, nonetheless, received official credit for his 30 May victim early in June of 1918, and thus would have preceded Campbell by one day. Official credit for the 7 May victory came much later. In fact, it came over forty years later, remaining unconfirmed until new evidence was considered in January, 1960.[22]

The fact that Rickenbacker's 7 May kill required forty years to win confirmation warrants some explanation. On that memorable May morning in 1918, Rickenbacker, Captain James Norman Hall, a veteran of the Lafayette Escadrille who achieved fame in the postwar years as the co-author of *Mutiny on the Bounty,* and Lieutenant Eddie Green were sitting on alert when they were warned that enemy aircraft were approaching the battle lines. The trio raced to their Nieuports and took off to intercept the hostile planes. Ten minutes later the Americans spotted below them a biplace Albatros apparently working with German artillery. Before the three could plunge down upon what appeared to be a helpless victim, the sharp-eyed Rickenbacker noticed four Pfalz fighters climbing to break up the attack. After signaling to draw his mates' attention to the new situation, Rickenbacker dove upon the rearmost Hun pursuit, and in his words: "at 200 yards I pressed my trigger and watched my tracer bullets speeding ahead into the Pfalz's wings. My gun continued to fire steadily until I had approached to within 50 yards . . . then the enemy plane turned over and fell into a Vrille." Because of the whirling combat around him, the flier did not follow the wounded German aircraft down and was uncertain as to its fate. Green also shot down a Pfalz in the fight, but Hall was last seen going down in a spin "with his upper wing gone."[23] The confirmation of Rickenbacker's Pfalz would ultimately depend upon Hall, but that individual was down behind the German lines and feared dead.

The courageous Hall, his upper wing shredded by the strain of the dive on the enemy pursuits, had managed to land in one piece, but was captured immediately. He was released after the Armistice and visited with his old squadron mates for a short time. He testified then that he had seen Rickenbacker's Pfalz "burst into flames and crash, burnt to a crisp." He also stated that a few hours after the fight he had had lunch with the German pilots and that they admitted having lost two aircraft in the battle. One, of course, was the plane destroyed by Green, but the other, undoubtedly, was Rickenbacker's victim. All of this was put in the form of an affidavit, and Rickenbacker in December, 1918, sought confirmation of the 7 May claim. Unfortunately, in the confusion arising from the post-Armistice rush to return to the United States, the affidavit became lost. It was not until 1958 that it came to light again. Finally, on 20 January 1960, Secretary of the Air Force Dudley C. Sharp directed that Edward V. Rickenbacker's records be corrected to show that "on 7 May 1918, in the vicinity of Pont-a-Mousson, France, he destroyed an aircraft in aerial combat. . . ."[24]

Eddie Rickenbacker, who would end the war as "America's ace of aces," was born in Columbus, Ohio, on 8 October 1890, the son of William and Elizabeth Reichenbacher. When his father died, Eddie, then twelve years old, dropped out of school and worked at various jobs to help support the family. While still in his teens he took a position with the Frayer-Miller Air-Cooled Car Company, a move which proved to be a turning point in his life. In his spare time he took correspondence courses in mechanical engineering and draftsmanship to help him in his job. Through his experience in the engineering of automobiles he became keenly interested in motor racing and, from 1910 on, was a consistent winner on the racetracks of America. In 1914 he set a world record of 134 mph, and by 1917 he was earning approximately $40,000 per year as a race driver.

When America entered the war Rickenbacker was in England under contract to prepare a racing team for the Sunbeam Motor Company. While in England he had observed a great deal of that country's aeronautical progress and returned to the United States enthusiastic with the idea of developing a flying unit composed entirely of race drivers. He believed that their quick reflexes, knowledge of motors, and familiarity with high speeds would enable them to learn more quickly how to fly. The project made no impact on Washington, and Rickenbacker returned to Europe as a chauffeur with General Pershing's staff. Meanwhile he changed his name from the Teutonic sounding Reichenbacher to an Americanized version, Rickenbacker. Even so, like many other Americans with German names, he was on several occasions pestered by secret service men.

While serving as a chauffeur for the aviation officers assigned to Pershing's headquarters, Rickenbacker continued to plead for an opportunity to get into aviation. In August, 1917, he was given his opportunity and entered the 2nd AIC at Tours. With his finely tuned reflexes and ability to make split-second decisions, an ability developed on the racetracks, he had little difficulty in learning to fly. Because of his great knowledge of engines he was sent to Issoudun as an engineering officer upon completion of the preliminary course at Tours. Eager for combat, engineering was not the job he wanted, and on his own time he completed the advanced flying program and finally persuaded his commander to send him to Cazaux for gunnery training. In March, 1918, he succeeded in winning a combat assignment and reported to Major John Huffer's 94th Aero Squadron, then based at Villeneuve-les-Vertus. His maturity, patience, familiarity with engines, and quick reflexes made him one of the great fighter pilots of the war.[25]

Throughout the month of May, the 94th and 95th Aero Squadrons continued to fly patrols, as well as a few escort missions, over the relatively quiet Toul sector. Although the group produced no aces other than Peterson, Campbell, and Rickenbacker, other pilots were learning their trade and destroying an occasional enemy aircraft. Lieutenants Edward Buford, John A. Hambleton, and John Mitchell, of the 95th Aero, and James Meissner, of the 94th Aero, scored their second victories during the month. Six others broke the ice with one enemy plane each.[26] To most fighter pilots the first kill always seems the hardest to win. It frequently requires several missions before the ordinary pilot even "learns to see" other aircraft in the air. Even such extraordinary hunters as Rickenbacker and Campbell were gently chided by their patrol leader, Lufbery, when they failed to observe numerous Allied and German aircraft on their first war flight.

The growing list of victories achieved by the two squadrons, however, was not without casualties. In addition to Captain James Norman Hall, who lost a wing and was forced down behind enemy lines on 7 May, five others were lost in combat. On 3 May Lieutenant Charles Chapman of the 94th Aero was shot down and killed while attacking a German two-seater. A short time later Lieutenants Richard Blodgett, of the 95th, and Paul B. Kurtz, of the 94th, were killed in action, and Lieutenant Wilfred V. Casgrain, of the 95th, became a prisoner of war.* In the middle of May the group lost its most revered and experienced flier—Major Raoul Lufbery.

The irrepressible Lufbery had been the Lafayette Escadrille's most brilliant star before transferring to the green 1st Pursuit Group as officer in charge of instruction. He was born in France, 21 March 1885, the third son of Edouard Lufbery, an American who had settled in France, and his French wife, Annette. His mother died when Raoul was less than a year old, and the father, unable to earn a living and care for the boys, placed them in foster homes. In 1890 Edouard Lufbery remarried and the following year returned to the United States, where he took up residence in Wallingford, Connecticut. Still uncertain of his financial potential, he left Raoul and his brothers with their grandmother. They were still separated eleven years later when the second Mrs. Lufbery died, leaving five small children of her own. Meanwhile, young Raoul had gone to work in a chocolate factory in Blois and sent a part of his meager earnings to his father in America.[28]

By 1904, no longer burdened with family responsibilities, Lufbery left France at the age of nineteen and began a career of travel and adventure. During the next several months he journeyed throughout the Mediterranean and the Near East, working at various jobs to pay for his adventures. In 1906 he traveled to the United States, where he hoped to be reunited with his father. Unfortunately, the elder Lufbery had returned to France at the same time, and the two never met again. Young Lufbery remained in Wallingford for about two years, waiting for the return of his father. Early in 1908 he got "travel fever" again. During the next few months he visited Cuba and worked in a New Orleans bakery and a San Francisco hotel. Later the same year he joined the United States Army, and was sent to the Philippines, where he

* In addition to the casualties listed above, Lt. Willard D. Hill, of the 94th, was wounded by an explosive bullet while flying over Montsec on 27 May. On 6 June the ace, Douglas Campbell, received a wound in the back and was returned to the U.S. Four other 1st Pursuit Group pilots were lost in June.[27]

distinguished himself as a marksman. When his enlistment period expired, he toured Japan, China, and India. The year 1912 found him in Calcutta, where he saw his first airplane, a French Bleroit, and made the acquaintance of the famous French pilot, Marc Pourpe. Although Lufbery had had no experience with machines, he persuaded Pourpe to hire him as a mechanic and helper. He quickly learned all there was to know about the Bleroit and toured the Far East with the French aviator. The summer of 1914 found the pair back in France.[29]

As the guns began thundering in August, 1914, Lufbery, then twenty-nine, began a new adventure. His friend Pourpe immediately joined the French Air Force and was assigned to Escadrille N. 23. As an American, Lufbery had to enlist in the French Foreign Legion to serve; in a short time, however, he was able to transfer to Escadrille N. 23 and was assigned Pourpe's mechanic. Pourpe was killed in combat in December of 1914, and Raoul Lufbery, determined to avenge his death, applied for flight training. His request was granted, and after several months of training he was assigned to a bombardment unit. After some six months of bombardment work he was sent to pursuit school. On 24 May 1916 he was assigned to Escadrille Lafayette N. 124, where he began the heroic exploits which won him acclaim as one of the great aerial duelists of the war with seventeen confirmed victories. For these deeds he was awarded the Croix de Guerre, with ten palms, the Medaille Militaire, and was named Chevalier of the Legion of Honor. In addition, he was the first American to receive the British Military Cross. In January, 1918, he was commissioned a major and assigned to the 1st Pursuit Organization Center to work with the new American squadrons at the front.*

Raoul Lufbery's fabulous career of adventure came to an end in a French flower garden on Sunday, 19 May 1918. At 10 A.M., as the church bells in the nearby city of Toul rang out the call to late Mass, an alert was sounded for a German two-seater recon-

---

* Lufbery's fellow pilots insist that he actually shot down more than forty German planes, a claim substantiated by entries in *Nieuport 124 Journal de Marche,* the official day-by-day account of squadron activities. The reason for only seventeen confirmed victories is that the French required three separate witnesses to the event. Balloon, artillery, or infantry personnel could qualify, but fellow pilots were excluded. Naturally, any victory taking place behind the German lines was certain to be unconfirmed.[30]

naissance plane headed for the area, apparently on a photographic mission. Antiaircraft guns opened fire and seemed to score a hit; the plane, identified as an Albatros, went into a spin. The German recovered at a low altitude, however, and started climbing toward the lines. A novice American pilot sent up to intercept the Hun used up his ammunition while at extreme range, and it appeared that the enemy aircraft would escape. It was at this point that Major Lufbery, his own Nieuport out of commission, borrowed a machine in front of the operations hangar and took off in great haste. About six miles from the airdrome he overtook the Albatros at 2,000 feet altitude. Lufbery made one firing pass at the enemy and then swerved away, apparently to clear a jammed gun. A few moments later he made a second attack from the rear, and his own plane was seen to burst into flames. Seconds later, spectators on the ground were horrified to see the American without parachute either fall or jump from his burning aircraft to his death. His body fell in a little flower garden in the tiny village of Maron while his plane, crashing a few hundred yards away, burned to ashes. His squadron mates, rushing to where he lay, found that French peasants had already covered his body with flowers. His death was a tragic shock to the young American pilots, but the colorful Lufbery had done much to instill his aggressive spirit in the new squadrons at the front.[31]

The 1st Pursuit was brought to full strength on 31 May 1918, when the 27th and 147th Aero Squadrons, now fully trained, reported ready for action at the Toul airdrome. Commanded by Major Harold E. Hartney and Major G. H. Bonnell, veteran transfers from the RFC, these squadrons were more than pleased to get out of the mud and dust of Epiez and into the big roomy Gengault field with its stone barracks, steel hangars, and concrete sidewalks. A few experienced pilots from the 94th and 95th Squadrons were temporarily assigned to the newcomers to serve as patrol leaders. The 27th Aero Squadron began active operations on 2 June, when an early morning patrol consisting of Lieutenants Alfred A. Grant, Robert F. Raymond, Jason Hunt, and C. A. McElvain and led by Lieutenant Thorne Taylor, of the 94th Squadron, toured the front lines. A similar situation existed in Bonnell's 147th Squadron. Gradually the new squadrons were weaned from the experienced pilots of the two older squadrons and began an active patrol of the lines from Pont-a-Mousson, on the Moselle River, to St. Mihiel, fifteen miles to the east on the Meuse River. In addition to line patrols the squadrons flew several escort missions for two-seater Spads and Salmsons of the American observation squadrons based in the Toul area.[32]

The front remained comparatively quiet during the near perfect weather of the month of June, 1918. Aerial combat was at a minimum, but Hartney's raw 27th Squadron scored its first victory and suffered its first loss on 13 June. An Albatros was brought down over Lorry with Lieutenants John MacArthur, Kenneth Clapp, and E. W. Rucker sharing the credit. Lieutenant W. H. Plyler came down behind German lines on the same day and was made a prisoner of war.[33] On the next day Bob Raymond destroyed an Albatros. Nearly two weeks later, on 25 June, Major Hartney, already an ace with the British, destroyed a German fighter for his sixth victory, and MacArthur turned an enemy two-seater into a fiery wreck.[34] By the end of the month, the 1st Pursuit Group had "brought down 58 Hun planes, 27 of which were confirmed."*

At the same time American pursuit units were taking their first uncertain and wobbly steps at the front, American observation aviation was also testing its combat wings. The initial observation squadron to arrive at the front was the 1st Aero Squadron, which took station at Ourches, about twelve miles southwest of Toul, on 4 April 1918. This unit, which had flown JN-2's and JN-3's in the punitive expedition against Pancho Villa in Mexico in 1916, had been based at Columbus, New Mexico, when war was declared. Under Major Ralph Royce, the 1st Aero Squadron sailed for France on 13 August 1917, thus becoming the first combat flying unit of the American Expeditionary Force to reach Europe. After stops at Liverpool and LeHavre the organization arrived at Avord, France, on 13 September 1917. With only three weeks of preliminary training in Bleriots, Penguins, and Nieuports, the

* The reason for the unusually large number of unconfirmed victories might be the rather strict rules for confirmation set up by the Air Service. In order to obtain a confirmation under these rules, it was necessary to "obtain besides the testimony of the pilots and observers concerned, one or more written confirmations given by any one of the following: (a) of witnesses of the combat, (b) when in our lines, of witnesses of the wreck of an enemy aircraft in the approximate locality and of the same type (airplane, balloon, zeppelin) claimed to have been destroyed, (c) in special cases, testimony of captured aviators."[35]

squadron moved to Amanty in October for training in observation work. Flying obsolescent French AR's (Avion Renault), the unit received instruction in radio and gunnery and participated in maneuvers with ground troops to acquire experience in reconnaissance and in coordinating artillery fire. On moving to the battle area in April, 1918, the 1st was given a complement of Spad 11's, a two-seater biplane long since discarded by the French as grossly underpowered; but they had retained some of their AR's. Thus the American observation squadron was to have two strikes against it at the beginning.[36]

Despite its ancient equipment, the 1st Observation Squadron began operations on 11 April 1918, when several pilot-observer teams flew reconnaissance patrols over the Seicheprey-Flirey area. The unit had its first encounter with the enemy on the following day when First Lieutenant Arthur J. Coyle was attacked by three enemy pursuit planes but managed to escape with only one bullet hole in his plane. From that time until the end of the war the 1st Squadron saw almost continuous service as a corps observation unit, and from its ranks came many of the AEF's squadron, group, and wing commanders.[37]

The 12th Aero Squadron, under the command of Major Lewis H. Brereton, arrived at Ourches on 3 May 1918, and started operations immediately. A few days later the 12th and 1st Squadrons became a part of the newly created I Corps Observation Group. On 8 May, Major Royce, a veteran of the Mexican border troubles, became commander of the new Group, and "Judge" Coyle took over the 1st Aero Squadron. Three weeks later Major Harry B. Anderson's 88th Aero Squadron moved to Ourches airdrome and was assigned to the I Corps Observation Group. Seldom has any military organization gone into combat with more out-of-date equipment than did these squadrons. The 12th was supplied with AR's, "Antique Rattletraps," as the pilots called them. These two-seaters, powered by a 190-h.p. Renault engine and equipped with an ancient wheel control, had been relegated to training duty for months in the French Army. Worse still was the plight of the 88th, which had been given French-built Sopwith 1½ Strutters, 120-h.p. LeRhone-powered crates of 1915 design. The DH-4's being produced in the United States factories were months from delivery, and the Air Service was forced to accept the leavings of British and

French air forces.[38] It was indeed fortunate that the Americans were assigned to a quiet sector.

Squadrons of the I Corps Observation Group operated mainly over the narrow front occupied by the 26th U.S. Division between Flirey and Apremont on the southeastern flank of the St. Mihiel salient. The group was under the tactical control of the French XXXVII Army Corps and under the administrative control of the American I Army Corps. For the most part the pilots had never served on the front. Nearly all of the observers, on the other hand, had seen service with French squadrons, and their experience thereby gained proved of great value.[39]

From a command point of view, the work of the I Corps Observation Group in the Toul sector was comparatively unimportant. There were no marked opportunities for obtaining information of significant value because no active ground operations occurred during the two and one-half months the group operated from the Ourches airdrome. In the air the enemy was weak, and the two American pursuit squadrons based at Toul were sufficient for the aerial defense of the sector. Yet to the raw American observation squadrons, the period spent in the quiet sector was invaluable as a training ground for the fierce battles of Chateau-Thierry, St. Mihiel, and Meuse-Argonne. The types of missions performed were of five types:

(1) *Short-range reconnaissance:* These flights were prearranged single-aircraft visual reconnaissance over small areas of the lines, or immediately back of them. The observer directed the pilot where to fly by hand signals or via a gosport tube and had a radio transmitter for one-way communications with the Command Post or the Division with which they were working. Upon landing, the observer filled out a form which described the flight and any noteworthy event observed.

(2) *Long-range reconnaissance:* The same general type of mission except it encompassed a larger area behind the lines. The observing aircraft carried no radio (to prevent enemy radio interception), and was escorted by several other observation aircraft for formation security.

(3) *Photographic reconnaissance:* Resembled a long-range reconnaissance very closely. The lead plane was equipped with a camera, the observer having determined by measurement the number of plates and camera magazines required for the areas to be photographed.

(4) *Artillery Adjustment:* Preparation of this sort of mission was similar to the short-range reconnaissance. The observer of the single air-

craft would direct, via radio, the fire of an artillery battery which had initially determined the location of its target by map co-ordinates only. The pilot would fly back and forth at a low altitude (3,000 feet or less) within sight of the target, while the observer estimated the required corrections and transmit them back to the battery.

(5) *Contact Patrols:* These were also single aircraft missions and flown to establish, by aerial observation, the exact location of the front lines, and to drop messages to advanced elements of troops. The theory was that, upon receipt of the proper Very light signal from the aircraft, the infantrymen would display cloth panels which "staked" the front lines. This was critical during advances or retreat because commanders needed to know where their men were. In practice this type of patrol was rarely effective because the ground units never seemed to have received any training in procedures.[40]

There were two distinct kinds of observation squadrons in the American Air Service. Corps observation squadrons were assigned to duties in the immediate vicinity of the battle line such as direction of artillery fire, contact patrols, and short-range reconnaissance. Generally, one squadron was assigned to each division of troops. Army observation squadrons, on the other hand, were given long-range visual and photographic missions and usually worked with army headquarters.

On 13 June the 12th Aero Squadron was moved to Flin airdrome near Vathemenil, a little to the southeast of Luneville in the Baccarat sector. Officers and men alike were disgusted upon their arrival to find that the airdrome was far from ready for operations. A few newly constructed hangars were available, but the landing field had to be leveled, and offices and barracks had to be constructed. With the hard-working Anderson leading the way the squadron set about the task of completing the job. Spirits were quickly lifted when, a few days after their arrival at the new base, the old AR's were replaced by eighteen new Salmson 2A2 airplanes. The Salmson was a fast, first-line observation aircraft powered by a reliable 260-h.p. radial engine. It was armed with a front-firing Vickers, plus two Lewis machine guns mounted in the observer's cockpit. At last the squadron would be able to compete on an equal basis with the best enemy aircraft. The 12th Aero was assigned to work with the 42 U.S. (Rainbow) Division then in training in the Baccarat area. Like the Toul sector, this proved to be an inactive area, and the squadron was to perform much the same type of combat training as before.[41]

Two other corps observation squadrons, the 90th and the 99th, began operations in the Toul sector in June, 1918. The 90th Aero, commanded by Major John L. Dunsworth and equipped with old two-place Sopwiths, arrived at Ourches on 13 June and immediately prepared for action. Three days later, Major Dunsworth and his observer, Lieutenant N. B. Adams, led a three-ship patrol over the lines between Apremont and Xivray. No aerial opposition was encountered, but the plane manned by Lieutenants Merrett White and T. N. Hendricks was damaged by archie. Later that same day a second patrol of five planes, led by Lieutenants Harold E. Greist, pilot, and Fred Vinson, observer, toured the same sector without incident. On 20 June First Lieutenant W. G. Schauffler became squadron commander replacing Major Dunsworth, who would soon become the commander of the 96th Day Bombardment Squadron. Schauffler, a recent transfer from the 1st Aero Squadron, had seen service on the Mexican border and "had the honor of being the first pilot of an American squadron to fly over the front." Under his able leadership the 90th, soon to be known as the "Pair of Dice" squadron, worked several months in the Toul area. As Leland Carver, the squadron historian, stated: "from the air, every stick and stone of the sector became familiar to the pilots and observers, and the 'V' in the woods north of Flirey was to direct many a pilot toward home and safety after his first trip over the lines."* This familiarity with terrain would be of great significance during the St. Mihiel campaign in September, 1918.

The 99th Aero Squadron, commanded by Major Arthur Christie, arrived in the Toul sector on 1 June 1918, and was based at Amanty. This squadron, equipped with Salmson aircraft, made its first war flight on 22 June, when three planes, flown by Lieutenants Clarence C. Kahle, Harry H. Nutt, and Sterling Alexander, reconnoitered the battle area in the vicinity of the Moselle River. Work

---

* Carver, of Detroit, Mich., a pilot in the 90th Squadron, served with the French ambulance service for several months before America entered the war. In the summer of 1917, he enlisted in the U.S. Air Service at Paris and took his pilot training at Tours and Issoudun. After a brief tour with the French and gunnery training in Italy, he joined the 90th Aero Squadron. He served on the Toul front, St. Mihiel, and Meuse-Argonne and, after being shot down and wounded on 4 November 1918, became the squadron historian.[42]

in the Toul region was of short duration, for on 1 July the squadron was transferred to Luxeuil-les-Bains, some sixty miles south of Nancy. On 15 July one flight from this squadron was sent to train with the U.S. 5th Division in the Vosges mountains near Epinal, where it remained until the end of August.[43]

The history of army observation in the AEF during the spring of 1918 is the story of the 91st Aero Squadron. This rather remarkable unit was organized at Kelly Field, Texas, on 20 August 1917, and started its movement to the war front on 30 September. After spending nearly a month of "drill and guard duty" at Garden City, Long Island, the squadron embarked for Europe on the R.M.S.S. *Adriatic* on 27 October. "At Halifax," according to the squadron historian,

the convoy of seven ships was picked up, and a quiet, uneventful trip was ended on November 10th, when Liverpool with her curious floating docks, her cobble-stoned streets, and her smoky skies greeted the travellers. The stay here was short, however, for at 3:15 P.M. the Squadron pulled out of Liverpool, arriving at Southampton by midnight. The following day HMS Huntscraft No. E 216, which in spite of its name proved to be a cattleship, started with the 91st for Havre, arriving after numerous delays, at 8:30 A.M. of the 13th. Everyone was allowed to "rest" at the Rest Camp there until 3:30 the next morning, when the Squadron left to take the "40 hommes, 8 Cheveaux" express for their destination, A.E.F. Headquarters at Chaumont, where they arrived at 10:30 P.M. of the 15th.[44]

The nucleus of the squadron, which included everyone but the flying officers, arrived at Amanty (Meuse) on 14 December 1917, and was placed under the temporary command of Major Joseph T. McNarney. Pilots began to arrive early in February, 1918. Major John N. Reynolds, a regular army officer and pilot in the 1st Aero Squadron in Mexico, took command on 24 February. Reynolds' first task was to solve a morale problem among the pilots. As the squadron history states, "A more disgruntled crowd of officers can hardly be imagined, as they had been taken from the chasse (pursuit) class at Issoudun, the hoped for goal of every flyer, and sent to what they expected to be an observation squadron flying A.R.'s." The personality of "Major John," however, was to work wonders, and within a few weeks the aviators were convinced that the 91st was the best army squadron on the front.

The 91st Aero Squadron received Salmson 2A2's late in April, and moved to Gondreville-sur-Moselle, located about three miles east of Toul, on 24 May 1918. Although the squadron was eager to begin active service, there were still further delays. A full complement of observers was not obtained until the first week in June, and the unsatisfactory quality of propellers furnished by the French did not permit safe flying until they were replaced a few days later. The first war flight of the squadron took place in the late afternoon of 7 June, when a formation of four Salmsons, escorted by a flight of Spads from the 1st Pursuit Group, went over the lines at 10,000 feet. Although no enemy air activity was encountered, almost every plane was damaged by very heavy and accurate antiaircraft fire.[45]

During the remaining part of June, the 91st Aero Squadron, acting under orders of the Eighth French Army, made numerous visual and photographic reconnaissance flights into the Etain, Conflans, and Metz areas. These missions deep behind the German lines were not without casualties. On 12 June Lieutenant Blanchard P. Battle, pilot, and Captain Joseph F. Williamson, observer, failed to return from a protection mission. A few days later it was learned by way of a note dropped by a German flier that the two were prisoners of war. On the same day Battle and Williamson were lost, Lieutenants Willis A. Diekema, pilot, and William Badham, observer, ran into heavy antiaircraft fire over Arneville, and, with their radiator punctured, some thirty holes in the Salmson, and a "furrow through the pilot's helmet," were forced down. Fortunately, Diekema was able to get back to the Allied side of the lines before his engine gave out. On 13 June a three-ship formation from the 91st was attacked by a flight of Pfalz fighters a few miles west of Metz. Lieutenant Victor H. Strahm and his observer, Captain James Wallis, became separated in the fight from the rest of the formation and suffered heavy damage before driving off three attackers. Meanwhile, Lieutenants John Lambert, pilot, and Howard T. Baker, observer, escorted by Lieutenants H. A. Schaffner, pilot, and Walter Bender, observer, fought a ten-mile running battle with five Pfalz pursuits. During the fight Baker shot down one of the attackers. No confirmation could be secured, however, as the action took place several miles behind enemy lines.[46]

Certainly, the deep penetrating 91st Aero Squadron found the Toul sector less "quiet" than did the corps observation squadrons.

This is understandable because it was necessary for the army observation unit to range over the very nest of the Hun *Jagdstaffeln*. By the end of the month the squadron was rapidly becoming a seasoned outfit.

American day bombardment had its beginning on 18 May 1918, when the 96th Aero Squadron, commanded by Major H. M. Brown, was moved to Amanty airdrome, near Gondrecourt. This squadron, the first in the United States Air Service to have bombardment as its sole mission, was organized at Kelly Field, Texas, in August, 1917, and sailed for England on R.M.S.S. *Adriatic* in late October. Although scheduled to receive its advanced bombardment training in southern England, plans were changed, and the unit was sent immediately to France and stationed at the 7th Aviation Instruction Center at Clermont-Ferrand. Here the squadron trained, for the most part, in the popular Breguet—the aircraft they would use later in combat. During the six months spent at Clermont-Ferrand the mechanics of the squadron, in the words of Bruce C. Hopper, "acquired a complete knowledge of the Breguet day bombardment plane and of the Renault motor by daily visits to the nearby Michelin factory where the planes were assembled. The experience thus gained by assisting in the construction of the planes and assembling the Renault motors in the factory proved of immense value when the squadron was sent to the Zone of Advance."*

Brown's 96th Aero Squadron faced real problems during its first weeks at the immense tree-surrounded Amanty airdrome. The flying equipment consisted of ten old instruction bombing planes, type Breguet 14-B2, which had 300-h.p. type 12 FEV Renault motors. They had been transferred by the 7th Aviation Instruction Center. Since these particular planes had been in training service since December of 1917, they were in poor condition. It proved impossible to secure Breguet spare parts, and the squadron's mechanics, under the leadership of Master Sergeant James Sawyer,

* Bruce C. Hopper, a pilot with the 96th Aero Squadron throughout its war operations, probably rolled up more bombing missions than any other American pilot. Later he was assigned the task of writing the history of American day bombardment in World War I, and the article cited here is an excerpt from his unpublished manuscript, "When the Air Was Young: American Day Bombardment, A.E.F., France, 1917–1918," written at the end of the war. After the war, Hopper served as professor of government and international affairs at Harvard University.[47]

were forced to use pieces of discarded French farm machinery. As recorded in the squadron history,

Part of a weather-beaten harvester was used for a tail post for one of the planes; wagon tires were cut up and used for tail skids, and pieces of an ox-cart tongue were employed to reinforce wing spars on several planes. One of the planes carried brace wires which had once served on the telephone line of communications. Plane No. 4014 was crashed in a bad field and was salvaged for spare parts. Everyone of the remaining nine planes, when put on the available list, carried some part of plane No. 4014.[48]

Thus, by using an extraordinary amount of ingenuity the squadron was able to operate long before spare parts from the supply depot at Colombey-les-Belles were available.

Amid much fanfare and excitement the 96th staged its first operational raid on 12 June 1918. Late afternoon found eight Breguets loaded with bombs and ready for the long-awaited mission against a hostile target, in this case the railroad yards at Dommary-Baroncourt. Present to watch this milestone in American bombardment aviation were General Hugh Trenchard, commander of the British Independent Air Force in France, and several other high British, French, and American officials. The squadron was practically without precedent for guidance, being isolated from French and British bombing squadrons, and had only two pilots on its rolls who had ever crossed enemy lines. After much picture making, the eight teams of pilots and bombardier-observers prepared to take off.

Shortly after 4:00 P.M. Major Brown and his observer, Lieutenant Howard G. Rath, of Pasadena, California, led the flight into the air. Two planes were forced to return to the base because of engine trouble, but the other six finally reached the bombing altitude of 12,000 and proceeded to the target without further mishap. Although encountering a heavy and accurate barrage of archie over the target, the squadron, dropping on the lead of Rath, scored several hits in the railroad yards and warehouses located nearby. With the bombing run completed, Brown turned the formation for home. A short time after leaving the target area the flight was attacked by three German fighters; pilots closed in and held a tight formation, however, and the observers were able to beat off the attackers. One of the Breguets, piloted by Lieutenant Charles P. Anderson, received two explosive bullets in the engine but managed to reach Amanty. Three others ran out of fuel but made safe landings on the Allied side of the lines. Later that evening the entire squadron staged a grand party celebrating the "unqualified success of the first American bombing raid."[49]

Several other successful bombing missions were flown against supply dumps and communications lines during the next several days. On 14 June Lieutenants André Gundelach, pilot, and Pennington H. Way, observer, led a formation of five planes to Conflans, approximately fifteen miles west of Metz, and "successfully bombed the railroad yards and round houses" with 632 kilos of bombs. Although intense antiaircraft fire was experienced, no casualties were suffered. Four days later Lieutenant Thornton Hooper, with Rath acting as lead observer, led a five-plane attack on Conflans in which 780 kilograms were dropped on the railroad yards. On the morning of 25 June, Gundelach led a four-plane raid against the same target, but because of poor visibility only partial success was attained.[50]

Toward the end of the month the worn-out Breguets began to crack under the strain. On 22 June a strike against Conflans had to be called off when several of the pilots were forced to return to base before reaching the lines. Raids against the Longuyon rail center were aborted on 26, 27, and 28 June when a majority of the participating aircraft developed engine trouble.[51] Thus the end of June, 1918, found the American day bombardment program practically at a standstill because of lack of machines.

The Toul sector was also the scene of the development of several American Air Service Balloon companies. In fact, the first American air unit to go into action at the front was not the 1st Observation Squadron or the 94th Pursuit Squadron but the 2nd Balloon Company. On 26 February 1918, this company, commanded by Captain Ira R. Koenig, moved into position near Royaumeix, some eight miles north of the city of Toul, there relieving a French company. The 2nd Balloon Company worked at first with the 1st U.S. Infantry Division and, after 3 April, with the U.S. 26th Division. On 12 April the 4th Balloon Company, under the command of Captain Claude E. Smith, arrived at Lahaymeix, a half-dozen miles northwest of St. Mihiel, and was assigned to work with the 2nd

Division. Three days later Lieutenant Walter J. Reed's 1st Balloon Company took station at Baccarat, where it was assigned to the 42nd Division. These three companies, the only ones at the front until the end of July, were under the control of the I Corps Balloon Group at Toul.[52]

A balloon company normally consisted of 6 officers and 150 men equipped with two balloons, one of which was held at some distance to the rear in reserve. The balloon, attached to a cable, was sent up and hauled down by an engine-driven winch. It normally operated at heights of up to 3,000 feet. The two observers in the basket were in telephone communication with a chart room maintained by the company on the ground. In the chart room, observations were plotted and passed on to division headquarters. Under ideal circumstances a balloon company worked with a particular division; the two or three companies assigned to a corps reported to a Corps Chief of Air Service, usually through a Balloon Group Commander.[53]

The balloon observer, with his high-powered binoculars sweeping a radius of ten miles or more, had no picnic up among the clouds. When a kite balloon went up it attracted considerable attention from the enemy because of its effectiveness in securing and passing on information. Frequently, long-range guns were directed at this aerial observer, but more dangerous to the balloonist was the enemy pursuit plane with its incendiary bullets. If the aircraft successfully ignited the highly flammable, hydrogen-filled bag, only quick work could save the men in the basket. The time from the first flames and the ultimate explosion and fall of the balloon was rarely over fifteen seconds. Consequently, the observer usually took to his parachute first and asked questions later. Of course, if the attacking plane was spotted soon enough the balloon was hauled down where it might be better protected by the company's machine gunners on the ground. During its stay on the Toul front in the spring of 1918, the 4th Balloon Company lost one balloon to German artillery fire. No other casualties were suffered.[54]

The main mission of the balloon companies was to regulate artillery fire, locate targets, and report all activities in the enemy lines. The Toul sector proved a little too quiet for the training of balloon personnel since there was little artillery fire, almost no opposition from German aircraft, and very little troop movement. However, liaison methods were developed, and the crews got much valuable practice in the actual maneuvering of the balloon itself, experience which would pay dividends in the furious days ahead.

NOTES

1. Patrick, *Report to Commander-in-Chief,* 226.

2. "History of the First Pursuit Group" (Gorrell Histories, AS AEF, N, IV), 2.

3. *Ibid.;* see also Kenn Rust, " 'Aces and Hawks,' History of the First Fighter Wing," *Air Power Historian,* October, 1962, 214.

4. Rust, *ibid.*

5. "Chronology of Air Service Units Assigned to Armies to November 11, 1918" (Gorrell Histories, AS AEF, D, II), part I, 10.

6. Rust, "Aces and Hawks," *loc. cit.,* 214.

7. "History of the First Pursuit Group," *loc. cit.,* 3.

8. *Ibid.*

9. *Ibid.*

10. *Ibid.;* "History of the 94th Aero Squadron" (Gorrell Histories, AS AEF, E, XII), 2.

11. U.S. War Department, Office of Director of Air Service, "Brief History of Air Service, AEF."

12. "History of First Pursuit Group," *loc. cit.,* 3.

13. *Ibid.,* 4.

14. Barrett, *The First War Planes,* 110.

15. *Air Service Bulletin,* VII, No. 302 (31 October 1918), Information Section, AS AEF, now housed in the Jones Collection, USAF HD Archives, Montgomery, Ala.

16. The DSC citation is quoted in Stringer, *Heroes All!* 274.

17. Thomas G. Miller, ed., "Confirmed Victories of A.E.F. Pursuit Groups, 1918," *Cross and Cockade Journal,* Spring, 1962, 43.

18. James Norman Hall and Charles B. Nordhoff, eds., *Lafayette Flying Corps,* I, 382–84.

19. "Chronology of Air Service Units," *loc. cit.,* 8, 12.

20. "History of the First Pursuit Group," *loc. cit.,* 4–6.

21. See DSC citation in Stringer, *Heroes All!* 85; Rickenbacker, *Fighting the Flying Circus,* 120–26.

22. An excellent treatment of this whole controversy may be found in Maurer Maurer, "Another Victory for Rickenbacker," *Air Power Historian,* April, 1960, 117–24.

23. Rickenbacker, *Fighting the Flying Circus,* 60–61.

24. Maurer, "Another Victory for Rickenbacker," *loc. cit.,* 124.

25. Bruce Robertson, ed., *Air Aces of the 1914–1918 War,* 93–96.

26. Miller, ed., "Confirmed Victories of A.E.F. Pursuit Groups, 1918," *loc. cit.,* 43.

27. Miller, ed., "Casualties of A.E.F. Pursuit Aviation," *ibid.,* 34.

28. Philip M. Flammer, "Lufbery: Ace of the Lafayette Escadrille," *Air Power Historian,* January, 1961, 13–14.

29. Whitehouse, *Legion of the Lafayette,* 93–109.

30. Hall and Nordhoff, *Lafayette Flying Corps,* 328–38.

31. Herbert Malloy Mason, Jr., *The Lafayette Escadrille,* 284–86. See also Mitchell, *Memoirs,* 200–201.

32. See Operations Reports for the month of May in "History of 27th Pursuit Squadron" (Gorrell Histories, AS AEF, E, VI).

33. *Ibid.*

34. Hartney, *Up and At 'Em,* 160–63.

35. See "First Pursuit Group Memo No. 37, September, 1918" (Gorrell Histories, AS AEF, E, XIII).

36. "History of the 1st Aero Squadron" (Gorrell Histories, AS AEF, E, I), 1–5.

37. "Tactical History of Corps Observation" (Gorrell Histories, AS AEF, D, I), 6.

38. J. J. Sloan, "The 12th Aero Squadron Observation," *American Aviation Historical Society Journal,* Fall, 1964, 179.

39. Patrick, *Report to Commander-in-Chief,* 226.

40. Miller, ed., "Eyes of the Army: The Observation Corps," *Cross and Cockade Journal,* Spring, 1962, 80–81.

41. "History of the 12th Aero Squadron" (Gorrell Histories, AS AEF, E, III), 1–10.

42. Leland M. Carver, *et al., The Ninetieth Aero Squadron, American Expeditionary Forces,* 16–17.

43. "History of the 99th Aero Squadron" (Gorrell Histories, AS AEF, E, XV), 1–2.

44. "History of the 91st Aero Squadron" (Gorrell Histories, AS AEF, E, X), 1–3.

45. *Ibid.,* 5–6.

46. *Ibid.*

47. Bruce C. Hopper, "American Day Bombardment in World War I," *Air Power Historian,* April, 1957, 88.

48. "History of the 96th Aero Squadron" (Gorrell Histories, AS AEF, E, XIV), 4–5. See also "Raid Log of the 96th Aero Squadron," in the same volume.

49. *Ibid.*

50. *Ibid.*

51. *Ibid.*

52. John H. Tegler, "The Humble Balloon: Brief History—Balloon Service, AEF," *Cross and Cockade Journal,* Spring, 1965, 11–25.

53. Miller, ed., "Balloon Section, AEF," *Cross and Cockade Journal,* Spring, 1962, 90.

54. Tegler, "The Humble Balloon," *loc. cit.,* 1–2, 24.

VI

Ordeal by Fire: The Aisne-Marne Campaign

THE indoctrination period for American air units was all too short. In a desperate effort to win the war before the fresh tide of American men and resources could permanently tip the scales against them, the Germans began a series of titanic offensives in March, 1918, that reached a blazing climax at the Second Battle of the Marne in July. Hoping to crush the British and roll them back against the sea away from their French allies, Ludendorff launched his first blow against Amiens in the Somme on 21 March. The Germans had carefully trained their divisions in Hutier tactics, named for General von Hutier, which had been used so successfully at Riga and Caporetto. Their troops had been taught to forget all that they had so painfully learned about trench warfare and adapt themselves to mobility characterized by "short intensive artillery preparation, a creeping barrage, by-passing of strong points, massive infiltration, and continued forward movement." The campaign was successful in driving a deep salient into the British positions before the push was finally halted by Allied reserves on 5 April. Four days later Ludendorff struck his second blow at the Battle of Lys on a twelve-mile front just south of Ypres. This blow, too, came perilously close to success before British troops, with Haig's "backs to the wall" order ringing in their ears, brought the German avalanche to a halt on 29 April. The Allies had lost at least 350,000 men during the six weeks of fighting, the Germans not many less.[1]

Determined to pin down the French and draw their reserves away from the hard-pressed English in Flanders, Ludendorff now aimed a third knockout punch at the Aisne sector further to the east. This third great German blow, consisting of forty-two divisions, struck the French on 27 May. Moving on a twenty-five-mile front, the Germans wrenched the Chemin-des-Dames from the French, bought earlier at so great a price, and then plunged across the Aisne River. By 3 June, the slashing German divisions had reached the Marne at Chateau-Thierry, only fifty-six miles from Paris. A salient thirty-two miles deep at its maximum with a base of fifty miles had been hammered into the French lines before the latter, with valiant assistance from the oversized 2nd and 3rd U.S. Divisions, halted the drive.* During the next several days a fourth German offensive designed to expand the base of the Marne salient and link it with the Amiens bulge in the Somme area met only partial success.

Ludendorff had intended the Aisne drive only as a diversionary movement before turning back to the task of knocking the British out of the war, but its stunning success in reaching the Marne from Reims to Chateau-Thierry presented him with new possibilities. A second big offensive in the same area would certainly force the Allies to rush reinforcements from the western end of the front— and if they did not, a breakthrough to Paris was possible. This new offensive would necessitate a substantial build-up. The Germans, however, were unable to achieve any large degree of surprise this time. General preparations, usually well-kept secrets, leaked out of Berlin or were spotted from the air, while detailed plans were learned from captured prisoners. This information enabled the new Supreme Allied Commander Foch to rearrange his reserves and take other defensive measures.

It was into this tense situation along the Marne that many of the American ground and air units that had been testing their arms in the Toul sector were transferred in late June, 1918. The American air units—four squadrons of the 1st Pursuit Group and three squadrons of the I Corps Observation Group—together with some French

---

* Advance elements of the U.S. 3rd Division met the Germans in the streets of Chateau-Thierry on 31 May and then withdrew to the south bank of the Marne, where the division stoutly resisted all German efforts to establish a bridgehead. Checked at Chateau-Thierry on 1 June, the Germans wheeled toward Vaux and Belleau Woods where, by 4 June, the 2nd U.S. Division finally halted the drive. Fierce counterattacks by the 2nd Division and U.S. Marines attached to it recaptured Belleau Woods by 25 June.

outfits were organized into the 1st Brigade under Colonel Billy Mitchell and given responsibility for that portion of the battle area around Chateau-Thierry. The move to this new front was well planned. Several days before the transfer was made, Mitchell, along with Majors Atkinson and Royce, commanders of the pursuit and observation groups involved, "had visited the new sector, made liaison with the Army Aeronautics Commander of the Sixth French Army, and had reconnoitered the airdromes assigned to each group."[2] Mitchell described the actual details of the transfer in the following fashion:

I organized the movement of our air units from Toul to the Chateau-Thierry district in three echelons, a part from each group going ahead to the airdromes to which the planes were to fly, to prepare for their coming. The airplanes were then flown directly to their destinations, where the squadrons found arrangements already made for them and most of their mechanical personnel on the ground. The third echelon, called the rear party, remained at the old airdrome, cranked up the machines as they departed, picked up everything that was left, then proceeded in motor trucks to their new station.[3]

On 29 June, fifty-four Nieuports from the 1st Pursuit Group were flown the 140 miles from Toul to the new base at Tonquin without major mishap. Tonquin airdrome, a large smooth field, was located about twenty-five miles southwest of Chateau-Thierry. The officers were quartered in the "magnificent and historic Chateau de la Fertelle [an estate] over 900 years old." The enlisted men were billeted in the various private homes of Tonquin.[4]

There were other newcomers in the Marne district in late June and early July, 1918. In order to cover their substantial build-up in the weeks after the Aisne drive, the Germans had concentrated a huge mass of pursuit aircraft in the area. Operating with the German Seventh Army were *Jagdgeschwader* I (Goering) and *Jagdgeschwader* III (Lorzer) with an additional ten *Jagdstaffeln* organized in two *Jagdgruppen*. The German First Army had three *Jagdgruppen* totaling fifteen *Jadgstaffeln,* while *Jagdgeschwader II* (Berthold) and two *Jagdgruppen* worked with the Third Army. Thus some forty-six of the seventy-eight German fighter squadrons on the Western front, including all three of the famous "Flying Circuses," were located in the Chateau-Thierry sector early in July. It was to this battle area that the American 1st Pursuit Group came, almost entirely inexperienced and flying obsolete Nieuports, but eager and quite unaware of its unreadiness for the inferno ahead.[5]

The test against the new and dangerous enemy was not long in coming when, early in the morning of 2 July, a flight of eight Nieuports from the 27th Aero Squadron roared off the Tonquin airfield and climbed toward Chateau-Thierry. Led by Lieutenant Donald Hudson, of Washington, D.C., the flight droned on to the northeast. After about fifteen minutes the formation passed over the shell-torn city of Chateau-Thierry and swung to the east up the crooked dirty-brown ribbon of the Marne. The day was bright and sunny with only a few fleecy cumulus clouds scattered about to provide hiding places for enemy scouts. An occasional burst of archie was seen as well as a new antiaircraft shell known as the "Flaming Onion" which "burst with a crack like the high explosive 'Archie' but was of white smoke." Since the young 27th Aero pilots had never seen the "Flaming Onion" before, they noted with interest that "coincident with the explosion a ball of fire cork-screwed through the air in a horizontal direction along an ever widening circular path."[6]

No foreboding of disaster entered the minds of the eight pilots as they roared on to the east. Minutes passed; then, on reaching the little town of Dormans, some fifteen miles up the Marne from Chateau-Thierry, the formation banked steeply to the left and began its leisurely return flight. Five more minutes ticked away as the little Nieuports raced along at 120 mph. Then, just north and east of Chateau-Thierry, Hudson's sharp eyes caught nine black specks on the horizon. Moments later he tensed in the cockpit as he recognized the specks as the late-model Fokker D-7. Had he known the red Hun fighters swinging across his path were flown by the crack *Jagdstaffel* 4 of the Richthofen Circus and led by the famed Ernst Udet he would have been even more apprehensive. As it was, however, the eager young Americans, fresh from their successes against the tame German squadrons on the Toul sector, quickly accepted combat. Within seconds Nieuports and Fokkers were locked in a twisting, rolling, looping, and turning dogfight. At the end of the blazing thirty-five-minute duel two Americans had been shot down behind enemy lines—Lieutenant Edward Elliott was killed and Lieutenant Walter B. Wanamaker became a prisoner of war. Wanamaker was shot down by Udet to become the latter's thirty-ninth victory.* By the end of the war Udet had run his score to sixty-two, making him second only to the incomparable Baron Manfred von Richthofen in the German Air Force. The 27th Squadron pilots claimed four kills of their own in the epic air battle, but only two were ever confirmed. In spite of the odds, they had fought well against one of the finest German *Jagdstaffeln*. Yet, it was clear to most that, equipped with the old Nieuports and armed with the jam-prone American-built Marlin machine gun, the American squadrons would suffer heavy losses.

On the same day that the 1st Pursuit Group moved to Tonquin, Royce established his I Corps Observation Group headquarters at Saints, a short distance to the north. Within a few hours the 1st and 12th Aero Squadrons arrived and prepared for immediate operations. The airdrome was situated on a large level wheat field which had only recently been harvested. The hangars, already erected by the French, were the standard type of large Besseneaux canvas shelters; all was well camouflaged. The enlisted men, for the most part, were billeted in a group of farm buildings bordering the airfield, while the officers were quartered in the nearby villages of Saints and Mauperthuis.[8]

The sector of the front to be covered by the observation squadrons extended from Chateau-Thierry northwest to Courchamps, a distance of ten miles. On 30 June, most of the pilots and observers of the 1st and 12th Aero Squadrons conducted flights over the front lines to familiarize themselves with the new sector. When, on 1 July, the U.S. 2nd Division launched its attack on Vaux, some three miles west of Chateau-Thierry, the aviators of the two squadrons were called upon to provide infantry contact patrol. Despite the fact that these squadrons had had little experience with moving troops in the Toul district, they performed their jobs in a creditable fashion. The Vaux experience would be of great benefit later in July when the whole Marne front became fluid.[9]

The I Corps Observation Group had barely unpacked at Saints when, on 6 July, it was moved again, this time to Francheville, a small village to the northwest of Coulommiers. On the same day the 88th Squadron, by then under the command of Captain Ken-

---

* After the war Wanamaker had a long and distinguished career as a common pleas judge in Akron, Ohio. During Ernst Udet's frequent visits to the U.S. during the period between the two world wars, he and Wanamaker became fast friends.[7]

neth P. Littauer, a veteran of scores of observation missions with the Lafayette Flying Corps, arrived to bring the group to full strength. The sorely needed group was assigned immediately to the I Army Corps, consisting of the U.S. 26th Division (which had just replaced the 2nd Division) and the French 167th Division, operating in the vicinity of Chateau-Thierry. "Judge" Coyle's 1st Aero Squadron was given responsibility for all corps missions, including adjustment of heavy artillery fire, surveillance of hostile artillery, and visual reconnaissance of the entire front. The 12th, commanded since 1 July by Captain Stephen H. Noyce, was assigned to work with the 26th Division while the 88th operated with the 167th Division. Because of the inability of the 88th's old Sopwiths to carry the latest camera equipment the other two squadrons were made responsible for all photographic work.* The 88th was reequipped with Salmsons during the latter part of July.

For the Americans, operations in the Chateau-Thierry–Marne-Vesle sector were divided into three periods: (1) the preparation for the expected German drive, which came on 15 July; (2) the crushing of that offensive and the preparation for the Allied counteroffensive, which began on 18 July; and (3) the counteroffensive itself, from Soissons to Chateau-Thierry, with the subsequent retreat of the Germans to the line of the Vesle River and finally to the Aisne River. Each of these periods "called for a somewhat different disposition of the air forces to effect the best results."[11]

The first phase of the campaign was primarily defensive. During the first two weeks of July the unstable state of the sector made it imperative that frequent photographs be secured not only of the first-line position but enemy rear areas as well. The observation group aircraft were kept in the air from dawn to dusk in carrying out these missions along with the ordinary visual reconnaissance patrols. Because of the considerable distance between the Franche-

* Owing to the great need for mature flying officers in higher Air Service echelons, the I Corps Observation Group was to undergo several command changes during the six weeks of the Aisne-Marne campaign. On 1 July Maj. Ralph Royce was made chief of Air Service, I Army Corps, and moved his headquarters to La Ferte-sous-Jouarre, where he worked closely with Mitchell's 1st Brigade and the Army Corps Commander. Maj. L. H. Brereton served as group commander from 1–7 July; Maj. Melvin A. Hall from 7–16 July; Maj. Joseph T. McNarney from 16 July–1 August; and Capt. Stephen C. Jocelyn from 1 August until the end of the campaign.[10]

ville airdrome and the target areas, an advance landing field was established at Morass farm, near La Ferte-sous-Jouarre. Two aircraft from each squadron were sent there shortly after daybreak each day. Supplies for the operation were transported by motor truck from the Francheville base, and a radio station was established. Thus, in radio communication with both group and corps headquarters, pilots and observers stood by to fly "command mission"—flights ordered by headquarters to investigate rapid changes in the tactical situation on the ground.[12]

The large concentration of aggressive German *Jagdstaffeln* in the Chateau-Thierry area caused the inexperienced corps observation squadrons some difficulty in carrying out their long-range photographic assignments. Although efforts were made to provide fighter escort from the equally inexperienced 1st Pursuit Group, which had now moved to Saints, little success was achieved. Time wasted in rendezvous with the friendly pursuit flights cut deeply into the cruising range of both. A policy gradually adopted was that of sending a number of observation aircraft on each photographic mission, the leading airplane of the formation being equipped for the photographic work contemplated with the others acting as biplace protection.[13] This tactic freed the pursuit squadrons from the difficult close-support task and enabled them to operate offensively, a role they performed much more effectively.[14] For whatever reason, observation losses in the first phase of the bloody campaign were light. Several observation aircraft were hit, but only two observers were wounded. Losses in the second and third stages proved to be more severe.

If observation squadron casualties were light during the first two weeks of July, the same could not be said for American pursuit units. Not only was the inexperienced 1st Pursuit Group facing the best in the German Air Force, but they were doing so in an obsolescent aircraft. In addition, pursuit pilots were made somewhat more vulnerable by the necessity of providing close escort protection for observation planes. Also, patrol tactics learned on the Toul front proved faulty. The small three- to five-ship formations used in the early part of July simply could not cope with the large hunt formations used by the German Circuses. Finally, the group had to operate at maximum range from airfields much too far from the battle lines. All of this would be corrected eventually, but before the changes could be made the 1st Pursuit had to pay dearly. In addition to several wounded, Lieutenants Wanamaker (27th), William Chalmers (94th), Carlisle Rhodes (95th), and Stuart Mc-Keown (95th) were shot down behind the German lines and captured, while Lieutenants Edward Elliott (27th), Maxwell Parry (147th), Sidney Thompson (95th), and Quentin Roosevelt (95th) were killed in action.[15]

One of the group's most shocking losses was young Quentin Roosevelt, of the 95th Aero Squadron. As the son of former President of the United States Theodore Roosevelt, Quentin had a difficult job in making his squadron mates accept him as an ordinary pilot. Throughout his Air Service career he had found that no officer wanted the responsibility of assigning him to hazardous duty. In fact, it had been a real struggle for him to escape a desk job to take flight training. Soon after his assignment to the 95th Aero Squadron, he was made a flight leader over his own protest. Believing himself unqualified, he turned the leadership over to a more experienced pilot, Lieutenant Edward Buford, once he was in the air and flew as a wing man in the rear of the formation. Rickenbacker later wrote: "Gay, hearty and absolutely square in every thing he said or did, Quentin Roosevelt was one of the most popular fellows in the group."[16] Yet, Quentin was courageous to the point of recklessness in trying to gain a reputation on his own merit rather than that of his father.

On 10 July, in a rather unusual manner, Roosevelt gained his only victory as a war pilot. After becoming separated from his 95th Squadron formation near Chateau-Thierry he attached himself as the last man in a second formation which he believed to be friendly. He was apparently unnoticed by anyone in this flight. Several minutes passed before he realized that the formation was proceeding north and well behind enemy lines. Suddenly, to his horror, he saw that each of his new "friends" bore huge Maltese crosses on wings and tail! Young Roosevelt's reaction was to fire a long burst into the Fokker immediately ahead of him and then make a hard, diving turn toward home. Glancing back over his shoulder he watched the Hun explode in flames. The formation leader apparently did not realize what had happened, for Roosevelt was not pursued as he continued his strut-straining dive to the south.[17]

Roosevelt's fabulous luck did not last. Four days later he was killed when once again he became separated from a flight led by Lieutenant Buford and was attacked by seven "red-nosed Fokkers" of *Jagdstaffel* 21. A German wireless message received a few hours after the fight indicated that Roosevelt had been shot down by Sergeant Karl Thom, one of the top aces of the Richthofen Circus.[18] German records, however, give the credit to Sergeant Christian Donhauser, of *Jasta* 21, who ended the war with fifteen victories.

Although facing great odds (estimated by the French as four to one), the 1st Pursuit Group was not without some success against the enemy in the first phase of the Chateau-Thierry campaign. During the fifteen days, pilots of the group were to score some nine victories. No new aces appeared, but Lieutenant John MacArthur, of Hartney's 27th Aero Squadron, pushed his score to four, while Lieutenants Ralph O'Neill, of the 147th, and John Mitchell, of the 95th, each destroyed their third enemy aircraft.

In order to regain control of the air over Chateau-Thierry, a British Air Brigade under General "Boom" Trenchard was moved to Tonquin from the Somme area on 7 July. To make room for the one hundred-plus Sopwith Camels, Bristol fighters, and Handley-Page bombers, the American pursuit group was transferred to Saints airdrome, which had just been evacuated by the I Corps Observation Group. At Saints, according to the 27th Aero Squadron historian: "part of the officers were located in the Hotel de Marie. This famous hotel was once used as an Arabian Hospital and to the sorrow of those unfortunate officers who entered the arms of Morpheus there, the Arabs left their friends the justly celebrated 'cooties.' The men were billeted in a large farm house, but because of the heat many simply used pup tents in the open."[19]

The 4th Park Squadron reported to Saints about the same time and was placed under Captain John Rankin, former supply officer of the group. From that time, this organization became an essential and integral part of the 1st Pursuit Group. It salvaged all planes, procured all supplies, and took charge of road building and transportation.[20]

An event of considerable importance to the 1st Pursuit Group occurred on 5 July, when Eddie Rickenbacker ferried in the first Spad 13. By the middle of the month, about twelve of these first-line French fighters had been delivered to the 94th Aero Squadron, and the old Nieuport 28 was on its way out. The Spad 13 was a rugged little biplane, powered by an 8-cylinder, liquid cooled, 220-h.p. Hispano-Suiza engine, with a top speed of 138 mph.[21] The other three squadrons were not reequipped with the new machine until early August. Not all of the pilots in the group were enthusiastic about the change. The 94th, now commanded by Captain Kenneth Marr, and the 95th, which had had the most trouble with the Nieuport's tendency to shed its upper-wing fabric, were delighted with the sturdy, fast-diving Spad. On the other hand, the 27th and 147th, whose British-trained commanders perhaps better understood the advantages and limitations of the rotary-engine fighters, were outspoken in their criticism of the trouble-prone 220-h.p. Hispano-Suiza engine in the Spad and its relative lack of maneuverability. Major Bonnell, commander of the 147th, was so critical that he was given another assignment and was replaced by one of the 94th Aero Squadron Flight Commanders, Lieutenant James Meissner.[22]

During the Chateau-Thierry campaign the "Hat-in-the-Ring" squadron played a less decisive role in the actions of the group than it had performed in the Toul sector. Perhaps the most important reason for this relatively quiet role was the fact that it received the new Spads in July and was in the process of making the transition from the Nieuport. Another factor may have been that some of the squadron's top pilots were out of action. Douglas Campbell had been wounded in June and had returned to the United States, while several other experienced pilots had been given roles of leadership in other pursuit squadrons. Then, early in July, Rickenbacker was ordered to a hospital in Paris where he spent several weeks recuperating from a mastoid operation. During the entire five weeks of fighting in the Marne-Vesle area the squadron scored only three victories and lost five pilots.[23]

Toward the end of the second week in July, Allied headquarters became convinced that the long-anticipated German drive to expand the Chateau-Thierry salient was imminent. On the afternoon of 14 July the American observation group was ordered to make a deep photographic penetration of the German rear. Although this mission was hotly contested by antiaircraft fire and fighters, the photography plane returned to the airdrome with more than twenty-five excellent plates. The information obtained indicated that the big push would likely occur within twenty-four hours, "for his [the enemy's] troop movements and occupation of hitherto unused battery positions were manifest."[24] The interpretation of the photographs was correct.

Shortly after midnight, 15 July, the big German offensive, known by history students as the Second Battle of the Marne, got under way. "The whole sky was lighted up by the artillery on both sides," wrote Billy Mitchell:

Rockets and signals were appearing everywhere; searchlight beams were sweeping the sky; the buzz of airplanes going and coming, and the noise of their bombs dropping covered the whole of the line. As yet we were uncertain where the main attack was being made. . . . I called up our pursuit group and observation group on the telephone and ordered them to have everything ready to operate by daylight.[25]

But the question was where would the main German attack come and where would the squadrons be needed most? A 3:00 A.M. conference with Major Gerard, commander of French air units in the sector, revealed that, because of a mix-up in orders, the French Air Force would not be able to go into action for several hours. Gerard suggested that the American and British squadrons patrol the skies immediately but admitted that he did not know where the main German attempt to cross the Marne was taking place. Rather than risk heavy casualties in aimless patrols, Mitchell proposed a reconnaissance mission to find out what the enemy was doing. This plan was agreed to, and Mitchell hurried to Saints airdrome to borrow a Spad. Unwilling to risk sending a junior officer on the mission, Mitchell, the direct actionist, decided to make the search himself.

The American Air Commander's idea was to patrol the Marne until he found the main enemy attempt to establish a bridgehead. Taking off alone at dawn, Mitchell flew north until he hit the Marne; then he wheeled right and followed the stream toward Epernay. The ceiling was low, "between three hundred and twelve hundred feet," and he had to hug the winding, steep-banked stream to avoid becoming lost in the clouds and haze. At first he could see little troop movement and no air activities at all. Near Jaulgonne, some seven or eight miles upstream from the town of Chateau-Thierry, he met a few Fokkers, who either did not see him or, if they did, paid him no attention. Still he could see no significant troop movements; then,

Suddenly as I rounded a turn of the river east of Dormans, I saw a great mass of artillery fire hitting the south bank, and, spanning the river, five bridges filled with German troops marching over. I looked everywhere for German airplanes but there were none in the sky at the time. I received no anti-aircraft fire and apparently no attention was paid me, although I flew within five hundred feet of the bridges.[26]

These bridges were of pontoon construction. The 1st Brigade Commander had found his target and now hurried back to the 1st Pursuit Group airdrome, where he ordered an aerial attack on the bridges. A few minutes later he reported his findings to the Allied high command.

From the news brought back by Colonel Mitchell and other information collected in the early hours of the attack, the German plan became obvious. By hitting hard both east and west of the cathedral town of Reims, Ludendorff hoped to pinch off that strong point and widen the Marne salient. He believed that such action would draw in vast reserves from the Somme front, where still another hammer blow was scheduled to fall shortly. Of course, if the Allies did not so react, the prospect of a breakthrough to the French capital from the Marne was excellent.

What the German Commander did not know was that Marshal Foch and his redoubtable lieutenant, one-armed General Henri Gouraud, commander of the French Fourth Army, had devised an ingenious defense in depth. Nor could he know that the flood of fresh American troops now arriving in the area would preclude the necessity of any significant transfer of French and British reserves from the west. Certainly, he had no idea that his punch of fifty-two divisions would be brought to a grinding halt in three short days and that within a month the entire salient would be neutralized.

Mitchell's early morning order to attack the pontoon bridges at Dormans was carried out with dash and enthusiasm. Over twenty years later Harold Hartney wrote,

I shall never forget July 15, 1918, as long as I live. It seemed as if the whole German Army, in desperation, simply hurled itself at our part of the lines around Chateau-Thierry. Our boys were in the air practically all the time. I turned my own machine over to one of the pilots. Frantic orders came through asking us, high flying pursuit planes, to skim the ground and try to fix the position and extent of the German advance, to try and determine how far over the Marne the Boche had reached. It was the ultimate of frenzied excitement. Allied troops of all kinds were rushing by us in both directions, French going back on relief, waves of Americans going forward. It was the climax of the war.[27]

Both observation crews and fighter pilots were in the air constantly, the former working with artillery batteries and trying to keep track of the German movements, the latter valiantly attempting to maintain control of the air and strafing troops on the ground. Hartney noted that the boys were magnificent, but he singled out one for special mention:

MacArthur, particularly appointed himself a committee of one to stop the whole German Army by strafing the troops crossing the bridges at Dormans and elsewhere on the Marne. . . . Time and again he came in, filled up with gasoline and bullets and rushed out again. He flew a total of seven and a half hours, emptying all his ammunition on the ground troops and hurrying back for more.

Even Hartney could not stand the excitement any longer and made two flights in the battle area in an unarmed Sopwith Camel. As he stated later: "with no armament, all I could do, with fully armed German planes dashing at me from all sides, was to take a quick 'look-see' and run like hell toward home."

Strangely enough, in the more than a score of aerial combats no confirmed victories were scored by the Americans; nor did they lose a man. However, as Major Hartney pointed out, the

damage to our machines got so bad that I finally had to forbid them to go out any more because all of them had so many bullet holes in their wings and vital parts that I was afraid they would fall apart from bullet-hole fractures and we would be out of the battle entirely.[28]

Mechanics and fitters of the 1st Pursuit Group worked through the night of 15 July getting the riddled airplanes ready for the bitter air battle which would come the next day.

Toward noon on 15 July, as American and French air units were bombing and strafing the pontoon bridges over the Marne, Billy Mitchell made an important decision. Instead of devoting the entire energy of the Allied air forces to tactical interdiction of the battle lines at the river, why not attack the enemy's great supply base at Fere-en-Tardenois, located some twelve miles northeast of Chateau-Thierry? After making a few quick notes on this strategic

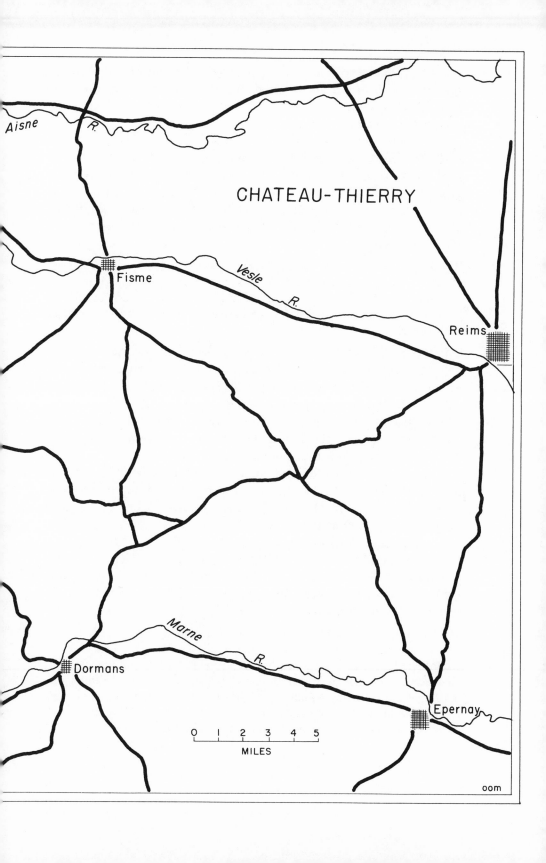

CHATEAU-THIERRY

Aisne R.

Vesle R.

Fisme

Reims

Marne R.

Dormans

Epernay

0 1 2 3 4 5
MILES

oom

possibility, he drove to the headquarters of Marshal Foch, where he conferred with Major Armengaud, the staff liaison officer for aviation. Mitchell's plan was accepted and the decision was made to launch the air attack the next day.[29]

The attack on Fere-en-Tardenois would serve two purposes. First, the destruction of the German stockpile of supplies would take much of the steam out of the Boche drive across the Marne. Second, the air strike against the great supply depot would tie down most of the German air forces to defensive action and would indirectly cover the Allies' own offensive plans in the sector. As Mitchell noted,

It was quite evident that, as the Germans were attacking at the salient of which the base was formed by Soissons on one side and Reims on the other, if we could get in from either base, we could turn the whole German position and if successful, attack them from the rear and perhaps destroy their whole army.[30]

Undoubtedly, Foch had already seen this opportunity. Aerial reconnaissance reports that the Soissons side of the German flank was weakly held merely confirmed his decision to make his strongest counterattack there, along the Aisne River. The shift of large numbers of troops to the Soissons flank would necessitate controlling the air in that area; the Fere-en-Tardenois operation would, to a great extent, accomplish this objective.

Since the Americans had no bombardment aviation in the Marne district, British and French units had to be called into the Fere-en-Tardenois operation. Apparently, the Germans were completely surprised by the first attack, which occurred at high noon on 16 July. Although the British alone lost twelve planes in the raid, the mission served its purpose. Not only was vast destruction caused at the supply base, but Germans immediately began to concentrate their air forces to protect this vital area. The 1st Brigade Commander elatedly commented:

We had found the Achilles' heel of the German position north of the Marne and had seized the initiative in the air. . . . It is the first case on record where we, with an inferior air force, were able to put the superior air force on the defensive and attack whenever we pleased, without the danger of the Germans sending great masses of the pursuit aviation over to our side of the line. What we could do if we had one thousand good airplanes instead of a measly two hundred and fifty![31]

Despite the lack of bombing aircraft, American air units contributed in a substantial way to stopping the German three-day offensive. Pilots of the 1st Pursuit Group flew scores of strafing, escort, and offensive patrols over the Fere-en-Tardenois–Epernay–Chateau-Thierry Triangle during the daylight hours of 16 July–17 July. They had learned some valuable lessons during those early weeks and now applied them. They flew in squadron-size formations of twelve to fifteen airplanes, if at all possible. These formations were usually echeloned in flights of five, with one flight remaining high to act as cover. Their early experiences had also taught them to refrain from trying to out-dive the fast sturdy Fokker D-7 in their fragile little Nieuports. Undoubtedly, their best possibility of staying alive was to take advantage of the extreme maneuverability of their slower machines.

During the brief German offensive, pilots of the 1st Pursuit Group destroyed eight enemy aircraft. Of these, Hartney's 27th Aero shot down five, while the 95th got two, and the 147th destroyed one.[32] Lieutenant John MacArthur, of the 27th, became the group's first ace since its arrival on the Marne by shooting down a "Hun two-seater" over Norey on 17 July. Lieutenant Jerry Vasconcelles, a little later to be the commanding officer of the night-flying 185th Aero Squadron, described his own first victory in his combat report of 16 July 1918:

Our formation was going west toward Chateau-Thierry south of the Marne. Two (2) biplace E.A. started north directly under us. I dove straight on the rear machine firing about 90 rounds. I saw the observer drop into the cockpit. I then passed over the machine and when I turned the machine was going down in flames. I watched it crash and burn in a woods just south of the Marne in the region of Dormans at 18 h 10.[33]

Despite the group's success in the Second Battle of the Marne, there was cause for gloom in the Hotel de Marie at Saints. Lieutenant Daniel W. Cassard, of the 147th, met his death in aerial combat, and Lieutenant B. Malcolm Gunn, of the 27th and Chester, Pennsylvania, was shot down and killed while engaged in a strafing mission on 16 July. Late in the afternoon on the same day Lieutenant Robert "Bugs" Raymond was shot down and captured when an eleven-plane formation led by Lieutenant Fred Norton became involved in a battle royal with a dozen Fokkers at 18,000 feet over

Chateau-Thierry. Hartney, accompanying the formation in his gunless Camel, described the action:

I can remember enemy and friendly ships in about equal numbers, whirling around madly with streaking tracer bullets flying all over the place and that familiar and highly distressing zip-zip-zip of bullets whistling past your ears. In no time at all we were down to 1,500 feet and over Epernay where I didn't believe there were any Germans. And here Lieut. R. L. "Bugs" Raymond, made his exit from active service in the jolly old war.[34]

According to Raymond's own report after the war his conqueror had been Udet himself.

In the early morning hours of 18 July, the French Tenth Army struck at the German's Soissons flank with terrific force. Despite a cloudburst which drenched the area, the U.S. 1st and 2nd Divisions in the van of the giant counterattack made rapid progress in the first hours. Because a mix-up in orders sent British squadrons to Reims, Mitchell's airmen had to bear the brunt of the air action over the advancing Allied forces. For a time in the course of the battle, everything seemed to hang in the balance. Would the Germans make a stand and hold their positions, or would they retire rather than face being cut off in the Marne area? The Allied high command could get no answer to this question; yet, it was extremely vital to know the German intentions as quickly as possible. To get the necessary information Mitchell ordered his chief of attack aviation, Major Lewis H. Brereton, to arrange for the required reconnaissance mission.[35]

Brereton called in his chief of operations, Captain Elmer Hazlett, and the two discussed the possibilities. Both agreed that obtaining the necessary information would involve a squadron of twenty-five planes, with a likely loss of eight to ten planes and their crews. Could the already depleted observation forces stand such a loss? After further discussion the pair decided to make the perilous flight alone and hurried to the Francheville airdrome, where a Salmson two-seater had been ordered in readiness. Within a short time the pair took off and climbed toward the battle area to the northeast. Hazlett, acting as the observer, realized that without fighter escort it was useless to keep searching the skies for enemy Fokkers. He therefore concentrated his attention on the ground, charting and mapping everything he could observe. Despite their precarious tour through a hostile sky, he allowed the whole panorama to seep into his mind:

Imagine the solid and continuous barrage of thousands and thousands of shells bursting in a line for miles and miles, the barking cannons on each side, like so many ferocious dogs spitting fire, roads filled with on-marching troops, coming up in formation from both sides, walking, as it were, into that veritable valley of death and destruction; the air filled with hostile planes and our whole safety depending upon the supposition of being alone and so far behind the lines that the Germans would not realize the presence of an enemy plane.[36]

After what seemed hours the Salmson settled gently to the friendly sod of the home airdrome. The audacious pair had completed one of the great flights of the war and had secured the vital information needed. The answer: the enemy was retreating on all fronts.

The third phase of the Marne-Vesle campaign, the Allied counteroffensive, was now under way. The American I Corps Observation Group would play an important role in this phase. Basic plans for the coming operation had been received by the group on the afternoon of 17 July, only a few hours before the big push on the German right flank was launched:

Liaison was effected immediately with all corps and divisional posts of command. The area was divided into zones, each zone to be covered by one group of the corps artillery in the work of neutralizing the artillery of the enemy. Copies of this map were prepared for the use of the squadron observers in the work of surveillance. This plan permitted the location of an enemy battery in action by the observer. He could then signal this information to the corps artillery group concerned, which would immediately take it under fire.[37]

Although attempts had been made during the preceding two weeks to fix plans for the rapid adjustment of roving batteries against targets signaled from the airplane, no significant success had been attained; thus, there was no real provision for handling a mobile warfare situation such as occurred in this third phase. Plans had also been made for infantry contact patrols.

Perhaps one of the most vital chores performed by the corps observation squadrons was that of infantry contact. Here the American squadrons faced serious problems. Without a doubt, the most serious difficulties encountered in these patrols were the direct result of the infantry's lack of training in carrying out their part in response to the signals of the air observer. Although some American divisions, namely the 26th and 42nd, had been given a certain amount of training with the Air Service, it was insufficient to insure success in determining location of the ground troops by observation aircraft. Most infantry units were not equipped with the necessary supply of flares and panels for marking out the lines. Even after these shortages were remedied the aircraft observer received poor response to his call for panel display. Consequently, in the majority of infantry contact patrols the observer was forced to descend to altitudes varying from 150 to 500 feet and face galling machine gun and rifle fire while locating the front lines of the friendly troops by distinguishing their uniforms.[38] Needless to say, this work was extremely hazardous. On 18 July, Lieutenant Floyd E. Evans, pilot and flight commander in the 88th Aero Squadron, was hit by ground fire and received a severe leg wound while flying an infantry contact mission. He became dizzy from pain and loss of blood, but with Lieutenant H. W. Merrill, his observer, offering encouragement and direction, he managed a landing in friendly territory before losing consciousness. On the next day an 88th Squadron plane manned by Lieutenants Philip R. Babcock, pilot, and Howard T. Douglas, observer, had its "intake manifold . . . shot away and a strut shattered"[39] by ground fire but landed safely at an auxiliary airdrome. Not all were so lucky, however, for on 20 July, Lieutenant John Boldt, an observer with the 1st Aero, was killed by machine gun fire from the ground.[40]

In the opening days of the Allied offensive, I Corps Observation Group airmen met with considerable success in the regulation of artillery fire on enemy batteries. As gun batteries began moving forward in the pursuit, however, it became increasingly difficult for the Air Service to maintain communications, and in only a few cases were observers successful in directing the fire of a battery on a fugitive target. In order to improve this situation each squadron assigned a trained observer to corps artillery command posts to act as an Air Service liaison officer. Although this helped some, inadequate radio equipment and poor telephone connections prevented any effective cooperation. All was not black, however, for during the advance to the Vesle River, observation aircraft continued to operate as information agents for artillery commanders.[41]

During the first two weeks of the drive, the advance was so rapid that it became impossible to take photographs of all the territory on the line of march, and photo missions were limited to procuring pictures of certain areas chosen by the Army and Corps G-2. Weather conditions frequently hampered the execution of these missions, but on the whole, valuable results were obtained. In the latter part of July, the photographing of oblique views at very low altitudes became customary, for such photographs proved of great value to the command in planning future operations. Up until this time, all aerial photography had been vertical.[42]

As the Allies pushed past Fere-en-Tardenois and on toward Fismes, on the Vesle, American corps observation casualties increased sharply. On 25 July Lieutenants Alfred N. Joerg and John J. Bradford, of the 12th Aero, were shot down and killed. Three days later the squadron lost two airplanes and three crew members when attacked by the enemy in the neighborhood of Fere-en-Tardenois. In a recent letter, Lieutenant Stephen W. Thompson described the fight in which he destroyed two German planes:

I was sent up to adjust artillery fire with Lt. John C. Miller as pilot. Lts. Alfred B. Baker and J. C. Lumsden went along in another plane. We ran into [an enemy] circus.

The whole fight took place near the ground at Fere-en-Tardenois. The clouds were about 800 feet high. We could see the barrage of shells bursting below us.

Lt. Lumsden was killed and Lt. Baker was taken prisoner. After the war Lt. Baker told me that Oberleutnant Leonhardt* was given an Iron Cross for shooting Miller and me down.

The first plane that dived on us I shot down; it never came out of the dive . . . as did the second plane . . . but the third plane hit my machine gun. I could not pull the trigger. They were shooting explosive bullets. One struck part of our plane and exploded. The slug went into my right leg; fortunately it had exploded first. Lt. Miller was shot in the stomach with a bullet that exploded there. Yet he managed to bring the plane down and land on the bank of the Ourcq River. This was behind our lines. Lt. Miller was taken to a dressing station where he died.

Miller and I were given official credit for these two airplanes.†

* This probably refers to Oberleutnant Erick Loewenhardt, who led *Jasta* 10 and had fifty-three victories at the time of his death in October, 1918.

† Thompson had some claim to have been the first American Air Service man to shoot down an enemy plane. While flying as a volunteer observer with a French squadron he destroyed a German on 5 February 1918.[43]

Photography missions continued to attract the most attention from enemy pursuit aviation. On 1 August a photo plane from the 1st Aero Squadron, escorted by two protection planes from the same squadron, was attacked by nearly a score of Fokkers in the vicinity of Soissons; two of the Salmsons were shot down. Lieutenants Ernest Wold, James Wooten, Walter B. Miller, and John Sykes were killed, and the observer in the third plane, Lieutenant Earl B. Spencer, was severely wounded.[44]

Although the I Corps Observation Group operated for a brief time with the U.S. divisions on the Soissons flank, most of its work during the Aisne-Marne counteroffensive was with the U.S. I Army Corps pushing northeast from Chateau-Thierry toward Fismes on the Vesle River. In order to stay abreast of the rapidly moving ground forces, Coyle's 1st and Noyce's 12th Aero Squadrons moved from Francheville to Morass farm on 2 July. On 2 August the I Corps Observation Group moved to May-en-Multien, just north of Meaux; on 10 August it changed bases again, this time to Coincy, five miles southwest of Fere-en-Tardenois, and on 12 August, with the offensive at an end, the group was sent to Chailly-en-Brie "to await orders to proceed to another sector."[45]

Meanwhile, on 30 July, Littauer's 88th Aero was relieved by a French squadron and four days later moved to Ferme-de-Graves, where it became the nucleus squadron of Major Joseph T. McNarney's newly created III Corps Observation Group. The field, located five miles southeast of the city of Chateau-Thierry, was the farthest point of the German advance in that sector, and had been vacated by them at the beginning of the Allied counteroffensive. According to the squadron historian, "The ground was covered with shell holes which had recently been filled with soft earth; and although it was a very large field, the shell holes made good landings difficult." Squadron officers and men were quartered in nearby farmhouses, all of which were "riddled with shell holes and the poor quality of billets . . . lost the billeting officer most of his popularity."[46] The 6th Photo Section joined the observation squadron a few days later, and after that Littauer's outfit was responsible for most of the photography work of the entire III Corps.

Pursuit pilots found the nineteen days of the Allied drive even more hectic and bloody than the first two stages of the Aisne-Marne campaign. The 1st Pursuit Group worked continuously from dawn until well after dark, with some pilots flying as many as three or four two-hour missions per day. During the last several days they even began the transition to the Spad from the little torque-prone Nieuport. In some cases the test ride in the new machine was also a flight in the battle zone. Engine settings, location of instruments, feel of controls, visibility, climbing attitudes, stall characteristics, and a dozen other items required the full attention of the pilot in his first few rides in any fighter. To ask that he be thrust into combat where he must keep his eyes constantly searching the sky ahead and behind, above and below—while he at the same time is familiarizing himself with the cockpit and the airplane—is murder. Usually, however, the Spads were accompanied by Nieuports.

The group was asked to perform all types of missions from low-level strafing to escort of photography planes to medium- and high-altitude offensive patrols intended to win and hold the skies against the Loewenhardts, Udets, and Bertholds. They had learned that survival rested, to a considerable degree, on large formations with a high flight to protect against surprise; even then, however, the fighting was bitter and the casualties were high. From the beginning of the Allied counteroffensive on 18 July, until its end on 6 August, the American pursuit group destroyed sixteen enemy planes while losing fifteen pilots killed or captured. In addition, several others were wounded but made it back to friendly territory. Because of the prevailing westerly winds in that area of France almost all combats tended to drift well behind the German lines. Consequently, disabled pilots with damaged planes were usually lost, even when successful in getting down in one piece.

Peterson's 95th Aero, the "Kicking Mule" squadron, lost Lieutenant Grover Vann, killed in action, and Lieutenants Paul Montague and George Puryear, captured. In addition, Lieutenant John Hambleton, soon to command the 213th Aero, was wounded, as was Lieutenant Clarence S. Gill. Lieutenants James Knowles and Walter L. Avery destroyed enemy planes over the Chateau-Thierry-Bouvardes area on 25 July, and on the next day Sumner Sewall, later to be governor of Maine, shared the destruction of a Boche airplane with four others. Avery's victim fell behind Allied lines, and the pilot, Lieutenant Karl Menckhoff, commanding officer of *Jasta* 72 and a thirty-nine-victory ace, was captured. The German ace was understandably chagrined to learn that he had been knocked down by a comparative beginner.[47]

The best victory-loss ratio was scored by Jim Meissner's 147th, which chalked up five victories while losing only one pilot, Lieutenant John H. Stevens, who failed to return from a mission on 31 July. No less than nine pilots shared in the destruction of the five enemy aircraft, with Ralph O'Neill, of Nogales, Arizona, scoring his fifth kill to become the squadron's first ace. On 24 July, Lieutenant Wilbert W. White, a New York City boy, scored his first two victories in a torrid aerial duel with enemy Fokkers over Chateau-Thierry. At the time of his death in October, 1918, he was one of the ranking U.S. aces with eight official victories.[48]

The 94th "Hat-in-the-Ring" Squadron, almost completely equipped with Spad 13's, seemed in a strange state of lethargy throughout the period. Several missions were flown but few combats took place. Only one enemy aircraft was shot down, by Lieutenant H. Weir Cook, but on the other hand, only one flier was lost. That one man, however, was Alan Winslow, who had scored the first victory for the group on that misty Sunday in April at Toul. Late in the afternoon of 31 July, a patrol from the 94th had engaged several enemy pursuits a few miles behind enemy lines, and Winslow was last seen falling into the deepening twilight below. His squadron mates anxiously searched for him for several minutes, then, being low on fuel, returned to their base. With the faint hope that the popular Chicago boy would eventually show up at Saints airdrome, now cloaked in darkness, flares were fired periodically to guide him home. He did not come and it was feared that he was dead. A few weeks later, however, a letter came from Winslow himself, from a German hospital, stating that his left arm had been shattered by a bullet during the combat and that the arm had been amputated. He, of course, remained a prisoner until the end of the war.[49]

The aggressive 27th, rapidly becoming one of the very best fighter squadrons on the front, was to down seven Huns during the offensive but was also to lose nine officers killed or captured and one wounded. The first blow came at 7:00 P.M. on 21 July, when a patrol consisting of Lieutenants MacArthur, Norton, Roberts, Dawson, and Miller encountered a storm and high winds several miles south of Soissons. As the five struggled against the gale which was blowing them deeper into German territory, they were jumped by seven Albatros fighters. Only L. H. Dawson and Ivan Roberts returned from the ensuing battle. John MacArthur, who had become an ace only three days before, was shot down and killed as was Fred Norton, a great football player in his college days and one of the squadron's most experienced patrol leaders. Zenos Miller crashed and was taken prisoner. Two Germans were believed to have gone down in the fight.[50]

With the increased losses in July came fresh but raw and inexperienced replacements from Issoudun and Cazaux. All were eager and willing, but none had any real idea of what aerial combat was all about. Squadron commanders or veteran flight leaders usually took these new pilots on "cook's tours" of the sector where they might become familiar with terrain features and learn to "see" other aircraft in the air. Some commanders, such as Harold Hartney, would take the newcomers up for mock dogfights. In these sham battles the recruit became quickly aware that he was easy prey unless extremely alert and led by an experienced patrol leader. Among the nine new pilots who reported into the 27th Squadron a day or two after the disaster which cost the lives of MacArthur and Norton were Lieutenants Frank Luke, a boastful blond Arizonian, and Joseph F. Wehner. Much would be heard of both in the weeks ahead. Hartney's opening comments to the nine young men were designed to jar them out of their complacency and prepare them for the hard days coming up:

You men stand in front of me today [but] within two weeks each and every one of you will be dead—cold dead—unless you weigh what I say.

You are going to be surprised in the first, second or third trip over the line and, despite all I can say right now, you will never know there is an enemy ship near you until you notice your windshield disintegrating or until a sharp sting interrupts your breathing.

School is over. You have a man's job . . . so when you get up there over the lines you find you want to come back that means you're yellow. I do not ask you to be brave enough to go over, I only ask you to have enough guts to come back and tell me so and get to hell out of this outfit . . . you are in the 27th in name only. When you have shown your buddies out there that you have guts and can play the game honestly and courageously, they'll probably let you stay. You'll know without my telling you when you are actually members of this gang. It's up to you.[51]

Of the nine only three survived until the Armistice, but the six who died had accounted for twenty-six victories.

Air fighting reached a crescendo on 1 August, when six pilots

from the 27th Aero were shot down in a tremendous air battle near
Fere-en-Tardenois. The reconnaissance report on that disastrous
flight read simply:

Protection Patrol—7h05 to 9h05; 18 planes. Lieutenants Grant, Daw-
son, Martin, Donaldson, Hunt, McElvain, Whiton, Vasconcelles, Nevius,
Beauchamp, Hudson, Polk, Rucker, Clapp, Roberts, Wehner, Sands,
Luke. To protect two (2) Salmsons (French Photographic Planes) in
Fere-en-Tardenois region. Altitude 3000 meters. Lts. Hunt, Martin, Mc-
Elvain, Whiton, Beauchamp, Sands did not return and are not heard
of as yet.[52]

As the two observation aircraft were working over slightly different territory between Fere-en-Tardenois and Fismes the fighter escort was divided into two groups. Three circuits were made into
German territory and out again in order to give the observers time
to change film. Up to this point no aerial opposition had been met.
Shortly after 8:00 A.M. a fourth circuit was begun; at 8:10 A.M. it
happened. Suddenly one of the formation was attacked by eight
"Checker Board Squadron" Fokkers. Soon the sky was full of Fokkers and Albatros fighters,* and even flights of two-place Rumplers
and Hanoveraners. In the blazing air battle, formations on both
sides broke up into a series of individual dogfights.[53] Lieutenant
Donald Hudson's combat report catches some of the chaos and
confusion of the fight:

We were attacked by 8 Fokker biplane Chasse machines east of Fere-en-
Tardenois at 8h10. I tried to bank to the left and fell into a spin, when
I came out of the spin there were 4 E.A. on my tail. I tried to turn again
but fell into another spin, I was followed by the 4 E.A. down to 1000
meters. As I was coming out of the spin a machine was headed straight
at me. I fired and he turned to the left, I turned a little to the left and
turned back again being right on his tail, I fired about 20 rounds into
him. He fell off slowly on his right wing and went into a spin. I turned
on the other machines and went into a spin, when I came out, the other
machines were climbing up. Just as the fight began, I saw an E.P. [enemy
plane] fall off on his right wing and spin in exactly the same manner as
the machine I shot down. I saw something else fall in flames. A Spad
passed within 20 feet of my right wing, falling on its back. My engine

---

* According to recent research by the editors of *Cross and Cockade Journal,*
these planes were from *Jagdstaffeln* 17, 4, 6, and 10, all top-quality units of the
German Air Force.

was boiling and I could not climb as my Nourrice was empty, and by using the hand pump I could just keep going. Then northeast of the railroad between Fere-en-Tardenois and Spaonay, I encountered a Rumpler biplane at between 100 and 200 meters. He passed me on the right and banked up to give his observer a good shot at me. I turned and got on his tail and followed him in a circle firing right into the cockpit. Suddenly his right wing came off and he crashed. I was being fired at by machine guns on the ground and was essing when I noticed another Rumpler under me to my left. I turned down and fired at the observer. He disappeared and the machine crashed just beside the railroad embankment. I circled the machine once to see if either the pilot or the observer got out, but they did not. Confirmation for three (3) requested.[54]

Indeed, the casualties in the fight had been high. Lieutenants Jason Hunt, Charles B. Sands, and A. L. Whiton were dead; R. C. Martin and Charles A. McElvain* were down in enemy territory and prisoners. Lieutenant Oliver Beauchamp was killed when his bullet-riddled plane crashed on the home airdrome. Sands, Whiton, and Beauchamp had been in the squadron less than one week. Despite its shattering losses, the outnumbered 27th had protected the two photography planes and had at the same time brought down "six Hun attackers." Jerry Vasconcelles, Ruliff V. Nevius, Ivan Roberts, and Don Hudson had scored victories, the latter getting three confirmed kills to become the squadron's second ace.[56]

Three Air Service balloon companies, under the over-all leadership of Lieutenant Colonel A. J. Paegelow, operated in the Aisne-Marne sector during the Chateau-Thierry campaign. Captain Ira Koenig's 2nd Balloon Company moved to Viller-sur-Marne late in June, and some of its aerial observers worked with a French balloon company during the attack on Vaux on 1 July. Six days later the company scored a first, although a dubious one, when they lost their first balloon to enemy aircraft. Lieutenants Leo Murphy and Malcolm Sedgwick, the observers at the time, were forced to jump, thus becoming the first Americans to do so. A few days later the

---

* McElvain fought a long duel with Lt. Alfred Fleischer, of *Jasta* 17, before running out of fuel and landing in German territory. As he glided in for a landing with a dead engine, Fleischer held his fire and landed beside him. The two became friends and after World War II, McElvain, then head of a mortgage company in Chicago, managed to bring Fleischer to the U.S. to live. The German pilot's son, now an American citizen, is employed by McElvain's firm.[55]

company lost a second balloon to a flight of five Spads wearing the Maltese Cross* of the German Air Force.[57]

The 1st Balloon Company reported on 19 July, and the two companies worked with American divisions throughout the counter-offensive of late July and early August. Since the infantry was constantly moving forward, the balloon crews found it necessary to move their position almost daily. Most of the moves had to be made at night because the observers were continuously directing artillery fire and spotting the infantry line during the daylight hours. In the course of the offensive the 2nd Balloon Company moved a total of forty miles, "passing through Bouresches, Epieds, Beuvardes, Villers-sur-Fere, Fere-en-Tardenois"[58] and on to the vicinity of the Vesle River. Early in August, Captain Claude Smith's 4th Balloon Company joined the operations near the Vesle River. During the five weeks of the campaign the three balloon companies lost eight balloons to enemy aircraft and had one balloon damaged by artillery fire. In all, twelve observers were forced to make parachute jumps.[59]

The giant Allied vise squeezing the entire Marne salient from Reims to Soissons slowly reduced the bulge until, by 6 August, the Germans retired to the high ground north of the Vesle River, thus bringing to an end the main Aisne-Marne offensive. Eight U.S. divisions (270,000 men) and a number of British had participated, but the bulk of the troops had been French. The campaign ended with two U.S. corps in the line, Soissons captured, and the Vesle reached. Indeed, the battle had far-reaching results. It eliminated the threat to Paris, upset Ludendorff's plan to attack the British again in Flanders, gave the Allies important rail communications, demonstrated the effectiveness of American troops on the offensive, firmly established Allied unity of command, and so dimmed German hopes for victory that even Ludendorff no longer hoped for more than a stalemate thereafter.

Despite their relative lack of training the American air units had performed well. The 1st Pursuit Group had flown hundreds of

---

* Craig S. Herbert, historian of the National Association of American Balloon Corps Veterans, in his article, "Humble Balloons—Corrections," *Cross and Cockade Journal,* Winter, 1966, 345, agrees that the Spads were flown by German pilots, but states that they still carried the French cockade rather than the black cross. Several Spads had been captured by the Germans in their drive toward the Marne.

strafing, escort, and patrol missions and had destroyed thirty-eight enemy aircraft while losing thirty-six pilots. The 1st Corps Observation Group had carried out its assignment with the loss of eleven men and had learned many valuable lessons. These two groups, plus the three balloon companies, would form the veteran nucleus for an ever expanding Air Service during the final campaigns coming up in September, October, and November.

NOTES

1. Hanson W. Baldwin, *World War I: An Outline History,* 140–43.

2. Capt. Phillip Roosevelt, "History of the Air Service Operations at Chateau-Thierry" (Gorrell Histories, AS AEF, C, I), 1–2.

3. Mitchell, *Memoirs,* 208.

4. "General History of the 27th Aero Squadron" (Gorrell Histories, AS AEF, 1918, N, V), 6. See also "Tactical History of American Pursuit Aviation" (Gorrell Histories, AS AEF, 1918, D, I), 6.

5. Miller, ed., "The Last Knighthood," *Cross and Cockade Journal,* Spring, 1962, 25.

6. "History of the 27th Aero Squadron—Operations in the Chateau-Thierry Sector" (Gorrell Histories, AS AEF, E, VI), 1–2.

7. *Ibid.;* H. Hugh Wynne, "A Brief History of the 27th Aero Squadron—First Pursuit Group, AEF," *Cross and Cockade Journal,* Summer, 1960, 13–15; Hartney, *Up and At 'Em,* 171–73.

8. "Tactical History of Corps Observation" (Gorrell Histories, AS AEF, D, I), 20.

9. *Ibid.,* 181–82.

10. Miller, "Eyes of the Army: The Observation Corps," *Cross and Cockade Journal,* Spring, 1962, 82–88.

11. Patrick, *Report to Commander-in-Chief,* 228.

12. "Tactical History of Corps Observation," *loc. cit.,* 20–25.

13. *Ibid.*

14. Patrick, *Report to Commander-in-Chief,* 229.

15. Miller, "Casualties of A.E.F. Pursuit Aviation," *Cross and Cockade Journal,* Spring, 1962, 34.

16. Rickenbacker, *Fighting the Flying Circus,* 193.

17. *Ibid.*

18. *Ibid.,* 194–96; Harold Buckley, *Squadron 95,* 94–95.

19. "General History of 27th Aero Squadron," *loc. cit.,* 6.

20. "History of the First Pursuit Group" (Gorrell Histories, AS AEF, N, IV), 8.

21. *Ibid.,* 7–8; Rust, "Aces and Hawks," *Air Power Historian,* October, 1962, 217.

22. Hartney, *Up and At 'Em,* 195–96.

23. "History of the 94th Aero Squadron" (Gorrell Histories, AS, AEF, E, XII), 5–6.

24. Roosevelt, "History of the Air Service Operations at Chateau-Thierry," *loc. cit.,* 4.

25. Mitchell, *Memoirs,* 219–20.

26. *Ibid.,* 220–22.

27. Hartney, *Up and At 'Em,* 180.

28. *Ibid.,* 180–81.

29. Levine, *Mitchell,* 121.

30. Mitchell, *Memoirs,* 222.

31. Quoted in Levine, *Mitchell,* 123.

32. "Victories and Casualties" (Gorrell Histories, AS AEF, M, XXXVIII), 15–38.

33. See Combat Reports in "History of the 27th Aero Squadron—Operations in the Chateau-Thierry Sector," *loc. cit.*

34. Hartney, *Up and At 'Em,* 181–82.

35. Levine, *Mitchell,* 124–25.

36. *Ibid.,* 125–26.

37. "Tactical History of Corps Observation," *loc. cit.,* 26.

38. *Ibid.,* 27.

39. "History of the 88th Aero Squadron, Chateau-Thierry Operations" (Gorrell Histories, AS AEF, 1918, E, IX), 2–3.

40. "Victories and Casualties," *loc. cit.,* 71.

41. "Tactical History of Corps Observation," *loc. cit.,* 20–23.

42. *Ibid.*

43. Quoted in James J. Sloan, "The 12th Aero Observation Squadron—Part II," *American Aviation Historical Society Journal,* Spring, 1965, 51–52.

44. "Victories and Casualties," *loc. cit.,* 71.

45. "Tactical History of Corps Observation," *loc. cit.,* 21–24.

46. "History of the 88th Aero Squadron," *loc. cit.,* 3–4.

47. "History of the 95th Aero Squadron" (Gorrell Histories, AS AEF, E, XIII), 1–6. See also Buckley, *Squadron 95,* 109; "German Army Air Aces," *Cross and Cockade Journal,* Autumn, 1962, 216.

48. Miller, "Confirmed Victories of A.E.F. Pursuit Groups, 1918," *Cross and Cockade Journal,* Spring, 1962, 44.

49. Rickenbacker, *Fighting the Flying Circus,* 203–204.

50. See Combat Reports of Lts. Roberts and Dawson in "History of the 27th Aero Squadron—Operations in the Chateau-Thierry Sector," *loc. cit.,* IX; Hartney, *Up and At 'Em,* 187–88.

51. Hartney, *ibid.,* 188–89.

52. Reconnaissance Report for 1 August 1918, in "History of the 27th Aero Squadron," *loc. cit.*

53. "History of the 27th Aero Squadron—Operations in the Chateau-Thierry Sector," *loc. cit.,* 2–3.

54. *Ibid.,* Combat Report for 1 August 1918.

55. See Williams R. Puglisi, ed., "The 27th Black Day," *Cross and Cockade Journal,* Spring, 1965, 13–15.

56. "History of the 27th Aero Squadron—Operations in the Chateau-Thierry Sector," *loc. cit.,* 2–4; Hartney, *Up and At 'Em,* 190–91.

57. Tegler, "The Humble Balloon," *Cross and Cockade Journal,* Spring, 1965, 13–15.

58. *Ibid.*

59. Patrick, *Report to Commander-in-Chief,* 230.

Salmson 2A2, of the 90th Aero Squadron, St. Mihiel, France, 1918.

Avion Renault E-2. *U.S. Army Air Forces.*

10th Balloon Company on the move. *U.S. Army Air Forces.*

Spad XVI. *U.S. Army Air Forces.*

Salmson-12, "B" Flight, 90th Aero Squadron, Ourches, France, July, 1918. Note the "Pair-of-Dice" markings of the 90th Squadron. *Courtesy Leland M. Carver.*

Italian instructors and American trainees at gunnery school, Furbara, Italy, June, 1918. Left to right: Italian instructor, Lt. Watkins, Lt. Carter, Italian instructor, L. H. "Tiny" Wingate, Red Foster, Schulz, George Baxter. *Courtesy Leland M. Carver.*

Salmsons of "B" Flight, 90th Aero Squadron, Ourches, France, July, 1918. *Courtesy Leland M. Carver.*

Fokker D-7 with "Bucking Mule" markings of the 95th Aero Squadron.
U.S. Army Air Forces.

Nieuport training planes at the 3rd Aviation Instruction Center, Issoudun, France.
U.S. Army Air Forces.

13-meter French Nieuport used by American pilots at gunnery school, Furbara, Italy, June, 1918. *Courtesy Leland M. Carver.*

French-built Salmson manned by a crew from the 91st Observation Squadron. *U.S. Army Air Forces.*

Nieuport-28. Squadrons of the American 1st Pursuit Group flying this obsolescent fighter suffered heavy losses during the early phases of the Chateau-Thierry campaign. *U.S. Army Air Forces*.

At this Production Center at Romortantin airplanes and engines received from the U.S. were assembled and then sent to their destinations. *AEF-1917–21*.

Savoia-Verduccia (with plywood fuselage), Italian observation plane, Furbara, Italy, June, 1918. *Courtesy Leland M. Carver.*

Caproni bomber at airfield in Northern Italy. American pilots serving on the Italian front flew this type of aircraft on several long bombing missions across the Adriatic. *U.S. Army Air Forces.*

Halberstadt C-5, a popular German observation plane of 1918.
U.S. Army Air Forces.

Lt. Elliott W. Springs standing beside his Camel. An ace with twelve victories, he was one of the original war birds to train in England during the fall and winter of 1917. *U.S. Signal Corps.*

1st Lt. Clifford D. Allsopp, of the 11th and 96th Aero Squadrons, and 1st Day Bombardment Group, France and Italy, 1917–18. *Courtesy Clifford D. Allsopp.*

Lt. Frank Luke, of the 27th Aero Squadron, ranked first among American aces at the time of his death, 29 September 1918. He was posthumously awarded the Medal of Honor. *U.S. Signal Corps.*

French Spad pursuit plane, 1918. *Courtesy Leland M. Carver.*

Maj. Harold E. Hartney, an ace with six victories, was commander of the American 1st Pursuit Group during the St. Mihiel and Meuse-Argonne campaigns. *U.S. Signal Corps.*

Lt. H. E. Goettler won the Medal of Honor while searching for the "Lost Battalion" during the opening days of the Meuse-Argonne offensive. He was killed in action on this mission. *U.S. Army Air Forces*.

Salmson observation plane with the markings of the 91st Aero Squadron, after a landing accident. *AEF-1917–21*.

"A" Flight of the 148th Aero Squadron. Left to right: Lt. Lawrence Wyly, Lt. Louis Rabe, Lt. Field Kindley (flight commander), Lt. Walter Knox, Lt. Jesse Creech. Remaisnil, Somme, France, 14 September 1918. *U.S. Signal Corps.*

Crew from the 166th Aero Squadron preparing to take off in their DH-4.
U.S. Army Air Forces.

Maj. Gen. Mason M. Patrick was given the American Air Service command in Europe when leaders such as Foulois, Mitchell, and Bolling quarreled over air policy. *U.S. Army Air Forces.*

Brig. Gen. Benjamin D. Foulois was made chief of Air Service, Zone of Advance, in August, 1918, with all tactical units not otherwise assigned under his command. *U.S. Signal Corps.*

Eddie Rickenbacker standing in the cockpit of his Spad pursuit plane. *U.S. Signal Corps.*

Lt. Everett R. Cook, commanding officer of the 91st Aero Squadron, standing beside a Spad 13. Although the 91st was equipped with Salmsons, Cook made frequent flights in the Spad. *U.S. Army Air Forces.*

Lt. Col. John Paegelow (center) commanded the American balloon groups at the front during the fall of 1918. *U.S. Army Air Forces.*

Loading bombs on a Breguet, the most popular bomber used by the American Air Service. *U.S. Signal Corps.*

Capt. Jerry Vasconcelles (left) and 1st Lt. Donald Hudson standing in front of a Sopwith Camel. Both pilots were aces with the 27th Aero Squadron before transferring to the 185th. *U.S. Signal Corps.*

3rd Aviation Instruction Center, Issoudun, France, one part of the largest flight training complex of the AEF. *U.S. Signal Corps.*

Col. Thomas Milling (left) and Gen. William Mitchell (center) with a French flying officer. When Mitchell became chief of Air Service, Army Group, on 14 October 1918, Milling was given command of air units in the First Army. *U.S. Army Air Forces.*

Jenny (JN-4) taking off on a training flight. *U.S. Signal Corps.*

Wreckage of a German plane shot down by Lt. Frank Luke, September, 1918. *U.S. Signal Corps.*

Sopwith Camels, of the 148th Aero Squadron, taking off at an airdrome near the English Channel for combat patrol on the British front. This squadron ranked second only to Rickenbacker's 94th. *U.S. Signal Corps.*

Officers of the 90th Aero Squadron, around October, 1918. Left to right:
Alan Lockwood, Percy Schuss, William Schauffler, John Sherrick, Fred Tillman, Van Hayden. Capt. Schauffler was a highly effective squadron commander during the fierce air battles of September and October, 1918. Lt.
Tillman won the DSC in June, 1918, for carrying his wounded pilot to safety
through heavy machine gun fire after their plane had been shot down. *Courtesy Fred. A. Tillman.*

Muddy conditions prevailed
at the 1st Air Depot, Colombey-les-Belles, during September, October, and November,
1918. The Besseneaux can-
vas-covered hangars in the
background usually accom-
modated six aircraft and
could be dismantled and
moved very quickly. *AEF-
1917–21.*

American balloon crew preparing for a training mission at Costuidan, France. *U.S. Army Air Forces.*

Handley-Page bomber under construction. Thi huge plane was used extensively by British Gen. Hugh "Boom" Trenchard's Independent Air Force. *U.S. Signa Corps.*

Observers preparing to ascend in a balloon. *U.S. Signal Corps.*

Group from the 20th Aero Squadron standing in front of an American-built De Havilland-4. *AEF-1917–21*.

Lt. Field E. Kindley, of the 148th Aero Squadron, with his mascot "Fokker" in the cockpit of a Sopwith Camel. *U.S. National Archives*.

VII

Lull Before the Storm: The Build-up for St. Mihiel

THE five weeks following the Aisne-Marne campaign saw a drastic reorganization of American land and air forces and intensive planning for the first big American offensive. The conduct of American units in the Marne offensive had strengthened Pershing's case for an independent American Army and a separate sector on the Western front. Actually, this had been the original plan, but it had lapsed in the crisis produced by the German offensives in the spring and early summer of 1918. As the danger subsided, Pershing pushed the issue again. Marshal Foch was willing to listen and, after a series of conferences, agreed to the organization of the U.S. First Army, assigning it to the St. Mihiel sector. On 10 August the First Army was formally organized, and within a short time most of the American divisions then in France were assembled in the Toul–St. Mihiel area.

While the Allied offensive to neutralize the German salient on the Marne was at its height, Foch had called a conference of his commanders to plan future Allied operations. He proposed first to reduce the three great German salients in order to improve lateral communications between Allied sectors, shorten the line, and set the stage for a general offensive. By the end of August two of the three salients had been wiped out. The Marne bulge had been choked off by 6 August, and within ten days a combined British-French force had flattened the Amiens angle. This left only the St. Mihiel salient, assigned to the Americans on Pershing's request.

The St. Mihiel salient was created by the German General von Falkenhayn's attempt in 1914 to take the French fortress town of Verdun by a converging maneuver. The northern force under the Crown Prince was stopped early, but the southern force under General von Strantz was not stopped until it had taken the ancient city of St. Mihiel on the east bank of the Meuse River.[1] The rupture in the battle line formed by von Strantz' advance was generally known as the St. Mihiel salient. The salient thus created was approximately twenty-four miles across the base and about fourteen miles deep. It extended from Les Eparges (some twelve miles southeast of Verdun) via Saint Mihiel and Seicheprey to Pont-a-Mousson on the Moselle River, a distance of about forty miles. Its primary strength lay in the natural defensive features of the terrain itself. The western face of the salient extended along the rugged, heavily wooded eastern heights of the Meuse River. The southern face followed the heights of the Meuse for about five miles to the east, and then crossed the plain of the Woevre, including within the German lines the detached heights of Loupmont and Montsec, which dominated the plain and afforded the Germans unusually good facilities for observation. In this area the autumn rains normally began about the middle of September, after which the Woevre plains became very difficult to negotiate.[2]

The value of the St. Mihiel salient to the German high command was the fact that it protected the strategic railroad center of Metz and the Briey iron basin. It also interrupted traffic on the main Paris-Nancy railroad, cut the Verdun-Toul railroad, and threatened the Allied territory in its vicinity, especially west of the Meuse. Its reduction was imperative before any substantial Allied offensive could be launched against the Briey-Metz region or northward between the Meuse River and the Argonne Forest toward the general area around Sedan.

Preliminary plans for the St. Mihiel drive called for a major attack by fourteen American and three French divisions. Many obstacles were met in setting up this operation, most of them arising because the American forces were unbalanced in favor of infantry; that is, they lacked sufficient artillery, air, tank, and various other types of units to round out an operational field army. This state of affairs resulted, mainly, from the previous demands of the French and British that the United States give priority to infantry and machine gun units. The French now came to Pershing's aid by providing over half the artillery needed, plus about half the airplanes and tanks. The American Commander's determination to build up an independent American force capable of major operations seemed about to bear fruit.

Preparation for the attack against the St. Mihiel salient was well along when, on 30 August, Foch, anxious to take advantage of the successes around Amiens before the Germans recovered, proposed to reduce the size of the St. Mihiel operation and disperse excess American units among the French and British armies. To exploit the recent successes was of course sound and fully appreciated by Pershing, but he stubbornly refused to let his Army fight, except as an independent force.[3] Two days later he agreed to a compromise plan which left his First Army intact but limited the objective of the St. Mihiel operation so that the American Army could undertake a major offensive between the Meuse River and the Argonne Forest about ten days later. Although the St. Mihiel effort was now subordinated to the Meuse-Argonne operation, it was still very important because it was the first major American effort.

The offensive plan required two nearly simultaneous attacks. Major General George H. Cameron's V Corps would assault the west face of the salient while Major General Hunter Liggett's I Corps and Major General Joseph T. Dickman's IV Corps were driving against the southeast flank. Both forces were to meet approximately in the center of the salient, thus pinching off all enemy forces caught in the angle. Meanwhile the French Colonial II Corps would make a secondary attack against the point of the bulge, following up and exploiting the success of the two main attacks.[4]

As Pershing wrestled with the Allied high command over an independent army and sector responsibility, the American Air Service on the French front was undergoing a rapid expansion. In fact, while the 1st Pursuit Group was being forged into a combat organization in the flames of the Chateau-Thierry district, two new fighter organizations were taking shape in the quiet St. Mihiel area. On 29 July, the 2nd Pursuit Group was formed at the Toul airdrome. It was commanded by Major Davenport Johnson, a former commander of the 95th Aero Squadron, and consisted originally of the newly arrived 13th and 139th Aero Squadrons, plus the veteran

103rd, better known as the Lafayette Escadrille. At Vaucouleurs, a dozen miles to the southwest of Toul, Major William Thaw, one of the first members of the Lafayette Escadrille and more recently commander of the 103rd, was busy organizing the 3rd Pursuit Group. One of Bill Thaw's first actions as a group commander was to trade one of his original squadrons, the 49th, to Johnson for his old outfit. By the middle of August both groups were completed: the new 2nd Pursuit Group included Captain Charles J. Biddle's 13th, Captain Ray Bridgeman's 22nd, First Lieutenant George F. Fisher's 49th, and Captain David E. Putnam's* 139th; the 3rd Pursuit Group included Major John Huffer's 93rd, Captain C. Maury Jones's 28th, Captain Robert Rockwell's 103rd, and Captain John A. Hambleton's 213th Aero Squadrons. The two new groups were in turn subordinated to a command called the 1st Pursuit Wing, which by the time of the St. Mihiel drive also included the newly organized Day Bombardment Group. "This wing was an approximation of the type of tactical organization which the French had evolved by early 1918, combining pursuit planes and light bombers into a mobile and flexible support force for offensive operations."[5] All of the pursuit squadrons in this Wing were equipped with Spad 13's.

During August the 1st Pursuit Group, still based at Saints in the Chateau-Thierry sector, also underwent a change of command. Bert Atkinson, soon to become a lieutenant colonel, left to take command of the newly created 1st Pursuit Wing. Replacing him as group commander was Major Harold E. Hartney, the extremely able squadron commander of the 27th Aero. Captain Alfred A. Grant, a regular army officer and the senior flight commander, moved up to Hartney's old job.[6]

Born in Canada and educated at the universities of Toronto and Saskatchewan, the thirty-year-old Hartney was well fitted for his new position. He had spent one year in the Canadian infantry and twenty-three months in the Royal Flying Corps, including time on the staff of the School of Special Flying, Gosport, England. During his service with the RFC he had shot down five enemy planes and had continued to fly combat missions after his transfer to the Amer-

---

* Putnam was merely the acting commander of the 139th in the absence of Maj. L. C. Angstrom, who had become ill on 25 June and would not return until 13 September, during the height of the St. Mihiel campaign.

ican Air Service to take command of the 27th Aero Squadron. In June, 1918, he scored his sixth aerial victory on the Toul front. Even after he became a group commander on 21 August 1918, he led an active combat role displaying "that dearest commodity in a leader of fighting men, the thorough knowledge of his profession gained by experience."[7] Hartney was respected by all of his fighter pilots, and he handled with equal effectiveness the steady orthodox fliers and the wild and undisciplined Frank Lukes. Following his example, all of his squadron commanders such as Peterson, Rickenbacker, Meissner, Grant, and Vasconcelles continued in fighting roles.

The 1st Pursuit Group continued to operate on the Chateau-Thierry front throughout the month of August. When the battle line moved across the Vesle River, approximately fifty miles from the Saints airdrome, it became necessary for the group to establish a refueling station and temporary landing strip at Coincy, the recent base for several German *Jagdstaffeln*. Lieutenant Frederick Ordway, of New Hampshire, a member of the 27th Aero Squadron, was put in charge of this station, and it was from here that most of the alert operations were carried out.[8] During the last three weeks of the month, air fighting tapered off sharply. Lieutenants Harold Buckley, the future author of *Squadron 95,* and Walter L. Avery were to score the group's only victories during the period when they knocked two "Boche machines" down on 10 August. On the same day their 95th Squadron teammate, Lieutenant Irby Curry, was killed in action. Lieutenant William M. Russell, whose war letters were later published in book form, was lost on 11 August. The only other combat losses for the month came when Lieutenants Alexander Bruce and Walter W. Smyth, of the 94th, collided with each other while attacking an enemy formation. Both were killed.[9]

Although the squadrons of the newly created 2nd and 3rd Pursuit Groups hurried the seasoning process during the hot August days, only the 103rd could be considered an experienced outfit when the big September offensives began. This squadron, sporting the "Indian Head" insignia and made up largely of Lafayette Flying Corps personnel, was to provide much of the leadership for the raw American combat units. Such individuals as Ray Bridgeman, Robert Rockwell, Robert Soubiran, John Huffer, Ken Marr, Seth Low, David McK. Peterson, Charles Biddle, Dudley Hill, Hobie

Baker, and C. Maury Jones served as squadron commanders, while Thaw, Biddle, and Hill led pursuit groups. From the time of its transfer to the American Air Service in February until the middle of August the squadron had served in the Champaigne, Aisne, Ypers-Lys, and Toul sectors and had destroyed twenty-one enemy aircraft. In addition, several of its pilots had scored victories while still with the French. Lieutenant Paul F. Baer, with eight official victories, led the squadron scoring until he was shot down near Armentières and seriously wounded. After that, Lieutenant Edgar Tobin, a native of San Antonio, Texas, became the 103rd's hottest pilot. In one month, 11 July to 11 August, Tobin scored five victories in the Toul area.[10]

The other three squadrons of Thaw's 3rd Pursuit Group had practically no experience when called upon in the St. Mihiel offensive. Huffer's 93rd began operations from Vaucouleurs on 11 August, and was joined by the 213th three days later. Maury Jones's 28th Aero was not ready to begin combat work until 2 September, only ten days before the big drive started.[11] Fortunately, little air opposition was encountered in those last days of August and the opening days of September; consequently, the group suffered few casualties. The 103rd lost two men; the 93rd lost one. No confirmed victories were achieved; however, Lieutenant Christopher W. Ford, of the 213th, did score a "probable" when he "fired 300 rounds" into an "enemy biplane" and saw it spin down out of control.[12]

Davenport Johnson's 2nd Pursuit Group was little, if any, better prepared for the bloody September. His senior squadron, the 139th, began operation in the Toul sector on 30 June. The 13th Aero, commanded by the veteran Captain Charles Biddle, had reached Toul in late June but was not fully equipped with Spads and ready to begin combat patrols until early August. The 49th Aero Squadron arrived on 16 August, and the 22nd was ready for operations five days later.[13]

The 139th Aero Squadron was organized at Kelly Field, Texas, on 21 September 1917, and had trained at the RFC's Taliaferro Field, near Fort Worth. Under the command of Major L. C. Angstrom, the squadron had arrived in Liverpool on 5 March 1918. For the next several weeks, squadron personnel were trained at Romsey, England, and Tours, France, before moving to Issoudun for final training. In May the outfit was transferred to Vaucouleurs, where it was equipped with Spad 13's. Since squadron mechanics were unfamiliar with the Hispano-Suiza 220-h.p. engine, several French mechanics were temporarily attached to the unit. On 30 June the 139th moved to Toul, where it became the pioneer squadron of the 2nd Pursuit Group.[14]

The squadron made an auspicious beginning in its war operations; only hours after its arrival at Toul, Lieutenant David Putnam, a recent transfer from the French Air Service, scored his ninth and the squadron's first air victory when he shot down a German Rumpler over the village of Vieville-en-Haye. On 29 July, Lieutenant Arthur R. Brooks, soon to be a flight leader in the 22nd Aero, destroyed a Fokker in the Buxieres area near St. Mihiel. A few days later, Captain Ray Bridgeman and Lieutenant Vaughn McCormick, also destined to become squadron commander and flight leader, respectively, in the 22nd, downed two Rumplers over the front lines. Putnam, now acting as Squadron Commander in place of the gravely ill Angstrom, was to chalk up the squadron's fifth and sixth victories on 15 August and 22 August. The 139th lost one pilot when, on 17 July, Lieutenant Henry G. MacClure crashed and was captured while protecting a deep reconnaissance mission. This increased tempo in the air action indicated a new German concern for the American build-up then taking place in the Toul sector.[15]

Despite its late start, the 13th Aero Squadron also made headlines in August. In twenty-eight-year-old Charles Biddle the squadron was blessed with outstanding leadership. After graduating from Princeton University and Harvard Law School, the Andalusia, Pennsylvania, man was admitted to the bar in 1914. He practiced law until the spring of 1917, when he joined the French Air Service. Upon completing his flight training at Avord, Pau, and Le Plessis-Belleville he was assigned to Escadrille Spa 73 in July, 1917, as a pursuit pilot. His only victory with the French came in December, 1917, when he shot down an Albatros two-seater over Belgium. Biddle was commissioned a captain in the American Air Service in November, 1917, but remained with Escadrille Spa 73 until January, 1918, when he transferred to the Lafayette Escadrille. Five weeks later that squadron became the 103rd Aero Squadron. On 12 April he destroyed a Halberstadt two-seater, and a month later he was shot down in an attack on a German reconnaissance plane.

Although wounded, he was able to make a safe landing in "No Man's Land," and despite heavy German machine gun and rifle fire, managed to scramble the hundred yards to the security of the British trenches. He took command of the 13th Aero in June, and on 1 August scored the unit's first air victories by bringing down two Albatros scouts near Vieville-en-Haye, six miles west of Pont-a-Mousson. Captain Biddle became an ace on 16 August when, in attacking a Rumpler biplace, he killed the observer and forced the wounded pilot to land his slightly damaged plane behind the French lines at Nancy.[16]

In addition to his own offensive performance, Biddle was able to nurse his embryo squadron through August and early September without casualties. During the period, five of his eager cubs—Lieutenants Harry B. Freeman, William H. Stovall, John J. Seerley, Robert Stiles, and Charles W. Drew—cut their combat teeth by sharing in the destruction of two "Hun aircraft."[17]

The 22nd Aero had originally been scheduled to become a De Havilland bombing squadron, and some of the officers and most of the enlisted men had trained for several weeks with British bombing units. In July, however, plans were changed, and the squadron was reorganized as a pursuit outfit. By the middle of August, equipped with new Spad 13's and commanded by the veteran Ray Bridgeman, the 22nd was ready to begin its great adventure. Lieutenant John Sperry, a flight leader and recent transfer from the 139th, made the unit's first war flight over the lines on 16 August. The next several days proved to be frustrating, to say the least. According to the squadron historian,

The new Spads, with their H-S-220 engines, gave much trouble in leaky tanks, broken water pumps, clogged water systems, fouled carburetors, shorting magnetos, broken gun gears and inaccurate rigging. . . . The new fledglings had much difficulty in concentrating attention outside the plane's intricacies and the excitement offered by the activity of the lines; which, with guns needing wearing-in and motors everlastingly "konking out" caused no little uneasiness during the early trials. As the time grew nearer for the guns to announce the straightening of the St. Mihiel salient, the patrolling grew more vigorous in an attempt to perfect formations. The storm broke with much to be desired in the way of smooth running.

In spite of the early problems with the 220-h.p. Spad, Lieutenant Arthur Brooks brought down a Rumpler in flames for the squadron's first kill on 2 September. Two days later Brooks and Lieutenants Frank Tyndall and Clinton Jones swooped down on a Fokker which had just fired on an Allied balloon and sent it crashing into the village of Barnecourt.[18]

Maintenance of any semblance of formation in any World War I air combat was always difficult. Indeed, it was practically impossible for young pilots to keep track of their patrol leader unless he was identified by some easily recognizable marking or device. In order to standardize the distinguishing markings used by American squadrons, the Chief of Air Service, on 28 June 1918, issued a memorandum which read in part:

a) The plane of a flight commander shall have streamers attached to the tips of the lower wings and a streamer attached to the rudder.

b) The machine of a deputy commander shall have a streamer from the rudder only, the streamers to be made of some closely woven material which will not fray easily.

c) The plane of each squadron commander shall carry two bands of red, white and blue stripes running diagonally from the rear of the cockpit to the rear of the fuselage at the foot of the rudder post.

d) Group and higher organization C.O.'s may mark their planes at their own discretion.

The memorandum also advised that no squadron might place a distinctive insignia on its planes until the following conditions were fulfilled:

a) Observation Squadrons: After one month of service at the front, or immediately upon receiving citation in orders from higher authority for distinguished services.

b) Bombing Squadrons: After one month of service at the front, or immediately upon receiving citation in orders from higher authority for distinguished services.

c) Pursuit Squadrons: After being officially accredited with three enemy planes brought down in aerial combat; or immediately upon receiving citation in orders from higher authority for distinguished services.[19]

Six of the twelve American pursuit squadrons to be used during the St. Mihiel campaign had already qualified for a squadron insignia before the drive got under way. For example, the 103rd's "Indian Head," the 94th's "Hat-in-the-Ring," and the 95th's "Kicking Mule" insignia were well known in Air Service circles.

No American day bombardment units were engaged in the Chateau-Thierry campaign in July of 1918. The single squadron available, the 96th Aero, remained at Amanty throughout the summer from whence it made sporadic sorties against rail centers and supply depots in the Metz-Conflans area. In fact, American day bombardment practically ceased to exist on 10 July 1918, when a formation of six Breguets was forced down behind German lines.

That black July day dawned with low clouds and intermittent rain. Much to the disgust of squadron pilots and observers, it appeared that the scheduled raid against enemy railroad yards at Conflans would have to be cancelled. Nonetheless, they hung around the squadron operations room hoping that the weather would take a turn for the better. A torrid poker game held the attention of some of the aviators, while others planned an excursion to nearby Nancy for "a bath and a good French meal." Their Breguets were bombed up and ready, but the weather held constant. Then late in the afternoon the clouds seemed to lift, and Major Harry Brown, the squadron commander, made his decision to attempt the hazardous mission. At 6:05 P.M., six heavily laden Breguets, with Brown leading the way, lumbered into the air and were almost immediately swallowed up by the descending clouds. Brown set course for the target area to the northeast, and the bombers droned on at 100 mph. An hour later the clouds closed down to 300 feet, and the fliers could no longer maintain visual contact with the landscape below. Major Brown pressed on hoping there might be a break in the cloud cover over the target. What he did not realize was that a strong southwest wind had sprung up and his little formation was being blown deep into German-held territory. After nearly an hour the Squadron Commander shook his ailerons to signify he was lost. An 180° turn was made, but it proved "impossible to return [to the home airdrome] by compass before the gasoline was exhausted."[20] Since American aviators in World War I did not wear parachutes the only thing to do was attempt a landing through the thick soupy cloud layer. All six of the planes were able to work their way down through the overcast and made safe landings near a large city. Much to their chagrin the city turned out to be Koblenz, and all twelve crew members were captured within minutes. Strangely enough, the Americans did not try to burn their planes to keep them out of the hands of the enemy.

A few hours after the disaster, which all but wiped out the United States' only bombing squadron, Air Service headquarters received a humorous message from the Germans: "We thank you for the fine airplanes and equipment which you sent us, but what will we do with the Major?" Billy Mitchell angrily wrote in his diary,

This was the worst exhibition of worthlessness that we have ever had on the front . . . needless to say we did not reply about the major as he was better off in Germany at that time than he would have been with us.*

During the next three weeks the 96th was at an operational standstill. The Koblenz episode left the squadron with only one flyable aircraft and a sadly depleted reservoir of flying officers. Captain James A. Summersett acted as squadron commander until the arrival of Major J. L. Dunsworth on 16 July. The single Breguet was used for bombing practice and flight training until 1 August, when eleven new Breguet bombers were ferried over from the supply depot at Colombey-les-Belles.[22]

With the arrival of the new planes, the 96th Aero Squadron began raids against enemy targets once again. Since there were not enough aircraft available for operations in two flights, the squadron followed the practice of sending out all serviceable planes in one eight- to ten-ship formation. During the fourteen flying days of August, the squadron made twenty raids and dropped over twenty tons of bombs on such targets as Conflans, Etain, and Longuyon. On 20 August, a strike against the railroad yards at Conflans destroyed forty German airplanes standing in boxcars in the station, "and killed fifty workmen and soldiers."[23]

The first serious casualties suffered by the squadron after the July catastrophe occurred on 4 September. A formation of eight planes led by Lieutenant André Gundelach had just completed a

* The Mitchell account is somewhat at variance with the report made by Maj. Brown's observer, Lt. Harold MacChessney, who claimed that they landed near Ihmaret, a short distance from Koblenz. MacChessney stated further that he and Brown destroyed all instruments, maps, etc. and kept a crowd of soldiers and civilians at bay with the plane's guns. Then after dark the two crawled through their pursuers and evaded capture for nine days.[21]

bomb run on the railroad yards at Conflans when five Pfalz fighters were noticed climbing to cut off their retreat. In the words of the squadron historian, Gundelach immediately changed directions

to fly straight into the sun and the leading observer [Lt. Howard Rath] fired the six red flares to signify "enemy planes, close in." The enemy planes were from a much dreaded squadron whose markings were a red nose, white tails and a mottled brown fuselage. The enemy pilots concentrated their efforts to break up the Breguet formation by attacking from all sides. The observers were on the alert, however, and beat off the first rush easily. The combat then settled down to a running fight with the scouts diving in to fire their bursts, then zooming back to positions above and behind the formation. When the first formation of scouts, 5 in number, quit the combat, the observers were given a recess of 3 minutes. Other specks coming from the clouds were first thought to be Allied pursuit planes, but when they dived, guns wide open, the observers wisely decided the attack was being continued by another flight from the same red nose squadron. The attack was highly organized and continued as far as Verdun. One of the second 5 enemy planes was shot down out of control, and crashed in the vicinity of Frauville. 1st Lieut. Arthur H. Alexander, pilot, was shot in the small of the back, and though weakened from the loss of blood, managed to land his plane at the airdrome. His observer, 2nd Lieut. J. C. E. McLannan, was wounded in four places in the legs, one ball severing a small coin in his pocket and carrying the fragments through the wounds. 1st Lieut. D. D. Warner received a ball in the hip, which shattered his thighbone. 1st Lieut. Avrome N. Hexter was wounded in the head, the bullet tearing a furrow above his eyes.[24]

During the vigorous forty-minute battle the 96th had not followed its usual straight and level tactics, but had maneuvered constantly, up and down, left and right while always maintaining close formation. This new tactic had proved effective against an aggressive opponent, and because of their success, pilots and observers gained a new confidence which would give them some solace in the bitter campaign to open eight days later.

The 1st Day Bombardment Group was formed two days before the St. Mihiel offensive opened and included the veteran 96th plus two brand-new outfits, the 11th and 20th Aero Squadrons. In fact, the 11th, commanded by First Lieutenant Thornton D. Hooper, and the 20th, led by Captain Cecil Sellers, had not completed their squadron organization when the big guns started thundering. Some of their pilots and observers had seen active duty with French squadrons, but the vast majority would make their first war flight over the lines in the St. Mihiel drive. The 96th, commanded by Captain Summersett when Major Dunsworth became the new group commander, retained the reliable Breguets, but the two new squadrons were to give the Liberty-powered DH-4 its baptism of fire.

The armament [on the DH-4] was the same as the Breguet, save the pilot had two Marlin machine guns, synchronized to shoot through the propeller. The De Havilland 4 carried the British Wimpers bombsight attached to the outside of the fuselage. This sight permitted the observer to aim at the target while standing, a position which kept him in readiness to fight off an attack by hostile aircraft.[25]

The question in every bomber crew's mind was how will the American-built DH-4 perform as a bomber?

Army observation work during the summer of 1918, like day bombardment, continued to be the history of one squadron. That squadron, Major John Reynolds' 91st, was one of the outstanding Air Service units of the war. Based at Gondreville, near Toul, the squadron was responsible for all army photography work south of the railroad line running through Etain, Conflans, and Metz, a distance of twenty-five to thirty miles behind the German lines. At first the unit had tried to carry out its missions at an altitude of 10,000 feet, but intense antiaircraft fire caused this to be changed to 16,000 feet. Because of the Salmson's speed at high altitudes, squadron crews were comparatively safe from the Pfalz and Albatros scouts then based in the Metz district. Most of the missions made by the 91st during its early weeks on the front were conducted between 8:00 A.M. and 4:00 P.M. It was soon discovered, however, that operations at this time of day were relatively useless, as the enemy made most of its moves under cover of darkness. After a time, the practice of flying dawn and dusk patrols was begun, and this proved much more fruitful. The early morning flights were especially useful, since there was a chance to catch the tail end of German movements started the night before.[26]

As planning started for the St. Mihiel attack, the northern boundary of the 91st Aero's area of responsibility was removed, and "missions were flown to the limits imposed by fuel supply and the opposition." This made several tactical changes on photographic missions necessary. At first only one plane carried a camera on such flights, with two or three others going along for protection; however,

the cameras used were not too reliable, and, even when they worked, a Salmson only had space to carry 48 plates. This restricted the area that could be covered on a mission. Experiments were made with two aircraft flying a half-mile apart, each with a camera; with a whole flight equipped with cameras; changing the formation lead as each leader ran out of plates; and, finally, to a system of keeping the same flight leader throughout the mission, but having each plane photograph a prearranged section of the course flown. The aircraft not actually engaged in photography provided protection. . . .[27]

Daily penetrations deep behind enemy lines did bring losses. On 2 July a squadron plane was knocked down by enemy pursuits, and the observer, Lieutenant Franz F. Schilling, was killed. Although shot through the head and legs, the pilot, Lieutenant Howard Mayes, managed to make a safe landing and was taken to a German military hospital. Two weeks later a two-ship formation was attacked by four Fokkers at 16,000 feet and badly shot up. The first machine gun burst killed Lieutenant Frederick Hirth and creased his pilot, Lieutenant John Van Huevel, on both sides of his head, knocking him unconscious. Their Salmson fell 12,000 feet before Van Huevel recovered enough to regain control and struggle to the home field. Lieutenant Horace Guilbert, the pilot of the second plane, received three bullets in his "Teddy Bear" flying suit, while his observer had his windshield shot off and received seven holes in his machine gun *tourelle*. Lieutenant Al Lawson, one of the squadron's hardest-working young pilots, was wounded by archie on 30 July, but was back on active duty within a few days. On 14 August, a Salmson formation led by Reynolds was attacked by four Pfalz scouts, and in the ensuing fight Lieutenant Howard T. Baker was hit in the stomach. Although Baker's pilot, Lieutenant John Lambert, raced with full throttle for the home airdrome and medical attention, he could not save his teammate's life. One day later, Lambert, flying with a new observer, had his engine "quit cold" over Metz at 16,000 feet. In spite of a vigorous attack by six Boche pursuits, he managed to glide the fifteen miles to Allied territory. At this point Major Reynolds ordered him to take three days off "to get his mind off the war."[28]

September opened with a forecast of what was to come. On Labor Day four crews from the 91st Aero Squadron were bounced by a flock of Boche over Metz and in the resulting dogfight succeeded in bringing down three of their attackers. Since the fight took place fifteen miles inside the German-held salient, no confirmation could be secured. Two days later the same teams were challenged by three enemy pursuits north of Pont-a-Mousson. Lieutenant Raymond Sebring was fatally wounded on the first pass, and his pilot, Lieutenant Fred Foster, was forced to land his crippled Salmson behind German lines. Lieutenant Victor Strahm and his observer, Captain James Wallis, managed to shoot one of the fighters down in flames while still another was seen diving away trailing a long column of smoke.[29]

On 23 August, the 91st was joined by a second army observation outfit, the 24th Aero Squadron. This organization, however, did not receive its Salmsons until early September and was not able to begin war operations until 12 September, the first day of the St. Mihiel offensive. Some of the squadron's pilots and observers did fly a few patrols with the 91st.* On 1 September First Lieutenant Maury Hill, until recently a flight leader in the 91st, became squadron commander of the new outfit.[30] It might be noted parenthetically that no less than five squadron commanders came out of the 91st Aero Squadron.

During the first week of September, the 1st Army Observation Group, consisting of the 91st, 24th, and 9th Aero Squadrons, was formed under Major Reynolds. The latter squadron was a night observation outfit, the only one in the American Expeditionary Forces. Lieutenant Everett Cook, soon to be a captain, replaced Reynolds as commander of the 91st, and Lieutenant T. A. Box was made commander of the newly formed 9th Aero. Thus, on the opening day of the St. Mihiel battle three army observation squadrons were available, only one of which was experienced.[31]

For corps observation the late summer of 1918 was a time of reorganization, reequipment, and training. The U.S. First Army had just been created, and its Air Service included four corps observation groups. On being relieved from duty in the Chateau-Thierry

---

* Letter from Spessard L. Holland to author, 13 April 1965. U.S. senator from Florida and author of the Poll Tax Amendment, Holland served as an observer in the 24th Aero Squadron throughout the St. Mihiel and Meuse-Argonne campaigns.

area during the second week of August, the I Corps Observation Group, then under the command of Captain Stephen C. Jocelyn, moved to Biqueley, located some five miles south of Toul. This group now included the veteran 1st and 12th Squadrons and the new 50th Aero Squadron, plus two French escadrilles. The 50th, commanded by Captain Daniel P. Morse, a transfer from the 1st Aero and one of the first pilots over the lines back in April, was equipped with DH-4's. The IV Corps Observation Group had two DH-4 squadrons, John Gilbert Winant's 8th and Blair Thaw's 135th; the 90th, now rid of its conglomeration of Spad 11's, Sopwith B2's, and Breguets, and fully equipped with Salmsons; and one French observation outfit. Captain Martin Scanlon's V Corps Observation Group was made up of the Salmson-flying 99th and 104th and one French escadrille; it would be joined later by the 88th, which was still fighting in the Marne-Vesle region. The last group, an all-French organization, was assigned to the 2nd Colonial French Corps.

It was a matter of great concern to Billy Mitchell and other senior Air Service officers that so few of the observation squadrons about to be thrown into the inferno had had any real combat experience. In an effort to avoid some of the pitfalls encountered in the Chateau-Thierry campaign, a Wing Commander of Corps Observation was appointed to work directly with Mitchell. His duty, basically, was to exercise control over training and operating procedures of all corps observation in the First Army. The officer chosen for this task was Lieutenant Colonel L. H. Brereton, a former commander of the 12th Aero Squadron and more recently chief of Air Service, I Corps. During the succeeding weeks, this able flying officer, who would become one of the top air force generals of World War II, performed an effective role.[32]

Perhaps the most exciting news in corps observation during the summer was the arrival of the long-awaited American-built DH-4 with its 400-h.p. Liberty engine. This aircraft was capable of 125 mph, and as an observation plane could climb to 15,000 feet in a little over twenty minutes. The fully loaded DH-4 bomber was much slower and certainly less satisfactory. Although there were mixed feelings about the aircraft, a survey at the end of the war indicated that the day bombardment pilots were even less enthusiastic about it than were the observation boys; of course, not all who flew the machine had the same opinion. Comments ranged from those who saw it as "two wings on a hearse" and a "flaming coffin" to those who described it as the "best on the front." Captain John G. Winant, commander of the DH-4-equipped 8th Aero Squadron, argued that close formation was "impossible" because the location of the gas tank made such formation a blind job for the pilot. He was also critical of the plane's tendency to burn when the unprotected gas tanks were hit, but found the "most serious defect of the DH-4's as an observation aeroplane [to be] the distance between pilot and observer."[33]

On the other hand, Captain Daniel P. Morse, the able commander of the 50th Aero, found that all of his fliers liked the Liberty engine, and even though most would have preferred "armored or rubber-covered gas tanks," better pilot visibility, and armored seats, they believed the DH-4 was unfairly criticized. In conclusion Morse wrote,

Altogether the Liberty plane was considered the best on the front, and its excellent speed and climbing power were well demonstrated in actual combat with enemy planes. In spite of all the articles to the contrary, our pilots proved many times in actual fights that the Liberty, at low altitudes, where we did most of our flying, could outdistance and outclimb any plane the Germans had.[34]

Whatever might be final judgment on strength and weaknesses of the Liberty DH-4, it was considered by most to have excellent defensive armament. Percival Gray Hart, in his excellent book, *History of the 135th Aero Squadron,* wrote,

The ships were armed with four machine guns; two Marlins for the pilot, mounted rigidly on the cowl and synchronized with a Constantinesco hydraulic mechanism to fire through the propeller; and two Lewis guns for the observer.* These latter were mounted together on a frame, ar-

---

* The Lewis machine gun, invented by Col. Isaac N. Lewis, of the U.S. Army, was the weapon most generally used as a flexible gun on Allied aircraft. Originally a ground gun, the Lewis had been modified for the air by stripping its cooling radiator and adding a gas check to reduce recoil. The gun was fed by a drum magazine, a more desirable feed than any belt system for flexible firing aircraft weapons. Perhaps the only successful weapon of the fixed type before America entered the war was the Vickers then being used by both Britain and France. Although this gun was manufactured in the United States prior to April, 1917, the Signal Corps (then the parent of the air arm) found that the infantry branch of the Army had contracted for the entire Vickers production.   Consequently, the Signal Corps took up the development of the Marlin as an aircraft gun of the fixed

ranged so that their fire would converge at about 100 yards from the muzzles. The left gun could be fired by a wire control which led to a secondary trigger on the pistol grip of the right gun. Thus the guns could be fired either singly or together, by using the right hand only. They were mounted on a turret, which consisted of a metal hoop fitted over a steel band which was built around the rim of the rear cockpit. On the hoop were two curved spurs, extending upward for a foot or more, and serving as guides and braces for a U-shaped bar, hinged onto the upper hoop. In the middle of this bar the gun frame was pivoted by means of a large spike (attached to the frame by a universal joint) which went through a hole and was locked firmly in position. On the left side of the bar was a lever on which the observer's left hand always rested. By gripping the lever and the bar with a slight pressure the bar could be raised or lowered. Releasing the bar locked both bar and hoop. The observer could thus fire in any direction except through the wings or floor. A special stock was designed for the guns, against which the observer could lean to steady the guns while firing, although some preferred the regulation spade grip.

The Marlin guns operated on the recoil principle, and the ammunition was fed them by a belt made of clips and the bullets themselves. The Lewis gun was gas operated, and had magazines, each containing 97 rounds, which fastened on top of the guns. Four extra magazines were carried in a rack in the rear of the cockpit, and these could be substituted within seconds when those on the guns were empty.*

The first American DH-4 squadron to operate over the front was the 135th Aero, commanded by Lieutenant A. Blair Thaw, brother of Bill Thaw of Lafayette Escadrille fame. This squadron was organized at Rockwell Field, San Diego, California, in August of 1917, and went overseas in December of that year. For several weeks its ground crews and administrative officers trained with English DH-4 squadrons. Many of the 135th flying officers also worked in the British De Havilland program. In late July of 1918,

---

type. By December, 1918, no less than 37,500 of the fast firing (rate of fire about 650 rounds per minute) belt-fed Marlins had been produced by American companies—chiefly Marlin-Rockwell. Since American pursuit pilots used aircraft manufactured in England and France, most were equipped with the Vickers machine gun. About the time of the St. Mihiel drive, however, the Spad was converted to the use of the Marlin. Some French-manufactured 11-millimeter guns were used by American pursuit pilots for attacking enemy observation balloons.[35]

  * Hart was an observer in the 135th and served throughout the St. Mihiel and Meuse-Argonne operations. He was officially credited with one victory and won the DSC.[36]

the squadron moved to Ourches in the Toul sector, where it was equipped with the Liberty DH-4. The first combat sortie took place amid much fanfare and publicity on 7 August, when an eighteen-ship formation toured the front in the Nancy–Pont-a-Mousson area. General Benjamin Foulois, chief of Air Service, Zone of Advance, acted as Thaw's observer on that first operational mission, and Major Ralph Royce, chief of Air Service, I Army Corps, piloted one of the planes.[37]

On 16 August, Lieutenants Donald B. Cole, pilot, and Percival G. Hart, observer, were to fight the squadron's first air battle with enemy pursuits. In the fight Cole was wounded and his engine knocked out, but he managed to get back to the Allied trenches before being forced down. Five days later Lieutenants Robert D. Likely and Edward Urband scored the squadron's first aerial victory in a fight with a formation of Pfalz scouts over Thiaucourt. The squadron experienced no further losses until the beginning of the big St. Mihiel campaign. On 18 August, however, the 135th suffered a cruel blow when its popular commander, Blair Thaw, was killed in an accident. Thaw, with Lieutenant Cord Meyer acting as observer, was making a cross-country flight from Ourches to Paris when his plane developed engine trouble. In attempting a forced landing at Fere Champenois, he struck some telegraph wires and the plane crashed upside down. Thaw was killed instantly and Meyer was severely injured. Lieutenant (soon to be Captain) Bradley Saunders was then made squadron commander, a position he filled with distinction until the Armistice.[38]

While most of the American corps observation squadrons were training and conducting preliminary reconnaissance work for the upcoming St. Mihiel operation, one, the 88th, was suffering heavy casualties along the Vesle River in the Marne sector. On 9 August, Lieutenants Richard C. M. Page and John I. Rancourt, while conducting an unescorted reconnaissance over Fismes, were attacked by six Pfalz scouts. Although Rancourt was hit three times in the leg by the first burst of machine gun fire, by skilled maneuvering the pair shot down one of their tormentors and escaped. For this action both fliers were given the DSC.[39]

Two days later, on 11 August, the squadron did not fare as well. A formation of five Salmsons, engaged in a photo mission in the vicinity of Fismes, was intercepted by eleven German aircraft; when the shooting stopped Lieutenants Joel H. McClendon, Charles W. Plummer, and James S. D. Burns were dead, and Lieutenant J. W. Jordan was seriously wounded. Lieutenant Roger W. Hitchcock was piloting the plane in which Burns was killed, and although the latter's body jammed the controls, Hitchcock was able to bring the bullet-riddled plane home to Ferme-de-Greves. All of the officers mentioned above were awarded the DSC.[40]

During the next several days numerous aerial battles were fought without results. But on 2 September, Littauer's 88th Aero suffered a second disaster. A three-plane formation engaged in an artillery adjustment mission was jumped by eight aggressive Hun pursuit planes, and Hitchcock and his observer, Lieutenant Frank Moore, were shot down and killed. A second badly damaged plane flown by Page was forced to land at a French field near Reims. The German patrol leader, however, was hit several times and crashed near Romaine. Toward the end of August the situation became much easier for the 88th when several crack French pursuit outfits moved into the area and regained control of the air in the Marne region. On the day before the big St. Mihiel operation got under way the squadron received orders to move with all possible speed to Souilly, ten miles southwest of Verdun, to join the V Corps Observation Group.[41]

Early in August Colonel William Mitchell was made commander of the recently organized First Army Air Service, and on 26 August he moved his headquarters to Ligny-en-Barrois, in the vicinity of St. Mihiel, where plans for pinching off the German salient were developed. Two days later he announced the upcoming offensive to his staff. Lieutenant Colonel Thomas Milling, who had been in charge of American air activity in the Toul sector during Mitchell's tour at Chateau-Thierry, was made chief of staff of the First Army Air Service. Major Paul Armengaud, chief of the French Mission attached to the American Air Service, was named assistant chief of staff. Lieutenant Colonel Townsend F. Dodd was put in charge of the Information Section, and Major John A. Paegelow, who had done such a wonderful job of making do with nothing on the Marne, commanded the balloons. These men and their assistants comprised a highly efficient organization during the first big American effort in September.[42]

Mitchell developed a foolproof system of insuring that all orders were carried out. He composed them himself and then checked their receipt by field commanders. Believing that orders were disobeyed because of failure to deliver them or because of ambiguity, he devised a remedy of his own. "I always kept an officer at my headquarters, whose name I shall not mention, to whom I read all orders," Mitchell wrote. "If he could understand them, anybody could. He was not particularly bright, but he was one of the most valuable officers I had."[43]

Steps had been taken this time to avoid some of the confusion over chain of command which had prevailed in the Chateau-Thierry campaign. At that time ground commanders, both corps and army, had harassed air group commanders with demands for information and with conflicting orders. It was never really understood whether the 1st Air Brigade was tactical or administrative, though Mitchell himself believed it to be both. In the St. Mihiel effort the line of authority was clear.

By the time of the opening of the drive, Mitchell had under his direct control, or cooperating with him, the largest aggregation of air forces to engage in a single operation during World War I. The American Air Service contributed twelve pursuit, three day bombardment, ten observation, and one night reconnaissance squadrons. Also, Mitchell was assigned the French *Division Aerienne* (made up of forty-two squadrons of pursuit and day bombardment aircraft), two squadrons of French and three squadrons of Italian night bombardment planes, four squadrons of French pursuit working with the 1st Pursuit Wing, and twelve French observation squadrons. In addition, Mitchell was to have the support of eight night bombardment squadrons from Major General Hugh Trenchard's Independent Force of the Royal Air Force.* This heterogeneous American, French, British, and Italian force consisted of 701 pursuit, 366 observation, 323 day bombardment, and 91 night bombardment aircraft, making a total of 1,481. There were 30,000 officers and men to handle the planes, which were deployed on fourteen main flying fields.†

* Trenchard's Independent Force was not under the orders of the American First Army Air Service but voluntarily undertook missions in support of it.

† As assistant chief of staff, Air Service, Gen. Benjamin D. Foulois played a prominent role in training and sending forward reinforcements to the battle area. Although he took only an indirect part in making the operational decisions, those decisions would have had little chance of being carried out successfully without his skill in providing the necessary manpower and equipment.[44]

The concentration of these forces prior to the offensive constituted a major problem: since any unusual amount of aerial activity
in the St. Mihiel area would alert the German forces, the various
Allied air units had to be moved to the front with the greatest
secrecy. An example of this occurred on the night of 21 August,
when Mitchell called for Major Harold Hartney, commanding officer of the 1st Pursuit Group, to "come up quietly to a new sector
on the St. Mihiel salient" for a conference. Hartney described the
affair in the following words:

I slipped up in my car to Bar-le-Duc and there had my first real insight
into what goes on at Army Headquarters in preparation for a big assault.
I was fascinated. They had a large contour replica of the whole front,
complete with trees, hills, trenches and everything. It was like toy soldier
stuff but in deadly earnest. At dinner, with a flock of generals, we discussed the transfer of our group to a new field at Rembercourt where
we could take an immediate and vital part in the next big move of the
war—the St. Mihiel offensive.

Then after considerable discussion the American Air Commander
said,
    "Hartney, I want you to go over to that map and look at that tiny
field, then go back and prepare to slip in there overnight when I
give the word, without fuss of any kind. The enemy mustn't know
we are coming. Can you do it?"
    "Certainly," Hartney replied, "Our boys can land their Spads on
a dime and if there are small hills, so much the better, regardless of
the wind direction. How big is it?"
    "Thirty acres," Mitchell answered, "The only thirty acres left in
France, so don't squawk."[45]
    The little, bird-like, mustached Hartney assured Mitchell that the
move could be accomplished, and the next night, by truck and
plane, the entire group crept into Rembercourt without mishap.
Within twelve hours after the move, the 1st Pursuit Group was flying patrols over the new sector.[46] Other unit commanders were
briefed in a similar manner, and by the end of the first week of
September most squadrons were located at bases around the perimeter.
    In order to prevent enemy detection it was necessary for Allied
aviation to halt German reconnaissance of rear areas. Conse-

quently, pilots from the three American pursuit groups maintained a tight aerial security from Verdun to Nancy. Meanwhile, aircraft not in use on the patrols were carefully camouflaged and hidden in the trees bordering the airdromes.[47] The 1st Pursuit Group Commander wrote, "I had little fear the enemy would find our new location. I could hardly find it myself." To further minimize the possibility of the Germans detecting the new locations of Allied air squadrons, patrols were all on the Allied side of the lines and consisted of only one or two planes each. Despite the efforts at secrecy, however, some of the eager young pilots strayed over the German lines, and Lieutenant Norman Archibald, of the 95th Pursuit Squadron, was shot down by archie. Luckily, the innocent looking Archibald convinced his German captors that he was merely lost in a long flight from Saints, the former base of the 1st Pursuit Group; thus the recent air build-up in the St. Mihiel area remaind a secret.[48]

It was fortunate for Mitchell's plans that during the preparatory stage the enemy air force in the area of St. Mihiel was weak. At the time of the big Allied push, German air strength was estimated at approximately 213 aircraft, including 72 pursuit, 6 battle, 6 mosaics, 105 reconnaissance, and 24 bombing planes.[49] In addition, there was some evidence that the German pursuit units in the St. Mihiel sector were in the process of changing over to the Fokker D-7 from the older models of Pfalz and Albatros. Needless to say, an aircraft change-over during the middle of a battle presented problems.[50]

Since the American First Army was to attack an enemy salient, Mitchell planned to use his numerically superior air forces in much the same way he had successfully gambled with a smaller force at Chateau-Thierry in July. One-third of his force, or about five hundred planes, would be committed to ground support; the rest either simultaneously or alternately would attack the flanks of the salient and its primary bases, bombing and strafing installations, communications, and troop columns. Contrary to his original plans, this aerial blitzkrieg, the first in history, did not involve massive formations. As will be seen in the next chapter, low cloud ceilings and poor visibility during the brief campaign would prevent more than a few squadrons operating together.[51]

NOTES

1. C. R. M. F. Cruttwell, *A History of the Great War, 1914–1918*, 93–94.

2. A. J. Barnett, "Air Operations in the St. Mihiel Offensive," 2–3. This unpublished thesis is housed in the USAF HD Archives, Maxwell AFB, Montgomery, Ala.

3. S. L. A. Marshall, narrator, *American Heritage History of World War I*, 330–31. Henceforth, this book will be cited as Marshall, *World War I*.

4. U.S. Army War College, *Order of Battle of the United States Land Forces in the World War, AEF*, I, 97–107.

5. Thomas G. Miller, ed., "The Last Knighthood," *Cross and Cockade Journal*, Spring, 1962, 27.

6. "History of the First Pursuit Group" (Gorrell Histories, AS AEF, N, IV), 8–9.

7. Kenn Rust, "Aces and Hawks," *Air Power Historian*, October, 1962, 217–18.

8. "History of the First Pursuit Group," *loc. cit.*, 7–8.

9. "Victories and Casualties" (Gorrell Histories, AS AEF, M, XXXVIII), 26, 71–77.

10. "History of the 103rd Aero Squadron" (Gorrell Histories, AS AEF, E, XVI), 2–16.

11. U.S. War Dept., Office of Director of Air Service, "Brief History of Air Service, AEF," 14.

12. Kelly Wills, Jr., "History of the 213th," *Cross and Cockade Journal*, Summer, 1965, 122.

13. U.S. War Dept., "Brief History of Air Service, AEF," 14.

14. "History of the 139th Aero Squadron" (Gorrell Histories, AS AEF, XVII), 1–5.

15. *Ibid.*, 9–11.

16. "Victories and Casualties," *loc. cit.*, 8; Charles J. Biddle, *The Way of the Eagle*, 240–42. Since World War I Biddle has had a highly successful law practice in Philadelphia.

17. "Victories and Casualties," *loc. cit.*, 8.

18. Capt. Arthur Raymond Brooks, "22nd Aero Squadron," *Cross and Cockade Journal*, Summer, 1963, 109–12. This article is an excerpt from a history written by Brooks at the end of the war.

19. "Memorandum, Office of Chief of Air Service, AEF, 28 June 1918" (Gorrell Histories, AS AEF, A, IX), 100.

20. Bruce C. Hopper, "When the Air Was Young," 8–9.

21. Mitchell, "Before Pershing in Europe," 247.

22. Bruce C. Hopper, "American Day Bombardment in World War I," *Air Power Historian*, April, 1957, 89.

23. Hopper, "When the Air Was Young," 8–9.

24. "History of the 96th Aero Squadron" (Gorrell Histories, AS AEF, E, XIV), 15–16.

25. Hopper, "When the Air Was Young," 13.

26. "History of the 91st Aero Squadron" (Gorrell Histories, AS AEF, E, X), 3–7.

27. Miller, "Eyes of the Army: The Observation Corps," *Cross and Cockade Journal*, Spring, 1962, 86.

28. "History of the 91st Aero Squadron," *loc. cit.,* 7–8.

29. *Ibid.,* Operations Report, 4 September 1918.

30. Frederic P. Kirschner, "A Thumbnail Sketch of the 24th," *Cross and Cockade Journal,* Spring, 1964, 53.

31. "First Army Observation Group" (Gorrell Histories, AS AEF, N, XX), 1–8.

32. "Operations, First Army Air Service, 10 August–11 November 1918" (Gorrell Histories, AS AEF, C, III), 1–30.

33. Letter from Spessard L. Holland to author, 13 April 1965; letter from Lawrence Kinnaird to author, 26 April 1960; Capt. John G. Winant's Report on the DH-4 in "History of the 8th Aero Squadron" (Gorrell Histories, AS AEF, E, I).

34. Daniel P. Morse, *The History of the 50th Aero Squadron,* 26.

35. For a thorough discussion of aircraft machine guns used by the U.S.A., see Benedict Crowell and Robert F. Wilson, *How America Went to War,* V, *The Armies of Industry,* 399–407.

36. Percival G. Hart, *History of the 135th Aero Squadron,* 22–23.

37. "History of the 135th Aero Squadron" (Gorrell Histories, AS AEF, E, XVII), 1–6.

38. *Ibid.,* 6.

39. See DSC citation in Stringer, *Heroes All!* 305, 325.

40. "History of the 88th Aero Squadron" (Gorrell Histories, AS AEF, 1918, E, IX), 3–5.

41. *Ibid.,* 4–6.

42. "Operations of the First Army Air Service, 10 August–11 November 1918," *loc. cit.,* 7.

43. Mitchell, *Memoirs,* 234–35.

44. Patrick, *Report to Commander-in-Chief,* 230; Sam Hager Frank, "American Air Service Observation in World War I," unpublished dissertation, University of Florida, 312.

45. Hartney, *Up and At 'Em,* 213–14.

46. *Ibid.*

47. "History of the 27th Aero Squadron" (Gorrell Histories, AS AEF, E, VI), 22.

48. Hartney, *Up and At 'Em,* 214–15.

49. "Tactical History of the Air Service, AEF" (Gorrell Histories, AS AEF, D, I), 9–10.

50. "Tactical History of American Pursuit Aviation," *ibid.,* 12.

51. Brig. Gen. William Mitchell, "The Air Service at St. Mihiel," *World's Work,* August, 1919, 369–70. See also the summary of Mitchell's proposals for employing his air units in a memorandum to the Commanding General, First Army, dated 20 August 1918, reproduced in *Memoirs,* 235–37.

VIII

"He That Outlives This Day and Comes Safe Home": The First Day at St. Mihiel

THE flying officers of the 90th Aero Squadron glanced apprehensively at each other as the rain continued to beat against the paper-thin walls of their flight operations shack. Outside, the sod of Ourches airfield had turned into a sea of mud under the two-day deluge. A dozen Salmson biplanes waited, the bright red of their "Pair-of-Dice" insignia barely discernible in the eddying grey mist.

Ordinarily the young fliers would have simply shrugged their shoulders at the gloomy situation and trudged back to their makeshift barracks for another couple of hours' sleep. But this was 12 September 1918—D-Day for the big American offensive to neutralize the St. Mihiel salient held by the Germans, and the infant American Air Service was determined to carry out its assigned task in General John J. Pershing's master plan. Fair weather or foul, the long-awaited American drive was under way. The Army's big guns had been thundering away at the Hun trenches since 2:00 A.M., and sleep had been impossible anyway. It was now 5:00 A.M., and the 90th's first observation mission in support of the American 42nd (Rainbow) Division was scheduled to take off in a few minutes.

Despite the fact that only a few of the pilot-observer crews were to participate in the early morning missions, practically the entire squadron was crowded in the operations office, housed in a one-room hut-type frame building. A counter divided the tiny room in two parts. Behind the counter were three wooden desks and a telephone. One or two large sector maps were tacked to one wall of the room. On the opposite wall hung a huge Mission Board showing the planes and crews on duty for the day and the missions assigned to each team.[1]

As the minutes ticked by, Lieutenant Bill Gallup, the acting squadron commander filling in for the hospitalized Captain Schauffler, paced back and forth and eyed the telephone nervously. Some of the young men waiting reflected, undoubtedly, on yesterday's briefing in which French flying officers had given the impression that the average life of a flier in the type of work to be done "was 2½ hours."[2] A few men attempted stale jokes in subdued voices, but most simply stared at the Mission Board or idly studied the wall maps. Those posted to the first missions had already squeezed into fleece-lined "Teddy Bear" flying suits and were gathering flight maps, gloves, and other necessary items. A decision to go or not to go would have to be made shortly.

The 90th and its sister squadrons of the IV Corps Observation Group—the 8th, 135th, and one French Escadrille, all based at Ourches—had prepared for the moment for more than two weeks. A great deal of photography work had been carried out, and maps had been prepared for D-Day and H-Hour. Two days before the scheduled attack each team of pilot and observer had been assigned a particular task. On the night of 11 September, only a few hours before the big guns started blasting away at Hun positions, the squadron flying officers had met for a final briefing. The atmosphere had been tense as Major Joseph T. McNarney, group commander, stood before the big war map in the operations hut and outlined the next day's mission. Aviation, he had said, would be a "very essential part of the attack, and whatever the weather the missions were to be performed as long as it was physically possible for the planes to take off."[3] Indeed, aviation was on trial.

Other corps observation squadrons located at various airdromes around the perimeter of the St. Mihiel salient had been given much the same mission briefing and pep talk on the role of aviation on the night of 11 September. All waited impatiently on the grey, windswept morning of 12 September. Captain Arthur "Judge" Coyle's veteran 1st and Captain Steve Noyce's experienced 12th Aero Squadrons shared the Toul airdrome with the four pursuit squadrons making up the 2nd Pursuit Group.[4] Six miles south of Toul was the tiny airfield of Bicquely, the home of the DH-4-flying 50th Aero Squadron, whose only experienced flying officers were Captain Daniel Morse and Lieutenant Stewart "Jay" Bird, commander and operations officer respectively.[5] On the western flank of the St. Mihiel wedge the 88th, commanded by the incomparable Captain Kenneth "Kepi" Littauer, the 104th, led by Captain Clearton H. Reynolds (a recent transfer from the 91st), and the 99th, commanded by Captain James E. Meredith, were based at Souilly, some ten miles southwest of Verdun. Of these squadrons the 88th had had experience in the Chateau-Thierry campaign in July and August, while the other two were comparatively inexperienced. In fact, the 104th was to fly its first war missions at St. Mihiel. The squadron was in the process of moving to Souilly, and its first day of operations proved disastrous.[6]

The army observation group, charged with long-distance visual reconnaissance and photography for army headquarters, was located at Gondreville, near Toul, on the southern flank of the salient. Cook's veteran 91st was scheduled to do most of the real observation work, while the rookie 24th and 9th Aero Squadrons were to be used, primarily, as two-seater escorts for both observation and pursuit formations.[7]

Mitchell stationed his pursuit units around the flanks of the St. Mihiel salient in much the same manner that he located his observation squadrons. In addition to providing protection for the vital reconnaissance, infantry contact, and artillery adjustment performed by the observation units, pursuit was also charged with maintaining control of the air, strafing and bombing enemy troops, destruction of balloons, and preventing enemy aerial observation. To handle the pursuit mission Mitchell had pulled together an impressive collection of fighters. Seven French and three American pursuit groups of four squadrons each were scattered from Pont-a-Mousson on the east to Les Eparges on the west. Of the American units, Davenport Johnson's 2nd Pursuit Group was based at Toul on the eastern flank; Thaw's 3rd Pursuit Group was located at Vaucouleurs, twelve miles southwest of Toul; and Hartney's veteran 1st Pursuit Group flew out of Rembercourt on the western face of the St. Mihiel line. The 2nd and 3rd Pursuit Groups, along with the Day Bombardment Group, were administratively a part of Atkinson's 1st Pursuit Wing.[8]

The same rain that caused so much concern for the 90th Observation Squadron at Ourches was also lashing the airdrome at Toul,
where Captain Ray Bridgeman's 22nd Pursuit Squadron was waiting to carry out its early morning assignment. Although the squadron had been at the front some four weeks and had already scored
a couple of air victories against the Germans, it was still considered
a green outfit.[9] Captain Bridgeman, however, was an experienced
and highly skilled pursuit pilot. The Lake Forest, Illinois, boy, despite the fact that he "hated war with his whole soul," had enlisted
in the French service in July of 1916. He had served with French
Escadrille N-49 and for nearly a year in the Lafayette Escadrille.
He was described as one of the keenest pilots, one of the most aggressive fighters the squadron ever had, and earned the Croix de
Guerre, with star, for his action with the Lafayette Escadrille. In
February, 1918, he was commissioned a captain in the U.S. Air
Service and was made a flight commander in the 103rd Aero
Squadron. When it became apparent that experienced flying officers
would be needed to lead the newly created American pursuit units
he was made commanding officer of the 22nd Aero Squadron on
15 August 1918, a position held until the end of the war.[10] A few
years after the war he became a history professor at New York
University, where he continued to infect young Americans with his
high sense of idealism.

As Bridgeman stared through a broken window of the squadron's
operations hut at the row of eighteen dripping Spad 13 pursuit
planes sitting in the soft turf outside, he wondered whether it was
physically possible to get them into the air at the appointed time.
Even if his pilots could get airborne, would they be able to see anything and would they be able to land again after taking off? Then,
as he watched the soaking-wet ground crew put the finishing touches
to their preparation on the squat little fighters, he became vaguely
aware that the rain had turned into a fine mist and was now being
driven by a heavy southwest wind. Objects across the field became
distinguishable. It was now 5:30 A.M., and perhaps the first mission,
a patrol along the Flirey–Pont-a-Mousson line, could take off after
all. As he turned back to his pilots huddled about the room he
noticed that Lieutenant Vaughn McCormick, who was scheduled
to lead the patrol, had gotten up and was motioning for his flight to
get ready. After a few brief instructions about staying under the

cloud cover, the Commander waved good luck, and Lieutenants McCormick, Raymond J. Little, Watson La Force, John G. Agar, and Murray Tucker raced through the mud to their waiting machines. At 5:45 A.M. McCormick's Spad turned into the gale and began splashing forward across the soggy field. Bridgeman and the pilots of the 22nd not assigned to the first mission watched anxiously as the Spad, its Hispano-Suiza engine howling at full throttle, lumbered ahead toward the trees bordering the field. Would the fighter gain enough speed to become airborne and would the mud hurled forward by the wheels break the propeller? The little group of observers breathed a sigh of relief when, after what seemed an eternity, the little French-built plane groaned into the air. The whole agonizing process was repeated as each of the remaining four planes also struggled into the air. Despite poor visibility the five pilots quickly pulled into a loose formation and disappeared into the low-hanging mist within moments. In less than two hours one of the five would be dead.[11]

Twelve miles to the southwest of Toul, Lieutenant Gallup, of the 90th Aero, had made his decision for action. At 5:20 A.M., Lieutenant Loren Rohrer, of Giraud, Ohio, and his observer, Lieutenant Fred Vinson, of Milledgeville, Georgia, jockeyed their heavy Salmson biplane into the whirling mist and set course to the north and the Seicheprey area to fly an infantry liaison patrol for the 42nd Division.[12]

Before the day was over the "Pair-of-Dice" squadron made no less than twenty-six sorties, most of which were of the infantry contact variety. Forced to fly at altitudes of 100–1,000 feet because of low clouds and rain, the squadron, understandably, did not get through the day untouched. Earlier that morning, Lieutenants John Young, a pilot from Montpelier, Vermont, and Henry C. Bogle, an observer from Ann Arbor, Michigan, had had their radiator pierced by bullets fired from the ground. Bogle, presently a partner in a Chicago law firm, described that memorable mission in the following words:

As we approached the old "front line" we saw a dense pall of smoke mingled with the low cloud ceiling hanging over the entire battlefield. This cloud ceiling could not have been over three or four hundred yards above the earth, but Young kept the plane under it, and I think we must have flown through our own barrage, which as we approached the old familiar "V" in Flirey Woods, we could plainly see laying down its "surf" of white puffs along the ground in front of our troops. Already it had advanced some distance into the German lines. We proceeded to pass beyond the slowly advancing barrage and spent the next 1½ to 2 hours over "German" territory. We sent back wireless reports of the location of what appeared to be good targets, such as road intersections, concentration of retreating enemy, "pill boxes," etc. We saw what appeared to be good "hits" but had no means of knowing whether our messages had been of any service, or even whether they had been received. (We could of course send but had no means of receiving wireless messages.)

After about an hour of this, and after wondering whether we were making any real contribution, the two of us unanimously decided to conduct a personal vendetta, as Young had a good machine gun mounted in front and I had a double one mounted on the *tourelle* in my open cockpit, which enabled me to swing it from side to side and tilt it up or down. Young took the plane down even closer to the ground. We could plainly see the convoy of enemy horse-drawn vehicles in retreat along the road to Thiaucourt. Young pointed his plane down, cut loose on the convoy with his front gun and as he pulled out and started to climb slightly, I would cut loose with the rear guns. The convoy in confusion took to the fields. I can still remember one angry German driver, as he turned his horses off the road, looking up and shaking his fist at us . . . confusion we did cause and perhaps more at our last target, a German battery, at which the gunners manning same could be plainly seen. After we had unloaded our guns on them, I asked Young (through the speaking tube) to take the plane up so I could put a new belt of cartridges in the machine gun. He did this but this placed the plane on a straight path moving away from some machine gun position on the ground, making us almost a stationary target. Ping! From the shower bath of water we knew that the water-cooled motor of the Salmson had been pierced and it was likely to "freeze" in a few minutes. We were . . . one to two hundred meters from the ground when struck, and we could feel the plane start to settle. [After quick consultation the two decided to try to negotiate the five miles to friendly territory. Throttling the engine back to bare flying speed to avoid over-heating, Young nursed the plane to safety.] With the wheels of the plane just a few yards off the ground, several German infantrymen ran out from Flirey Woods on our left, doubtless to take us prisoner upon our expected imminent landing. They were disappointed. Within a few seconds we were passing directly through our own barrage with the 75's dropping under and on either side of us. Then appeared the American infantry coming up in columns of two—a welcome sight. Young made a three-point landing in what had been no-man's land two hours before, and we climbed out. The plane was undamaged except for the one hole piercing the radiator. . . .[13]

Once on the ground the pair hitch-hiked back to the squadron airfield, reporting in late in the afternoon.

Later in the same day the team of Lieutenants W. E. Kinsley of Winchester, Massachusetts, and William O. Lowe, of Fountain City, Tennessee, while flying at low altitude between Essey and Pannes, some two miles behind enemy lines, was attacked by a German Rumpler, and their plane suffered hits in the exchange of fire. With their cooling system shot out the American pair was forced to land at Menie-la-Tour, a short distance behind their own lines, where they called in the information they had been assigned to secure.[14]

Other squadrons of the IV Corps Observation Group were also active on the first day of the St. Mihiel drive. The 8th Aero Squadron was assigned to the 1st Infantry Division, striking northward toward Nonsard, and the 135th worked with the 89th Division two miles further to the right. Lieutenants James W. Bowyer and Arthur T. Johnson were the first team from the 135th to brave the elements when they struggled into the air at 5:30 A.M. The American artillery barrage was still under way when they reached the front a few minutes later. Because of the extremely low ceiling, Bowyer was forced to fly at treetop level as Johnson searched the ground below for the advancing American infantry. While hedgehopping along at this low altitude the pair fell victim to a once-in-a-million accident. Their American-built DH-4 was hit by one of their own artillery shells and crashed in flames. Both fliers were killed instantly.[15]

Although shocked at the manner of Bowyer and Johnson's death, crews from the 135th continued their low-level cooperation with the advancing infantry throughout the day; some pilots and observers flew as many as three patrols in the atrocious weather. It was late in the afternoon that the team of Lieutenants Jack Curtin and Percival G. Hart,* the latter on his third nerve-wracking flight

---

* Percival G. Hart, one of the most articulate officers to emerge from World War I, has described the radio communication system and techniques used in adjusting artillery fire on stationary targets in the following words: "Each observation plane had a standard sending key operated by the observer. He sent in Morse Code (this was studied assiduously in Observer's School, and tests had to be passed in both sending and receiving, although we never received in the air). The power

of the day, shot down an attacking Fokker D-7. Hart, the observer, described the action:

We were attacked by a single Fokker D-7 and were engaging in a running fight with it. The Fokker kept coming down on our tail in a straight line. I kept pumping bullets into him when he suddenly stopped and went into a spin with his plane smoking. The D-7 was about 75 feet away when I shot him down. He was close, but I couldn't see the expression on his face. You couldn't have seen over his engine, and besides, he would have had his face close to the machine gun sight.[16]

As Curtin and Hart turned toward home they were bounced by a flight of six Fokkers, and for a few moments the situation looked black. Before the Fokkers could make the kill, however, they were interrupted by a flight of American Spads. As the fighters broke up into individual dogfights the observation plane managed to make its escape.

Captain Winant's 8th Aero Squadron, working with the 1st Division, experienced great difficulty in contacting division and brigade headquarters, even when trying to report that the American artillery was hitting its own men. Most of the brigade seemed to have had no radios or no qualified radio operators. During the day Winant went so far as to send radio equipment and some of his own men to work with the infantry command posts. In spite of radio difficulties, pilots and observers were able to maintain some contact by dropping written messages (in cylinders attached to streamers) at 1st Division Headquarters. Late in the afternoon one team, of Lieutenants

---

came from a generator mounted on the side of the fuselage, which was activated by a propeller which rotated from the force of the air from the slip stream. An antenna was mounted on a large reel, and was unreeled after the plane was airborne. The length of the wire antenna governed the wavelength of the transmission. The signals were always sent as the plane flew toward the receiving station. On leaving the field a signal to the radio station (located near the artillery battery) would get an acknowledgment from the ground to verify that the signals were being received. Most wireless [messages were] to [artillery] batteries for the purpose of adjusting their guns on unseen (from the ground) targets. The batteries had white cloth panels approximately 10 feet square—and each with a special black marking to distinguish it. . . . The plane, flying a predetermined adjustment for the battery, would call the battery as it approached: 'ABC, ABC, ABC.' The battery would put out a side panel saying 'Battery ready.' The observer would fly over the target, identify it, and signal the pilot to fly back to the battery. He would then signal 'ABC, ABC, ABC, – – –, – – –' (the three dashes meaning 'fire'). The plane then would fly toward the target and the observer would note the error of the shell bursts (such as 25 meters left or right and 125 meters over or short). He would then radio this to the battery." See letter from Hart to author, 7 August 1967.

Horace W. Mitchell and John W. Artz, was shot down in a duel
with a Hun fighter. Artz, the observer, was badly wounded, and
both men were captured by the Germans.[17]

Major Jocelyn's I Corps Observation Group, working with the
2nd, 5th, 82nd, and 90th U.S. Divisions between Thiaucourt and
the Moselle River, found the heavy mist, low-lying cloud banks,
and intermittent rain a major handicap on that first morning of the
St. Mihiel attack. Yet, somehow most of the infantry liaison and
artillery adjustment missions were carried out successfully. Lieutenants William D. Frayne and H. C. French had the distinction of
making the first war flight for the rookie 50th Aero when they
braved the elements at 5:30 A.M. on that miserable Thursday morning for a reconnaissance mission with the 82nd Division. They were
also to make the squadron's last operational flight two days before
the Armistice. Frayne, presently an executive engineer with a large
Connecticut firm, was one of the original "Toronto Detail" that
trained in Canada and at the RFC schools in Texas in the late summer and fall of 1917. He later won his RAF wings in English flying
schools and was assigned to the 50th Aero Squadron in August,
1918. As a flight commander with that outfit, he became one of the
outstanding observation pilots of the war.[18]

One of the most important duties of military aviation in World
War I was the infantry contact patrol. Captain Daniel P. Morse,
squadron commander of the 50th Aero, described one of their
typical missions:

Flying over and reporting to division headquarters by wireless, the men
in the plane see . . . a panel, which means "Where are my front elements?" The observer sends down his "Understood" message and starts
off. He has a general idea where our front line troops should be, but it
is his job to find out their exact location, for it is evident from the panel
on the ground that the division does not know this and that communication is probably cut off. Flying perhaps at only 300 to 500 meters high
(he is within rifle and machine gun range up to 1000 meters) he approaches and flies across where No Man's Land should be. At the first
"Archie" burst, he knows he is where the enemy is, so turns and looks
on the ground for signs of No Man's Land. Probably not finding any,
he flies along where he thinks it should be and fires off his pistol rocket,
sending out luminous stars, like roman candle fireworks. He has guessed
right, for below him here and there appear white patches—the infantry

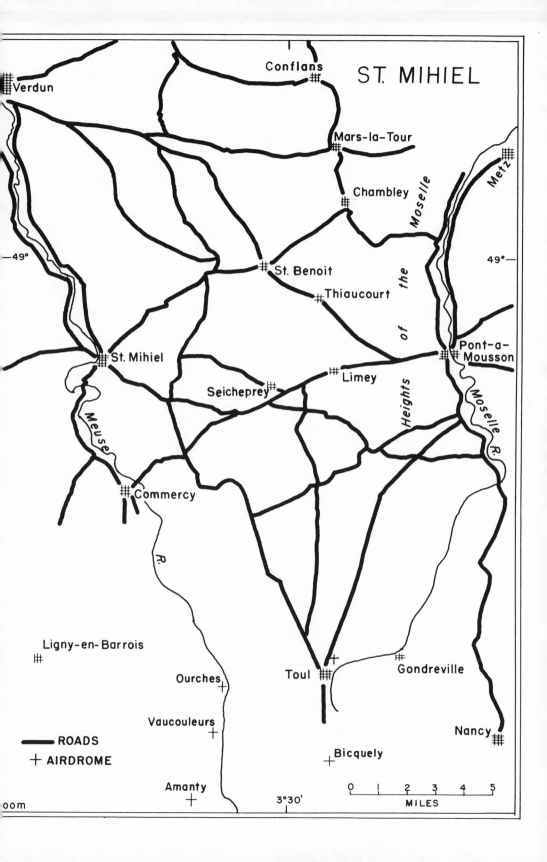

front line is showing its panels. The observer in the plane carefully charts each spot on his map, which forms a jagged line. He has "found" where our foremost troops are. He then shoots his "Understood" rocket and the panels disappear. Suddenly he may see from the midst of the white spots a rocket like a shooting star. His wireless gets busy at once, for that is the signal that our own artillery is falling on our troops. They had probably gone too far, or our artillery was ignorant of the fact that it was shooting short. The message is received at division headquarters and all work is stopped while they get word to the artillery to lengthen fire. . . . Or the observer may spot another peculiarly shaped and larger panel just in back of where the smaller panels were. He recognizes that immediately as meaning "We need ammunition." Suddenly that panel is taken up and another panel is put down. The observer knows that sign best of all, and without a moment's loss he turns and scans the sky. That panel had meant "Enemy aircraft approaching you." While his attention had been diverted to all the needs of the infantry, some enemy planes had tried to surprise him. But the men working the panels on the ground had seen them and warned our plane. A fight then follows, which decides whether or not the vastly important information is to reach division headquarters. It is the duty of the pilot and observer of our machines to get the information back safely and in the quickest possible times, so they fight a defensive fight. The pilot and observer know that if they do not get this information back it will not be known that our men need ammunition and that headquarters will not know the position of their front line.[19]

Obviously, in the rain, confusion, and poor radio contact during the first day at St. Mihiel the system worked less effectively than Morse's description.

During the first day of the offensive the veteran 1st and 12th Aero Squadrons flew continuously in support of the rapidly advancing infantry on the southeastern flank of the salient. An example of the wide variety of missions performed is indicated by the 12th's Operations Reports for 12 September which reads in part as follows:

Artillery surveillance:* mission not completed due to motor trouble— Time 6:05–8:30.

---

* The distance of radio communication depended somewhat on the altitude of the plane. In practice, when adjusting the batteries of 75-millimeter and 155-millimeter guns, the plane operated no more than one and a half miles in front of the receiving station and usually a little less than a mile. The receiving station, of course, was located at or near the gun battery. Although the French 75-millimeter gun had a range of over five miles, it was normally used at 1,800–4,200 yards.

Adjustment and Artillery Surveillance: Regnieville-Fay-en-Hay— 6:30–8:30–altitude 250 meters–visibility poor—Pilot, Lt. [C. E.] Gregory–Observer, Lt. [J. F.] Hyman–attacked by EA at 7:30–Enemy machine which was a biplace was hit and crashed in woods near Regnieville.

Adjustment of Artillery Fire: Pont-a-Mousson, Remenauville—Time 6:30–9:05–altitude 500–1600 meters–visibility poor—Pilot, Lt. [C. M.] Smith–Observer, Lt. [R. C.] Keeley.

Infantry Contact Patrol: Vieville-en-Hays, Bois-du-Four—Time 5:00–7:20–altitude, 300 meters–visibility, fair–Pilot, Lt. [Robert C.] Paradise–Observer, Lt. [B. S.] Wright. Troops failed to display panels when called for. Worked with 5th Division.[20]

In all, more than fifty individual sorties were flown by the I Corps Observation Group, but not without losses. Two 12th Aero planes engaged in reconnaissance duty on the 90th Division front near Vilcey were attacked by several enemy pursuit planes and were forced down a few hundred yards behind their own lines. The pilots, Major Brereton, recently appointed commander of the Corps Observation Wing, and Lieutenant Dogan Arthur, were unhurt as was Arthur's observer, Lieutenant Howard T. Fleeson. Captain Vallois flying with Brereton was slightly wounded.[21] Henry L. Stevens and his observer, Lieutenant E. H. Gardiner, of the 50th, failed to return from a 10:30 A.M. flight in support of the 82nd Division.[22] Then, toward the end of the day, Lieutenants Harry Aldrich and David Ker, of the 1st Aero, were shot down in flames. The gas tanks on the Salmson exploded a few feet before the plane plunged into the ground and Aldrich, the pilot, wounded in the legs and badly burned, was thrown clear. He undoubtedly would have been killed had the force of the explosion not broken his fall. Ker was killed in the flaming crash.[23]

On the western flank of the salient, Captain Scanlon's V Corps Observation Group was also having its difficulties on that raw September day. Due to bad weather during the second week of the month, the 104th Aero Squadron had been unable to ferry its planes to the Souilly airdrome, from which the group was to operate during the campaign. Fifteen pilots attempting to fly the squadron's Salmson two-seaters from their former base at Luxeuil to Souilly on the day of the attack met with mixed success. The first flight of eight planes ran into real trouble with the weather, and only Lieutenants John E. Coffin and Godfrey Jacoby landed safely at Souilly. Lieutenant Charles H. Ball attempted to land at Amanty and not only crashed his own plane but also wrecked two Breguets belonging to the 1st Day Bombardment Group. Lieutenants Raymond Davis, Earl S. Wallace, and H. P. Hauck also landed at Amanty and "broke propellers in the mud." Lieutenant Donald Johnson, lost in the rain and low clouds, strayed over German-held territory and was shot down and killed. A second formation of eight planes led by the squadron commander, Lieutenant C. H. Reynolds, had better luck and landed safely at Souilly at dusk on the opening day of the drive. Even this flight had to stop briefly at Ourches during a rain storm.[24]

In spite of the 104th's problems in ferrying planes, several of its observers did fly combat missions on the first day by sharing planes with pilots from the 99th and 88th Aero Squadrons. For example, Lieutenant Henry P. Full toured the corps front with Captain Kenneth Littauer, commanding officer of the 88th, and reported "considerable movement of enemy troops and burning villages." Lieutenant John W. S. Gilchrist, acting as observer for Lieutenant Joseph E. Eaton of the 99th, made a reconnaissance of the Rupt, Mouilly, St. Remy, and Domartin area southeast of Verdun. He noted that the American doughboys of the 26th Division were advancing rapidly and that several villages were on fire.[25]

The 88th Aero Squadron, only recently assigned to the V Corps Observation Group, was also in the process of moving up from the Marne area when the St. Mihiel offensive began. However, under the skilled leadership of Littauer, the transfer was made without a serious hitch, and elements of the squadron worked with the 26th Division as early as the first day of the campaign. Because of the crowded conditions of the Souilly airfield, the squadron was forced to move again two days later, this time to Pretz-en-Argonne, some ten miles southwest of group headquarters.[26]

The highly important task of long-distance reconnaissance of the enemy's rear areas during the American drive to pinch off the German-held salient was the responsibility of the First Army Observation Group. This organization, commanded by Major John Reynolds, had been formed around the veteran 91st Aero Squadron to which the 24th Aero Squadron and the 9th Night Reconnaissance Squadron were added. Owing to the inexperience of its flying personnel, Maury Hill's 24th was unable to participate to any great extent during the offensive. The 9th Squadron could not function at all because of the lack of training and night flying equipment. Most of the work of the four days required to neutralize the salient thus had to be handled by the 91st. Four French escadrilles regulated the army type of artillery fire.[27]

One of the most experienced units in the American Air Service, the 91st Squadron was well equipped for the role it was to play in the big offensive. Not only were most of its air crews veterans, but the squadron had been operating in the St. Mihiel district since its arrival at the front in the spring of 1918. The pilots and observers were familiar with every hill, woods, village, and stream in the area, and they were commanded by an inspiring leader, Lieutenant Everett Cook, who had been with the outfit throughout its war experience. He had served as a flight commander until his promotion to squadron commander early in September. Finally, the 91st had the advantage of operating out of Gondreville airdrome, one of the few in the area favored with good drainage and firm sod.[28]

According to Major Reynolds' original plan, formations of three planes were to take off at two-hour intervals to reconnoiter the German line of communications. It was felt that three planes were necessary since pursuit escort could not penetrate German lines to the fifty–seventy-five-mile depth the army observation aircraft would be required to go. Reynolds was certain that enemy fighters based in the Metz–Mars-le-Tour–Conflans region would vigorously resist all deep reconnaissance efforts.[29]

In spite of the dark rain clouds fanned by a strong southwest wind, two First Army Observation Group planes got into the air shortly after daybreak on the morning of the attack. One plane found a rift in the clouds through which it was able to descend and gather valuable information; the other was less fortunate and returned to the airdrome after an unsuccessful attempt to find an opening in the clouds and fog. Because of the adverse weather, Reynolds' plans for formation flying had to be abandoned. Luckily, the dud weather also interfered with German interceptors, and the group suffered no casualties during the day. Although photography was impossible, single planes were able to carry out visual observations to a depth of fifty miles. For example, one army observation team flying on a course from St. Mihiel, Etain, Briey, Donncourt, Gorse, and Pagny to Pont-a-Mousson at an altitude of 3,000 feet reported:

One train of general service wagons 2 km long west of Sleville (west of Briey) going west at 13:20. One general service train 2 km long on north side of road east of Bayonville at 13:38, standing but indicating they were going west. New material and intense activity at dumps south of Gondrecourt at 13:20. Great activity at dump south of Valleroy, engines running around quite a number of cars in the yards. A lot of material being removed from cars to the north side of the railroad tracks. On airdrome west of Briey (Latenfontaine) there were several large planes of dark steel blue color, probably bombers. In the valley of the Moselle there was nothing. . . .[30]

There were numerous similar reports dropped or radioed into army headquarters during the day.

Very early in the day information brought back by Air Service fliers indicated that the Germans were definitely withdrawing from the salient. It is now known that because of the heavy casualties experienced during the spring and early summer, the German High Command had planned to pull out of the St. Mihiel bulge should any real Allied pressure be applied there. This would enable them to reduce the length of the front and thereby economize on manpower. Allied aerial reconnaissance during the second week of September had provided some inkling of the imminent evacuation. Although the Germans expected the Allied attack they were surprised as to its timing and were caught in the process of withdrawing from the salient when Pershing threw his sledgehammer blow in the early morning hours of 12 September.

That bleak Thursday was also to be a day of mixed success for the hunters. Forty minutes after Vaughn McCormick's patrol had disappeared to the north into the heavy overcast, Captain Ray Bridgeman decided to make a personal reconnaissance over the front. Perhaps with first-hand knowledge of flying conditions in the Moselle River Valley area he could better advise the 22nd Pursuit Squadron patrols scheduled for later that morning. At 6:25 A.M. he buckled himself into the cockpit of his Spad, and after a brief check of elevator, aileron, and rudder controls he motioned for the crew chief to spin the propeller. The Hispano-Suiza engine coughed, then roared to life. After warming up the wet engine for a few moments he signaled for the chocks to be removed from the wheels and began taxiing slowly to the northeast end of the Toul airfield. On reaching the extreme boundary of the sponge-soft airdrome, Bridgeman turned into the strong southwest wind and slowly advanced the throttle. The snub-nosed little fighter picked up speed slowly but the gale-like wind would help. As he reached the middle of the field he eased the control stick forward slightly and felt the tail come off the ground. His speed continued to increase, and as the trees at the southwest corner of the field loomed near he gently pulled back on the stick. With more ease than he expected, the Spad deserted the mud and water and began a steady climb. After clearing the trees, the veteran flier began a medium turn to the left. With one circuit of the airdrome to get his bearings he set course to the northeast and immediately found himself in the rapidly moving low clouds. Visibility was indeed bad. Moving the stick forward slightly, he dropped down to 500 feet where he could see the earth below.

For the next several minutes Bridgeman skimmed on just below the cloud base. At 6:40 A.M. he sighted the Moselle just north of Dieulouard and banked to his left toward Pont-a-Mousson, five miles downstream. As the Spad roared on at 125 mph, Bridgeman's eyes searched the overcast for a possible break in the clouds. "Eternal vigilance is the price of life" was an airman's corruption of a well-known adage; a Hun pilot could be lurking in the fringes of the clouds to pounce on an unsuspecting victim. A minute or two later the American flashed over the Pont-a-Mousson bridge and hedgehopped on to the north toward the battle line. Three miles further on, in the vicinity of the village of Norray, he noted for the first time troops moving slowly northward down the river. These would be soldiers of the U.S. 82nd Division assigned to the extreme eastern end of the front. At the same time he saw several large fires in Norray. Off to the left he spotted a DH-4 observation plane bearing the markings of the 50th Aero Squadron (probably Lieutenants Frayne and French).

It was 6:55 A.M., and Captain Bridgeman had seen no sign of McCormick's formation; perhaps the flight was patrolling a little further to the west. As he banked steeply in that direction his eyes caught a glimpse of still another aircraft. Was it another DH-4? It was a two-seater, certainly, but not an American Liberty plane.[31]

As he maneuvered closer he recognized the stranger as a German Hanoveraner. The German had not yet spotted the approaching Spad, and Bridgeman was able to close the gap quickly and to fire "150 rounds at very close range from a good position." The stricken Hanoveraner "went straight down through the clouds as out of control." Because of the ground fog the American was unable to see the crash, but the German's plunge had taken place from an altitude of less than 500 feet, and a safe recovery would have been impossible.[32]

The flight was not over. Five minutes after the German two-seater dove through the mist to its destruction Bridgeman spotted an enemy Rumpler in the same area, but the Hun banked into a low cloud and escaped. At 7:10 the commander of the 22nd Squadron saw "5 enemy Rumplers in the region of St. Marie . . . but they retreated into their lines" too quickly for him to attack. Three brushes with enemy aircraft within twenty minutes had eaten deeply into Bridgeman's fuel supply, so at this point he elected to turn southward toward Toul. As he flew low over the battle line a bullet from the ground, very likely fired by an American soldier who mistook his Spad for an enemy aircraft, damaged his engine, and he was forced to land just outside Remenauville, a village which had been in German hands only two hours before.[33] Other than the engine the Spad was undamaged, and Bridgeman made his way to Toul by automobile to get the aid of his mechanics.

Bridgeman's joy over his early morning victory was short lived. On reaching the 22nd Aero Squadron Headquarters he learned that his friend, Vaughn McCormick, had been killed in a crash upon returning to the airdrome from his 5:30 A.M. patrol. The patrol had had several indecisive fights during the morning, and it was believed that McCormick must have been wounded, for his landing approach had been normal up to the time he turned into the wind to land.[34] McCormick, a flight commander, had been credited with two official victories before coming to the 22nd and was considered one of the squadron's most promising pilots.

Shortly after the first patrol from the 22nd Squadron took off, flights from Major Charles Biddle's 13th, Captain George Fisher's 49th, and Lieutenant David Putnam's 139th, all based at Toul, also braved the elements and headed for the front lines. Barrage patrols consisting of huge formations, stacked at altitudes from 3,000 to

15,000 feet over the battle lines, had to be abandoned because of the low clouds and poor visibility. Strafing of retreating German infantry and low-level reconnaissance, however, could be performed. Early patrols found the Vigneulles-St. Benoit road filled with the enemy's retreating columns, guns, and limbers. This road formed

practically a forced point of passage for such of the enemy troops as were able to escape from the point of the salient. All day [Allied] pursuit planes harrassed it with their machine gun fire, throwing the enemy columns into confusion.[35]

Toward dusk of that trying day at St. Mihiel the 2nd Pursuit Group and the American Air Service lost its leading ace: David Endicott Putnam was shot down and killed. A descendant of General Israel Putnam of Revolutionary War fame, David Putnam was born in Jamaica Plains, Massachusetts, in 1898. As an undergraduate at Harvard he was president of his class, an outstanding orator, and a fine athlete in swimming, football, baseball, and hockey. Early in 1917, before America entered the war, Putnam dropped out of school, hitchhiked to France on a cattleboat, and joined the French Air Service. On winning his brevet as an aviator at Avord in October, 1917, he was sent to Pau for advanced training in acrobatics.[36] In December he joined a French escadrille which was then based a few miles from Chalons, near the Meuse River. During the next six months he achieved a remarkable record as a pursuit pilot, shooting down eight enemy aircraft. In June, 1918, he transferred to Escadrille Spad 38, commanded by the great French ace, George Félix Madon, and five days later he single-handedly engaged ten German Albatros fighters. When the melee was over he had downed five of the ten, which at that time was the greatest score of victories credited to a pilot in a single engagement.* Late in June of 1918 he was commissioned a first lieutenant in the American Air Service and was assigned to the 139th Aero Squadron as a flight commander. He scored his ninth victory on 30 June, and by the end of August he had been credited with his eleventh kill. At the time of the St. Mihiel campaign he was acting as squadron commander, replacing Major Lawrence C. Angstrom, who was ill.

* Actually only one was officially credited to Putnam in this fight, but according to Hall and Nordhoff "there can be no doubt about the other four." Some sources list him as having thirty-four victories at the time of his death.[37]

On the fateful afternoon of 12 September, Putnam, with Lieutenant Wendel A. Robertson, of Fort Smith, Arkansas, took off on a special reconnaissance of the rapidly changing front line. Fifteen minutes later the two Spads were making a wide turn over the town of Thiaucourt when they were suddenly pounced upon by fifteen enemy fighters diving from the low clouds. In the fierce treetop dogfight which followed, Putnam managed to maneuver "behind one of the Boche fighters" and send it crashing into a small village for his twelfth victory.[38] Then, with the odds hopelessly against them, the two Americans zoomed into the overcast and escaped. A few minutes later Putnam, with Robertson tightly glued to his wing, dropped through the overcast only to see a lone American observation plane being harassed by eight Fokkers. Without hesitation the Massachusetts boy, followed by the faithful Robertson, dived into the fray below. This surprise attack caused momentary confusion in the Fokker formation and gave the hard-pressed observation plane an opportunity to make its dash to safety. Seconds later Putnam's Spad crashed a few hundred yards from the town of Limey. The tall blond New Englander had paid for his gallantry with his life—having been shot twice through the heart.[39] For his twilight action on 12 September he was to win the DSC and the gratitude of a team of observation fliers.

Planes of the 3rd Pursuit Group flying out of Vaucouleurs also entered the aerial battle early. As the 93rd Aero Squadron historian narrates,

At 4:30 A.M. the field was a scene of officers and mechanics busily engaged in making final preparation for take-off. Specific instructions had arrived at the operations office, and the flight leaders had final conferences with their pilots before leaving. The first show was a strafing mission—"the 93rd Squadron will furnish a patrol of six machines to attack with machine guns, a concentration of German troops on the road between Chambley and Waverly." [40]

Shortly after 6:00 A.M. the first patrol, led by Lieutenant Chester Wright, became airborne during a brief lull in the rainstorm. Two nerve-shattering hours later the pilots found their way home again having "successfully fulfilled their mission."

A second flight led by Lieutenant Leslie J. "Rummy" Rummell and consisting of Lieutenants Charles R. D'Olive and Paul Cox, took off at 9:50 A.M. This turned out to be one of the most thrilling patrols made by any squadron during the whole miserable day. Rummell's description of the resulting air battle is a classic of clarity and color:

It was a reconnaissance mission that I set out on about ten o'clock with Lts. Cox and D'Olive following me. There were clouds at less than 400 meters and a fine rain which stung our faces like needles. I shall hurry over the preliminaries; how I lost Lts. Cox and D'Olive in the clouds, how I gained my objective, made the necessary observations and started back. It was then that I glanced inside the cowling of my machine at my pressure gauge, and looked up again to find a speck, a German scout I soon decided, among the clouds, above and in front of me. I climbed, turning slightly away from the other machine, which started to climb toward me. He was some 500 meters and about on my level, with the clouds above, below and around us both. I recall that I was surprised at that very instant to find how calm and collected I was. I thought I would be scared stiff; I felt that I ought to be but I wasn't. Nobody is I guess when he gets that far. What followed I did without reasoning. It just seemed to be the thing to do. The Hun was coming toward me, climbing in such a way as to head me off if I kept straight on. Right along my line of flight was a cloud, a small one, which I saw I could get around. I turned and dodged around the cloud, climbing all the time, evidently giving the German the impression I was running away, for when I completed the circuit, I found the enemy machine going in the direction he had last seen me take. I was now above and behind him, and, most important of all, unnoticed. The rest was easy. I came down on him, opening with both guns at a distance of 75 yards. The tracer bullets I could see enter his cockpit and the forward part of his fuselage. As I reached a point about thirty yards away from him, he seemed to pull the nose of his machine up; I followed with my tracers and became so intent on keeping those yellow streams flowing into him, that I almost drove my plane into his. Suddenly I did the only thing left to do. I dove underneath with full motor. When I looked back he had fallen into the clouds below us, lost to sight.

Then I was scared; and lost. I could see the ground only at intervals, and could recognize no landmarks. I resorted to the compass, and what I could see of the sun, keeping as much in the clouds as I could to avoid possible attack from enemy planes. Incidentally, those fifteen minutes I spent in the grey mist of the clouds, with no idea where I was, and almost as little of where I was going, with minutes of flying getting fewer as the gas became less, were a bit startling. My compass led me too far east, to where the front turned south toward Nancy. As I was flying south, I merely flew parallel to the lines for awhile, until, in one of my periodic dips, I discovered the trenches, and crossed over and picked out the only available spot for landing. This spot was, I found out later, on a slope of the Vosges Mountains. I crashed the machine, but not myself; and later, when our troops moved up, got confirmation on my first enemy plane. I was reported missing, too, because it wasn't until late that night that I could get word to the squadron.[41]

Before the war was over Lieutenant Rummell, with seven victories, ranked as one of the top pursuit pilots in the American Air Service.

During the hectic minutes in which Rummell fought his picturesque battle in the clouds, Lieutenant Charles D'Olive was also busy. While nursing a cranky engine he had lost his patrol leader in the clouds, and realizing it would be next to impossible to find the formation again, he decided to try to get his bearings by diving under the cloud layer. As he broke through the mist at 800 feet he was startled to find himself practically "on top of a Hun airplane."[42] In D'Olive's words,

The Hun never saw me . . . he must have been looking at troops on the ground. I dived through the cloud, caught up and came up underneath him. I saw the crosses on his wings, raised my nose a little, and when I was lined up with his propeller I started shooting. I think he must have been killed by the first burst because the plane went straight up, fell off, took three turns and hit the ground.[43]

This was the Suggsville, Alabama, boy's first aerial kill; he finished the war with five official victories.*

Major John Huffer's 93rd Squadron engaged in several missions during the daylight hours of that terrible Thursday. Perhaps typical of these was the mission which stemmed from an early afternoon order to fly at a "low altitude and straff [sic] the following towns: Vigneulles, St. Benoit, Dampvitoux, and Chambley, and roads and all concentrations of troops. . . ." Fourteen Spads took off in three flights to carry out the assignment. Lieutenant Walter Case's combat report graphically describes the flight:

Lt. [O. J.] Gude could not go any further than the lines on account of motor trouble, so we three that were left went on over and completed the

---

* The final victory lists for the American Air Service gives D'Olive credit for only four kills, even though five were confirmed in army orders. In 1962 D'Olive, then vice-president of Chamberlain Corp., Waterloo, Iowa, asked the Air Force to check its records. On 18 June 1963, some forty-five years after the war, his records were corrected to show the fifth victory.

mission. I did not know any of the enemy territory so I flew very close to Lt. [Harold] Merz, who was leading. I watched him and fired on almost every target he fired on. At one time we flew over a small town, where there were, to my judgment, about 3000 troops in the streets and outside of the town, together with many motor lorries. I piqued down and fired on the troops in the street which caused utter confusion, a great many of them trying to enter one door at once. I concentrated my fire on that door, killing and wounding many of them, I am sure, for I could see them fall, being at that time less than fifty meters high. Things were getting pretty hot for us there and we moved on. I saw a company of riflemen about a half mile from the village. As I looked at them I could see that they were all at ready and a second later I thought my time had come, for I could see the smoke coming from their rifle barrels. I piqued on them, firing both guns until I was about 150 feet from them, then had to pull up to keep from hitting the ground and crashing. At a very short distance from them I saw several motor trucks going north. I opened fire on one of them and saw the driver jump from one side and another chap from the other, as the truck hit a tree and stopped. I fired on numerous other small formations of the enemy. On our way home there was a great deal of rifle and machine gun fire and archie directed at us, luckily no one in the formation being touched, but Lt. Merz had a longeron shot in two by rifle or machine gun fire. Lt. [Lewis] Carruthers also picked up two bullets in his machine. Neither I nor my machine was touched.[44]

Indeed, the squadron that only four short weeks before had "lacked everything from experience to motors" had done well. At that time the squadron had available only six pairs of wheels, and when one plane returned from patrol Engineering Officer Lieutenant Charles "Bolsie" Boles and his ground crew had been forced to transfer its wheels to "another machine which had been made ready for the next 'show.' "[45]

Other squadrons of Bill Thaw's 3rd Pursuit Group were equally active. The 103rd flew several reconnaissance sorties during the morning hours and shortly after noon Rockwell led a fourteen-ship strafing mission against troops and motor trucks on the Pannes-Beney and the Chambley-Dampvitoux roads. On this flight the squadron became the first American unit in the St. Mihiel sector[46] to drop bombs from pursuit planes.* About the same time ten pilots

* In a recent letter to the author (14 August 1967) Lt. Charles R. D'Olive, whose 93rd Aero Squadron was also engaged in bombing, described the technique in this manner: "On the pursuit planes some of us used a little bomb rack that was adapted to a home made hangar under the gas tank of the Spad XIII. These held

from the 28th Squadron led by Lieutenants Charles Merrick and Thomas G. Cassady bombed and strafed the roads and villages between Ars and Pont-a-Mousson.[47] Later in the afternoon a ten-plane formation, again led by Merrick, picked its way through the rain squalls and German archie to blast troops and transports on the road north of Vigneulles. Five Spads had to return to base because of engine trouble, but the others continued to hunt targets of opportunity until their ammunition was gone. Merrick attacked a German Rumpler without success when his guns jammed.[48]

John Hambleton's 213th Squadron did not put aircraft in the air until 12:30 P.M., but during the afternoon the squadron flew no less than twenty individual sorties with varied success. The Squadron Commander's own reconnaissance report, describing one of the late missions, was typical of the day's action of

seeing wagons and limbers scattered along the roads from Vigneulles to Dampvitoux. The movement of troops was both ways, but the main current [was] entirely northward (thus, the Germans were definitely retreating from the salient). Fired into one convoy dispersing horses and men. Saw burning dumps at Vigneulles and in the vicinity. The rest of the patrol (seven had taken off) either through bad weather or motor trouble were unable to act within the enemy's lines.[49]

If possible, the weather situation on the Meuse River side of the St. Mihiel salient was even worse than that facing American units on the south and east portion of the battle lines. In the words of the 1st Pursuit Group Commander,

On the morning of September 12, our men were on the job long before daylight but, to the disgust of everybody the weather was atrocious—pouring rain, with low hanging clouds. This, however, was perfect for part of our plan—low flying. The pilots certainly flew low that day—they could not do otherwise—and the success of this new system (low altitude strafing and bombing attacks on troop convoys and trenches) pointed the way we followed until the end of hostilities. And by low I mean low. The clouds at times formed a solid mist at 100 feet and everything had to be done below that. This low flying by an entire group was a revolution in war-time flying.[50]

4—20-lb. Cooper bombs. For the bomb sight we just lined up the center section struts with the road—if we caught one with trucks, etc., and 'let go' from about 250–300 feet. I never had one misfire, except once when the mechanic failed to cut the safety wires that held the little propeller that had to spin off to un-guard the fuse." This was essentially the same system used by the American squadrons flying Camels on the British front.

In spite of the inclement weather the 27th, 94th, 95th, and 147th Squadrons each flew approximately twenty individual sorties without casualty.

Captain Alfred Grant's 27th Squadron was the first to take off from the tiny Rembercourt airfield when a patrol consisting of Lieutenants Jerry Vasconcelles, Frank Luke, K. S. Clapp, E. W. Hewitt, R. W. Donaldson, Donald Hudson, Leo Dawson, and Joseph Fritz Wehner ventured aloft at 7:30 A.M. Although Vasconcelles was nominally the patrol leader, the formation soon broke up into flights of one's and two's because of the weather. No enemy planes could be found, but members of the patrol discovered plenty of strafing targets along roads near Lamorville, Maizy, St. Remy, Combres, and Montsec.[51] Shortly before 8:00 A.M. Wehner spotted a German balloon in the vicinity of Montsec and fired 100 rounds of machine gun bullets into it. "The balloon did not burn but was immediately hauled down."[52]

Frank Luke, the blond Arizonian with a reputation for insubordination and reckless individualism, ran into three enemy aircraft near Lavigneville and chased them across the entire salient to the Moselle where they disappeared toward Metz. Luke's chagrin at losing the Hun planes was somewhat lessened when he spotted a German observation balloon some five miles north of Pont-a-Mousson. His combat report described the resulting action:

Saw enemy balloon at Marieulles. Destroyed it after three passes at it, each within a few yards of the balloon. The third pass was made when the balloon was very near the ground. Both guns stopped so pulled off to one side. Fixed left gun and turned about to make one final effort to burn it, but saw it had started. The next instant it burst into great flames and dropped on the winch, destroying it. The observer, Joseph M. Fox, who saw the burning, said he thought several were killed when it burst into flames so near the ground. There was a good field near our balloons so landed for confirmation. Left field and started back when my motor began cutting out. Returned to the same field, and there found my motor could not be fixed [they were still having trouble with the Hispano-Suiza 220], so returned by motorcycle. Attached you will find confirmation from Lt. Fox and Lt. Smith.* Both saw burning.[53]

Luke had wandered far from the area assigned to the 1st Pursuit Group and had made an unauthorized landing. But to him con-

---

* These two officers had been manning a nearby American balloon and had seen the destruction of the German balloon.

firmation of the destruction of the enemy balloon by eyewitnesses was imperative. While on a patrol a month before he had left his flight leader and later returned to base claiming the destruction of an enemy aircraft. At that time few had believed his story and "some of his fellow-pilots considered him a conceited braggart."[54] He was severely reprimanded several times for his contempt of authority, though he was considered by Hartney, the group commander, to possess the ideal combination of flying ability, marksmanship, and fighting spirit. Embittered by the attitude of many of his more orthodox squadron mates, Luke became even more of a lone eagle than before. During the St. Mihiel campaign he won the title "Balloon Buster," and in the next seventeen days, the last days of his life, he destroyed eighteen enemy aircraft.*

The first patrol from the 94th "Hat-in-the-Ring" Squadron did not get into the air until nearly noon, when Lieutenants Edward Rickenbacker and Reed Chambers took off on a volunteer mission. Rickenbacker had returned to the squadron only the night before after a mastoid operation and several weeks in a Paris hospital, and he was eager to tangle with the Hun again.[55] He was already an ace with six victories and had been made a flight commander a few days before his hospital confinement. Chambers, a twenty-four-year-old Onager, Kansas, boy, had not yet scored an official victory but had already developed many of the aggressive characteristics that eventually would make him a seven-victory ace.

Rickenbacker and Chambers found that even though the ceiling was only 600 feet, the visibility, in spite of the light rain, was adequate. Flying straight east to St. Mihiel, the pair crossed the Meuse River and turned down the river toward Verdun. Along this route Rickenbacker observed that "many fires were burning under us as we flew, most of them well on the German side of the river . . . villages, haystacks, ammunition dumps were being set ablaze by the retreating Huns."[56] After proceeding as far as Verdun they swung off to the east and at a low altitude passed over Fresnes and Vigneulles. The latter city, situated some fifteen miles east of Verdun and an equal distance north of St. Mihiel, was the objective of the converging American infantry corps. Like an irresistable pincers the eastern and western forces were drawing nearer and nearer to

* According to some lists Luke was credited with twenty-one enemy aircraft destroyed.

this point; those German troops still inside the salient would soon be caught in the noose.

As the pair turned south of Vigneulles they noted that the main highway running north to Metz was black with hurrying men and vehicles, and that guns, stores, and ammunition were being hauled away with all possible speed. Continuing on southeast down the St. Mihiel-Vigneulles road they observed that the Germans were in full cry to the rear. As the two Spads droned on at 125 mph, the pilots spotted an especially attractive target—"a whole battery of Boche three-inch guns was coming toward us on the double." In his book *Fighting the Flying Circus,* written a few months after the action, Rickenbacker described his attack on this half-mile-long convoy.

Dipping down at the head of the column I sprinkled a few bullets over the leading teams. Horses fell right and left. One driver leaped from his seat and started running for the ditch. Half-way across the road he threw up his arms and rolled over upon his face. He had stepped full in front of my stream of machine-gun bullets!

All down the line we continued our fire—now tilting our aeroplanes down for a short burst, then zooming back up for a little altitude in which to repeat the performance. The whole column was thrown into the wildest confusion. Horses plunged and broke away. Some were killed and fell in their tracks. Most of the drivers and gunners had taken to the trees before we reached them. Our little visit must have cost them an hour's delay.[57]

Then with ammunition running low the 94th Squadron pair dodged through the mist over the city of St. Mihiel and finally to the tiny little Rembercourt airfield hidden in the trees a few miles away. The highly significant information collected on the reconnaissance flight was immediately telephoned to army headquarters. Their observations merely confirmed what other pilots—both pursuit and observation—had been reporting throughout the morning. Indeed, it seemed certain that the enemy was actually quitting the St. Mihiel salient as rapidly as possible.[58]

The 1st Day Bombardment Group based at Amanty, fifteen miles southwest of Toul, also got its bloody baptism of fire on the first day of the St. Mihiel offensive. Commanded by Major John L. Dunsworth, the group had been organized only two days before the drive was launched and included the 11th, 20th, and 96th Aero Squadrons. Actually, the 11th and 20th Squadrons had not completed their squadron organization on that murky, muddy, and windy day. Some of the pilots and observers had seen combat service with French flying units, but most of them would see their first battle action during the next four days. The two new squadrons operated American-built DH-4 airplanes equipped with Liberty engines. U.S. Air Service squadrons had not used these planes before in bombing operations; consequently, mistakes were expected. Fortunately, both of these rookie outfits were commanded by able and experienced fliers—the 11th by First Lieutenant Thornton "Nap" Hooper, the 20th by First Lieutenant Cecil "Swede" Sellers. The veteran 96th Squadron, led by Captain James Summersett, had been stationed at Amanty since 18 May, and had been flying missions in the Toul sector since 12 June. Aviators in this outfit were thoroughly familiar with the St. Mihiel, Metz, Conflans, and Verdun area. The 96th was still equipped with Breguet-14 B-2 aircraft and had no intention of changing: even though squadron mechanics had been forced to improvise in making parts for these aircraft the flying personnel considered the Breguet a far better aircraft than the DH-4.[59]

Shortly before midnight on the night before the St. Mihiel drive the 1st Day Bombardment Group was instructed to prepare for an early morning mission to "bomb and machine-gun hostile troops in front of our advancing infantry." Since the 11th and 20th Squadrons were assigned to fly barrage patrols with the 2nd Pursuit Group, the entire burden of bombardment aviation would have to be shouldered by the 96th. To carry out the bombing assignment the twelve available Breguets were divided into flights of four each. Dunsworth and Summersett planned to send the flights off at thirty-minute intervals, "and thus keep the enemy troops under constant bombardment."[60] This close-in tactical work was undoubtedly General Pershing's idea, as Mitchell would have preferred making the rail centers of Conflans, Mars-Le-Tour, and Metz and the bridges over the Moselle the primary targets.

At 10:00 A.M. on the morning of 12 September, orders were finally received to attack troop concentrations in the town of Buxieres, six miles south of Vigneulles, and along the main roads in the area. Because of the strong wind and low ceiling, Summersett, in consultation with the Group Commander, decided it was impractical for even a four-plane formation to operate. Consequently, Lieutenants André Gundelach and Pennington Way, the leading team of the first flight, volunteered to attempt the mission alone, "and to determine, if possible, the best method of conducting troop bombing under the existing unfavorable weather conditions."[61] Within a few minutes the Breguet, laden with 32 antipersonnel bombs, waddled the length of the muddy Amanty airfield and climbed slowly to the north. It did not return. It was learned later that Gundelach and Way had reached their objective, dropped their bombs on the concentration of enemy troops, and begun their return to their home field. In the vicinity of Commercy, well inside their own lines, they were attacked by eight Fokker fighters and brought down in flames. Way, the observer, was killed instantly, while Gundelach died within a few hours after the crash. For their action they were posthumously awarded the DSC.[62]

The day's second bombing mission met with considerable success. At 1:30 P.M. nine planes, led by David H. Young, took off to bomb the troop center at Buxerulles. The formation passed directly over the city of St. Mihiel at 2:15 P.M., at less than 2,000 feet, but did not draw a single shot, "showing that the withdrawal from the salient had already begun."[63] Five minutes later, on the signal of Sam Lunt, the lead observer, the nine teams simultaneously dropped their bombs on the target town. Eight of the bombers returned to their home field; the ninth was forced to land at Vaucouleurs, the home base of Thaw's 3rd Pursuit Group.

A third bombardment mission flown during the day proved to be a nightmare of disaster. Since many of the planes used in the early afternoon had to be used again on that last raid, the flight did not get off until 6:35 P.M. Several of the Breguets broke propellers in the takeoff run on the soft field and never became airborne. Five planes led by Captain Summersett managed to get into the air and set course for Vigneulles, the assigned target, but because it got a late start the little formation did not reach the objective until after dark. There were many fires in the town, however, and Summersett had no difficulty in locating the target; thus, 1,150 kilograms of bombs were dropped on the northern part of Vigneulles and on the road to Hatten-Chatel. Since it was dark, results could not be ascertained. At approximately 7:30 P.M. the bombing formation left the area and headed for home. The Breguets were not equipped for night flying, and an attempt was made to land with the aid of ground flares. One of the planes landed safely, three crashed on the Amanty airdrome, and one machine, piloted by Lieutenant Edward Cronin, crashed in a ploughed field near Gondrecourt. Cronin was killed, but his observer, Lieutenant L. C. Bleeker, was uninjured.[64]

The end of the day found the 96th Squadron in bad shape, having lost three fliers and eight planes wrecked or out of commission. The clinging mud of the rain-soaked field "caused many broken propellers, and the high wind made it necessary for the mechanics to hold the wings while the planes were taxied to and from the starting line." In addition to the combat losses, a refugee Salmson, flown by a 104th Squadron pilot, attempted to land near the hangars and drifted into two Breguets loaded with bombs. All three aircraft were total wrecks, but fortunately the bombs did not explode.* Lieutenant James A. O'Toole, an observer in the 96th, was also lost while flying with Lieutenant G. M. Crawford of the 20th Aero Squadron. Their plane was shot down behind enemy lines; O'Toole was killed and Crawford was captured.

Tomorrow there would be more blood and more dying. Although there was sadness over those who had fallen on that opening day of the big battle, the young airmen—bombardment, observation, and pursuit alike—viewed it all with a certain philosophic fatalism. During the evening hours in the barracks, clubs, and cafes frequented by the winged warriors the refrain of an old song was heard:

> Stand to your glasses, steady!
> The world is a world of lies;
> A cup to the dead already
> And here is to the next that dies.[66]

* The constant breakage of propellers probably contributed to combat losses; resulting formations were so small that they were "ripe pickings" for enemy pursuits.[65]

Notes

1. Letter from Leland M. Carver to author, 30 April 1965.
2. *Ibid.*, 24 June 1965.
3. Leland M. Carver, *et al., The Ninetieth Aero Squadron*, 24–25.
4. "First Corps Observation Group" (Gorrell Histories, AS AEF, C, XII), 1–8.

5. Morse, *50th Aero Squadron,* 30.

6. "History of the 104th Aero Squadron" (Gorrell Histories, AS AEF, E, XVII), 4–9.

7. Miller, ed., "Eyes of the Army: The Observation Corps," *Cross and Cockade Journal,* Spring, 1962, 87.

8. "Operations, Air Service, First Army" (Gorrell Histories, AS AEF, C, III), 1–15.

9. "History of the 22nd Aero Squadron" (Gorrell Histories, AS AEF, E, V), 23.

10. Hall and Nordhoff, *The Lafayette Flying Corps,* I, 144–45.

11. "History of the 22nd Aero Squadron," *loc. cit.,* 23–27; see also the reconnaissance report for 12 September 1918.

12. Carver, *Ninetieth Aero Squadron,* 25.

13. Memorandum from Henry C. Bogle to author, 12 July 1964.

14. Carver, *Ninetieth Aero Squadron,* 26.

15. Percival G. Hart, "Observations from a DH-4," *Cross and Cockade Journal,* Winter, 1961, 234.

16. *Ibid.*

17. "History of the 8th Aero Squadron" (Gorrell Histories, AS AEF, E, I), 111.

18. Morse, *50th Aero Squadron,* 30; see also letter from Morse to author, 14 June 1965.

19. Morse, *ibid.,* 14–15.

20. "Operations Reports of the 12th Aero Squadron, 10 August–11 November 1918" (Gorrell Histories, AS AEF, E, III).

21. *Ibid.*

22. Morse, *50th Aero Squadron,* 31.

23. George B. Richards, compiler, *War Diary and Letters of John Francisco Richards II, 1917–1918,* 166.

24. "History of the 104th Aero Squadron," *loc. cit.,* 4–15.

25. *Ibid.,* 8–12.

26. James J. Sloan, "History of the 88th Observation Squadron," *American Aviation Historical Society Journal,* Fall, 1960, 196.

27. Sam Hager Frank, "Air Service Observation in World War I," unpublished dissertation, University of Florida, 325.

28. "First Army Observation Group" (Gorrell Histories, AS AEF, C, VIII).

29. Frank, "Air Service Observation," 325–26.

30. "Operations, Air Service, First Army," *loc. cit.*

31. Bridgeman Memorandum, undated.

32. "History of the 22nd Aero Squadron," *loc. cit.,* 23–28.

33. *Ibid.,* see Bridgeman's combat report.

34. *Ibid.,* see Lt. R. J. Little's reconnaissance report.

35. "Tactical History of the Air Service" (Gorrell Histories, AS AEF, D, I), 10–11.

36. Robertson, *Aces of the 1914–1918 War,* 101–102.

37. Hall and Nordhoff, *The Lafayette Flying Corps,* 395–98.

38. Air Service, First Army, AEF, G.O. No. 9.

39. See DSC citation in Stringer, *Heroes All!* 323; Robertson, *Aces of the 1914–1918 War,* 102.

40. "History of the 93rd Aero Squadron" (Gorrell Histories, AS AEF, E, X), 5.

41. *Ibid.,* 6–7; see also Rummell's reconnaissance report for 12 September 1918.

42. *Ibid.,* 7.

43. Vance Bourjaily, "Memoirs of an Ace," *Esquire,* August, 1964, 31–32.

44. "History of the 93rd Aero Squadron," *loc. cit.,* 8.

45. *Ibid.,* 4.

46. "History of the 103rd Aero Squadron" (Gorrell Histories, AS AEF, E, XVI), 10.

47. "History of the 28th Aero Squadron" (Gorrell Histories, AS AEF, E, VII), 6.

48. *Ibid.,* reconnaissance report.

49. Reconnaissance report in "History of the 213th Aero Squadron" (Gorrell Histories, AS AEF, E, XXI).

50. Hartney, *Up and At 'Em,* 216.

51. See reconnaissance reports for Lts. R. W. Donaldson, K. S. Clapp, J. F. Wehner, and Frank Luke in "History of the 27th Aero Squadron," *loc. cit.*

52. *Ibid.,* combat report for Joseph F. Wehner, 12 September 1918.

53. *Ibid.,* for Frank Luke, 12 September 1918.

54. Hartney, *Up and At 'Em,* 250–88.

55. Rickenbacker, *Fighting the Flying Circus,* 230–32.

56. *Ibid.,* 233.

57. *Ibid.,* 233–34.

58. *Ibid.,* 234.

59. Hopper, "American Day Bombardment," *Air Power Historian,* April, 1957, 88–90.

60. "Tactical History of the Air Service," *loc. cit.,* 6.

61. *Ibid.*

62. See DSC citation in Stringer, *Heroes All!* 172–73, 408.

63. Daily Log of the 96th Aero Squadron in "History of the 1st Day Bombardment Group" (Gorrell Histories, AS AEF, N, XV), 23.

64. *Ibid.*

65. Hopper, "American Day Bombardment," *loc. cit.,* 93.

66. Song quoted in Leighton Brewer, *Riders of the Sky,* 119.

IX

St. Mihiel: The Bloody Mopping Up

FRIDAY 13 September dawned wet and cloudy, with a treacherous wind still blowing and five lonesome Breguets on the alert at the 96th Squadron hangars. These five were all the hard-pressed ground crews, by working throughout the night, could get ready for action on that second day at St. Mihiel. The ground crews and flying officers alike nervously waited out the morning but no mission orders came. Finally, at 3:15 P.M. instructions were received to strike the roads between Chambley and Mars-la-Tour, some ten or twelve miles west of the German stronghold of Metz. A few minutes later the five bombing planes, led by Lieutenant Bradley Gaylord, years later to be an air force general, and his observer, Lieutenant Howard Rath, attempted to take off to carry out the assignment. Four escaped the clutches of the mud; one, however, was forced to land before reaching the battle line. The other three continued the mission and successfully bombed German troops in the Chambley area from an altitude of 3,000 feet. On turning for home the little formation was attacked by fifteen enemy pursuit planes. Although one of the enemy aircraft was shot down immediately the German formation continued to press its attack in a highly aggressive fashion. Within a matter of minutes the Breguet carrying Lieutenants Thomas Farnsworth and Robert Thompson went down out of control near the village of Charey. Moments later a second bomber, manned by Lieutenants Stephen Hopkins and Bertram Williams, spun down in flames over Dommartin. Miraculously, the team of Gaylord and Rath fought its way through

175

the enemy patrol and eventually returned to Amanty without serious damage.[1]

DH-4's from the 11th and 20th Aero Squadrons continued to fly barrage patrols along the lines, supposedly as protection for the Spads of the 2nd Pursuit Group. The idea was to frustrate surprise attacks from the rear, but according to Lieutenant Clifford Allsopp, a pilot in the 11th Squadron, "the arrangement was a great flop."[2] The De Havillands simply could not keep up with the pursuits.

Down below, the American ground forces were turning the offensive into a rout. By the end of the first day's fighting, most units had reached the objectives set for the second day. General Pershing therefore ordered the schedule stepped up. On the morning of 13 September the U.S. 1st Division, advancing from the south, reached Vigneulles and joined the U.S. 26th Division driving in from the west. By the end of the day virtually all objectives had been taken and the salient had been reduced.[3] The next two days were devoted to mopping up.

Even though the land operation was nearly complete by nightfall of the second day, the air forces were to see considerable action during the next several days. There was abundant evidence that the German air units based at Mars-la-Tour, Metz, and Steney were being reinforced on the second day of the battle. In fact, Freiherr Oscar von Boenigk's *Jagdgeschwader* II had been flown in from sectors further to the west and was now based at Steney, near Metz. This *Jagdgeschwader* consisted of four crack *staffeln* of Fokker D-7's—*Jastas* 12, 13, 15, and 19. Included in its ranks were such multiple aces as Franz Büchner, Georg von Hantelmann, and Josef Veltjens.[4]

Because of the continuing bad weather, American observation units ran into relatively little aerial opposition on 13 September. The 8th Squadron lost a Salmson in a running fight with a Fokker formation; the pilot, Lieutenant Hilery Rex, and the observer, Lieutenant William F. Gallager, were killed.[5] Late in the afternoon Lieutenants Wilber C. Suiter and Guy E. Morse, of the 135th Squadron, were shot down by Fokker D-7's over their own airdrome. Suiter was shot through the head and Morse was catapulted from the plane when it crashed. Both were killed. This was the first time during the St. Mihiel campaign that German fighters appeared over Allied air bases.[6] A crew from the 91st Aero Squadron made the only kill scored by observation units when it shot down an attacking pursuit plane in the vicinity of Rembercourt during the afternoon.[7]

Corps observation squadrons worked effectively with the rapidly advancing infantry division throughout the day. Perhaps the outstanding piece of work done was a low-level oblique photography mission carried out by Lieutenant Leland Carver, pilot, and Lieutenant Gustav Lindstrom, observer, of the 90th Squadron. Braving terrific ground fire, Carver and Lindstrom photographed every town and village in the U.S. 42nd Division sector.* Friday, the 13th, proved not so lucky for a 50th Squadron crew engaged in a similar mission for the 82nd Division near the Moselle. Lieutenant F. B. Bellows, observer, was mortally wounded by rifle fire from the ground. His pilot, Lieutenant David Beebe, made an emergency landing just behind the American lines in an effort to save Bellows' life but to no avail.[9]

During the day, pursuit flying was once again confined to relatively low altitudes and small formations. Although most of the pursuit work, as on the first day, was dominated by strafing and bombing troops and horse-drawn wagon convoys, there was some dogfighting with the newly arrived *Jagdstaffeln*. Shortly after 5:00 P.M., Lieutenant Charles D'Olive, of the 93rd Pursuit Squadron, momentarily lost from his own patrol, attached himself to a 103rd Squadron patrol just as the latter dove from a low cloud into a Fokker formation. Teaming with Lieutenant George W. Furlow, of the 103rd, he sent three black-crossed enemy aircraft crashing into the outskirts of the little village of St. Benoit on the main Vigneulles-Chambley highway.[10] At approximately the same time, Lieutenant Frank O'D. Hunter, later a general officer in World War II, burned a German fighter and then joined his 103rd Squadron teammate, Lieutenant Gorman Larner, to cut a Fokker out of a formation of six, sending it spinning down over the town of Chambley. Five minutes later, Lieutenant Hugo Kenyon, also of the 103rd, brought down an Albatros over St. Julian, some two miles south of Chambley.[11] Lieutenants Lewis Carruthers and Lowell Harding, of the 93rd, teamed up to destroy still another enemy fighter in the

---

* For this photographic mission the twin Lewis guns in the observer's cockpit were replaced by cameras so that oblique pictures could be made from extremely low altitudes. Apparently, only Lt. Carver's plane was so equipped.[8]

vicinity of Woel.[12] A flight of 13th Squadron Spads, led by Lieutenant J. Dickinson Este and consisting of Lieutenants J. J. Searley, Rob Roy Converse, David W. Howe, and Frank K. Hays, fought a flaming air duel with a flight of Fokkers some two miles north of Chambley and blasted three of them out of the sky.[13]

These successes scored practically on top of the German airfields at Mars-la-Tour, however, were not secured without a bloody price. Lieutenants Eugene Jones, 103rd Squadron, Wayne D. Stephenson, 28th Squadron, and Frank Sidler, 213th Squadron, were killed in action. Rob Roy Converse, 13th Squadron, and Lieutenant C. F. Nash, 93rd Squadron, did not return from the flight and were later reported as prisoners of war.[14] Thus the American Air Service lost a total of fourteen pilots and observers on that black Friday in September.

On Saturday, 14 September, the third day of the St. Mihiel offensive, the sun appeared for the first time in the campaign. Although masses of broken clouds still dotted the sky, the ceiling was high and visibility was good. Squadrons of the 1st Day Bombardment Group would operate as a unit for the first time on that day. The 11th and 20th Squadrons, flying Liberty planes, had been used as biplace fighter outfits on the first two days of the drive, but on the evening of 13 September, they were instructed to prepare for a bombing mission. The raid, a strike against Conflans, was scheduled for the morning of 14 September. All the night of 13 September squadron trucks hauled bombs from the depot at Colombey-les-Belles, about fifteen miles to the east. By daybreak, after many hours of hard work and after consuming gallons of strong coffee, the armorers and mechanics had the DH-4's ready for their first bombing mission.[15]

The conditions under which the De Havilland squadrons operated in the St. Mihiel campaign were far from ideal. In the case of the 20th Squadron, with the exception of the commanding officer, none of the pilots or observers had flown over the lines. Some had never flown in Liberty planes, and none had had any opportunity to learn about handling the DH-4 loaded with bombs; the first flight was the real thing. Lieutenant C. G. Stephens was killed on one of the first bombing raids when his heavily laden plane stalled on the takeoff and crashed on the field. His observer, Lieutenant J. J.

Louis, was seriously hurt in the accident. Despite this early morning disaster, the 20th, under the leadership of Cecil Sellers, staged several successful attacks on the railroad centers in the Etain-Conflans area during the day.*

Unshaken by its heavy losses on the first two days of the offensive, the 96th Squadron welcomed the clearing weather of the third day. Without a doubt the improved visibility would bring intense activity on the part of enemy fighter pilots, but at least the squadron would be able to operate at a higher altitude. Ten planes were ready for the first raid on the morning of 14 September. The formation, which left the ground at 6:40 A.M. with Lieutenant David H. Young in the lead, dwindled to three planes before reaching the lines north of Verdun. In spite of such meager support, Young continued on to the objective. Conflans, the target, was concealed by several layers of fleecy clouds, but "a favorable opening permitted the formation to descend below the clouds and the lead observer, First Lieutenant S. M. Lunt, scored a perfect hit at the neck of the railroad yards."[17] Although under heavy attack by a flight of Fokker D-7's, Lieutenant Bruce Hopper was able to maneuver his Breguet over the city so as to give his observer the opportunity to obtain photographs of the bursts. Then the three planes pulled into a tight formation and began a game of hide and seek with some twenty enemy pursuits in the broken clouds. The observers kept up a constant fire with the *tourelle* guns while the pilots dodged in and out of the cloud alleys.[18] Forty-five minutes later the little formation landed at the big Amanty airdrome without casualties. Two other missions were carried out by the squadron during the day, bombing troops at Vitronville and Arnaville on the Moselle River.[19]

The 11th Aero Squadron did not escape so easily during its baptism of fire as a bombardment outfit. A formation of seven DH-4's succeeded in bombing Conflans from a high altitude without interference except for rather inaccurate antiaircraft fire. As the flight, led by Lieutenant Roger F. Chapin, turned away from the smoking railway center the archie suddenly ceased and fifteen "extravagantly painted" Fokker single-seaters dived into the American's defensive "V."[20] It became quickly apparent that the red-nosed Fokkers were being handled by highly skilled fighter pilots and just as obvious

---

* Of the eight raids made during the first three days of the squadron's experiences as a bombing unit Sellers led all but one.[16]

that the inexperienced 11th Squadron's defensive fire was not being used to the best advantage. One pilot noted that each fighter "attacked with a quick climbing turn, a short burst of fire, a stalling turn, a sharp side-slip toward the other side of the 'V,' and a repeat of the same maneuvers. Thus one fighter could attack both sides in a single pass." One of the colorful adversaries was shot down in flames, but the whole American formation was soon in real trouble. All of the Liberty planes were heavily damaged, and two, manned by Lieutenants Fred Shoemaker, Robert Groner, Horace Shidler, and Harold H. Sayre, were sent crashing to the earth. Only the timely, though unexpected, arrival of a patrol of Spads averted further disaster.[21] The 240-pound Shoemaker and his observer, Groner, survived the crash and were made prisoners of war. Shidler also managed to land in one piece and had time to bury his dead observer before being captured.[22]

Because German fighter pilots tended to concentrate on the deep probing day bombardment aircraft, casualties in the corps and army observation squadrons were comparatively light. One plane each from the 91st and 24th Aero Squadrons did not return from late afternoon missions, and an observer from the 99th was fatally wounded. Nonetheless, observation aviation came close to losing one of its outstanding fliers during that bright sunny day when Captain Kenneth Littauer, commander of the 88th Squadron, was shot down. The popular New York City man had volunteered to fly escort for a 99th Squadron Salmson assigned to photograph the Conflans area. Only minutes after the two observation planes had reached their objective they were attacked by five fiercely aggressive fighters. Although his observer, Lieutenant Theodore E. Boyd, was painfully wounded in the arms and legs on the first pass, Littauer's marvelous flying skill saved the day. Maneuvering his big two-seater with the agility of a fighter, the Lafayette Flying Corps transfer managed to beat off repeated attacks. While he fought his one-sided duel with the fighters, the photography plane was able to escape with its pictures. Although his own plane was riddled with bullets and his radiator punctured, Littauer managed to make a forced landing a short distance behind the American line. For this action on 14 September 1918, both Littauer and Boyd were to receive the DSC.[23]

Observation squadrons were, on the whole, able to perform much effective work on that relatively clear Saturday. Infantry contact patrols and fugitive target duty remained difficult because the ground troops were reluctant to display panel markers, but photography and long-range visual reconnaissance proved fruitful. Each of the squadrons flew a score or more individual missions during the day.[24]

During the four days of the St. Mihiel campaign only on 14 September did the American fighter squadrons have an opportunity to devote their energies to their normal work of fighting in the air. Large concentrations of enemy pursuit machines were met, and savage combats ensued. At least four new Hun organizations were definitely identified, but the Germans were greatly outnumbered. The Allies had at last gained aerial supremacy. Layers of broken clouds made for excellent ambush and surprise tactics on both sides—especially in the area covered by Atkinson's 1st Pursuit Wing. A 28th Squadron formation consisting of Lieutenants Charles Merrick, Tom Cassady, Eugene J. Hardy, Henry C. Allien, Louis Moriarity, and William T. Jebb ran into a flight of Fokkers near Vilcey-sur-Troy and shot down "one red-nosed Boche."[25] A little later Lieutenant George Wood of the same squadron was shot down and taken prisoner. Lieutenants Charles Grey, Samuel Gaillard, and Roland W. Richardson of the 213th Squadron engaged a Fokker "painted red with the exception of the tail, which was light color." After each pilot had taken turns in raking the German with machine gun fire, it was seen to go down in a deadly spin, marking the squadron's first aerial victory of the war.[26]

The unlucky 13th Aero Squadron was involved in one of the wildest dogfights of the day when fifteen Spads, led by Captain Charles Biddle, the handsome Princeton graduate, encountered a large formation of Fokkers over Lake Lachaussee. Before the skirmish was over, two Germans had been sent crashing from 7,500 feet and four Americans had been lost. Lieutenant Leighton Brewer, years later an English professor at Boston University, described the action:

We were given a low patrol, 2500 meters, and we were flying this when we were attacked by a bunch of red-nosed Fokkers. We lost four planes in one minute! I was flying between a couple of men who were shot down, but I got only one bullet in the tail of my plane. The first indication I had of the thing was seeing a red Fokker with a white fuselage, standing on its nose and spraying the fellow in the back of me with bullets. Two Fokkers with red wings and noses, and white fuselages, came down on us and they shot down the men on each side of me. Charlie Drew, George Kull, Buck Freeman and "Steve" Brody were all lost. Drew was badly wounded, Kull was killed and the other two were prisoners.*

In his book *The Way of the Eagle,* Biddle, one of the great fighter pilots of the war and onetime commander of the 4th Pursuit Group, ascribes these early losses to overeagerness and inexperience.[28]

Other squadrons in the 1st Pursuit Wing were also busy. Lieutenants Hugh Fontaine and Hugh Brewster, of the 49th Squadron based at Toul, teamed to destroy two enemy aircraft over Chambley. Arthur Brooks, of the relatively inexperienced 22nd Aero, entered his name on the list of aces when he and squadron mate Philip Hassinger downed two German fighters in the vicinity of Mars-la-Tour. In the rolling, twisting battle over the Hun airdrome Hassinger was shot down and killed. During the engagement the squadron, led by Captain Bridgeman, managed to fight off twelve Fokker D-7's and protected a pair of Salmson observation planes.[29]

While there were fewer air battles on the western face of the St. Mihiel salient patrolled by Hartney's 1st Pursuit Group, a number of German planes as well as an enemy balloon were destroyed. Shortly after 8:00 A.M. on the balmy third day of the offensive, Rickenbacker scored his seventh aerial kill when, flying a single-ship volunteer mission, he pounced upon four scarlet Fokkers and picked off the rearmost man. This was his first victory since returning to the front and was very nearly his last, as the three remaining Fokker pilots maneuvering with consummate skill, according to Rickenbacker, "whipped their machines about me with incredible cleverness." After what seemed to be minutes of vision-dimming turns, he slipped out of their noose and "with motor full open and nose straight down" made his escape.[30]

Rickenbacker's victory was not the only reason for celebration at Rembercourt that night. Lieutenant Wilbert W. White, of the 147th Squadron, knocked down a balloon and an enemy aircraft over Chambley,[31] while Frank Luke continued his hot run on German "sausages" by flaming two in a midmorning flight.[32] In fact, so

---

* Several years after the war Brewer wrote the long epic poem *Riders of the Sky,* one of the finest pieces on World War I air fighting.[27]

many balloons were brought down by the group during the St. Mihiel drive that it is doubtful whether the enemy received much information from this source of observation on the western side of the salient. Luke and Joseph Fritz Wehner, of the 27th Aero Squadron, were the chief exponents of "balloon busting." The former, who conceived the tactic of attacking balloons at dawn and dusk when the attacker was difficult to see, shot down eighteen enemy aircraft (all but four of which were balloons) during the last three weeks of September. Eight of these victories were scored during the four days of the St. Mihiel drive. Wehner generally acted as cover for the Arizona maverick during these actions and ran his own score to five before he was shot down and killed on 18 September, while trying to save Luke from attacking pursuits. Eleven days later Luke himself was dead, but not before he had made the German Air Force pay dearly for his friend's death and had won the Medal of Honor en route.[33]

Sunday 15 September marked the end of the St. Mihiel offensive. Despite the rain and low clouds, American pursuit aviation was eminently successful, scoring fifteen victories while losing only one pilot. Biddle's 13th Aero Squadron attained a measure of revenge for their heavy losses of the previous day when a patrol led by Hank Stovall intercepted a flight of their old red-nosed adversaries over the Corney-Vaux area. During the savage fight three Huns fell to the guns of Stovall, Leighton Brewer, Murray K. Guthrie, and Frank Hays. A few minutes later Major Carl Spaatz, attached to the 13th for the St. Mihiel effort, scored the squadron's fourth victory of the day.[34] Spaatz, a tough regular army officer destined to be chief of staff of the yet unborn U.S. Air Force, had taken a three-week leave from his duties as commander of the Issoudun flying schools and had come to the front to take part in the big campaign as a fighter pilot. At his own request he had been attached to Biddle's outfit "as a lieutenant."* During his brief stay with the squadron, he destroyed two enemy aircraft and won the deep respect of the younger fighter pilots, many of whom had served under him at Issoudun.

---

* Actually, Spaatz was under orders to return to the United States to oversee pursuit training there. It was to prepare himself for this important role that he sought combat duty in September, 1918.[35]

Other fighter pilots braved that dreary Sunday morning sky in search of enemy aircraft. Shortly before noon, Lieutenants Wendel Robertson and H. A. Garvie, still angry over the loss of their respected 139th Squadron Commander, David Putnam, who had fallen on the first day of the battle, sent two enemy scouts down out of control. During the early afternoon, Lieutenants Chester Wright and Henry Lindsey, of the 93rd, shot down an airplane in the neighborhood of Charey.[36] Wild, talkative Lieutenant Jacques Swaab of the 22nd, who had been slightly wounded a few days before the St. Mihiel campaign opened, returned to action and in epic battle at 15,000 feet over Cirrey destroyed three enemy fighters.[37] By the end of the war the colorful Swaab had run his score to ten official kills.

With Lufbery and Putnam dead, a dozen pursuit pilots now sought the title of American "ace of aces." The 94th Squadron's Eddie Rickenbacker took the lead momentarily on 15 September when, on a volunteer patrol, he plunged into a formation of Fokkers and sent one down in flames. The enemy aircraft, which crashed behind enemy lines near Bois-de-Warville, ran his score to eight.* Only Lieutenant Elliott Springs, then serving with the 148th Aero Squadron on the British front, had more official victories, having scored his ninth on the same day. But Frank Luke was catching up rapidly; he burned three more balloons during the day, while his partner Joe Wehner flamed another.[39]

Unlike the pursuit squadrons, day bombardment and observation units encountered only light aerial opposition on the last day of the offensive. The 1st Day Bombardment Group carried out raids on the marshalling yards at Arnaville and Longuyon and bombed the bridges along the Moselle between Arnaville and Corney. Although the midday mission was attacked by nine enemy fighters, no casualties were suffered.[40] The bomb missions, however, were something less than a complete success because formations were greatly weakened in each raid with several planes either unable to take off or forced to return from mechanical problems.† At least some of these

---

* Rickenbacker described his 15 September kill as his seventh, but recent official sources list this victory as his eighth.[38]

† Capt. Cecil Sellers and his observer, Lt. K. G. Payne, won the DSC during the day when theirs was the only plane of a 20th Squadron formation to reach the target at Conflans. Four enemy aircraft were met and driven off in their dash to the objective. Three more Huns were encountered as the pair left the target area; they were able to nurse their badly shot up DH-4 back to Amanty, however, and landed safely.

failures were due to gross overloading of the DH-4's. Unfortunately, many operational decisions were being made by "swivel chair commanders" who understood little, if anything, about planes, weather problems, and aerial opposition.[41] The Air Force did not make this mistake in World War II, for all operational commanders from squadrons to air forces were flying officers.

In spite of the dud weather conditions, corps and army observation units were able to carry out several worthwhile oblique picture missions in addition to the usual visual reconnaissance flights. One 91st Squadron and two 99th Squadron fliers were wounded in brushes with enemy aircraft, but no planes were lost during the day. While dodging through the late afternoon mist, Lieutenants Roe E. Wells, pilot, and A. W. Swineboard, observer, had the distinction of scoring the first official kill made by the rookie 24th Squadron when they shot down an attacking fighter.[42]

Although the four days of the St. Mihiel drive were usually plagued by wind, rain, and low clouds, the nights were for the most part clear. The British Independent Air Force cooperating with the American effort made nightly forays to Conflans, Longuyon, Metz, and other points on the railway along which the Germans were moving up reserves. Meanwhile, the French and Italian night bombardment squadrons also attacked these same strategic points as well as enemy concentration centers and command posts near the front lines. In the absence of night reconnaissance units, planes of the French night bombardment forces kept watch over the enemy's movements, in addition to their primary mission of bombing.[43]

Under Major John Paegelow, a veteran of over thirty years in the regular army, fifteen American and six French balloon companies took part in the St. Mihiel operation. Weather conditions during the first two days of the drive seriously limited operations, but with visibility improving on 14 September, balloon observers were able to "adjust artillery fire and send to various Army Corps and divisional staffs much valuable intelligence."[44] From 12 September to 16 September no less than ten American balloons were burned by German fighters, and Lieutenants Byron T. Burt, of New York City, and James A. McDevitt, of Cincinnati, Ohio, earned DSC's for remaining aboard burning balloons until the last second to transmit vital information before parachuting to safety. In the gales of the first day of operations one balloon was blown into German territory, and its two-man crew was captured when the cable broke.[45] Despite the atrocious weather and muddy roads, balloon company crews managed to keep pace with the fast moving infantry until the balloon line finally stretched from Pont-a-Mousson to Verdun. The salient had been flattened.

As Colonel Billy Mitchell, nattily dressed in a new uniform, gathered his staff around him at Ligny-en-Barrois on the night of 16 September to read General Pershing's congratulatory letter, he had every reason to be proud of the First Army Air Service in its initial effort as an independent organization. The letter read:

Please accept my sincere congratulations on the successful and very important part taken by the Air Force under your command in the first offensive of the First American Army. The organization and control of the tremendous concentration of Air Forces, including American, French, British and Italian units, which has enabled the Air Services of the First Army to carry out its dangerous and important mission, is as fine a tribute to you personally as is the courage and nerve shown by your officers a signal proof of the high morale which permeates the service under your command.

Please convey to your command my heartfelt appreciation of their work. I am proud of you all.[46]

Indeed, the Air Service had held command of the air throughout the St. Mihiel offensive. In the words of one historian,

During the four days between September 12 to September 16, American aviation had made 3300 flights over the battle lines, were in the air 4000 hours, fired 30,000 rounds of machine gun ammunition and over 1000 individual bomb attacks were made during which 75 tons of high explosives were dropped. Twelve enemy balloons and more than sixty enemy planes were destroyed working in conjunction with the French and British aviators, notwithstanding unfavorable weather, the Air Service successfully executed the majority of its missions.[47]

Mitchell's skill in marshalling and controlling so large and heterogeneous a force was surprising; in short, "St. Mihiel was as promising a debut for the Air Service as for the First Army."[48]

Although the land campaign to neutralize the St. Mihiel salient was completed by daybreak of 16 September, Allied air units continued to operate in the sector for several days. During this period bombardment aviation continued to suffer heavy losses.

On Monday, 16 September, the 1st Day Bombardment Group, encouraged by the first good visibility in four days, attempted three separate missions against marshalling yards, supply depots, and troop concentrations. The DH-4's of the 11th and 20th Aero Squadrons again had difficulty staying in the air, or for that matter getting airborne at all, and the first two raids were carried out almost entirely by the sturdy Breguets of the 96th. On the third mission, a strike against Conflans, only two planes from the 20th and four from the 11th crossed the line, and none reached its primary target.[49] This poor performance was in no way owing to a lack of persistence or courage on the part of the flying officers, as indicated by the case of a 20th Squadron team made up of Lieutenants A. F. Seavers and John Y. Stokes. The pair found themselves alone near the target area when one plane after another had been forced to turn back with mechanical trouble. For a time Seavers, the pilot, had attached himself to a formation from another squadron, but as this second formation neared Etain his plane was hit by antiaircraft fire and thrown out of control. By the time he had regained control he had fallen away from the protection of the other planes. With a crippled plane and a damaged and sputtering engine, the team continued on toward the secondary target, the marshalling yards at Etain. Finally, just before the objective was reached, the engine quit running entirely. Only after gliding on over the target and dropping their bombs did the pair turn back toward Allied lines, some seven miles away. To complicate matters even more they were then attacked by an enemy fighter. While Stokes kept up a fierce defensive fire, Seavers struggled without success to start the Liberty engine. After a long glide the DH-4 crashed in a forest just inside the Allied lines. Seavers and Stokes, miraculously uninjured in the incident, were recommended for the Medal of Honor but were instead awarded the DSC.[50]

That same late afternoon raid against Conflans proved disastrous to the hard-hit 96th Squadron. Only four aircraft reached the target, and all were shot down, three of them in flames. At first the eight crew members were listed as missing, but it was soon learned that Lieutenants Charles P. Anderson, Hugh Thompson, Raymond C. Taylor, William Stuart, Newton Rogers, and Kenneth P. Strawn were dead. The other two, Lieutenants Charles Codman and Stuart McDowell, were captured. This blow put the squadron completely out of business for the next several days. The 96th had lost sixteen pilots and observers and fourteen planes in five days, a rate of loss never equalled before or after by any other outfit in the AEF.[51]

It rained on 17 September, and no bombing missions were flown. The rest was badly needed. One 11th Squadron flier summed up the attitude of most of the bombardment boys when he stated,

We thanked the Lord for this favor, though we did it shamefacedly, because we realized that our blessing was the curse of the fellows who were holding their places so wonderfully in the mud and slime of the trenches.[52]

The respite was short indeed, for on the next day the two De Havilland squadrons were ordered to attack targets in the Mars-la-Tour and Lake Lachaussee area. The 11th Squadron historian caught some of the drama of the situation when he wrote,

The sky was overcast with heavy clouds that made the weather look impossible for our kind of work. All morning we waited for the word to go, but nothing happened. About two thirty in the afternoon Hooper [the squadron commander] came hurriedly from his little shack that served as office, bedroom, dining room and general quarters. "We've got to go," he said, and in reply to hurried questions he added, "to La Chaussee." There was a hasty glance at the maps we all carried, as we picked out the objective. It proved to be a small town not far behind the lines. "I know this is murder," said Hooper, "but the swivel chair commanders don't know it, and all we can do is go and trust to luck." That was Hooper's savage comment as he fastened on his helmet and goggles. We tried to persuade him to stay at home, as he was not required to make the raid and there was no point in his taking such chances, but he refused to hear of it and merely said, "I can't send you fellows over unless I go myself." He went, but did not come back.[53]

Seventeen aircraft took off, one crashed shortly after leaving the field, and ten others failed to reach the assigned target, although some did bomb a secondary objective. Of the six DH-4's that hit the primary target only one, manned by Lieutenants Vincent P. Oates and Ramon H. Guthrie, returned. In all, ten flying officers were lost. The casualties included the squadron commander, two flight leaders, and the lead observer of the 11th Squadron; two of the teams had been captured and the other three had been shot down in flames during the blazing air battle with eleven Hun pursuit planes.* The German fighter pilots had found the DH-4's Achilles' heel, its unprotected gas tank located so dangerously between pilot and observer. The battered 11th Squadron was withdrawn from operations to await reinforcements in aircraft and flying personnel.

First Lieutenant Charles L. Heater was assigned to command the 11th Aero Squadron on 21 September. Except for the arrival of this rather remarkable young air officer, the morale and effectiveness of the squadron might have been shattered for the remaining weeks of the war. Heater, a native of Mandan, North Dakota, was a senior at Purdue University when America entered the conflict. He immediately dropped out of school and enlisted in the military service. During the summer of 1917, he attended the aviation ground school at Cornell University, and in September of that year he was one of the 150 war birds sent to England for flight training. Upon completing his training in various two-seaters, including DH-4's and DH-9's, he was assigned to Squadron 55 of Trenchard's Independent Air Force. After thirteen combat missions with the British the twenty-four-year-old Heater transferred to the American Air Service, then operating in the St. Mihiel sector. On taking over the crippled 11th, Heater stoutly refused to commit the squadron to further action until it was brought into shape. For this action he won the loyalty and respect of the officers and men but did not add to his popularity with "the generously hated group commander."[55] Within a short time he was to dress the "Jiggs" squadron into one of the top bombardment outfits on the front, and he himself later destroyed four enemy aircraft.

The heavy casualties experienced by the day bombardment group during the middle of September led to a conference between Major Dunsworth and the squadron leaders to determine some better tactical doctrine. In nearly every case the bloody disasters had occurred in formations weakened by accident and mechanical failures or scattered by bad weather. Larger formations were obviously needed. Group formations of a mixture of Breguets and De Havillands had not proved too successful because of differences in air-

---

* In the hectic air battle, Lts. Thornton Hooper, pilot, Ralph Root, observer, Roger F. Chapin, pilot, and Clair B. Laird, observer, were captured. Lts. Lester S. Harter, pilot, McRae Stephenson, observer, John C. Tyler, pilot, Harry N. Strauch, observer, Edward B. Comegys, pilot, and Arthur R. Carter, observer, were killed.[54]

craft performance. Since the 96th was again supplied with a full complement of Breguets but was short of flying personnel, a situation which was reversed in the DH-4 outfits, it was decided to supplement the 96th with enough crews from the other two squadrons to make up one large Breguet formation. The remaining teams from the 11th and 20th were to be used in one large Liberty plane formation. This tactic, with a few modifications, was used for the rest of the war, as Summersett's 96th never received adequate replacements.[56]

During the next few weeks it was determined that all formations should fly in a "V" with the rear of the "V" closed. Airplanes in the formation were numbered as follows:

$$
\begin{array}{ccccc}
 & & 1 & & \\
 & 3 & & 2 & \\
 5 & & 12 & & 4 \\
 7 & & & & 6 \\
 9 & 11 & & 10 & 8 \\
\end{array}
$$

According to the "Manual of Instructions for Day Bombardment," prepared by Lieutenant Colonel Thomas Bowen and Captain Bruce Hopper,

Number 1 is the Leader and flies at the lowest altitude; Numbers 2 and 3, 4 and 5 are similarly placed pairs and should fly at the same altitude, numbers 2 and 3 about 50 meters higher than Number 1 and about 30 meters to the right and left of Number 1 respectively. Number 4 takes the same position relative to Number 2 as Number 2 does to Number 1. Number 5 takes the same position as Number 3.

Formations should be as compact as possible, especially when dropping projectiles; during a combat, formations should close up. Too much emphasis cannot be laid upon training of Day Bombardment pilots in formation flying. If the pilots maintain a regular echelonment in height, in case of emergency they can close upon the Leader by diving. The Leader should never open his throttle wide, and observers should always warn the pilots when their own, or any other airplane appears to be getting out of formation. It is fatal for an airplane to leave formation, and the airplane should not break formation; the formation should not be broken up to protect an airplane which has dropped out.[57]

Less than a week after the reduction of the St. Mihiel salient, the American First Army, four corps strong, was moved west of the

Meuse River and prepared for the plunge into the Argonne Forest area. Colonel Mitchell made arrangements to cover the new thrust by moving his aviation units in the same direction. On 23 September the day bombardment group was shifted from Amanty to Maulan airdrome, ten miles south of Bar-le-Duc. This small airdrome was perched on top of a narrow ridge and was surrounded by deep wooded glens which increased the hazards for the brakeless aircraft of the period.[58]

During the week following the close of the St. Mihiel campaign American pursuit units were also redeployed to the west for the Meuse-Argonne effort. Atkinson's 1st Pursuit Wing Headquarters was transferred from Toul to Chaumont; the 2nd Pursuit Group went to Belrain, about ten miles west of the town of St. Mihiel; and the 3rd Pursuit Group moved to Lisle-en-Barrois. Hartney's 1st Pursuit Group, already based to the west of the Meuse, remained at Rembercourt, a few miles south of Verdun.

In order to camouflage the forthcoming offensive in the Argonne, all three groups continued to fly patrols to the east of the Meuse. These patrols frequently encountered opposition, and in the ten days before the beginning of the Meuse-Argonne effort pilots of the American pursuit groups destroyed twenty-one enemy aircraft while losing approximately half that number. One of those shot down behind enemy lines was the 95th Squadron's Waldo H. Heinrichs, who, when his new Marlin machine guns jammed, was cut out of a Spad formation and riddled by seven German Fokkers. Heinrichs, a history professor at Middlebury College (Vermont) after the war, described his precarious situation in the following terms:

An explosive bullet hit me in the left cheek and knocked out sixteen teeth, breaking both jaws and then tearing through the windshield, breaking it also. I remembered spitting out teeth and blood and turned again for our lines. Pulled a "reversement" and came out underneath the chap who was firing at me from behind. Two more explosive bullets hit me in the left arm, tearing through and breaking the left elbow. Two broke in the right hand and nearly took off the right small finger. Another hit me in the left thigh, one in the left ankle, and one in the right heel. Two more hit me in the leg. Six of the ten wounds were from explosive bullets. Tried to yank the throttle wide open but got no more speed out of the plane; seemed that it wouldn't work at all. Saw my arm hanging broken at my side.

The blood which I spat out blinded my goggles so I threw them over my helmet. Dove for the ground and pulled out just before I crashed into the woods and fortunately found an open field directly in front of me. Dove under telegraph wires, fearing lest with dead motor the wires would catch and spin me over. Right wing crashed through a telegraph pole about two inches in diameter and broke it off. Machine came to rest with dead motor five yards from the edge of the field. Broke the gas lead from the top tank and gasoline spilled over me and into the cockpit. Reached for the matches in my overalls pocket but my left arm was unable to hold anything. Tried to hold the match box in my teeth but my whole mouth was blown away. Fortunately (as it proved later) I did not think to hold the matches between my knees. Sixty infantrymen with rifles lined on me came running out of the woods. I loosed my safety belt and as I moved up on the edge of the cockpit saw a pool of blood swishing around in the bottom of the plane. Surrendered by holding my right arm over my head and the Germans gave me first aid immediately, putting a tourniquet on my left arm and left thigh. They were very kind to me but left me lying in the field for two hours before stretcher-bearers, one of them wearing the Iron Cross, took me to a field hospital about two miles away in Gorize. I could see the balloons along the line waving idly in the afternoon sun. The war was over for me.[59]

The German Air Force was also making readjustments during those September days. On 20 September, elements of *Jagdgeschwader* I, the old Richthofen Circus, now commanded by Hermann Goering, began arriving in the Metz area. Within a few days the entire Circus consisting of the deadly *Jagdstaffeln* 4, 6, 10, and 11, commanded by Ernst Udet, Ulrich Neckel, Arthur Laumann, and Ernst Wedel, respectively, had arrived.[60] These units, plus the crack *Jagdgeschwader* II and a few less well-known outfits that were already in the area, would face the Americans until the end of the war.

American corps observation underwent a substantial reorganization in preparation for the big offensive ahead. The I Corps Observation Group, still commanded by Steve Jocelyn and made up of the 1st, 12th, and 50th Squadrons and one French escadrille, was shifted to Remicourt, a few miles south of Verdun. Major Martin Scanlon's V Corps Observation Group, composed of the 99th and 104th Squadrons plus two French outfits, was stationed at Foucaucourt in the same general area. The newly created III Corps Observation Group, headed by Captain Littauer, was moved to Souilly during the third week of September. This organization consisted of the 88th, commanded by Lieutenant Floyd Evans after Littauer's promotion to group commander, William Schauffler's 90th Squadron, and two French units.[61] The IV Corps Observation Group, now made up of the 8th and 135th Squadrons and two French squadrons, remained at Ourches and continued to work in the St. Mihiel district. It did not participate in the Meuse-Argonne.[62]

On 21–22 September the 24th and 91st Squadrons of the First Army Observation Group moved from Gondreville to Vavincourt, west of Verdun. Due to a shortage of pilots, two days were required to ferry the planes to the new field. The 9th Aero Squadron, now reequipped for night reconnaissance, had been transferred to Vavincourt a day or two before. Pilots accustomed to the big and smooth Gondreville airfield were disgusted with the new location. In addition to being rough and poorly drained, the field was situated near the junction of two major roads which made it an easy target for German bombers. It was only twenty-five miles from the front lines, however, and the squadrons based there were able to operate throughout the Meuse-Argonne campaign without further moves.[63]

Colonel Mitchell moved his First Army Air Service Headquarters from Ligney-en-Barrois to Souilly, where he completed plans for the Meuse-Argonne operation. He would enter this final campaign with a much smaller force of aircraft than he had had at St. Mihiel. Since the French had withdrawn most of their forces, Mitchell's initial strength was about 800 planes. About 600 of these were American, and prospects of further reinforcements from the rapidly expanding Air Service were good.

NOTES

1. Hopper, "American Day Bombardment," *Air Power Historian*, April, 1957, 93.

2. George A. Moreira, "Clifford Allsopp and the 11th Aero Squadron," *Cross and Cockade Journal*, Autumn, 1961, 184.

3. Marshall, *World War I*, 322.

4. Miller, ed., "Last Knighthood," *Cross and Cockade Journal*, Spring, 1962, 27.

5. Operations Report for 13 September 1918, in "History of the 8th Aero Squadron" (Gorrell Histories, AS AEF, E, I).

6. Hart, "Observations from a DH-4," *Cross and Cockade Journal*, Winter, 1961, 334.

7. Air Service, First Army, AEF, G.O. No. 21, cited in "Victories and Casualties" (Gorrell Histories, AS AEF, M, XXXVIII). Unless otherwise noted, all future references to First Army General Orders confirming air victories will be found in this volume, and citations will be limited to the General Order Number.

8. Carver, *The Ninetieth Aero Squadron,* 29; see also letter from Carver to author, 8 August 1967.

9. Morse, *50th Aero Squadron,* 31.

10. G.O. Nos. 6 and 14.

11. G.O. Nos. 8 and 13.

12. *Ibid.*

13. Combat Reports for 13 September in "History of the 13th Aero Squadron" (Gorrell Histories, AS AEF, E, III).

14. Miller, ed., "Casualties of A.E.F. Pursuit Aviation," *Cross and Cockade Journal,* Spring, 1962, 34–37.

15. "History of the 20th Aero Squadron" (Gorrell Histories, AS AEF, E, IV), 3–5.

16. *Ibid.,* 3–4.

17. Hopper, "American Day Bombardment," *loc. cit.,* 93.

18. *Ibid.*

19. *Ibid.,* 94.

20. *The 11th Aero Squadron,* 151.

21. Moreira, "Clifford Allsopp and the 11th," *loc. cit.,* 184–85.

22. *The 11th Aero Squadron,* 8.

23. Hall and Nordhoff, *Lafayette Flying Corps,* 315–18; Stringer, *Heroes All!* 66, 145.

24. Frank, "American Air Service Observation in World War I," unpublished dissertation, University of Florida, 321.

25. Reconnaissance report for 14 September, 1918, in "History of the 28th Aero Squadron" (Gorrell Histories, AS AEF, E, VII).

26. Reconnaissance report for 14 September 1918 in "History of the 213th Aero Squadron" (Gorrell Histories, AS AEF, E, XXI). See also Kelly Wills, Jr., "Richardson's Remembrances," *Cross and Cockade Journal,* Summer, 1965, 112–13.

27. Leighton Brewer, "How It Was," *Cross and Cockade Journal,* Spring, 1962, 69.

28. Charles J. Biddle, *Way of the Eagle,* 254–55.

29. G.O. No. 7.

30. Rickenbacker, *Fighting the Flying Circus,* 240; G.O. No. 8.

31. G.O. Nos. 8 and 10.

32. G.O. Nos. 6 and 12.

33. Kenn Rust, "Aces and Hawks," *Air Power Historian,* October, 1962, 218–19.

34. G.O. No. 7.

35. Brewer, "How It Was," *loc. cit.,* 70. See also letter from Gen. Carl A. Spaatz to author, 24 August 1965.

36. G.O. No. 17.

37. G.O. No. 28.

38. G.O. No. 6.

39. G.O. Nos. 6, 12, and 9.

40. "Summary of Operations of the 1st Day Bombardment Group" (Gorrell Histories, AS AEF, C, VIII), 3.

41. *The 11th Aero Squadron,* 153.

42. Frederic P. Kirschner, "A Thumbnail Sketch of the 24th," *Cross and Cockade Journal,* Spring, 1964, 54.

43. Toulmin, *Air Service, AEF,* 369; Patrick, *Report to Commander-in-Chief,* 232.

44. "Tactical History of Air Service, AEF" (Gorrell Histories, AS AEF, D, I), 9.

45. Miller, ed., "Balloon Section, AEF," *Cross and Cockade Journal,* Spring, 1962, 90–91.

46. Mitchell, *Memoirs,* 250.

47. Bissell, *Brief History,* 63.

48. Craven and Cate, *AAF in WW II,* I, 14.

49. Miller, ed., "Ordeal of the 1st Day Bombardment Group," *Cross and Cockade Journal,* Spring, 1962, 8.

50. "History of the 20th Aero Squadron," *loc. cit.,* 3–4; Stringer, *Heroes All!* 252, 277.

51. Hopper, "American Day Bombardment," *loc. cit.,* 94.

52. *The 11th Aero Squadron,* 153.

53. *Ibid.*

54. *Ibid.,* 153–57.

55. *Ibid.,* 157–59. For a chronology of Heater's career see letter from Heater to author, 12 May 1965, and Air Service Questionnaire, 9 March, 1965.

56. Miller, ed., "Ordeal of the 1st Day Bombardment Group," *loc. cit.,* 9.

57. Cited in Bruce Hopper, "When the Air Was Young: American Day Bombardment, A.E.F., France, 1917–1918," an unpublished manuscript in the Library of Congress, Washington, D.C.

58. Hopper, "American Day Bombardment," *loc. cit.,* 94.

59. Buckley, *Squadron 95,* 133–35.

60. N. H. Hauprich, *et. al.,* "German *Jagdstaffeln* and *Jagdgeschwader* Commanding Officers, 1916–1918," *Cross and Cockade Journal,* Autumn, 1961, 267–68.

61. "History of the III Corps Observation Group" (Gorrell Histories, AS AEF, C, XII), 214.

62. Frank, "Air Service Observation in World War I," 347–48.

63. *Ibid.,* 363.

X

Forgotten Squadrons: Americans on the British Front

WHILE American air units under Billy Mitchell were fighting against heavy odds at Chateau-Thierry, two new American pursuit squadrons began their combat service with the British forces in the Flanders area. These two squadrons, the 17th and 148th, were at the same time the most publicized and the most neglected of all American combat units. They gained some fame, in a sense, from the immortal stories of Elliott White Springs which were mostly concerned with the 148th Squadron. On the other hand, Air Service historians have tended to neglect the British-trained, British-equipped, and British-commanded units because they were out of the mainstream of the American story. It is only natural that attention has been concentrated on the graduates of Issoudun who fought in the Toul, Chateau-Thierry, St. Mihiel, and Meuse-Argonne sectors as a part of the American Army. Yet, the 17th and 148th compiled outstanding records in their four-month service with the British Expeditionary Forces. With a score of sixty-four official victories, the 148th ranked a close second to the famous 94th "Hat-in-the-Ring" Squadron, which was credited with seventy aircraft destroyed, and the 148th's record is all the more remarkable when remembering that the squadron was in combat only four months, compared to the seven months of service by the 94th. The 17th was to chalk up a total of fifty-four confirmed kills to rank with the very best pursuit squadrons.[1]

The 17th Aero Squadron (originally called Company M, then

Company B, and still later the 29th Provisional Squadron) was organized on 13 May 1917. Its personnel came from thirty-five states of the Union, Puerto Rico, Mexico, and Canada and made up one of the first groups to report to the then unfinished Kelly Field in Texas. After a few weeks of fighting Texas heat, snakes, and tarantulas, the squadron, on 2 August 1917, was sent to Canada to train with the Royal Flying Corps. Two months later the 17th, then under the command of Major Goeffrey Bonnell, who had had war experience with the British, returned to the RFC's Hicks Field, Fort Worth, Texas. By this time several partially trained flying cadets had been assigned, and by 1 November the squadron had a full complement of flying officers. Several of these pilots would remain with the 17th throughout its war service. Flight training continued through the autumn with an unusually large number of "forced landings." In fact, so many of these "forced landings" occurred "in the neighborhood of a girls school not many miles away [from Hicks Field], that all engine trouble came to be looked upon with suspicion."[2] Sometimes these romantic adventures were in the form of cross-country training. As one pilot put it,

Every morning we would pick out our favorite mechanic, generally a sergeant by now—tell him to put on his best uniform and tie his Stetson hat in the fuselage and off we would go. In those days "aviators" were pretty rare and you could land on any vacant field near a big farm house or on the edge of a town and a reception committee including the mayor, the wealthiest men and the prettiest girls would soon be out to see the curiosities.[3]

Captain Martin Scanlon became squadron commander in November, and in late December the outfit, complete with pilots and ground crews, moved to Garden City, New York, to await passage to the war theater. After two weeks fighting the bitter cold, accentuated by a coal shortage, the 17th embarked on the *Carmania*. The unit landed at Liverpool on 25 January, and immediately went into rest camp at Romsey to await further orders.

The 17th Aero was one of the first to go overseas as a complete unit, and the men hoped to go into action as a squadron. In early February, when it became apparent that the U.S. Air Service would not be able to accept or equip them, as it could not handle the Americans who had gone to England earlier as cadets, the 17th

Squadron ground crews were broken up into flights for further training with active British squadrons. Headquarters Flight went to 24 Squadron, "A" Flight to 84 Squadron, "B" Flight to 60 Squadron, and "C" Flight to 56 Squadron, all then flying combat in the Flanders area. The pilots were scattered about the various flying schools in England for further flight training. Some eventually saw active service with RFC operational squadrons.[4]

For the next five months the 17th Aero Squadron ground crews were integrated into the British combat units. In the words of Lieutenant Frederick M. Clapp, adjutant and squadron historian,

These spring months were one of the busiest and most exciting times the R.A.F. had ever known and, during them, the enlisted men of the 17th Squadron learned much more than the mere care of their machines. They knew now what it meant to send out patrols and move incessantly from one aerodrome to another at the same time. And that knowledge gained in actual experience was, if possible, even more valuable to them than the knowledge they gained of service machines and engines.[5]

On 20 June 1918, the now veteran ground crews were pulled together once again and sent to Petite Synthe, near Dunkirk, to organize for combat as the 17th Aero Squadron. The unit was equipped with Sopwith Camels powered by 110-h.p. LeRhone engines. In a day or two a few of the squadron's original pilots, along with several others from the casual officer's pool, reported to Petite Synthe. On 1 July Lieutenant (soon to be Captain) Samuel B. Eckert was assigned as commanding officer.[6]

Sam Eckert, a former commander of the U.S. 9th Aero Squadron, had been at Dijon, far to the south, when notified of his new command and had flown to Petite Synthe in the rain to take over. Like all pilots, ground officers, and enlisted personnel in the 17th Squadron, he was British trained. The Chester County, Pennsylvania, man had seen combat service in S.E.-5's with 84 Squadron, RAF, at Bertangles and had flown Camels while with 80 Squadron, RAF, at Chateau-Thierry "during some of the fiercest and most decisive fighting" of the German push in that sector.[7]

The 148th Aero Squadron was activated at Kelly Field on 11 November, exactly one year before the Armistice. On the next day the squadron's enlisted men, under the supervision of Lieutenant Charles H. Marshall, were ordered to the Royal Flying Corps fields at Fort Worth for their technical training. These fields, generally known as Taliaferro Fields, consisted of Everman, to the south of the city, Benbrook to the west, and Hicks to the north.

The first stop for the men was at Everman, where they were placed under the charge of Captain Vivian Drake, of the RFC, for instruction in the rudiments of airplane engines and rigging. After a month of school work the non-technical men such as cooks, motorcycle drivers, and clerks were sent to Benbrook for practical instruction. Something went wrong, however, and instead of instruction, fatigue was their lot most of the time; to make matters worse, "this was coupled with some very cold weather and unfloored tents on a cold hillside."[8] In January, 1918, the squadron was moved to Hicks Field and placed under the command of Major Cushman A. Rice. A number of flying cadets were attached and the squadron was given eighteen JN-4 Jennies. During the next few weeks the outfit made rapid progress toward becoming an effective organization.

On 14 February the 148th received its overseas orders and entrained for Garden City. After a tiresome five-day train ride and a week's wait at the Port of Embarkation, the squadron sailed on the S.S. *Olympia,* "possibly the best steamship in the transport service." The unescorted *Olympia* docked at Liverpool on 6 March, and the 148th was sent to Flower Down Rest Camp near the historic old English city of Winchester. A short time later a move was made to Romsey Rest Camp near Southampton where the pilots were withdrawn and sent to English flying schools for further training. Only one, Lieutenant William J. Cogan, ever returned to the outfit after it began its independent war work. A few days after its pilots were removed the squadron sailed for LeHavre with only its ground officers and enlisted men.[9]

For the next three months the 148th Squadron's experiences paralleled those of the 17th. The organization was divided into three detachments sent to three British fighter squadrons for their final operational training. These detachments left LeHavre for the front on 20 March, one day before the massive German offensive in the Somme. Headquarters and "A" Flight, under the direction of the squadron adjutant, Lieutenant George Brown, on orders to join 54 Squadron then stationed at Ham, ran into trouble immediately. By the time their troop train reached the vicinity of the front on the

Somme, the German forces were already shelling their destination at Ham. Consequently, on the morning of 22 March their train was halted at Chaulnes, a few miles to the west. Throughout most of the day the tired, hungry, and half-frozen Americans remained in, or near, their "Chevaux 8 Homme 40" cars waiting for the transportation officer at Chaulnes to make a decision. In the words of one squadron member,

The sound of a continuous barrage from the big guns filled the air. . . . By now Chaulnes was in a fever of excitement. Troop trains were being rushed through the town on the way to the Peronne and St. Quentin Fronts in a vain hope to stem the Hun tide. Box cars and coaches, filled with refugees and their few valued belongings, were moving westward through the point.[10]

Still there was no decision on what to do with the Americans. Finally the 148th detachment set up a temporary camp some 100 yards from the railroad station and got ready for the night. It was here that the squadron suffered its first battle casualties when a German night bomber dropped three bombs into their tents, killing ten men and wounding eight others.* Strangely enough, this unfortunate incident claimed more lives before the 148th ever fired a shot than the squadron lost in all the months of combat ahead.

After the disaster on the night of 22 March, the detachment was diverted to Bruay, some forty miles south of Dunkirk, where most of the men were assigned to the S.E.-5 flying 40 Squadron, commanded by the great ace, Major R. S. Dallas.† Some thirty men were moved to the opposite side of the field where they learned their trade with 4 Squadron, Australian Air Force, then using Sopwith Camels. Since it was planned that the 148th would be assigned Camels when it began operation as an independent squadron, Headquarters and "A" Flights were assigned, early in June, to 208 Squadron for further work in the latest type of Camels.[11]

The other two detachments were also assigned to Camel outfits. Flight "B", under the leadership of Lieutenant William R. Everett,

---

* Those killed were Pvts. John E. Allen, Harry Boerstler, Walter T. Cohee, Garry Crist, Archie Henderson, Jesse L. Koopman, Clarence M. Jones, Alek Miller, George E. Ostrander, and Patrick Rogers. Only the heroic work of Lt. William R. Cravens, the 148th Squadron's medical doctor, saved several others who were seriously wounded.

† Dallas had been credited with thirty-nine victories before being shot down on 1 June 1918.

supply officer of the 148th, was assigned to the veteran 3 Squadron. As the German drive continued toward Amiens, this squadron was forced to evacuate its airdrome at Albert. After approximately two months of jumping from one airdrome to the next with this organization, Flight "B" was transferred to 70 Squadron, then based at Remaisnil, to continue the learning process on Clerget-powered Camels. At Remaisnil Lieutenant Everett was replaced as supply officer by Lieutenant Rawolle Lochridge, son of Brigadier General P. D. Lochridge, a member of the Supreme War Council. The third detachment, made up of Flight "C" under the command of Lieutenant Thomas Blake, the gunnery officer, was attached to the crack 43 Squadron which was also flying Camels. Like other British fighter units in the Somme area, this squadron was forced to make frequent moves to avoid being overrun by the enemy's land forces. While they were assigned to this squadron, the American mechanics were given charge of the planes being flown by American-born officers serving with 43 Squadron. Three of these officers —Lieutenants Henry R. Clay, George C. Whiting, and Erroll H. Zistel—later joined the 148th.[12]

By late June, 1918, the ground personnel of the 148th were considered fully trained, and on the last day of the month the various detachments were reassembled at Cappelle airdrome near Dunkirk.[13] The new squadron commander was Lieutenant Morton L. Newhall. Like the 17th Aero Squadron's Sam Eckert, "Mort" Newhall was also British trained. He had seen combat service with 3 Squadron and 84 Squadron of the RAF and had served briefly as the senior flight commander in the 17th American Squadron.[14]

At about the same time flying officers began to arrive, and within a few days the 148th had received its entire complement of twenty-one pilots. All of the fliers were products of British flying schools, and several had seen active service with RAF operational squadrons. Eight of the pilots—Lieutenants Bennett Oliver, Elliott Springs, Field Kindley, Erroll Zistel, George Whiting, Henry R. Clay, Lawrence T. Wyly and Harry Jenkinson—had gone to England with the original war bird contingent in September of 1917. Oliver, Springs, Kindley, and Zistel had already scored victories while flying with the English; thus, the 148th was staffed with men with battle experience, and their knowledge was soon to be passed on to the newer pilots. Elliott Springs was given command of "B"

Flight, while Henry Clay led "C" Flight. The Yale-educated Oliver was made "A" Flight commander, a position he was forced to relinquish after only a few days because of illness. Field Kindley, the man with a slow Arkansas drawl and lightning-like reflexes, replaced him as flight commander and led "A" Flight until the end of the war.[15]

Early in July the 148th received nineteen second-hand Sopwith Camels powered with 140-h.p. Clerget rotary engines. Although leftovers, these Camels were all the British had to give at the time. The Clerget Camel* was capable of approximately 110 mph in level flight and could climb to 10,000 feet in a little less than ten minutes. It was armed with twin synchronized Vickers guns mounted in front of the pilot. The Camel was extremely tricky to fly because of the powerful gyroscopic forces created by the rotary engine—the whole engine which was attached to the propeller spun around a fixed crankshaft. Castor oil was used in most rotaries "because it would not mix with and dilute the fuel-air mixture in the crank case."[16] Needless to say, castor-oil fumes had some effect on the pilot's digestive system. Although considerably slower than the British S.E.-5, the German Fokker D-7, and the French Spad-13, the Camel had no peer in maneuverability when handled by an experienced pilot. In the words of one RAF fighter pilot, the Camel "was unquestionably the greatest plane at the front—and that includes the German planes. . . . In a fight it could turn to the right faster than any other plane. . . ."[17] Indeed, more planes were shot down by the Camel than any other plane in the 1914–1918 war. It could not match the operational ceiling of the Fokker and Spad, however, and in the summer of 1918 it was considered obsolescent by many. According to some fliers, "A Camel pilot had to shoot down every German plane in the sky in order to get home himself, as the Camel could neither outclimb nor outrun a Fokker."[18]

Whatever their view of the Camel might be, the ground crews proudly painted the squadron's markings on the "new" aircraft. The 148th had been given a solid white equilateral triangle as its squadron insignia. This triangle was carried on each side of the fuselage behind the RAF roundels. Individual plane letters were painted on both sides just forward of the roundels and immediately

* The name "Camel" came from the distinctive humped fairing over the nose guns.

behind the cockpit. The 148th's sister squadron, the 17th, based across the canal in Petite Synthe, carried a white dumbbell instead of the triangle. Since the pilots of the two American outfits on the British front had trained together, the two squadrons were to stage a good-natured rivalry to see which could send the most Huns crashing into the green French-Belgian countryside. As the "Dumbbells" and the "White Triangles" were frequently engaged in the same missions, the contest became intense.*

During the opening days of July, pilots of the two American squadrons practiced formation flying and air-to-ground firing "on the silhouetted plane" in the marsh nearby at St. Pol. After a few days of this type of work the Yanks began line patrols over the front from Nieuport, on the Belgian Coast, to Ypres.[20] These patrols, mainly for training purposes, were made daily to acquaint the newer pilots with the front. This part of the line had been relatively quiet throughout the war, and only rarely was an enemy plane sighted. Such practice was in keeping with the British philosophy of introducing men into combat gradually. One American pilot who had trained in England summed up the RAF attitude:

Another valuable idea with the British was that upon being posted to an active squadron, except in extreme emergencies, a new pilot would spend two or three weeks in acclimation. A great deal of attention was given to formation flying, combat tactics, and becoming familiar with the terrain, the equipment, the personnel and to the degree possible, with the opposition.[21]

It was while flying one of the "quiet" line patrols on 13 July 1918 that Lieutenant Field E. Kindley chalked up the 148th American's first air victory when he caught a German Albatros D-3† at 12,000 feet over Ypres. His combat report tells the story of this action:

At 8:57 A.M. I saw E.A. [enemy aircraft] below us between Poperinghe and Ypres. An Albatross came out of the clouds between me and my formation. After climbing head-on over him, I half-rolled and shot two bursts of one hundred rounds into him at point blank range. Soon he

---

* On being transferred to the American Air Service on the Toul front in November, 1918, the squadrons were given more sophisticated insignia—the 148th, a Liberty Head, and the 17th, a Great Snow Owl.[19]

† The Albatros D-3 was considered the best German fighter in the first part of 1917. Its speed of 120 mph gave it a decided advantage over Allied machines in operations when it first came out. Baron Manfred von Richthofen flew this type before the Fokker triplane became popular.

and another E.A. were on my tail, diving vertically at me. Of course, I was watching them and when the one I had fired two bursts at tried to come out of his dive, I saw his tail come loose and he went down in a vertical dive with the tailplane hanging to his fuselage. He continued to dive vertically through the clouds and to the best of my knowledge, must have crashed not far from the lines South East of Ypres. By this time three E.A. were firing upon me and I maneuvered my way through the clouds back to the lines and rejoined my formation.[22]

The kill, Kindley's second, was confirmed, and a few hours later the 148th Squadron Headquarters received the following telegraphic message from Brigadier General E. R. Ludlow Hewitt, Commanding Officer, 10th Brigade, RAF: "Please convey my congratulations to the 148th Squadron and Lieut. Kindley for marking up the first point scored against the enemy by American Air Service."[23] For a few days the slender, hawkeyed Kindley was the toast of the American squadrons then operating on the British front.

Field Kindley, the only child of George C. and Ella S. Kindley, was born on a farm near Pea Ridge, Arkansas, on 13 March 1896 —practically on top of one of the great battlefields of the Civil War. He may have imbibed some of the atmosphere of battle which still clung around the area for he, too, was to win fame in the deadly game of war. His mother died when he was two and one-half years old, and a short time later his father, a school teacher, took a position as an education supervisor in the Philippine Islands. Young Kindley lived with a grandmother in Bentonville, Arkansas, until he was seven years old, when he joined his father in Manila. After some five years in the Philippines he returned to the United States and made his home with an uncle in Gravette, Arkansas, where he lived until his graduation from high school. Like many farm and small-town boys of that period, Kindley learned to use firearms at an early age, a knowledge which paid huge dividends later in France. After graduation from high school he moved to Coffeyville, Kansas, where he became part-owner and operator of one of the first motion picture establishments in southern Kansas. Here this handsome and tremendously magnetic young Arkansan so won the hearts of the local townspeople that after his death they honored him by giving the magnificent new senior high school, built in 1929, his name.[24]

When America entered World War I, Kindley enlisted in the

Kansas National Guard and shortly thereafter was sent to Fort Riley for infantry training. He was never too happy with infantry life and infantry training—especially close-order drill. When a notice was posted on the barracks bulletin board describing the aviation branch of the Army Signal Corps and asking for volunteers, he was an interested reader.[25] One of his infantry buddies remembers the slender, blue-eyed Kindley standing in front of the bulletin board reading and re-reading the notice, then snapping his fingers briskly and declaring, "that is what I'm going to be."[26]

Within hours after reading the aviation notice Kindley had made application to transfer to the signal corps. A few days later, on 15 August, he became a member of the Signal Enlisted Reserve Corps and was ordered to the School of Military Aeronautics, University of Illinois, for ground training. He apparently showed real promise in the ground-school program for he was one of the original war bird cadets sent to England for flight training in September of 1917.[27] From this point on, Kindley's story was pretty much the story of the other war birds told so charmingly in the diary of one of them, John MacGavock Grider.[28] After completing his training on Rumpties, Avros, Pups, and Camels, Field Kindley was commissioned a first lieutenant in the American Air Service on 15 April 1918. For several weeks thereafter he ferried aircraft from England to the battle front. Like others employed in this work, he had some difficulty with bad weather and mechanical failures which resulted in forced landings. On 5 May 1918 his career as a war pilot almost came to an end before it started when, in a heavy fog and low ceiling, he crashed a Camel into the Cliffs of Dover.

After a short time in the hospital, Lieutenant Kindley was released and assigned to 65 Squadron, RAF, then fighting in the Flanders area. Here, under the careful tutelage of veteran British fliers, he rapidly developed into a superb fighter pilot. On 26 June, less than a week before his transfer to the 148th American, Field Kindley scored his first air victory by shooting down Leutnant Wilhelm Lehmann, the commanding officer of the famed *Jagdstaffel* 5, in a fierce dogfight over Albert.[29]

When "Bim" Oliver was forced to enter an English hospital late in July of 1918, Kindley became flight commander in the 148th American. Although there were a half-dozen Ivy League college men available for the position, the choice of the Arkansan was a popular one. Because of his flying ability, leadership qualities, and great personal charm Kindley was admired and respected equally by the pilots and the ground personnel who kept the planes in flying condition.[30] Before the end of the war he scored twelve official air victories, a number exceeded only by Rickenbacker, Luke, Lufbery, and George Vaughn in the American Air Service.

After a few days of line patrols the 17th and 148th were considered ready for offensive patrols and escort missions. Their first escort work was to protect British DH-9 bombers on raids against the Belgian cities of Zeebrugge, Ostend, and Bruges. A typical raid on Bruges, located about fifteen miles inland from the English Channel and twenty-five miles behind the German lines, is described in the following 148th Squadron report:

With the D.H. 9's at fourteen thousand feet and the Camels above at fifteen thousand to sixteen thousand feet, over thirty planes in all, it made an imposing array as they proceeded along the coast past the Middlekirke "Archie-battery." . . . On they went past Ostend and then over Zeebrugge, where the mole and the two British concrete-laden battleships could be plainly seen. Finally, turning along the border of Holland, with the Island of Flusting seeming just beneath, the bombers would fly straight across Bruges on their way home, picking out their targets carefully and watching the flames and puffs of smoke as the high explosive bombs fell on the railway stations, ammunition dumps, and sometimes buildings which were not quite as warlike looking. The "nines," having a greater speed than the little Camels, would "open up" and leave their protectors behind as they "legged it" for home. But the Camels did their own share of hurrying. Soon the familiar marshland of the Yser came into view, and it was not long before they were safely over the Lines, landing a few minutes later on their airdrome at Dunkirk [in the case of the 17th the landing was at Petite Synthe].[31]

Although heavy antiaircraft fire was encountered on these raids, no American planes were lost in escort activity during July, 1918.

During the week following Field Kindley's 13 July kill, pilots of the 148th collected both bets and drinks from their friends at Petite Synthe. But on 20 July their superiority was seriously challenged when the 17th Squadron's Lieutenant Rodney D. Williams, of Wales, Wisconsin, sent a Fokker down out of control over Ostend. The modest Williams was given an impromptu fête at dinner in the 17th's mess which, according to Frederick M. Clapp, he took with obvious embarrassment. Sergeant [Hayden C.] Kellum drew a large ink sketch of the memorable "scrap" from the descriptions brought in by the pilots. Ultimately it was framed and hung in the Mess with the legend: "Our First Hun."[32]

It was the "Dumbbells' " turn to collect from the "White Triangles." Some of the joy was missing from the occasion, however, for the 17th had also lost its first pilot on that midmorning flight. Lieutenant George Glenn, described as a "Son of Virginia, and a charming fellow," had been shot down from 20,000 feet in the vicinity of Ostend.[33] He was later reported killed in action.

Although no further aerial successes came to either squadron during the last ten days of July, there was plenty of excitement for all. Both squadrons were based in the proximity of Dunkirk and they were to have a ringside seat for the German's nightly air raids on the docks and supply depots. Since both Cappelle and Petite Synthe were old established British airdromes, buildings were well sandbagged, aircraft were protected by revetments, and each squadron had its own dugout. Consequently, officers and men could, with relative safety, watch the "aerial spectacle of the searchlights, the bursting barrage of 'Archie,' and the red glare and deafening crash of bombs. Now and then, the Huns would come droning over the airdrome, and the men would duck into the dugouts or the ditch at the side of the field."[34]

The airdrome's facilities occupied by the American squadrons were excellent for a battle area. For example, the officers and enlisted men of the 148th American were "quartered in Nisson Huts. The Officer's Mess was in a Nisson Hut, and their ante-room, a recreation room, in another hut of the same make." Both the mess and the anteroom were comfortable and attractively arranged. "The walls were painted white, with black trimmings, and the windows were curtained with chintz. For furniture they had comfortable wicker chairs. With a phonograph and a piano, their quarters were complete."[35] From these halls, as from a hundred squadron meeting places all across France, there echoed such songs as:

> A Mademoiselle from Armentières
> Parlez-vous;
>
> A Mademoiselle from Armentières
> Parlez-vous;

> A Mademoiselle from Armentières
> Sold herself for souvenirs
> Hinky dinky, Par-lez-vous.

But the favorite may have been:

> The young aviator lay dying,
> And as under the wreckage he lay,
> To the mechanics assembled around him
> These parting words did he say:

> "Two valve-springs you'll find in my stomach,
> Three spark plugs are safe in my lung,
> The prop is in splinters inside me,
> To my fingers the joy-stick has clung.

> "Take the cylinders out of my kidneys,
> The connecting rods out of my brain;
> From the small of my back take the crankshaft
> And assemble the engine again." [36]

July had been a breaking-in period for the 17th and 148th American Squadrons; August would see air action on the British front increase sharply. At Petite Synthe, 1 August dawned warm and hazy with a light westerly wind. The first patrol of nine machines left at 8:00 A.M. and climbed toward the battle lines to the northeast. Sixty minutes later they encountered three Fokker triplanes and a Fokker biplane in the vicinity of LaBassée; in the resulting dogfight Lieutenant Robert M. Todd, of Cincinnati, Ohio, chalked up the 17th Squadron's second air kill. His combat report told the story:

While on offensive patrol 8:00–10:00 A.M., August 1, 1918, our formation met three triplanes and one Fokker biplane at 14000 to 16000 feet. The leading three of our formation dived on the E.A. and when the E.A. turned, I dove on the nearest triplane, opening fire at about 100 yards range. The triplane pulled up, allowing me to get within 25 yards of him, and my next burst sent him down out of control. While watching him, I went into a spin accidentally and pulled out of it at about 6000 feet. While still diving, I saw the triplane crash into a wood near Provin . . . This was about 8:50–9:00 A.M.[37]

Thirty minutes later the American formation, while cruising at 15,000 feet, came upon three Fokker D-7's and a Pfalz scout near Hallebeke. In a series of individual dogfights Lieutenants William

H. Shearman, M. K. Spidle, and Ralph D. Gracie each sent down an enemy aircraft "out of control." None of these were ever confirmed, but there could be little question that the war had started in earnest for the 17th American.[38]

Out of this fight a new confidence was born. In the wild dogfight the comparatively green American squadron had held the upper hand, and

when the patrol returned and the pilots crowded, all excitement, into the adjutant's office, filling its warm sunniness with the icy chill of the upper air that still clung to their flying clothes, one was put to it, for a moment, to disentangle the tactics of the battle or its results from their furious colloquies, one with another, in which emphatic gestures illustrated, with fantastic vividness, side-slips, rolls, zooms, stalls, dives, loops, vertical banks, and all the tension and determination and lightning-quick reactions of imminent danger defied and overcome.[39]

Two days later pilots of the 17th scored the squadron's third and fourth official victories and surged far ahead of their 148th Squadron rivals when Lieutenants W. J. Armstrong and Merton L. Campbell shot down a Fokker triplane and a Fokker D-7 near Roulers.[40] Frederick Clapp, the squadron adjutant, barely had time to record the new successes, however, before the 148th narrowed the gap once again. Less than an hour after Armstrong and Campbell's victims plunged into the Belgian countryside, Field Kindley and Elliott Springs knocked down a pair of Fokker biplanes in the outskirts of Ostend to shove the "White Triangle's" score to three.[41] Springs's victory was his fourth; Kindley's kill was his third. The good-natured race was picking up speed with the ultimate result being trouble for German air units in the Dunkirk-Ostend area.

During the week following the big 3 August battle, the two squadrons settled down to routine patrols along the British line from Zeebrugge to Mount Kemmel. Although only a few enemy planes were seen on these flights, the 17th Squadron did engage in several aerial battles. Murray K. Spidle was shot down and killed on 4 August. Three days later the 17th got a measure of revenge when Lieutenant Lloyd A. Hamilton's "C" Flight spotted eight Fokkers at 8,000 feet over Armentières and dived out of the sun into their ranks. During the fight Hamilton, who claimed four victories while flying with 3 Squadron, RAF, sent one enemy Fokker plummeting into the lush farmland below. Meanwhile Merton

Campbell crashed two others, one of which plowed into the ground nose first. These victories ran the squadron's total to seven.[42]

Several other pilots scored hits on the fallen victims, but under the British confirmation system the kill went to the pilot who had scored the most telling blows; in case two or more pilots were equally responsible for the destruction, fractional credit was given. Two pilots sharing equally in the destruction of an aircraft would each be credited with one-half of a victory. On the other hand, two pilots contributing equally to the shooting down of an aircraft on the French end of the front (for example, Meuse-Argonne) would each be given full credit. The squadron, of course, would be credited with only one official kill. An extreme example of this occurred on 2 October 1918, when seven pilots from the 28th Aero Squadron combined to shoot down a German plane in the Argonne area. Each of the pilots were given credit for one kill. Statistics indicate that the 1st Pursuit Group destroyed 203 aircraft, but individual pilots in the group were credited with 296 victories; the 2nd Pursuit Group had 132 victories, while its pilots had 230; and the 3rd Pursuit Group got 87 kills, and its pilots were credited with 132 aircraft downed. It was apparent that the debriefing officers were taking the easy way out and simply not making a serious effort to determine who rendered the death blow. Things finally got so bad that the 1st Pursuit Group issued a memorandum to the effect that no more than three pilots would be credited in the destruction of an enemy aircraft. Unfortunately, the other two groups took no such action. (A breakdown of squadron victories compared with individual pilot victories in Table I.) The 17th and 148th Squadrons operating under the stricter rules in the Flanders sector were, understandably, somewhat disgruntled by the situation. Also, since they were somewhat isolated from the American Air Service command they did not receive their fair share of American decorations. Although the two squadrons could claim more than a dozen aces in their ranks, only a few Distinguished Service Crosses were received. Many fliers serving in the Toul–St. Mihiel–Verdun area were awarded the DSC for one plane shot down.

On 8 August 1918, the British began their big move to wipe out the Amiens salient which had been driven into their lines by the German spring offensive. To cover the massive attack on a twenty-five-mile front from Albert to Roye the Allied command assembled an air armada of over 1,000 British and French airplanes. The Germans countered this move by rushing many of their best air units into the area. It was into this flaming battle that Mort Newhall's 148th American Squadron was dispatched three days after the campaign opened. The move was, more or less, at the squadron's own request. During the nearly four weeks of war flying over the comparatively calm Nieuport-Ypres front, during which time only "three Huns were brought down," the pilots had begun to chafe at their inability to "get fights." Believing the squadron was ready for a more active role, Major Harold Fowler, who was then in charge of American aviation with the British, had requested that the 148th be assigned to the Amiens sector, and the request had been granted.[43]

Pilots of the 148th made the move to Allonsville, their new base near Amiens, without a hitch on 11 August. The ground crews found the seventy-five-mile move to the south in truck convoy more complicated, and some elements did not arrive until late afternoon of the next day.[44] Nonetheless, the squadron was able to start combat operations immediately. The new field, popularly known as "Horse-Shoe Woods" because of the shape by which the woods could be identified from the air, was in the very heart of the sector; from this point the squadron would certainly "get a fight."

The 148th Squadron was stationed at Allonsville only seven days, but during that hectic week its pilots destroyed at least six enemy planes. Their first victories occurred on 13 August, just two days after their arrival at the little "Horse-Shoe Woods" airdrome, when a patrol led by Field Kindley spotted six enemy machines cruising at 6,000 feet a little north of Roye. In order to give the impression that he had not seen them, the Arkansan turned to the north and led his Camels behind some clouds as the Germans, four Halberstadt two-seaters and two Fokker D-7's, approached the lines. Then turning his patrol, Kindley dove through the clouds on an intercept course with the enemy. As the Americans dropped through the fleecy cloud screen they found themselves practically on top of the German formation and opened fire immediately. The first dive and zoom accounted for three enemy aircraft and possibly a fourth.[45] The other German planes fled to the east while the Americans followed their stricken victims down. Lieutenants Kindley and Lawrence T. Wyly were credited in RAF communiqués with one official victory each when their opponents crashed near the front lines. Lieutenants George C. Whiting and George V. Seibold shared in the destruction of another. Later in the afternoon Lieutenant Harry Jenkinson sent an enemy aircraft down in flames, but no confirmation was ever received.[46]

This auspicious beginning at Allonsville was marred when Lieutenant Wyly failed to return after shooting down his Halberstadt— the first of his four confirmed kills. On the next day, however, the squadron received a telegram stating that he was safe. His engine had quit as he followed his victim down and he had been forced to make a dead-stick landing just on the Allied side of the lines. When Kindley went with a touring car to pick up the "missing warrior" he found that Wyly had made friends with an antiaircraft machine gun company and "was having the time of his life popping away at Hun planes as they came within range."[47]

On 15 August the Knights of the White Triangle scored again when "A" and "B" Flights patrolling east of Chaulnes encountered fifteen Fokker D-7's high over the battle lines. The Americans, well aware of the superior performance of the Fokker at high altitudes, led their opponents down to an altitude more to their own advantage before accepting combat. In the twisting dogfight which ensued, Lieutenants Jesse O. Creech, George Seibold, and Harry Jenkinson each managed to bring down a "Hun machine."[48] During the fight the squadron suffered its first casualty when Wyly was hit in the arm and, for the second time in three days, was forced to land just inside Allied lines. After a few days in a field hospital the indomitable Wyly was ready for another crack at "the Boche."[49]

Three days after the Chaulnes fight, Lieutenant Henry Clay, the Fort Worth, Texas, lad who commanded "C" Flight, shot down a Fokker near Noyon[50] to score the squadron's tenth victory and its seventh since moving to Allonsville. Clay was one of the original war birds and had once been a pupil of Captain Edward "Mick" Mannock, the great British ace. Before coming to the 148th he had served with 43 Squadron, RAF, where he was credited with at least one kill. Because of his even temperament and his "wonderful knowledge of aerial strategy," Clay was frequently given the role of leading squadron-size formations. Before he left the 148th American to become commanding officer of the newly created 41st

Aero in November, he had pushed his personal victory total to eight and ranked as one of the top U.S. aces.

On 18 August, after only a week at Allonsville, the 148th was moved to Remaisnil, some seven miles northwest of Doullens, and attached to the 13th Wing, RAF, British Third Army. The squadron continued to operate with the 13th Wing until its transfer to the American Air Service in the Toul sector during the last weeks of the war. From the beautiful tree-surrounded airfield at Remaisnil the 148th, during the next four weeks, flew many low-level bombing and strafing missions in support of the Allied push toward Cambrai.[51]

Meanwhile, on 13 August, Sam Eckert's 17th Aero Squadron, still operating from Petite Synthe on the English Channel, staged one of the most audacious raids of the first world war—a strike against the German airdrome at Varssenaere. This large airfield, located a short distance southwest of Bruges, was the home of five squadrons of Fokkers and Gothas. Original plans had called for a low-level surprise attack by four Camel squadrons—a number which was cut to three when the 148th American was transferred out of the 65th Wing and sent to Allonsville. The operation was finally limited to 210 and 213 Squadrons, RAF, and the 17th American. The three squadrons were to rendezvous over the Channel and then fly inland to attack the airdrome at dawn. Each Camel was to carry four twenty-pound Cooper bombs, "with the exception of the flight commanders' which were to carry phosphorus bombs to be dropped on or near the machine gun implacements that guarded the airdrome."[52] In order to perfect the plan, a practice flight under the supervision of Colonel Cunningham, the wing commander, was made over the British airdrome at Andembert, near Calais.

After several postponements from bad weather, the scheduled raid was finally set for 13 August. Just before daylight on that fateful morning, twelve Camels, led by Lieutenants Lloyd Hamilton and Weston W. Goodnow, left Petite Synthe and disappeared into the predawn mist. For two long hours 17th Squadron mechanics and ground officers paced up and down the hangar line and anxiously watched the sky to the north. Then one by one the pilots came back, their little LeRhone-powered Camels badly shot up, but no one injured. The raid had been a smashing success. The two RAF squadrons had dropped their bombs and climbed up to act as protection for the 17th Squadron, which then roared in at an extremely low altitude to drop their bombs on the Chateau, which served as an officers quarters, hangars, workshops, and barracks. With Hamilton leading the way, the pilots then made pass after pass across the airdrome at treetop level, shooting at planes lined up "with engines warming up preparatory to taking off, as well as enemy mechanics and pilots scattered about the field." The Royal Air Force Communiqué for the day described the results in succinct terms:

The following damage was observed to be caused by the combined operation: a dump of petrol and oil was set on fire, which appeared to set fire to an ammunition dump; six Fokker biplanes were set on fire on the ground, and two destroyed by direct hits from bombs; one large Gotha hangar was set on fire and another half demolished; a living hut was set on fire and several hangars were seen to be smouldering as the result of phosphorus bombs having fallen on them. In spite of most of the machines taking part being hit at one time or another, all returned safely, favorable ground targets being attacked on the way home.

Months later a captured German revealed that no less than fourteen aircraft had been put out of action. Reports coming in from Belgium also indicated 120 soldier-mechanics and 30 pilots had been killed by the raid. Even Air Service, AEF, Headquarters, located far away on the French front, noted the occasion and wired congratulations to the 17th for its signal accomplishment.[53]

In addition to the Varssenaere airdrome raid the 17th American engaged in several fights during the second week of August. Merton Campbell and Lieutenant Glen Wicks each destroyed an enemy plane, running the squadron total to nine, now one behind the 148th. On the darker side, Ralph Gracie, one of the squadron's original pilots from the Taliaferro days at Fort Worth, was shot down and killed on 12 August. Two days later Lieutenants Lyman E. Case and William Shearman were also lost. While escorting RAF bombers in a raid against submarine shelters, marine works, and docks in the Bruges-Ostend area, Lieutenants William J. Armstrong, Ralph Snoke, and Harris Alderman were wounded in an aerial battle with enemy scouts. Armstrong was rather seriously injured and barely managed to get home again before landing heavily on top of a British DH-9. The other two were less seriously hurt. Alderman, better known by his squadron mates as Aldy, had been wounded by a bullet which had ricochetted through his fuel tank and struck him "where he sat." Out of this superficial wound came one of the amusing stories of the air war.

It seems that all three wounded officers were sent to Queen Alexandra Hospital near Dunkirk to recover. A day or so later, King George V visited the hospital and on touring the wards came upon the American fliers. The King chatted briefly with each pilot and asked about their wounds. When he reached Aldy no wound was visible so he asked, "and where were you wounded?" According to the squadron historian, "Aldy had a terrible moment of self-consciousness, but his quick-witted reply was: 'Over Ostend, your Majesty.' The King understood. A smile of delighted amusement crept over his face and spread to the faces of the officers of his suite. Aldy's wound became, from that moment, as it were, a public possession and its exact location was always thereafter described in polite society—for had not a king understood?—as, 'Over Ostend.' "[54]

On 18 August, the 17th Squadron was ordered to move to Auxi-le-Chateau in the Amiens area to participate in the Cambrai drive. Here its work was varied, with a mixture of low-level strafing and bombing missions and medium-altitude offensive patrols getting most of the attention.[55] Thus the two American squadrons were once again operating in the same sector and engaged in the same type of duty.

In the battle for Bapaume and Cambrai the American air units ran into a high quality of pursuit opposition. Almost daily they fought crack *Jastas* which they identified as "Orange Tails," "Orange Bands," the solid red planes of the old Richthofen Circus, and the famous "Blue Tails." Occasionally they saw the "White Tails," "Black and White Checkered," and the "Black Tails."[56] As might be expected, losses in the comparatively untried American squadrons were heavy. During the first week the 17th lost ten pilots killed, wounded, or missing, including two of the three flight commanders.

First of the flight leaders to be lost was Lloyd Hamilton, the squadron's nine-victory ace. He was shot down by ground fire on 24 August as he zoomed away from a balloon he had just set on fire. It was later learned that he had been killed in the crash. Lieutenants Merton Campbell, of Royal Oak, Michigan, and George Wise, a Washington, D.C. aviator, were also lost in the squadron's first four days at Auxi.[57] But the worst was yet to come.

Without a doubt the 17th Squadron's most tragic experience occurred on 26 August. It had rained the previous night, and a gusty wind had begun to blow at dawn, "getting stronger and gustier as the day advanced." Low broken clouds streamed thickly up from the southwest over the rolling hills beyond the airdrome. The Besseneaux hangars "bulged up and flapped [and squadron] tents were all swollen on one side and lean and caved in, against the wind, on the other." Trees surrounding the field groaned under the impact of the wind which was "blowing in fits at seventy and eighty miles an hour."

Late in the afternoon the telephone rang, and Wing Headquarters reported that some of its low strafers (they turned out to be Camels from the 148th American) were under heavy aerial attack along the Bapaume-Cambrai Road. Would the 17th Squadron go to the rescue? The squadron answered affirmatively, and within a matter of seconds the pilots, led by Lieutenant William D. Tipton, "B" Flight commander, were sprinting toward their waiting Camels. A moment later eleven LeRhone engines roared to life, and the pilots prepared to taxi in to takeoff position. Because of gusty conditions it was necessary for mechanics to hold tightly to the wing tips of each Camel until it could be turned into the hurricane-like wind.

Tipton, who had been moody and silent since the death of his friend Lloyd Hamilton two days before, got the formation away in good shape, and the eleven fighters quickly disappeared over the treetops to the east. One plane turned back almost immediately with engine trouble and a half-hour later still another returned with jammed guns. Then there was silence except for the howl of the wind. Two hours passed. Finally Weston Goodnow and Ralph Snoke circled the airdrome and landed in the heavy wind. The latter's plane was riddled with bullet holes, and both fliers looked dazed. Several minutes later Lieutenant Frank Dixon hedgehopped over the trees and landed smoothly in the middle of Auxi airdrome. The ground crews waited patiently, but no other Camels appeared.[58]

In the operations tent Sam Eckert and Frederick M. Clapp, the adjutant, slowly pieced together the story of the disaster from accounts given by the stunned trio who had survived the battle. On reaching the Quéant area, the formation had spotted a lone Camel from the 148th Squadron under attack by five Fokkers and had dived to the rescue. No sooner had they joined the battle when they were jumped by several other Fokker formations which slid through a rift in the clouds with guns blazing. In a matter of moments the nine Camel pilots found themselves fighting for their lives against some fifty enemy pursuits. Although the Americans fought fiercely, such an unequal contest could have only one result. Disaster. Lieutenants Tipton, Robert Todd, Henry Frost, Howard Bittinger, Laurence Roberts, and Harry Jackson all were sent crashing to earth, the latter three killed. Tipton, Todd, and Frost were made prisoners of war. Despite the odds the 17th had fought well. Frank Dixon claimed the destruction of two enemy planes, and before going down Tipton shot down two, while Todd got one. All of these kills were eventually confirmed in RAF Communiqués.[59]

The British wisely withdrew the shattered 17th Squadron from action for several days while replacements in pilots and aircraft came in. One of the new flight leaders was the redoubtable Lieutenant George Vaughn, the New Yorker who was already an ace with 84 Squadron, RAF. Vaughn was given command of "B" Flight and eventually became America's fourth ranking ace with thirteen air victories. Lieutenant William T. Clements transferred from the 148th Squadron to take over Hamilton's old "C" Flight.*

Mort Newhall's 148th American survived the bombing, strafing, and low-altitude offensive work in the Cambrai push in much better shape than did its sister squadron. During the month at Remaisnil (18 August–20 September) the squadron shot down thirty enemy aircraft while losing only six pilots. The "White Triangles" suffered their first air casualty on 24 August, when Lieutenants George Seibold and Jesse Creech were surprised by three Fokkers while on a strafing mission in the front lines. In the treetop-level battle Sei-

* After his release from the Air Service, Vaughn returned to Princeton University and completed his work for a B.S. degree in February, 1920. During the early 1920's he worked for both Western Electric and Westinghouse as a research engineer. In 1928 he organized and became president of the Eastern Aeronautical Corp. This was the first commercial company to build a hangar at Newark Airport and subsequently absorbed the General Aviation Co. In 1931 Franklin D. Roosevelt, then governor of New York, appointed Vaughn to the New York State Aviation Commission. Vaughn is now vice-president of the Academy of Aeronautics at La Guardia Airport.[60]

bold, who had destroyed three enemy planes since joining the 148th, was shot down and killed just inside the British lines. Creech, who would end the war with seven victories,[61] managed to nurse his badly damaged Camel back to Remaisnil and made a safe landing. On a later strafing sortie, Lieutenant Marvin Kent Curtis,* an Amherst College man, was caught in exactly the same manner and went down inside the German lines to become a prisoner of war.[62]

On 2 September 1918, while participating in the Drocourt-Quéant Battle, the 148th American experienced its most severe combat loss of the war. Two flights of Camels had been engaged in bombing and strafing the retreating Germans along the main highway between Albert and Cambrai. On turning toward their home field, the American pilots became very apprehensive of the low broken clouds over No-Man's Land. This cloud formation was, of course, the perfect setup for a German aerial ambush. With every pilot warily searching each cloud the two flights cruised steadily westward toward Remaisnil. Flight "A," with Kindley leading, had reached the protection of a large bank of clouds a little south of Romaucourt, while "B" Flight, under Elliott Springs, was still below and behind. Suddenly, a dozen Fokker D-7's dropped from a low-hanging cloud into the middle of Springs's flight. Kindley caught the action out of the corner of his eye just as his own flight entered the cloud ahead. Without hesitation he abandoned the safety he had reached by banking his fighter sharply to the right and plummeting down to aid the hard-pressed members of "B" Flight, who were now fighting for their lives. The other four members of "A" Flight followed their leader into the melee. More Fokkers dived into the battle from the clouds above, and for a few seconds the sky was full of flashing wings and tracer bullets. Kindley picked out a Fokker which was close on the tail of a friendly Camel and fired a short burst into its engine and fuselage. The German machine rolled over on its back and burst into flames. Lieutenants Charles McLean and Walter Knox also tallied victories, but the rescue attempt was too late to prevent heartbreaking losses.[63]

* According to the *148th U.S. Aero Squadron Bulletin,* Kent Curtis became an insatiable world traveler after the war. He made at least one trip around the world, spent many weeks with Nordhoff and Hall on Tahiti and months with American writers in Paris, later hobnobbing with Ernest Hemingway in Florida. Between the two wars several of his books were published, and at the time of his death he ran a boys' camp in Minnesota.

Lieutenants Linn H. Forster, J. D. Kenyon, Oscar Mandel, Joseph E. Frobisher, and Jesse Creech did not return from the fight. Creech landed safely inside British lines, while Kenyon and Mandel were taken prisoners. The other two were killed. Frobisher, wounded three times in the abdomen, died in a Canadian Army hospital, and Forster was fatally injured when he crashed behind the German lines.[64]

Field Kindley's victory ran his score to five, making him the squadron's second ace, but the one-sided battle came close to claiming his life. "Upon landing," he wrote,

I found 36 holes in my bus. Ten had burst on the butt of my guns and the splinters sprinkled my face, while one bullet went through my goggles missing my temple by ¼ inche [*sic*]. My machine could not be flown again. . . .[65]

Apparently the close call did not shake his confidence, for four days later he sent a Fokker down "out of control" over St. Quentin Lake for kill number six.[66]

The 148th American was indeed a hot outfit during the first three weeks of September. Following its flight leaders, the squadron downed seventeen German planes, mostly Fokker D-7's, with its Vickers machine guns. A friendly rivalry had developed within the organization, and by the end of its stay at Remaisnil, on 20 September, four pilots had achieved acedom. Elliott Springs, the irrepressible "B" Flight commander, led the pack with nine, but was followed closely by Kindley with eight, Clay with six, and Creech with five. Several others had been credited with two or more triumphs.[67]

As the Allied armies slowly forced the Kaiser's forces back on the Canal-du-Nord section of the Hindenburg Line, many of the fighting squadrons were moved closer to the battle lines. On 20 September the 148th American was transferred to Baizieux, five miles west of the city of Albert. At the same time Eckert's 17th Squadron was moved to the Soncamp airdrome near Doullens. Since the Clerget- and LeRhone-powered Camels used by the two American outfits were relatively short ranged, these moves were imperative. From their new bases, the 148th and 17th were called upon time and again for work of the most dangerous type, "bombing and strafing at low altitudes, keeping the Hun observation balloons out of the sky, and driving the Fokkers back so the British observation planes might carry on their work unmolested."[68] Of all these tasks the low-level bombing and strafing of troops and equipment proved the most hazardous. The attacking plane was not only vulnerable to small arms fire from the ground but was easy prey for any aircraft that might pounce on it from above.

Pilots of the 148th arrived at their new home in a somewhat depressed frame of mind. On the last patrol from Remaisnil, from which they were to land at Baizieux, Lieutenant Harry Jenkinson was shot down in flames despite the valiant efforts of Elliott Springs to save him. Flight "B" had been attacked by a *Jagdstaffel* of Fokker biplanes over the Canal-du-Nord, and as the battle raged still more enemy planes dove into the melee. While Jenkinson was blasting away at one of the enemy fighters, two others succeeded in getting on his tail and opened fire. Springs, himself hotly engaged, spotted his friend's predicament and whipped around in a stall turn to shoot down one of the attackers. But before he could deal with the second Fokker, he was horrified to see Jenkinson's Camel erupt into a searing ball of fire. With the wind-whipped flames flowing like a river through the cockpit, the popular Jenkinson, one of the original cadets who had gone to England for flight training and a veteran of scores of air battles while serving with both British and American squadrons, had absolutely no chance for survival.[69]

Grief stricken over Jenkinson's fate, Springs felt no elation or sense of triumph as his own victim spun down to a fiery crash near the Canal-du-Nord for his tenth official victory. Perhaps the most famous of the Americans who served on the British front, Elliott White Springs was born at Fort Mill, South Carolina, in 1896. The son of a wealthy textile tycoon, he was educated at Asheville, Culver Military Academy, and Princeton. Shortly after America entered the war, an aviation ground school was established at Princeton University, and though he had not yet completed his senior year, Springs enlisted and received his preliminary aviation training on his own campus. In September, 1917, he and 209 other cadets, including Lloyd Hamilton, Laurence Callahan, Field Kindley, George Vaughn, and John MacGavock Grider, were sent to England for flight training. For the next several months Springs attended flying schools at Stamford, Hounslow, Thetford, London, Colney, and Ayr, where he became a legend for his flying ability, pranks, and his skill in mixing South Carolina eggnog and mint juleps. Springs was perhaps the leading personality in Grider's famous war diary.[70]

While in training, Springs attracted the attention of Major William "Billy" Bishop, the famous Canadian ace, and when the latter returned to France in 1918, as commander of 85 Squadron, RAF, he took the South Carolina boy along. Springs's early training with Bishop and Mick Mannock paid off richly; by the time of his transfer to the 148th American at the end of June he had been credited with the destruction of four German aircraft. On 3 August he became the 148th Squadron's first ace by downing a Fokker near Ostend. At the end of hostilities he was tied with Kindley as ace of the squadron with twelve confirmed kills. In November, 1918, Springs was given command of a squadron, and shortly thereafter he was promoted to captain.[71]

After being released from the service, Springs, the maverick spirit, spent several years barnstorming about the United States. For a time he returned to a more sedate life with his father's textile company but soon grew restless and wandered about the world looking for new adventures. While recovering in Paris from stomach ulcers, he tried his hand at writing and was quickly a success. His first publication, *War Birds: Diary of an Unknown Aviator,** serialized in *Liberty* magazine in 1926, was followed by *Nocturne Militaire, War Birds and Lady Birds,* and a half-dozen other novels about World War I aviation. At the death of his father in 1931, Springs became president of the Springs Cotton Mills and within a few years had expanded the industry into a vast textile empire. His catchy, sometimes risqué, advertising program won national attention.†

Soon after its arrival at Soncamp airdrome, the 17th Squadron made a valiant effort to get back in the race with its sister outfit. Following the 26 August disaster, the squadron had been temporarily withdrawn from combat while it was reequipped and reor-

---

* This was the Grider *Diary;* Springs's work was mainly an editing job.

† During World War II Springs served as executive officer, Charlotte AFB, Charlotte, N.C. Until his death in 1959 he continued his interest in aviation, working with young men and women in the South Carolina district of the Civil Air Patrol.[72]

ganized. During this brief lull the "Dumbbell" outfit had fallen far behind the 148th. Lieutenants Howard Burdick, Howard C. Knotts, and William T. Clements[73] had scored successes during the middle of September, but at the time of the 17th's move to its new base it could claim only twenty-four official victories, compared with its rival's forty kills. The gap was narrowed somewhat when, on 22 September, Eckert's outfit opened its Soncamp chapter with a flourish. While on a morning patrol in the Cambrai area, George Vaughn saw fifteen Fokker biplanes dive on Clements' "C" Flight several thousand feet below him. Although greatly outnumbered, he led his "B" Flight impetuously to the attack and, in the furious tracer-marked air battle, shot down one of his adversaries in flames and crashed a second. Lieutenant Glen Wicks got a third, while Knotts blasted two others.[74] For Vaughn it was victories number eight and nine; for Knotts kills number three and four. The squadron total now stood at twenty-nine.

The Cambrai success, however, was not without its price: Lieutenants Theose E. Tillinghast and Gerald P. Thomas had gone down under Fokker guns. Thomas, the quiet blond from Flushing, New York, was killed. Tillinghast, a frail boy from Westerly, Rhode Island, was made prisoner after landing his badly damaged Camel inside the German lines. A few days after his capture he managed to escape through a hole in the roof of the farmhouse in which he was being held and contacted the Belgian underground. Early in October he was put in touch with the Belgian engineer charged with maintaining the electrical fence guarding the frontier and, equipped with rubber gloves, wire cutters, and a map of the wire barrier, he escaped to Allied lines.[75]

During the last week of September the 17th ran into aggressive German patrols almost daily. On 24 September four enemy planes from the crack "Blue Tail" *Jagdstaffel* were shot down.[76] Four days later, Lieutenant Burdick shot down an LVG two-seater in flames and sent a Fokker biplane crashing into No-Man's Land. In the same fight Vaughn forced a German observation plane down "out of control" for his 10th and the squadron's 34th victory.[77] The 17th Squadron had destroyed twelve enemy machines in eight days but lost ground to the slashing "Knights of the White Triangle," who smashed fourteen in the same period of time.

Without a doubt, the 148th's most successful air combat while based at the dreary little Baizieux airfield occurred on 24 September. The story of this fight can best be told through the experience of one of the pilots. It was 7:27 A.M., and the "White Triangle" outfit was Hun hunting a few miles west of Cambrai and not far from the battle lines. The squadron was divided into three flights of five planes each, and fifteen pairs of eyes were scanning the cloudy sky in an effort to spot an enemy formation. Suddenly Lieutenant Field Kindley, whose "A" Flight along with Springs's "B" Flight was flying top cover, tensed in the tiny cockpit of his British-built Sopwith Camel. Several thousand feet below a half-score of German single-seaters were roaring down out of a nearby cloud to attack the 148th's bottom or decoy flight, led by Lieutenant Henry Clay. Kindley hastily glanced over his shoulder to see if the other four pilots in his formation were in position. Then, after wagging his wings as a signal, he whipped his Camel over and down in a "power on" dive to break up the enemy attack on the outnumbered Americans below. As the Arkansan held his sturdy little machine in the wing-straining dive he noted with increasing apprehension that the enemy planes were Fokker D-7's of the "Blue Tails" Squadron. His apprehension was justified, for the "Blue Tails" *Jasta* was equaled only by the Richthofen Circus in the German Air Force.

As Kindley's flight leveled out a few hundred feet behind the Fokkers, the latter banked steeply and began a sharp turn to the right. The enemy had seen the trap and the dogfight, or *Kurven-kampf* as the Germans called it, was now under way. Elliott Springs's flight now entered the picture as did still other Fokkers. Within seconds there were fifteen Camels and some twenty Fokkers in the fray. Camels and Fokkers alike twisted, half-rolled, turned, and dived. Field Kindley, a superb flier, stayed glued to the tail of one of the Fokkers. Finally, after several hard turns the German stalled, and the American squeezed the trigger of his twin Vickers machine guns mounted in front of the cockpit. Tracer bullets ripped into the fuselage of the German fighter and smoke began to pour from its engine. Then, as the Hun went into a slow spin, the boy from the Ozark Mountains finished him off with another long burst of machine gun fire. A few minutes later the Fokker crashed and burned, thus becoming Kindley's ninth official victory.[78] Other

148th pilots, fighting effectively in teams for the first time, were also doing well, and seven enemy machines flamed out of the fight, or spun down out of control.

As quickly as the dogfight had begun it broke up, and the victorious 148th Squadron pilots raced home in high spirits. They had met the best and won. In addition to Kindley's victim, Springs, Knox, Clay, and Wyly each had destroyed one plane, while Lieutenant Errol Zistel had blasted two out of the sky.[79] Springs's kill was his eleventh; Clay's was his seventh.

Although several of the American Camels were badly shot up, only Zistel failed to return to Baizieux. In breaking off combat, his badly damaged machine went out of control and, in his words forty-six years later,

that is the last I recall until regaining consciousness in a casualty clearing station near Bapaume. I was told I had been brought in there by a British Labor Battalion group, four days before, who had observed my right lower wing collapse and my falling into the remnants of a shell torn tree, which had evidently broken my fall. A concussion of the brain appeared to be my severest injury at the time.[80]

Proof that the 148th American's smashing success on 24 September was no fluke was furnished two days later when the squadron again encountered the German "Blue Tails" over the Bourlon Woods, a little north of the Arras-Cambrai Road. In the vicious dogfight which ensued four German fighters fell under the guns of Lieutenants Kindley, Creech, Wyly, and Orville A. Ralston.[81] Three days later Lieutenants Louis Rabe and Charles McLean sent two more Fokkers flaming to the earth a short distance to the north of Cambrai.[82]

Friday, 27 September 1918, was a red-letter day in the life of Field Kindley. As this young man pulled on his fleece-lined flying suit at 8:15 A.M., he could not have realized that within three short hours he would establish himself as one of the great air heroes of the war. At 8:20 A.M. he strolled to the flight line to make a last-minute check of his plane before leading his flight on a scheduled strafing and low-level bombing mission. Upon reaching the hangar area, he found his crew chief still fussing with the Clerget engine of his Camel. As he waited for the mechanic to finish, he idly played with "Fokker," his English Bull Terrier, and glanced about the flying field. Nearby several other Camels were being warmed up for the morning's mission. Across the field a squadron of British S.E.-5's were also getting ready for a patrol over the front lines. Perhaps he was a bit envious as he watched those sleek little machines roar down the field and climb gracefully to the northeast— for the S.E.-5* was considered by many to be the finest Allied pursuit plane operating in 1918. A few minutes later the crew chief signaled that everything was ready, and all thoughts of the S.E.-5's were forgotten. As Kindley buckled his safety belt and tested the Camel's controls he noted the time was 8:35 A.M. After a glance around the field he signaled the other pilots in his formation to prepare to taxi out for takeoff. At 8:40 A.M., "A" Flight, with throttles full on, roared into the air and climbed toward the battle lines.[83]

Twenty minutes after takeoff, Kindley spotted a heavy concentration of German transports on the railway near the village of Marcoing. Although greatly annoyed by the barrage of archie being thrown up to protect the transports, Kindley dived to 800 feet before releasing the four twenty-five-pound bombs which he carried under the fuselage. Other pilots followed their leader, and soon more than a dozen of the transports were in flames.

As Kindley climbed away from the burning transports he caught sight of an enemy observation balloon and turned to pour 200 rounds of "Buckingham" into it. The balloon did not burn but the Hun observers jumped and it was pulled down immediately. At 9:05 A.M. he found a number of German troops marching along a highway and roared down to strafe them from a very low altitude. A few seconds later he silenced a machine gun nest which had been holding up a British infantry advance. At this point the boy from the Ozarks climbed to 2,000 feet to look for another target. Meanwhile other pilots in the patrol were searching for targets of their own. At 9:10 A.M. Kindley noticed a well-camouflaged machine gun nest a little to the east of his position, and as he turned to attack it he heard that "familiar popping behind." A German Halberstadt two-seater had slipped in on the tail of his Camel and was already firing before Kindley was aware of its presence. The American ace slammed his little fighter over into a vicious right turn; then as the heavier German machine overshot its mark, he whipped sharply to

---

* This compact scout-fighter, built by Royal Aircraft Factory, was considerably faster than the Camel and much more maneuverable than the Spad.

the left and rolled out directly under and a little behind the Halberstadt. The two Vickers guns on the Camel roared, and in a few seconds the "Boche burst into flames" and crashed from 800 feet for Kindley's eleventh victory.[84] But the morning was not over. In spite of heavy counterfire, the young officer continued to press his attack on the retreating German infantry until his ammunition was exhausted. At this point he turned toward home. At 10:10 A.M., while still in the vicinity of the battle lines, he noticed two Fokkers picking on a lone comrade, and disregarding empty guns, he dived into the middle of the dogfight, hoping to "frighten them off." The audacious bluff worked, for the Fokkers turned east and left the scene. Twenty-five minutes later the exhausted Kindley made a safe landing at Baizieux.[85] For his morning's work he was awarded an Oak Leaf Cluster to the DSC and the British Distinguished Flying Cross.[86]

During the same morning Elliott Springs and Henry Clay shared in the destruction of a Halberstadt biplace machine over Fontaine–Notre Dame.[87] For Springs the kill was number twelve, his last as he was transferred out of the 148th a few days later and given the command of a newly organized squadron on the French front. Command of "B" Flight was given to Lieutenant Laurence K. Callahan, a close personal friend of Springs and a veteran of many air battles with 85 Squadron, RAF, as well as with the 148th American. Callahan had been credited with the destruction of several enemy planes while with the British and ended the war with a total of five victories.[88]

During October the British gradually pushed the Germans back toward Cambrai, where the latter made a stand for a time along the Sheldt Canal. Then the Kaiser's army gave away, continuing its retreat. For a while the battle line bent around Cambrai on each side, with the Germans still holding the city. In this phase of the fighting the 17th and 148th were sent over to do low reconnaissance, as well as the usual bombing. The pilots scanned the roads leading into Cambrai from the east for signs of German evacuation of the town and dropped their bombs on "troops and transports, who were seen making their way toward Le Cateau on the long straight French road." Finally, when the enemy could hold the city no longer, the lines straightened out miles to the east and the Allied advance continued. As the infantry surged past Cambrai the 148th was again moved up and this time to shell-torn Bapaume in the middle of what a short time before had been No-Man's Land.[89] Eckert's 17th Squadron remained at Soncamp.

Mort Newhall's warriors found the new airdrome at Bapaume a very unpleasant place. They had left civilization behind and were "surrounded for miles by the desolate country" so commonly found in the wake of warring armies. The airdrome had been covered with shell holes, but through the constant work of hundreds of Chinese coolies, the holes had been filled in. Squadron personnel were housed in British "bell-tents," which proved something less than comfortable in the cold, rain, and fog of late October. The mud was thick and it was necessary to construct walks of corrugated iron and boards from the tents to the hangars and the airplanes. Although the pilots managed to get into the air almost every day, flying conditions were bad. Pilot logbooks were full of such comments as "dud weather," "testing weather," and "very bad weather."[90]

Because of poor flying conditions, comparatively few air-to-air battles occurred during October. The 17th lost two pilots—Lieutenants Harold D. Shoemaker and Howard C. Knotts, the latter an ace—while the 148th lost Lieutenant Walter R. Avery. The Boston-born and Tufts-educated Avery managed to escape from his Hun captors and was in the process of working his way back to the squadron at the time of the Armistice.[91] During these dreary October days the "Dumbbells" destroyed four enemy machines, with George Vaughn running his score to thirteen and Howard Burdick getting his eighth. The 148th was credited with ten enemy aircraft during the same period, but seven of these were knocked down on 28 October.

Shortly before noon on that crisp October morning, Lieutenant Kindley led the "Knights of the White Triangle" on their last and, perhaps, most successful mission of the war. The great struggle was rapidly coming to a close, and during the last several days the German pilots had demonstrated a surprising reluctance to engage in air combat. With this in mind the 28 October mission, an offensive patrol, had been carefully planned to pull the enemy into battle. The squadron's three flights, commanded by Kindley, Callahan, and Lieutenant Thomas L. Moore,* crossed the lines at different

---

* Moore had replaced Henry Clay as commander of "C" Flight when Clay had been transferred out of the 148th Aero Squadron to take command of one of the new American pursuit squadrons.

altitudes with Kindley's "A" Flight acting as bait for the trap. On reaching No-Man's Land, members of the squadron noticed seven Fokkers "some distance to the east," and the decoy plan was put into operation. After firing a Very signal pistol to warn Moore and Callahan, Kindley led his flight of four machines down to an altitude of 3,000 feet, where he pretended to be looking for German two-seaters. The upper flights, keeping careful watch upon the lower one, climbed gradually until there was a space of 7,000 feet between them and the decoys. This apparent lack of cohesion between the flights was maintained for over an hour as the flights patrolled back and forth over the lines. Gradually Kindley's flight ventured toward the Fokkers, who were some distance above and east of them but still several thousand feet below the upper flights. This was a dangerous game. Should the Fokker pilots take the bait and dive to the attack the flights of Moore and Callahan would have only seconds to make their kill. Should they fail to time their plunge of several thousand feet accurately, Kindley and his comrades in the decoy formation would suffer heavily. Minutes ticked by and still the enemy did not take the bait. At last, just as the Americans were about to give up the plan, the German fighters slanted down on Kindley's flight at a steep angle. The 148th Squadron flights above had been watching carefully and "like swiftly falling arrows, true to the mark" they were on the Fokkers almost before the Germans started firing on the bottom flight. Meanwhile, pilots in the decoy flight had become aware of their danger and had turned sharply to meet the attack as the Germans leveled out behind them. The surprise from above was complete; one after another of the Germans went crashing to the earth, now very close below.[92] The fight was over in a few seconds, "and there on the ground, within a radius of one thousand yards, were seven crashed Hun planes,"[93] mute evidence to the success of a well-planned attack. Tom Moore, Jesse Creech, Field Kindley, Larry Callahan, and George Dorsey were each credited with one official kill, while Clayton Bissell, perhaps the hottest pilot in the squadron during the month of October, destroyed two.[94] Bissell, destined to be a major general and the commander of the U.S. Tenth Air Force in the Far East during World War II, ended the war with five official victories. Kindley's victim marked his twelfth confirmed kill and tied him with the now departed Springs for the squadron lead.

Although Kindley's decoy flight suffered some hits, the stunning squadron success was achieved without the loss of a single pilot. The Camel flown by Lieutenant John R. Hogan, a handsome aviator from Montclair, New Jersey, was practically shredded by bullets but managed to return to Bapaume airfield.[95] Lawrence Wyly had a forced landing with a bullet hole in his Clerget engine but returned to his home station later in the afternoon. Indeed, the destruction of seven Fokkers in one blow was a fitting *coup de grace* for the hard-fighting 148th.

On 1 November the 17th and 148th Aero Squadrons were transferred to Toul airdrome, about 150 miles east of Paris, where they were assigned to Major Charles Biddle's newly organized 4th Pursuit Group for work in the Meuse-Argonne drive. They had served brilliantly in the Somme-Albert-Cambrai area and carried with them the thanks and best wishes of the British when they were sent to Pershing. The commanding general of the Royal Air Force made this quite clear in a letter to General Mason Patrick, chief of Air Service, AEF, when he wrote:

Now that the time has come when Nos. 17 and 148 Squadrons return to you, I wish to say how magnificently they have carried out their duties during the time they have been lent to the British Aviation.

Every call has been answered by them to the highest degree, and when they have arrived with you, you will have two highly efficient squadrons filled with the offensive spirit.[96]

Unfortunately, the 17th and 148th Squadrons never got to try their spurs on the American Front. At Toul they were given Spad-13's, and before they could complete their transition work in the French-built fighter, time ran out for Kaiser Wilhelm II's war machine. Had the war lasted a little longer they would have undoubtedly "continued in the Fourth Pursuit Group the high reputation which they enjoyed in the BEF."[97]

NOTES

1. According to "Victories and Casualties" (Gorrell Histories, AS AEF, M, XXXIII), the 148th was ranked first with seventy-one; the 94th was credited with sixty-four; and the 27th and 17th tied with fifty-four victories. W. P. Taylor and F. L. Irvin, compilers, of *History of the 148th Aero Squadron,* credit the 148th with sixty-six victories, as does Robert E. Rogge, in "A History of the 148th Aero Squadron," *Air Power Historian,* July, 1962, 157. James J. Sloan, in "The 148th

American," *American Aviation Historical Society Journal,* Winter, 1959, credits the squadron with only sixty-three. See Table I.

2. Frederick M. Clapp, *A History of the 17th Aero Squadron,* 3–8.

3. Letter from William P. Taylor to author, 17 June 1964. Taylor later flew combat with the 148th Squadron.

4. Clapp, *History of the 17th,* 9–11.

5. *Ibid.,* 12.

6. *Ibid.,* 12–15.

7. *Ibid.,* 15.

8. Taylor and Irvin, *The 148th Aero Squadron,* 3.

9. *Ibid.*

10. *Ibid.,* 8–9.

11. Sloan, "148th American," *loc. cit.,* 255.

12. Rogge, "History of the 148th," *loc. cit.,* 16.

13. "History of the 148th Aero Squadron" (Gorrell Histories, AS AEF, E, XIX), 12–20.

14. Clapp, *History of the 17th,* 15.

15. Taylor and Irvin, *The 148th Aero Squadron,* 21–22.

16. Rogge, "History of the 148th," *loc. cit.,* 159. For a technical discussion of the whole problem of lubrication see David R. Winans, "World War One Aircraft Fuels and Lubricating Oils," *Cross and Cockade Journal,* Autumn, 1961, 225–39.

17. A. J. Lynch, "Interview with Leftenant Richmond Viall, 46 Squadron, RAF, 25 August 1961," *Cross and Cockade Journal,* Autumn, 1961, 243–44.

18. Rogge, "History of the 148th," *loc. cit.,* 160.

19. Taylor and Irvin, *The 148th Aero Squadron,* 21–24.

20. *Ibid.*

21. Letter from Charles L. Heater to author, 12 May 1965.

22. Combat Report, 13 July 1918, in Kindley Records File, Field E. Kindley Memorial High School, Coffeyville, Kans.

23. Telegram from Brig. Gen. E. R. Ludlow Hewitt, commander, 10th Brigade, RAF, to 148th American Aero Squadron, 13 July 1918. Kindley Records File.

24. James J. Hudson, "Captain Field E. Kindley: Arkansas' Air Ace of the First World War," *Arkansas Historical Quarterly,* Summer, 1959, 4–5.

25. *Ibid.,* 6–8.

26. Author's interview of Bruce Bently, Coffeyville, Kans., 2 January 1958.

27. Hudson, "Capt. Field Kindley," *loc. cit.,* 6–8.

28. [Grider] *War Birds: Diary of an Unknown Aviator.*

29. Combat Report, 26 June 1918, in "Combat Records, Americans with the RAF" (Gorrell Histories, AS AEF, B, XIV); William R. Puglisi, "German Army Air Aces," 227, *Cross and Cockade Journal,* Autumn, 1962, 227.

30. Taylor and Irvin, *The 148th Aero Squadron,* 21–25; see also letter from Rickenbacker to author, 19 April 1958.

31. Taylor and Irvin, *ibid.,* 24.

32. Clapp, *History of the 17th,* 24–25.

33. *Ibid.*

34. Taylor and Irvin, *The 148th Aero Squadron,* 25.

35. *Ibid.*

36. These songs are quoted in many squadron histories. The versions used here are from Leighton Brewer's *Riders of the Sky,* 111–12.

37. Combat report, 1 August 1918. All combat reports for the 17th Aero

Squadron pilots are listed in "History of the 17th Aero Squadron" (Gorrell Histories, AS AEF, E, IV).

38. Combat reports of Shearman, Spidle, and Gracie.

39. Clapp, *History of the 17th,* 29.

40. Combat reports, 3 August 1918.

41. Combat reports, 3 August 1918, cited in "History of the 148th Aero Squadron," *loc. cit.* All ensuing combat reports for pilots of the 148th are from this source.

42. Combat reports, 7 August 1918.

43. Taylor and Irvin, *The 148th Aero Squadron,* 25.

44. Francis L. "Spike" Irvin, "War Diary, 1918–1919," Irvin Collection. Sgt. Maj. Irvin was in charge of the 148th Squadron orderly room and was in a position to note most of the significant events in the unit's war career. He presently lives in Arlington, Vt.

45. Taylor and Irvin, *The 148th Aero Squadron,* 26–27.

46. "Victories and Casualties," *loc. cit.,* 44. This source lists all victories officially confirmed by the RAF; see also the combat reports for the 148th.

47. Taylor and Irvin, *The 148th Aero Squadron,* 27.

48. Combat reports, 15 August 1918.

49. "History of the 148th Aero Squadron," *loc. cit.,* 23.

50. Combat report, 18 August 1918.

51. "History of the 148th Aero Squadron," *loc. cit.,* 23–25.

52. "History of the 17th Aero Squadron," *loc. cit.*

53. *Ibid.,* 30–32.

54. Clapp, *History of the 17th,* 33–35.

55. "History of the 17th Aero Squadron," *loc. cit.,* 43–48.

56. Sloan, "148th American," *loc. cit.,* 257.

57. "History of the 17th Aero Squadron," *loc. cit.,* 57; see also combat report for Lt. J. F. Campbell, 24 August 1918.

58. Clapp, *History of the 17th,* 40–42; see also combat reports, 26 August 1918, for Snoke, Goodnow, and Dixon.

59. *Ibid.;* Miller, "Confirmed Victories," *Cross and Cockade Journal,* Spring, 1962, 58.

60. "History of the 17th Aero Squadron," *loc. cit.,* 61.

61. Miller, "Confirmed Victories," *loc. cit.,* 60. Robertson, in *Aces of the 1914–1918 War,* credits Creech with eight victories.

62. "History of the 148th Aero Squadron," *loc. cit.,* 34–35; *148th U.S. Aero Squadron Bulletin,* No. 21 (May, 1959), 3–4. This publication is edited and produced by Capt. Neil Goen, of Melbourne, Fla. Goen, a ground crew enlisted man in the 148th in France, has in recent years been secretary-treasurer of the 148th Association. Because of his tireless work, the 148th has been one of the most active of all the World War I squadron associations.

63. Hudson, "Capt. Field Kindley," *loc. cit.,* 18–19; combat reports, 2 September 1918, for Kindley, McLean, and Knox.

64. Taylor and Irvin, *The 148th Aero Squadron,* 33–34; Ralph Brady, "Cheating Death in the Skies," *148th U.S. Aero Squadron Bulletin,* No. 31 (September, 1961), 5–6.

65. Letter from Field E. Kindley to Uther Kindley, 30 September 1918, Marion Wasson Collection, Fayetteville, Ark.

66. Combat report, 6 September 1918.

67. Miller, "Confirmed Victories," *loc. cit.,* 59.

68. Taylor and Irvin, *The 148th Aero Squadron,* 30–31.

69. *Ibid.,* 35.

70. See [Grider] *Diary of an Unknown Aviator.*

71. William E. Barrett, "The War Bird Who'll Never Die," *Cavalier,* March, 1960, 31–35.

72. *Ibid.,* 33–36.

73. Combat reports for 13, 17, and 18 September 1918.

74. Combat reports, 22 September 1918.

75. Clapp, *History of the 17th,* 47.

76. Combat reports, 24 September 1918. The squadron history lists five enemy aircraft as destroyed in this battle; RAF communiqués, however, confirmed only four.

77. Combat reports, 28 September, 1918.

78. Combat report, 24 September 1918. See also Hudson, "Air Knight of the Ozarks: Captain Field E. Kindley," *American Aviation Historical Society Journal,* Winter, 1959, 233–34.

79. Combat report, 24 September 1918. The official squadron history lists seven victories in the fight. RAF communiqués credit one each to Kindley, Springs, Clay, Knox, Wyly, and Zistel, for a total of six.

80. Letter from Errol H. Zistel to author, 8 July 1964.

81. Combat report, 26 September 1918.

82. Combat report, 29 September 1918.

83. Memorandum, "A Day in France," in Kindley Records File.

84. Memorandum, "An Oak Leaf Job," in Kindley Records File.

85. *Ibid.*

86. Hudson, "Air Knight of the Ozarks," *loc. cit.,* 247–48.

87. Combat report, 27 September 1918.

88. Miller, "Confirmed Victories," *loc. cit.,* 60.

89. Taylor and Irvin, *The 148th Aero Squadron,* 41–52.

90. "History of the 148th Aero Squadron," *loc. cit.;* Irvin, "Diary," 1 October–28 October 1918.

91. Walter R. Avery, "World War I Story." This manuscript, describing Avery's escape efforts, is housed in the Avery Collection, Boca Raton, Fla.

92. Hudson, "Capt. Field Kindley," *loc. cit.,* 25–26.

93. Taylor and Irvin, *The 148th Aero Squadron.*

94. Combat report, 28 October 1918.

95. Flight logbook for John R. Hogan.

96. Letter from Gen. J. N. Salmond to Gen. Mason Patrick, quoted in Taylor and Irvin, *The 148th Aero Squadron,* 51.

97. Miller, "Last Knighthood," *loc. cit.,* 31.

XI

Service with Allied Units

SERVICE WITH THE FRENCH

ALMOST LEGENDARY in its romantic appeal in the annals of the Air Service was the Lafayette Escadrille, an organization of American volunteers who flew for France long before the United States entered the war. In the last forty-odd years, scores of books and articles, such as Arch Whitehouse's *Legion of the Lafayette* and Herbert Malloy Mason's *Lafayette Escadrille,* have kept the picture of these intrepid young daredevils bright in the public eye. Perhaps the most famous study, however, is James Norman Hall and Charles B. Nordhoff's *Lafayette Flying Corps,* a two-volume work published shortly after World War I. In their classic, Hall and Nordhoff did not limit themselves to the Lafayette Escadrille but told the story of the entire Lafayette Flying Corps, a larger organization consisting of all American volunteers in the French aviation service. A large number of these fliers were never in the Escadrille at all but flew as individuals in various French pursuit, bombardment, and observation squadrons. Since much of the activities of the Lafayette Escadrille and the Lafayette Flying Corps occurred before the American Air Service was organized in the AEF, their story will be held to a minimum in this study.

The idea of an all-American squadron in the French service seemed to have been conceived by Norman Prince, a pioneer American aviator, who arrived in Paris in January of 1915. He immediately went to work to get the French government to organize such a squadron and was soon joined in the effort by Frazier Curtis,

233

Elliott Cowdin, William Thaw, James J. Bach, and Bert Hall. The latter three, who had served in the French Foreign Legion, had transferred to aviation in December of 1914 and had already begun their flight training at Buc. Prince, Cowdin, and Curtis joined the French Air Service in March, 1915, and were sent to Pau where they were soon joined by Hall and Bach. Thaw had gone to the front with a French combat squadron with the idea of joining the others if the American Escadrille became a reality.[1]

Prince, scion of a wealthy Massachusetts family, was well equipped to carry on his crusade for the all-American unit. He graduated with honors from Harvard in 1908, and three years later took his law degree from the same university. For a short time he practiced law in Chicago, where he became interested in aviation as a sport. Much of his youth had been spent in his family's second home at Pau, France. During this time he had made many friends and had learned to speak French fluently. With these obvious advantages the twenty-seven-year-old Prince effectively pressed his case in the spring of 1915.[2]

Meanwhile, another American citizen—Dr. Edmund Gros, one of the leaders of the American Ambulance Service in France and later a major in the U.S. Air Service—was also dreaming of an American squadron. Several American volunteers had already distinguished themselves as members of the French Foreign Legion, where they did not have to relinquish their United States citizenship, and scores more were arriving in France to drive ambulances. Perhaps, as Gros reasoned, this abundant supply of eager young men would accept a more active war role as members of a flying unit. Gros joined forces with Prince, Cowdin, and others in pushing the flying squadron project. Working through a contact in the French Department of Foreign Affairs, the Americans finally convinced French officials of the advantages of the plan, and on 21 March 1916, the *Escadrille Americaine* came into being.[3]

One month later, on 20 April, the new squadron, officially designated as N 124, was sent to the front. Captain Georges Thenault, the squadron commander, and his chief assistant were French, but all of the pilots were American citizens. The first seven members of the unit were Norman Prince, William Thaw (who had transferred from Escadrille N 65), Elliott Cowdin, Bert Hall, James McConnell, Kiffen Rockwell, and Victor Chapman. Two of the original proponents of the idea were missing: James Bach, while flying with a French Escadrille, had been captured; Frazier Curtis had been injured in a flying accident. Soon the squadron ranks were filled with the likes of Raoul Lufbery, Didier Masson, Chouteau Johnson, Dudley Hill, Paul Pavelka, Clyde Balsley, and Robert L. Rockwell.[4]

Kiffen Yates Rockwell, of Asheville, North Carolina, who had joined the French Foreign Legion with his brother soon after the war started, shot down the first enemy plane credited to the *Escadrille Americaine* on 18 May 1916. While firing only four rounds he killed both the pilot and the observer and sent the German two-seater crashing into the cathedral town of Thann.[5] A French forward observation post telephoned confirmation to *Escadrille Americaine* Headquarters in Luxeuil, so the news beat Rockwell home. Thenault recommended him for the Médaille Militaire, and his brother sent to Paris for a bottle of eighty-year-old bourbon—"a treasure beyond price in France." After some discussion, "it was decided to ration the liquid gold one drink at a time to a pilot whenever he had a confirmed kill. Rockwell drained his two ounces and the bottle was put away."[6] "All Luxeuil," according to James McConnell, "smiled on Kiffen—especially the girls."[7]

From the first the *Escadrille Americaine* was a pursuit, or chassé, outfit equipped with Nieuports. Within a matter of weeks the squadron's exploits had attracted wide attention, and many Americans sought to join its ranks. It was soon evident that the unit could not accommodate all those who wished to volunteer, and this brought about the formation of the larger organization known as the Lafayette Flying Corps.

As vacancies appeared in the *Escadrille Americaine,* replacements were furnished from the corps, where Americans were attached as individuals to work with various French combat units. A committee consisting of Dr. Gros; Jarousse de Sillac, a French official; and W. K. Vanderbilt, a wealthy American then living in France, handled the selections. Vanderbilt spent much of his personal fortune in financing the project and was made honorary president of the organization.[8]

Within a short time an elaborate and smoothly operating organization was developed. The typical American aspirant reported to a

Lafayette Flying Corps official in New York who passed on his credentials, provided him with a physical examination, and sent him up for a flight aptitude test at Mineola field.

If satisfactory, he was then sent to France, where he reported to Dr. Gros, was given a second physical examination, and signed his papers of enlistment. He did not have to pledge allegiance to the French Government, so did not lose his American citizenship. If he was found to have no aptitude for flying he was released.[9]

Most of the young volunteers trained under the old Bler it system of progressing from penguins and rouleurs to more advanced aircraft on which they were breveted as qualified aviators. From the Bleroit school, the Lafayette men were usually sent for a brief preliminary course on Nieuports at Avord, thence to Pau, where they were taught to fly service-type planes. When the budding warriors finished at Pau, they were considered ready for combat and were sent to a replacement pool at Le Plessis Belleville. From this center they were assigned to squadrons at the front, in some cases to the *Escadrille Americaine,* but usually, as the corps increased in size, to one of the French combat units.[10]

In all, a total of 267 Americans enlisted in the Lafayette Flying Corps; of these, 43 were released because of illness or injuries, or were "washed out" for flying ineptness during their training days. Of the 224 remaining, 5 died of illness and 6 by accident; 15 were taken prisoner, 19 were wounded, and 51 were killed in action against the enemy. Some 180 served in combat roles with the French. Members of the LFC, which included the *Escadrille Americaine,* officially destroyed 199 enemy aircraft and claimed many more which could never be confirmed.[11]

The corps produced several brilliant fighter pilots. Ace of the organization and perhaps the best known was Raoul Lufbery, who was credited with seventeen air victories while flying with the *Escadrille Americaine.* Indeed, he must have drained Rockwell's bottle of vintage bourbon. Frank L. Baylies, of New Bedford, Massachusetts, served with both Escadrille Spa 73 and Escadrille Spa 3 (the famous *Cigonnes* or Stork squadron) and chalked up twelve confirmed kills before he died in combat with four German fighters on 17 June 1918. Baylies was the highest scoring ace to serve only with the French. Other top pursuit men, to name only a few, were

David Putnam, a twelve-victory ace killed at St. Mihiel while lead-
ing the U.S. 139th Aero Squadron; Thomas Cassady, the Spencer,
Indiana, youth who later flew with the U.S. 28th Squadron; G. De-
Freest Larner, who ended the war as an eight-victory ace with the
U.S. 103rd Squadron; and such crack fliers as Paul Baer, of Fort
Wayne, Indiana, and William T. Ponder, of Mangum, Oklahoma,
both of whom served with the U.S. 103rd.

Not all of the LFC men were pursuit pilots. Some, like Kenneth
P. Littauer, of New York City, preferred observation work. Kepi,
as his LFC comrades called Littauer, flew at the front in the old
twin-engine Caudron, "and was one of the few men who had actually flown it who could be found to praise this leisurely and vulnerable bird." Once he got a bullet through the center of his wind-
screen, a fact which qualified him for the "wind-shield with hole
attached award." That he did his work well with Escadrille C 74,
and still later as a squadron and group commander in the U.S. Air
Service, is indicated by the fact that he earned the Distinguished
Service Cross, the Croix de Guerre (with palm and star), the
Belgian Croix de Guerre, and the *Chevalier d l'Order de Leopold.*
In the words of Hall and Nordhoff, "He never asked his pilots to
undertake a difficult and important mission without himself leading
them, although as a squadron and group commander it was really
his duty to remain on the ground."[12]

Of the original seven members of the *Escadrille Americaine,* four
lost their lives while serving with the French. Victor Chapman, the
New Yorker whose great-great grandfather was John Jay, the first
chief justice of the U.S. Supreme Court, was the first to die.[13]
Prince and Kiffen Rockwell followed him a short time later. The
likeable James Roger McConnell, a graduate of the University of
Virginia and a long-time resident of France, was the last to go
down. By the end of the war, William Thaw had become a lieutenant colonel, and Elliott Cowdin had become a major in the U.S.
Air Service.

During the fall of 1916 the German ambassador to the United
States "protested that Americans were fighting with the French and
that communiqués contained allusions to an 'American *Escadrille,*'
whose planes bore the insignia of the head of a Sioux Indian in
full war-paint and feathers."[14] Since the United States was not then
at war it was deemed advisable to drop the *Escadrille Americaine,*

and for a short time the unit was simply called by its official number, N 124. A little later Dr. Gros suggested the name "Lafayette Escadrille," and this name caught the public fancy in the years following World War I.[15]

When the United States entered the war, it was decided that Americans then serving with the French would be encouraged to transfer to their own Air Service, and a program was set up to implement the change-over. In October of 1917 a board, which included Major Edmund Gros, traveled from Verdun to the English Channel, stopped at all airdromes where Americans were fighting with French combat units, and examined those who wished to transfer. A list was compiled, and the board made its recommendation on 20 October. Strangely enough, many of the Lafayette men then recommended had to have waivers before being accepted in the Air Service. Several were considered too old for flying. Major Lufbery, for example, was thirty-two years old; Captain Robert Soubiran was thirty-one. Some were plagued with rather startling physical defects. Major William Thaw had poor vision in one eye, defective hearing, and a knee injury. Captain Dudley Hill's right eye was limited to finger perception only. Whatever their physical condition, however, these men, with their long combat experience, were too valuable to lose.

By Christmas of 1917, ninety-three members of the Lafayette Flying Corps were transferred to the U.S. Air Service, while twenty-six others joined the air arm of the U.S. Navy. The remainder elected to stay with the French. As the United States had no air squadrons ready for combat in December of 1917, some of those who had accepted commissions remained temporarily with the French. On 18 February 1918, the Lafayette Escadrille became the 103rd Aero Squadron. Commanded by Major Thaw, this squadron was attached to *Groupe de Combat* 15 and continued to operate under French orders until other American units could be readied for combat duty. Seventeen of the original pilots remained in the squadron, while others were sent to new pursuit outfits then being organized at the front.[16] This scattering of experienced pilots throughout the American Air Service was tremendously important in preparing the innocent air squadrons for Chateau-Thierry, St. Mihiel, and the Meuse-Argonne campaigns coming up. The 103rd was placed under American control on 1 July 1918, and shortly thereafter Thaw was made commander of the newly organized 3rd Pursuit Group.

Americans Assigned to French Squadrons Through the G.D.E.

In the early days of 1918, the U.S. Air Service found itself with a decided surplus of trained aviators but few service-type aircraft. As these fliers could not be used in the few American squadrons being organized at the front, they had to be held in the various training schools. To relieve this congestion at the instruction centers, and at the same time to make use of the impatient airmen, the French Air Service agreed to take a number of American pursuit pilots and bombardment teams. These individuals were thus incorporated into French escadrilles at the front. In this way both services would benefit, "for the American officers would receive valuable training under fire, and the French would add to their squadrons of cocks some hard hitting American eagles. . . ."[17]

This cooperation between the American and French Air Services was accomplished through the French *Groupe des Division d'Entrainement,* better known as G.D.E., a combination finishing center and replacement depot. Nestled around G.D.E. Headquarters were several flying fields equipped to provide the most advanced instruction on each type of machine and for each type of service. After achieving a proper state of efficiency, the Americans were dispatched to the front as individuals. The G.D.E. Center was first located at Le Plessis Belleville, Oise, but after the German drive of 21 March 1918, it was moved to Generville, Eure-Et-Loire, a small town some eight miles southeast of Chartres.[18]

To improve liaison with the French, an American Aviation Post was established at Generville on 2 June 1918. This post, officially under the Chief of Training at Air Service Headquarters in Tours, was attached to the *Groupe des Division d'Entrainement* and kept close track of all American officers fighting with the French. One of its earliest commanders was Captain Pierre de Lagarde Boal.[19]

In the course of several months, 150 American flying officers were assigned to French combat units through the G.D.E. program. Of these 52 were pursuit pilots, 44 were day bombardment pilots, 47 were day bombardment observers, 2 were night bombardment pilots, 2 were night bombardment observers, and the remainder were assigned to reconnaissance outfits. These aviators flew over 5,000 hours, engaged in over 200 combats, and made 1,020 bombing missions. Ten were killed or missing in action, two were taken prisoners, and nine others were wounded in combat. In contrast to this they destroyed fifty-one enemy planes and three balloons, all of which were confirmed by the French government.[20]

That the Americans fought well with their French comrades is indicated by the fact they earned four Distinguished Service Crosses, one Legion of Honor, and more than a score of Croix de Guerre awards. The following report tells the story of how two flying officers won their DSC's.

On the 9th of August 1918, the American day bombardment team of 1st Lt. C. Raymond Blake, pilot, and 2nd Lt. Earl W. Porter, observer, while on a bombing expedition at low altitude, was attacked by five enemy planes. Outnumbered and cut off from their group, they put up a desperate and gallant fire against the Germans. Their machine was riddled with bullets, and many of the controls cut, but Lieut. Blake skillfully kept it in action, while they shot down one of their adversaries and evaded the rest. Upon landing, Lieut. Porter was almost unconscious. It was found that he had been shot through the jaw, the bullet passing through his neck and lodging in his chest, in the early moments of the combat; but he had given his pilot no indication of this, and had continued firing, bringing down a German plane, until the blood from another wound filled his goggles and blinded him.[21]

The G.D.E. program continued in operation until the Armistice. During the fall of 1918, however, the American Air Service needed all available flying officers for its own vastly expanded combat effort, and by degrees it began to withdraw Americans operating with the French. By November of 1918, the G.D.E. program had practically ceased to exist.

Americans Assigned to French Squadrons through AEF Headquarters

In addition to those pilots and observers sent to the French front through G.D.E., 174 American observers were attached to various French observation squadrons through the Aeronautical Section of the French Mission in General Headquarters, AEF. The purpose of this move was to provide observers with war flying experience before their assignment to active American squadrons. Such an approach was necessary because of the meager training facilities which existed in the AEF during the winter and spring of 1917–1918. At that time the school for observation training at the 2nd Aviation Instruction Center at Tours was just being organized, as was the I Corps Aeronautical School at Gondrecourt.[22] Further, the finishing schools at Chatillon, Souge, Meucon, and Coetquidan were far from operational. The problem of training was even more complicated by the transfer of a large number of field artillery observers to the Air Service. None of these officers had had any air observation training.[23]

In the absence of any real observation school, a French squadron was withdrawn from the front and sent to Le Valdahon to instruct American air observers. When the preliminary course was completed, arrangements were made to continue their training in French squadrons on the front. The first of these observers was attached to French combat units on 20 January 1918, and the experiment proved to be an immediate success. Within a short time an agreement was worked out whereby approximately eighty places were made available in French escadrilles for American observers.[24]

The average stay with the French was approximately one month, though several remained much longer. Some Americans had outstanding records with the French. For example, Lieutenant S. W. Thompson, of White Plains, Missouri, shot down a German plane while on a volunteer mission with Breguet-123, and Lieutenant Fred Tillman, who eventually became operations officer of the American III Corps Observation Group, won the DSC, Legion of Honor, and Croix de Guerre (with palm).[25]

In spite of poor weather conditions during the late winter and early spring, the Americans averaged some ten hours of combat time while with the French. In addition to combat missions, other flying was carried on in liaison exercises with ground troops; this phase of work was "particularly important since French observation units, during the summer of 1917, had begun to establish very intimate relations with the Infantry and Artillery of the organizations to which they were attached."[26] Most of these American observers were eventually transferred to the 1st, 12th, 88th, and 91st American Squadrons then being organized in the Toul sector of the front. Consequently, these new units were much better prepared for active operations than might have been expected. As one writer stated: "The inexperience of the pilots was more than compensated for by the war experience that the observers had gained with the French."[27]

The number of American observers attached to the French for training increased steadily until mid-April, 1918, at which time eighty-eight were working with combat escadrilles. By 15 June, this number had decreased to seventy-one, and by 30 July the number was negligible. The last American observer was transferred from the French Air Service on 21 September. After August, not only were there not enough observers to fill the reserved spaces offered by the French, but there were not enough to keep American squadrons on the front up to their alloted strength.[28]

AMERICANS ASSIGNED TO ITALIAN SQUADRONS

The story of those Americans who served with Italian air squadrons in the Mediterranean area was, to a large extent, the story of Fiorello H. La Guardia. Undoubtedly one of the most colorful individuals ever to enliven the American political scene, La Guardia was an obscure lawyer serving his first term in the U.S. House of Representatives when President Wilson asked for a Declaration of War in April, 1917. Eager for action, the irrepressible "Little Flower" hurried to a Washington recruiting station early in July to apply for duty with the Air Service.*

La Guardia did not identify himself as a congressman from New York, and the recruiting people were not much interested in lawyers. But they were interested in anyone who knew how to fly, and the short, powerfully built La Guardia could make such a claim. Two years before, he had taken flight lessons at the Giuseppi Ballanca Flying School at Mineola, Long Island, and had managed to learn enough to solo. All this was in his favor when he applied for a direct commission in the infant air arm of the Army.[30]

When the Air Service discovered that the talkative La Guardia was a congressman and could speak Italian fluently, he was sent immediately to Major Benjamin D. Foulois, who was then chief of Air Service, with headquarters in Washington. Foulois told him of

---

* Finding that some of his constituents opposed the draft, Congressman La Guardia had promised that if he voted for conscription he would also join the service. Perhaps this had something to do with his early enlistment.[29]

plans being made to train pilots in Italy. Major R. C. Bolling had already been sent to Europe to collect technical information, buy aircraft, and arrange for the training of some American pilots overseas. Certainly, La Guardia would be a good man to help with the program in Italy.[31] A few days later the congressman from New York's 14th District received his commission as a first lieutenant and was sent to Mineola, where American personnel were being assembled for overseas shipment. There La Guardia, now a captain, helped Captain Leslie MacDill prepare for the transfer of a group of flying cadets to Europe.[32]

Strangely enough, La Guardia did not resign his seat in the House of Representatives when he reported for active duty. This dual arrangement, obviously, gave him far more authority and power than his military rank alone could command and led to some rather interesting incidents. For example, Captain La Guardia arranged first-class accommodations for all of MacDill's party on the Cunard liner *Carmenia*. After everyone was on the ship, the senior army officer aboard, a colonel, ordered all enlisted men down to the steerage. This included not only clerks but also cadets, for under the regulations of the time only commissioned officers went first-class. Putting on his second hat, Congressman La Guardia had a talk with the colonel, and the cadets stayed in first-class quarters.[33]

When the *Carmenia* arrived in England the contingent of cadets, soon to be identified as the war birds (made famous by Elliott Springs, John MacGavock Grider, Laurence Callahan, and others), was sent to British flying schools, but Captain La Guardia went to Paris. In France the Captain-congressman joined a second group of cadets bound for the Italian flying school at Foggia, 150 miles southeast of Rome. To Fiorello "it was something of a homecoming, for Foggia was his father's birthplace."[34]

Forty-six American cadets, under the command of Major William Ord Ryan, were already undergoing pilot training on Farman biplane pushers when La Guardia's detachment arrived in mid-October, 1917. Fiorello and his group of cadets immediately began the course, which started

with each student being given a ten-minute joy ride. Afterward the student flew with an Italian instructor in a dual-control plane until he was ready to solo. He then flew gyros to the left and gyros to the right, practicing quarter turns in a glide, and learned to execute various other maneuvers before finishing this phase of preliminary training with an "alinemento," consisting of a climb to 3,000 feet, a glide to 1,800 feet with the motor off, two figure "8's" at 1,800 with the motor on, and a double half-turn while gliding into the field. The student was then ready for his first brevet test, in which he was required to do two figure "8's" at 1,500 feet and then fly for forty-five minutes while maintaining a constant altitude of 3,000 feet. If he passed the test he was an "aviator."[35]

In the next phase of his training the student was required to complete a series of tests at high altitudes and land at a "strange airdrome." Finally, the trainee was required to take the "raid test" consisting of two cross-country flights over different triangular courses in one day. With this successfully accomplished, the cadet was rated a "Military Aviator" and was commissioned a second lieutenant. Because of extremely bad weather, La Guardia had some difficulty on his "raid test." On the second leg of the triangle the wind forced him off course and beyond the limits of his map. In attempting a landing to orient himself he crashed his Farman trainer. Although not seriously hurt he was forced to spend several days in the hospital.

Though only the second-ranking officer at Foggia, La Guardia, because of his congressional position and his Italian background, virtually took over American policy making in Italy. His affinity for breaking, or at least stretching, regulations kept the Air Service Headquarters in Tours in constant turmoil. When the food provided by the Italians proved to be bad, the aggressive little captain simply hired a caterer to feed the American cadets. When the American Quartermaster in the AEF received the bills for these unusual services he promptly summoned Captain La Guardia to Tours to explain. On arriving at headquarters, La Guardia was taken before a general, who charged him with breaking regulations. Captain La Guardia advised changing the regulations. In the outburst which followed, the general uttered something to the effect that the regulations were based upon law, whereupon La Guardia shot back that he would have Congress change the law. At this point an aide intervened to explain who the exasperating little captain really was. Congressman La Guardia was now given a seat and the conversation continued in a more friendly atmosphere.[36]

Whatever his Air Service superiors may have thought of him, the dynamic La Guardia won the hearts and friendship of the Italian people. Whenever his administrative duties allowed, he traveled to Rome, Turin, Milan, or Naples, making speeches to explain Wilson's war aims or urging the Italians to a greater war effort.[37] It is safe to say that the "Little Flower," who would one day be the mayor of New York City, did more than anyone else to harmonize relationships between the two nations.

Early in April, 1918, La Guardia arranged to have American pursuit pilots trained in aerial gunnery at Furbara, near Civitavecchia, on the coast a few miles north of Rome. The first class of twenty-five students entered the school on 24 April 1918, but because of a shortage of aircraft and other difficulties, the program was dropped in late September. Only fifty pilots received their gunnery instruction at Furbara.[38]

A plan for giving American pilots advanced training in Caproni bombers proved more successful. In this program, conducted by Italian instructors at Foggia, the student started with the three-engine, CA-350, and then moved up to the more powerful CA-450 or CA-600. One of the American pilots, Lieutenant Frederick K. Weyerhaeuser, a Yale graduate and heir to a lumber empire, described some of the problems associated with the Caproni:

The big Fiat motor on the 600's . . . had the bad habit of catching fire when throttled down for glides or descents. The principal trick to flying a Caproni was getting off the ground. You had three throttles and would start opening the two side motors little by little until the plane had good speed on the ground. Sometimes the rear motor would stop without your knowing it, while you were getting the side motors open; which could of course be mighty serious if you had a load of bombs in a small field.[39]

Most of the work in the huge CA-600 took place at Malpensa, an Italian school northeast of Milan. By the end of the war over seventy-five Americans had qualified in the big trimotor Caproni.

During the spring of 1918, United States–Italian relations were strained over the disposition of American pilots trained in Italy. In arranging for their training, the U.S. government had made it quite clear that the fliers would remain under American control, and upon completion of their training they would be assigned wherever needed by American squadrons. After several pilots trained in Italy were sent north to France for duty, the Italians mounted a campaign to have the graduates assigned to the Italian front. Also, they insisted that ground troops be sent to fight in northern Italy against the Austrians; indeed, Italian morale had been low since the Caporetto disaster of the previous fall. American policy, however, was to keep Americans together for operations on the Western front.[40]

Although they were not enthusiastic about this policy, the Italian high command had known about it from the beginning. Many Italian airmen at Foggia, however, had believed that they were training the Americans for service in Italian squadrons, and were disillusioned and disappointed when the graduates were sent to France for war duty. Their enthusiasm consequently declined, and for a time the training program lagged. Several Americans in Italy were sympathetic to the Italian request, and La Guardia worked hard to get permission to use some of the bombardment pilots on the Italian front. Finally, on 23 May 1918, General Pershing approved a plan whereby pilots then in Italy might be placed temporarily in Italian squadrons to complete their training through actual combat. His approval was given only, however, with the understanding that the fliers could be withdrawn from the Italian front at any time they were needed by American squadrons in France.[41]

On 20 June 1918, eighteen pilots trained at Foggia and led by Captain La Guardia arrived at Padua on the Italian front and were assigned to the various *squadriglias* of the 4th and 14th Bombardment Groups. These pilots did not have time to unpack their bags before they flew their first mission, for within a few hours of their arrival at Padua the entire detachment went over the lines in an attack on an enemy troop concentration at Falze di Piave. On the raid, each American was paired with an Italian pilot, and "excellent results were obtained, all machines reached their objectives, and many hits were made." Lieutenant Gilbert P. Bogert, of Glen Ridge, New Jersey, had one engine shot out of commission but managed to limp back to the Padua airdrome. Lieutenant Clarence M. Young, of Des Moines, Iowa, and his Italian crew failed to return from the mission, and it was later learned they had been forced down a short distance inside Austrian lines.[42] In a recent letter, Young, presently a vice-president of Pan American World Airways, described the flight that marked the end of his combat career with the Italian Air Force:

The plane which was assigned to me seemingly was not functioning normally because we could not climb to the prescribed altitude, nor could we maintain the same speed as the other aircraft. As a result we were behind and below the group as we crossed the lines, thus offering a wide-open invitation to the anti-aircraft gunners on the ground. They took advantage of it and succeeded in disabling our aircraft. We fell out of control for some distance, finally getting the plane righted but without power. We glided toward the Italian lines but we ran out of altitude and were forced to make a landing in a mud flat on the Austrian side of the Piave River. We were interned as prisoners of war, and stuck for the duration.[43]

A day or so after the Falze di Piave raid, Captain La Guardia returned to his administrative duties in Rome. From his headquarters there he was able to carry out diplomatic and public relations assignment and at the same time retain administrative control over the pilots at the front. The latter responsibility was difficult to handle from such a distance, and on 8 August, La Guardia, recently promoted to major, turned the Rome office over to Major Robert Glendinning and returned to the front. At Padua he set up, and took command of, a combat division to which all American pilots were assigned for administrative purposes. For operational control the pilots were attached to Italian bombardment *squadriglias* based in the Padua and Verona area. Seventeen Americans were assigned to the naval station at Poggia Renatico.[44]

Additional detachments of American aviators continued to arrive on the Italian war front. Nearly one hundred pilots served in the battle area, with a maximum at any one time being fifty-eight. Upon arrival at the front each pilot was paired with a veteran Italian pilot for a few flights. Then he was given command of a Caproni and an Italian crew for combat. In all, Americans took part in sixty-five bombardment missions, mostly at night, and flew 587 hours over the lines. Their principal targets were troop concentrations, munitions dumps, airfields, bridges, and railroad centers, but occasionally they were asked to land far behind the Austrian lines to deliver propaganda material, carrier pigeons, and supplies for Italian agents.[45]

Usually only two or three Caproni giants were dispatched on a mission, but on some operations much larger formations were used. On 17 July 1918, no less than fifty three-engine bombers and one hundred pursuit planes attacked the big Austrian naval base at Pola, across the Adriatic some sixty miles south of Trieste. Six Americans, Lieutenants Willie S. Fitch, Gilbert Bogert, Morton Downs, Raymond P. Baldwin, Donald G. Frost, and Harold F. Holtz, made the three and one-half hour flight.* Despite the mist over the target and heavy antiaircraft fire, the attack was successful, and all planes returned safely.[46]

Perhaps the most destructive raid participated in by American pilots in Italy was the 13 September strike against the Austrian air-field at Pergine, the home station of about eighty enemy fighters. The objective of the seventeen Caproni bombers on the mission was to draw the Austrians into the air where they might be engaged by a large number of British and Italian pursuits. None of the Austrians took off to intercept the formation, with the result the bombers caused "horrible destruction to the field." Several of the Capronis suffered heavy damage from ground fire, but all were able to return to their base.[47]

Early in October, Major La Guardia was recalled to the United States, and Lieutenant John W. Lowman assumed command of the combat division. During October and early November, American pilots flew numerous missions in the Asiago, the Grappa, and the Piave River sectors. With a raid against Palmonova on 2 November, only hours before Austria quit the war, American activities were concluded, and American pilots were rapidly withdrawn from Italy.[48]

In a little over four months of duty on the Italian front American pilots had destroyed three enemy planes. Lieutenant Alexander M. Craig shot down an Austrian scout on 24 June, only four days after the first American arrived at Padua. The other two were destroyed by Lieutenants James L. Bahl, Jr., and Dewitt Coleman, flying in the same plane on 27 October. In the vicinity of Vittorio Veneto, the American pilots were attacked by five enemy pursuit planes and managed to shoot down two before their own plane plunged to the earth in flames. Bahl and Coleman, the only American fliers

---

* According to Gilbert Bogert, only Lts. Fitch, Holtz, Downs, Bogert, and Paton MacGilvary made the flight. See letter from Gilbert P. Bogert to author, 8 October 1965.

killed in combat in Italy, were posthumously awarded the Italian Medal of Valor.*

SERVICE WITH THE BRITISH

In retaliation for the bombardment of London and various other English cities by German Gothas and Zeppelins, the British government, in the spring of 1918, decided upon an active strategic bombing program of their own. The result of this decision was the formation of the Independent Air Force operating directly under the Air Ministry in London and commanded by Major General Sir Hugh Trenchard. The hard hitting Trenchard, affectionately known as "Boom" by those who served under him, had "boomed" for such a force for several months. "The war can drag out indefinitely if we continue to hurl our weight against the German Army in the field," he had argued.

It can be won quickly by striking at the heart of that army through a relentless attack on its sources of supply. We have to have both day and night bombardment squadrons, with probably the greater number for day work. It is necessary that the enemy must always fear attack during all the twenty-four hours. If he does, he has to concentrate men and equipment constantly to repel attacks that may come to him at any hour. To tie up so much equipment and so many men in defense against possible attack is almost as great a feat as to destroy these men and equipment.[50]

It is little wonder that Billy Mitchell had been much impressed with the dynamic Englishman's strategic thinking during his visit in May of 1917.

During the fall of 1917 British and American officials discussed the possibility of a joint bombing program. These talks resulted, on 6 February 1918, in General Pershing's pledging of the greatest possible cooperation between American aviation and units of the Royal Air Force in the Toul-Nancy area.[51] Although the Independent Air Force had not yet been formed, this date may be said to have inaugurated American cooperation with that force.

Trenchard went to Nancy and organized the Independent Air Force on 5 June 1918. It was to be a tough organization made up

* Forty-one Americans, including La Guardia, received the Italian *Croix di Guerra,* and several administrative personnel were awarded the *Corona d'Italia.*[49]

of men who had been warned in advance that they were undertaking one of the most dangerous jobs of the war. Applications were submitted to Trenchard from volunteers who wanted to transfer from the regular air services to the IAF. He accepted those for whom he could provide planes. Although Trenchard asked for sixty squadrons, his strategic force never exceeded ten squadrons, but with it there came into being the modern concept of air power, and had the conflict lasted a few months longer, the airplane might have proved to be a decisive factor.

Individual American pilots and observers served in Trenchard's Independent Air Force almost from its beginning in June of 1918. There were three general classifications of Americans who served with this organization. Some were sent from the American forces in France to observe the methods used by the British without actual service over the lines. A second group was sent from English flying schools to day bombardment squadrons to be used in active service with the British until their services were needed by their own forces. This class was subject to immediate release after two months of active duty with the IAF. Fliers in the third classification were assigned to Independent Air Force night bombardment squadrons and were to remain until they were efficient enough to act as instructors to Americans in that branch, especially in Handley-Page machines. In all, thirty-six flying officers attached to the IAF under the last two classifications flew combat missions over enemy territory; of them, eighteen were either killed, wounded, or captured.[52]

In keeping with British policy, American pilots attached to the Independent Air Force were required to undergo a two-week indoctrination period before engaging in actual combat. During this interlude the newcomer practiced formation flying, studied maps and intelligence reports, and in general became acquainted with the tactics and bombing techniques employed by the unit to which he was attached. When the unit commander was convinced that the new pilot was ready for action, he was, under normal circumstances, paired with a veteran observer for his maiden operational flight. On his first raid he usually flew in a rear or wing position— not because this position was easiest to fly, but because it was less dangerous to the over-all formation should he make a mistake.

In July of 1918 the IAF consisted of three day bombardment and three night bombardment squadrons. Two of the day bombing units were equipped with DH-9's and the third one used DH-4's, powered by 275-h.p. Rolls-Royce engines. One of the night bombing squadrons was still operating with ancient FE-2D pushers, while the other two were equipped with the big twin-engine Handley-Page bombers. All six flew missions deep into German territory. During the last several months of the war the IAF made both day and night raids on Cologne, Frankfort, Darmstadt, Mannheim, Ludwigshafen, Stuttgart, Treves, and other industrial centers throughout the Rhine Valley and the Metz-Thionville area. Some of these flights were as much as 150 miles behind the nearest Allied lines and required four and one-half hours to complete.[53]

Lieutenant W. D. Dietgen was the first American pilot to serve with Trenchard's strategic force when he was assigned to the DH-9-flying 99 Squadron early in June, 1918. He was also the first American casualty when he was shot down on his first raid on 30 June.[54] By the end of July Americans were scattered throughout the IAF. Some ten pilots and three observers were working with night bombardment squadrons, but the majority were attached to the day bombing units.[55]

Since most German pursuit units were based very near the front lines, the early bombing raids in the Rhine area ran into relatively light opposition. The German fighters encountered generally made headlong attacks which the bombing formations combated effectively by going "into a circle, each on the other's tail." "This," according to one American participant, "seemed to give us the most effective use of the fixed Vickers gun mounted in front and the moveable Lewis gun with its 360° sweep in the hands of our observers."[56]

By the end of July the German Air Force was concentrating larger pursuit forces in the areas around the big industrial centers, and IAF casualties increased greatly as a result. At approximately the same time there was a marked change in German fighter tactics. Now pursuit pilots would harass the bombing formations from just outside effective firing range, thus seeking to induce the bomber crews to waste ammunition and fuel. In all too many cases the teasing was effective with the bomber squadrons becoming sitting ducks for the next German formation further along the route.[57]

Before the change in German pursuit tactics, an IAF squadron might lose one or two planes out of a twelve-ship formation. In late

July and August it was not uncommon for a squadron to lose half of its machines on a raid into the Rhine Valley. On 22 August, only two of a twelve-ship formation from 104 Squadron returned from a strike against the Mercedes plant in Mannheim.[58]

On that disastrous August day twelve DH-9's, organized as two flights and flying what was known as a double-diamond formation, took off from their Nancy airdrome at dawn. Two American pilots, Lieutenants Horace P. Wells and Linn D. Merrill, were flying wing positions in the second flight. Almost an hour was consumed as the heavily laden De Havillands circled Nancy, struggling to reach the 12,000 foot altitude necessary for the mission. With the bombing altitude finally achieved, the formation set course for the northeast and the Rhine Valley. Within minutes the bombers were under heavy fighter attack, and the two six-ship flights became somewhat separated. By the time the DH-9's had reached Karlsruhe on the Rhine the rearmost flight had dwindled to three aircraft—the Deputy Flight Commander Searle, a South African; and the two Americans. Wells and Merrill crowded close to Searle's lead plane, while their observers kept up a constant fire against nearly a score of attacking Fokkers.

With the formation decimated by the steady pursuit attack and with the weather ahead toward Mannheim becoming "soupy," the survivors were ordered to drop their bombs on a secondary target in the city of Karlsruhe and turn back. Although the battered squadron experienced intense antiaircraft fire over the city, no hits were suffered, and for the moment the fighters seemed to relax their pressure. Then, just as the Allied airmen had come to believe that they might get back to Nancy without further bloodshed, the sky suddenly filled with "what seemed like hundreds of fighters." Most of them concentrated on the three bullet-riddled ships in the rear flight. Searle was hit and went spinning down out of control, and Merrill disappeared leaving only Wells and his observer, Lieutenant John Redfield, of Montclair, New Jersey, to fight alone.[59]

With the odds now overwhelmingly against them, Wells and Redfield fought desperately. Wells described those last moments in the following words:

At that moment it wasn't a question of what you are going to get, or even if you are going to get it. It's just a question of when, and a hope and a prayer that it isn't a fire-ball. I continued evasive flying. They came at me from different angles. Jack was still going full out with his Lewis gun. While those in front engaged my attention one or two would slip upon my tail and let fly. Finally we got it. The first direct attack was two short bursts, and strangely enough, with my evasive flying timed with the bursts, he clipped one flying wire on each side of the plane. . . . The second burst went between my legs. Some bullets became imbedded in the sand cushion I was sitting on. This burst caught my radiator, oil tank and gas tank, all in a line, and we were enveloped in black fumes immediately. But good old Jack, who incidentally had been severely wounded in the left leg, seeing the trouble reached down, got his Pyrene fire extinguisher and reached clear around the side saying, "Wellsey, don't you want the fire extinguisher?" I said "No, I don't think we need it." We finally blew it out and looked around for some place to land. My first inclination was to get to hell away from there and go clear out in the sticks somewhere and try to run for it. Then it came to me that such was a foolish thought since Jack wouldn't be able to go. So we looked for something safe. I looked for Red Cross markings, hospitals, anything I could find.[60]

At that moment Wells spotted a huge Zeppelin airdrome directly below and immediately began a landing approach.

Meanwhile one of the enemy fighters escorted the DH-9 down— firing an occasional warning burst to prevent the American from changing his mind. The warning was unnecessary, for with his observer badly hurt Wells had no intention of attempting an escape. Within minutes the De Havilland settled gently in the middle of the big field at Baden-Baden, and with hundreds of German workers (the airdrome was a salvage depot) looking on, the Americans were taken prisoners.*

Several other Americans compiled distinguished records with the IAF. Lieutenant Linn D. Merrill, who had miraculously survived the 22 August disaster, was made a flight commander in 104 Squadron after only eight missions. At the time he was the senior surviving pilot. During his three months with 55 Squadron, Lieutenant P. M. Payson flew fourteen missions against such targets as Frankfort, Koblenz, and Stuttgart. In all, he spent sixty-four hours over German territory. Lieutenant C. L. Heater destroyed two enemy

---

* John Redfield's wounds were dressed immediately by a German doctor stationed at the Zeppelin base. Wells was introduced to the German fighter pilot who had forced him down. The latter apologized for having been forced to wound either of the Americans.[61]

aircraft while making thirteen long-distance raids with the same squadron and was awarded the British Distinguished Flying Cross. Early in September Heater was returned to the American Air Service, and shortly after St. Mihiel he took command of the 11th Day Bombardment Squadron. Still another young American who distinguished himself with Trenchard's forces was Lieutenant P. Sutherland. Although wounded in both arms and the right hand and bleeding profusely from a leg wound, Sutherland, an observer, shot down two enemy planes over the Rhine. He, too, won the British DFC.[62]

Eventually most of the surviving day bombardment fliers returned to the American Air Service and positions of leadership in the rapid build-up in bombardment aviation during the autumn of 1918. Although a dozen pilots and observers gained valuable experience with IAF night bombardment units, no American night bombing squadron was ready for combat at the time of Armistice. Despite the fact that the United States had fabricated parts for 101 Handley-Page aircraft and delivered them to England, few of the big bombers had been assembled by the end of the war. Had the conflict lasted until the middle of 1919, several squadrons of strategic bombers would have probably been in operation.[63]

In addition to the Americans who served with Trenchard's Independent Air Force, some 216 Air Service flying officers served with the various Royal Air Force squadrons as individuals. This arrangement was advantageous to both countries in the spring of 1918. The United States simply did not have room for these airmen in her few squadrons then in active operations. On the other hand, Britain could use the fresh American aviators to ease her own pilot shortage. Practically all of these fliers had been trained in British schools, so the transition to RAF service outfits was relatively easy. Most of the Americans were assigned to pursuit units, but a few were sent to bombardment and observation squadrons.[64]

The first American Air Service pilots were posted to British combat outfits in March of 1918.* During each succeeding month more Americans were gradually added to this initial force, the maximum number of forty-three being assigned in May. On 21 July it was

* These men consisted of the pilots of those squadrons (such as the 17th, 22nd, 28th, and 148th) which were at that time divided into flights for service and training with the British.

agreed that those Americans still serving with British squadrons (some eighty-eight had already been withdrawn and assigned to the 17th and 148th American Squadrons) should be automatically transferred to the American front two months after being posted to the RAF. The first pilots withdrawn under the July agreement were ordered to the American front on 12 September.

On 28 May 1918, Lieutenant Bennett Oliver, then serving with 84 Squadron, RAF, and who later flew with the 148th American, shot down a German Albatros to score the first victory achieved by an Air Service pilot attached to the British.[65] In all, the 216 pilots who served with the RAF officially destroyed 225 enemy aircraft while suffering 71 battle casualties. Among those who served at least a portion of their combat time with British squadrons were such men as George Vaughn, Elliott Springs, Field Kindley, and Clayton Bissell, but the pilot scoring the most victories while actually assigned to a British unit was Reed G. Landis, of Ottawa, Illinois. This strong-willed son of the famous Judge Kenesaw Mountain Landis* was one of the "orphans" who trained in England and who was lent to the British in the spring of 1918. He spent most of his active career with 40 Squadron, RAF, where he destroyed nine enemy planes and one enemy balloon. In September he was made commander of the U.S. 25th Aero Squadron. This unit, scheduled to fly S.E.-5's, did not get into action until 10 November, one day before the end of the war. Consequently, Landis had no real opportunity to add to the score he had run up with the British.[66]

---

* Judge Landis was perhaps best known as the commissioner of Baseball, having taken that post after the "Black Sox" scandal of 1919.

NOTES

1. Juliette Hennessy, "The Lafayette Escadrille—Past and Present," *Air Power Historian,* July, 1957, 150–51.

2. H. Hugh Wynne, "Escadrille Lafayette," *Cross and Cockade Journal,* Spring, 1961, 45.

3. Hennessy, "The Lafayette Escadrille," *loc. cit.,* 151.

4. Whitehouse, *Legion of the Lafayette,* 5–9.

5. *Ibid.,* 40.

6. Mason, *Lafayette Escadrille,* 63.

7. *Ibid.*

8. Edmund Gros, compiler, "A Brief History of the Lafayette Flying Corps" (Gorrell Histories, AS AEF, 1918, B, XII), 3–18.

9. Hennessy, "The Lafayette Escadrille," *loc. cit.*, 152.

10. *Ibid.*, 152–53.

11. *Ibid.*, 154.

12. Hall and Nordhoff, *Lafayette Flying Corps*, 315–18.

13. Wynne, "Escadrille Lafayette," *loc. cit.*, 43.

14. Hennessy, "The Lafayette Escadrille," *loc. cit.*, 154–55.

15. *Ibid.*

16. Gros, "Brief History of the LFC," *loc. cit.*, 5–20.

17. "History of American Aviation, G.D.E." (Gorrell Histories, AS AEF, B, XII), 1.

18. Director of Air Service, "Brief History of Air Service, AEF," 22.

19. "American Aviation, G.D.E.," *loc. cit.*, 1–2.

20. Director of Air Service, "Brief History," 22.

21. "American Aviation, G.D.E.," *loc. cit.*, 2–3.

22. Director of Air Service, "Brief History," 22.

23. Patrick, *Report to Commander-in-Chief*, 263.

24. Director of Air Service, "Brief History," 22–23; letter from Leland Carver to author, 26 January 1965.

25. Capt. F. W. Zinn, "Historical Notes on American Observers Attached to French Observation Squadron" (Gorrell Histories, AS AEF, B, XII), 17–20.

26. Director of Air Service, "Brief History," 23.

27. Zinn, "Observers Attached to French," *loc. cit.*, 4.

28. Director of Air Service, "Brief History," 23.

29. Fiorello H. La Guardia, *The Making of an Insurgent. An Autobiography, 1882–1919*, 161–65.

30. Maurer Maurer, "Flying with Fiorello: The U.S. Air Service in Italy, 1917–1918," *Air Power Historian*, October, 1964, 113.

31. *Ibid.*

32. La Guardia, *Making of an Insurgent*, 165–67.

33. *Ibid.*, 168.

34. Maurer, "Flying with Fiorello," *loc. cit.*, 113.

35. *Ibid.*, 114.

36. *Ibid.*

37. La Guardia, *Making of an Insurgent*, 183–85.

38. Maurer, "Flying with Fiorello," *loc. cit.*, 115.

39. F. K. Weyerhaeuser, "War Experiences, 1917–1918," 11. This is an unpublished manuscript at the Weyerhaeuser Co., St. Paul, Minn. The designations for the Caproni bombers were taken from the total horsepower of the three engines; for example, the CA-600 had three 200-h.p. engines.

40. See correspondence relating to placing American fliers on the Italian front in "History of Air Service Activities in Italy and American Pilots on the Italian Front" (Gorrell Histories, AS AEF, 1918, B, I), 82–95.

41. *Ibid.*, 82–95.

42. *Ibid.*, 2. A photostat of this document is in the Caproni Collection of the USAF HD Archives. See also letter from Gilbert P. Bogert to author, 28 October 1965.

43. Letter from Clarence M. Young to author, 30 September 1965.

44. Director of Air Service, "Brief History," 24–25.

45. *Ibid.* See also Willis Fitch, *Wings in the Night*.

46. "Air Service Activities in Italy," *loc. cit.*, 4–5.

47. *Ibid.*

48. *Ibid.*

49. Maurer, "Flying with Fiorello," *loc. cit.,* 4–5.

50. Quoted in William E. Barrett, *The First War Planes,* 140.

51. Letter from Pershing to Trenchard, 6 February 1918, in "Development of Air Service in England" (Gorrell Histories, AS AEF, B, II), 54.

52. "American Flying Personnel With the Independent Force, RAF" (Gorrell Histories, AS AEF, 1918, B, XII), 6.

53. *Ibid.,* 7–8.

54. *Ibid.,* 9–10.

55. "Report on Air Service Flying Training Depot in England" (Gorrell Histories, AS AEF, B, IV), 1–10.

56. "An Interview with Horace P. Wells," *Cross and Cockade Journal,* Winter, 1960, 86.

57. *Ibid.*

58. *Ibid.*

59. *Ibid.,* 87–88.

60. *Ibid.,* 88.

61. *Ibid.*

62. "American Personnel with the Independent Force," *loc. cit.,* 11–12.

63. Gorrell, *America's Effort,* 34.

64. "Air Service History, Headquarters, American Air Service With the B.E.F." (Gorrell Histories, AS AEF, B, XII), 10–12.

65. *Ibid.*

66. *Ibid.,* 24–25.

XII

Autumn Crescendo: The Meuse-Argonne

EARLY on the morning of 26 September 1918, the Meuse-Argonne offensive, the final campaign of World War I, was launched. An ear-splitting three-hour artillery barrage opened the attack, and at 5:30 A.M. the American infantry moved forward into No-Man's Land. The terrain through which the attack was to be made favored the German defenders. On the east were the rugged heights of the Meuse River; on the west was the high, rugged, and heavily wooded Argonne Forest. In the center of the twenty-mile front a ridge running roughly north and south dominated the valley of the Meuse on the east and the valley of the Aire River to the west. On this ridge were the German strong points of Montfaucon, Cunel, and Berricourt, which Pershing's three army corps would have to seize before any real progress could be made. Behind the whole front the enemy had organized a defense in depth. That defense, manned by elements of the German Third and Fifth Armies, comprised three well-established defense lines and a partially completed fourth, further to the rear, on ground of great natural strength. Both enemy flanks were well protected by the natural terrain. Consequently, the American Commander had no alternative but to move straight ahead against the German positions.

Strong as this defense system was, Pershing hoped that the weight of his initial drive would crash through the first three German lines without loss of momentum and thus open up the enemy's flanks to attack. Even if early success did not attend his first effort, he planned to pound away with his force of nearly one-half million men (eventually he would have over a million troops) until he had crossed the Meuse to the west of Sedan and cut the Sedan-Mézières railroad. British and French forces on his flanks would also go on the offensive at the same time the American First Army made its move.

The American Commander's hopes for an early victory were not entirely realized. The assault divisions promptly took the enemy's forward positions and at the end of the first day had made excellent progress except at two places, Montfaucon and the Argonne Forest. In the next few days the first two German defense lines were captured, but the advance ground to a halt in front of the third, upsetting Pershing's hopes for a quick breakthrough. The reasons for the collapse of this first phase of the campaign, other than stubborn enemy resistance, were many. Tank support proved inadequate, and supply broke down because of congestion and poor roads. Perhaps more important was the inexperience of several of the assault divisions that were receiving their first baptism of fire. Some had to be replaced by veteran outfits as soon as a lull in the battle permitted. By 4 October the campaign entered a second phase, a month of bitter fighting during which American troops advanced slowly, wearing out the enemy and enlarging the front of the attack. The third and last phase, beginning early in November, was a general assault by the AEF, which now advanced rapidly toward Sedan. The Armistice found elements of the 1st and 42nd Divisions within one mile of that vital strong point on the Meuse.

To cover the massive American offensive in the Meuse-Argonne sector, Billy Mitchell, promoted to brigadier general during the campaign, had a smaller force than at St. Mihiel two weeks earlier. Of the slightly more than 800 aircraft available for the difficult assignment, approximately three-fourths were flown by Americans. The French had withdrawn most of their own air units for service in other sectors. Although a few of the American air units were still comparatively inexperienced, several had fought at Chateau-Thierry, and almost all had served in the neutralization of the St. Mihiel salient. American pursuit, on entering the Meuse-Argonne, had, according to General Mason Patrick, "reached a stage at which it ranked in efficiency with the pursuit aviation of the Allied Armies . . . with pilots second to none."[1] Patrick could have made the same comment with regard to observation and bombardment.

Air Service plans for the employment of pursuit aircraft during the campaign reflected some new approaches. Hartney's 1st Pursuit Group was assigned to the task of clearing the front of German balloons and low-flying battle planes; Johnson's 2nd Pursuit Group and Thaw's 3rd Pursuit Group were to furnish high cover for these operations and escort the day bombardment group. The Spads of the latter two pursuit groups were also fitted with bomb racks and carried two twenty-five-pound bombs for the purpose of harassing the German infantry. In order to make aerial protection more quickly available to the advancing American doughboys, the 27th Squadron stationed one flight at a temporary landing field near Verdun. This unit, commanded by Jerry Vasconcelles, was within five minutes of the battle lines. The 95th Squadron established a forward alert field at Froides, and the 147th based one flight at Brabant-en-Argonne, also within a short distance of the front.

One of the most vital air operations on the first day of the big offensive was to put the German observation balloons out of action. At 4:00 A.M., shortly after the thunder of the Army's 2,700 big cannons signaled the opening of the campaign, eighty-one Spads of the 1st Pursuit Group took off from Rembercourt and headed toward the lines. It was still dark, but the Americans had no trouble in locating the trenches, for the tremendous artillery barrage had marked the front like a line of fire. The group was out early to catch the enemy balloons just at dawn when the attacker would be hard to see. The plan was eminently successful; within an hour no less than six German "sausages" fell in flames before the guns of Lieutenant Ivan A. Roberts, Jerry Vasconcelles, H. Weir Cook, Reed Chambers, Alexander McLanahan, and Harold Buckley.[2]

On the same mission Eddie Rickenbacker spotted a Fokker in the half light of that September dawn and shot it down on the outskirts of the little town of Damvillers, a dozen miles north of Verdun, for his eleventh victory.[3] The Ohioan had only the day before been made the commander of the 94th Aero Squadron, replacing Captain Kenneth Marr who was on orders to return to the United States to work in the air training program. Although he was the unit's junior flight commander, the aggressive Rickenbacker had been chosen to lead the squadron, which seemingly had never lived up to its early promise. At the beginning of the Meuse-Argonne drive, the "Hat-in-the-Ring" outfit lagged behind the 27th in its own group and the 148th Squadron on the British front, and its score was being approached by several other squadrons. When the war ended seven weeks later the remarkable Rickenbacker had pushed the 94th back into first place and won for himself the Medal of Honor.*

In all, Hartney's low-flying 1st Pursuit Group destroyed ten German aircraft on 26 September. During the day Lieutenants Alan Nutt of the 94th and Ivan Roberts of the 27th were shot down and killed, but considering the type of work being performed, casualties were surprisingly light.[4]

Units of Lieutenant Colonel Bert Atkinson's 1st Pursuit Wing were also active on that hectic first day of the drive. Elements of the 2nd Pursuit Group, patrolling at 14,000 feet over the lines between Grandpré on the western flank and Damvillers on the east, met with mixed success. *Jagdstaffeln* from the old Richthofen Circus were in the area, and the American offensive did not go without challenge. The 13th Aero Squadron, heavily hit during the St. Mihiel campaign, lost two men. Bridgeman's 22nd and Fisher's 49th each had a pilot killed, and Angstrom's 139th lost three.[5] Major Carl Spaatz, destined to be one of the great air generals of World War II, came close to losing his life that day. The hard-flying Spaatz, near the end of his three-week tour with the 13th Squadron, had just finished sending a Fokker crashing into the village of Flabas, ten miles north of Verdun, when two Fokkers swung in on his tail. Luckily he was spotted by his sharp-eyed squadron commander, Charles Biddle, who with Leighton Brewer and S. M. Avery dove to the rescue shooting down one of the Boche and chasing the other away.[6] The victory was Biddle's sixth. Other pilots were also busy, and at the end of the day a total of eight kills was claimed by the 2nd Pursuit Group.[7] A similar patrol by the 3rd Pursuit Group, led by its commanding officer, Major William Thaw, resulted in the destruction of three more German aircraft that same afternoon.[8]

The 1st Day Bombardment Group was also active the first day of the Meuse-Argonne offensive. During the morning all three squadrons bombed Dun-sur-Meuse, about twenty-five miles northwest of

---

* Rickenbacker's Medal of Honor was awarded for single-handedly attacking a group of five Fokkers and two Halberstadts over Billy and shooting two of them down. The decoration was not granted until 1931.

Verdun. A total of four and one-half tons of bombs were dropped on the railway center and a railroad bridge spanning the Meuse just west of the town. As the bombers left the target, the lead flight of six Breguets from the 96th Aero Squadron was hit by a dozen enemy pursuit planes. Although one observer, Lieutenant P. J. O'Donnell, was killed, the flight managed to shoot down two of the attackers and make its escape. The second flight of bombers was saved by the timely arrival of a flight of Spads from the 3rd Pursuit Group.[9]

Eight DH-4's from the 20th Squadron bringing up the rear of the group formation met disaster. This flight, led by Lieutenant Sidney Coe Howard, was just approaching the Dun-sur-Meuse target area when it was intercepted by approximately a score of Pfalz and Fokker fighters. Howard's observer, Lieutenant E. A. Parrott, was hit by the "first shower of shots from the attacking machines and fell jamming the controls [of the DH-4], thereby making a turn impossible."[10] With Howard firing his forward guns and struggling to free the controls, the De Havilland droned on deeper into enemy territory with the remnants of the shattered flights following in close formation. Finally, "after thirty-five minutes of utmost effort" the perspiring pilot managed to release the controls and turned back toward Allied lines. Hoping that Parrott might still be alive, Howard landed at the first available airdrome only to find that the observer had been killed instantly.[11] Five of the eight DH-4's failed to return from the disastrous mission. Three were seen to go down in flames, and some time later it was learned that Lieutenants Richard P. Matthews, Everett A. Taylor, David B. Harris, Earl Forbes, Philip Rhinelander, and Harry Preston had been killed, while Lieutenants Merian C. Cooper, E. C. Leonard, Guy Brown Wiser, and G. R. Richardson had been captured.[12] During the long flight, one enemy pursuit plane was shot down by the squadron.[13]

For his valiant attempt to save his formation Sidney Howard was recommended for the DSC. After the war he had a distinguished career as a journalist and playwright, his play, *They Knew What They Wanted,* published in 1924, winning a Pulitzer award.

As Pershing's infantry pressed forward in the predawn attack on 26 September, teams from army and corps observation units took to the air to provide the necessary photography, reconnaissance, artillery surveillance, and infantry contact work. Fog and haze hampered their work during the morning hours, and the rapid advance of the American infantry further complicated matters.* Nonetheless, by operating at dangerously low altitudes, observation crews were able to supply command posts with the necessary information. Several squadrons flew more than a score of individual sorties during the long day, but because most of the enemy pursuits were occupied in the Dun-sur-Meuse and Stenay areas, several miles behind the German lines, corps observation teams encountered relatively light aerial opposition. One Salmson from the 1st Aero Squadron was shot down over Varennes, and the pilot, Lieutenant John F. Richards, and his observer, Lieutenant Austin F. Hanscum, were killed.†

Reynolds' army observation group assigned to reconnaissance work over the German railway system in the Etain, Stenay, and Dun-sur-Meuse area, deep behind the lines, encountered stiff opposition. During the day Lieutenants Asher Kelty and Francis B. Lowry, of the 91st Squadron, were shot down and killed, while the 9th and 24th Squadrons each had a man wounded.[15] A team from the comparatively inexperienced 24th brought down an enemy aircraft over Doumprix.[16]

Despite the battle experience of the squadrons, corps observation work in the Meuse-Argonne campaign was something less than a complete success. Little of the fault, however, can be ascribed to the airmen. Several major problems plagued the boys in the De Havillands and the Salmsons. The rugged, heavily wooded terrain proved to be a serious handicap in locating friendly troops. This was especially true on the Argonne Forest flank of the American advance, which was being covered by the I Corps Observation Group. Bad weather prevailed throughout the 26 September–11 November period. Of the forty-seven days in the final campaign, only ten were considered favorable for observation work. Rain, low clouds, fog, and haze constantly interfered with the execution of photography missions, and in the final weeks only the most impor-

---

* Some infantry units advanced as much as seven miles on the first day of the Meuse-Argonne campaign.

† John Francisco Richards II was born in Kansas City, Mo., on 31 July 1894 and graduated from Yale University in 1917. In 1925 his war letters and diary were published by his father under the title *War Diary and Letters of John Francisco Richards II*. This item is one of the finest available on training and day-by-day activities of the American airman in France.[14]

tant objectives were photographed. Nothing but the heaviest rain or the thickest fog, however, prevented the visual reconnaissance missions, and the observation squadrons did provide much valuable service in that area.[17]

Perhaps the most serious obstacle facing corps observation was the inexperience of the ground troops with which they were working. Few of the assault divisions which opened the offensive had had any real battle seasoning, and the troops either did not understand the importance of infantry contact patrols or did not know how to maintain communications with the air observers. Lieutenants Forest McCook and Milton K. Lockwood, of the 50th Squadron, shot down in No-Man's Land on the third day of the offensive, found on talking with American doughboys that "not only had the troops in question never had instruction, actual or verbal, in coordination with the Air Service, but also that they had not the slightest knowledge of the meaning of any of the flares shot from planes."[18] In fact, many ground troops did not even recognize an American airplane. Some thought their own planes were to be identified by a star painted on the bottom surface of the lower wings, an insignia which had been used in the United States. Even as late as October, 1918, the red, white, and blue concentric circle insignia used by the Air Service at the front was practically unknown.[19] It is little wonder the uninstructed soldier failed to respond to the air observer's flare signals.

To improve the liaison with the ground forces, infantry contact schools were established at the airdromes of each observation group. In addition, considerable effort was made to clear up misunderstandings between the air and land forces; printed circulars on air cooperation were dropped from observation planes, and to improve recognition, the infantry division insignia was sometimes painted on the bottoms of observation aircraft.[20] Air observers were frequently sent to infantry units on short personal visits which were of value to both the Air Service and the infantry in promoting knowledge concerning the activities of each force. Whenever possible during the last month of the campaign, observation teams dropped chocolates, cigarettes, newspapers, and other reading material to the doughboys struggling in the mud below.[21]

As a result of these efforts to instruct and promote good will there was, in the last few weeks of the drive, an improvement in the effectiveness of infantry contact patrols. This was especially noticed by squadrons working with the veteran 1st, 2nd, and 42nd Divisions.[22] While there were still a good many instances in which observer teams were forced to fly at very low altitudes to locate the front lines by distinguishing the uniforms of ground troops, on the whole, marking the infantry line was easier than it had been at Chateau-Thierry and St. Mihiel.[23]

A combination of circumstances tended to nullify Air Service efforts to direct artillery fire on fugitive targets. As in the case of infantry contact patrols, the wooded terrain made the identification of targets difficult. Despite prior efforts to perfect radio transmission, artillery radio stations repeatedly failed to respond to calls from the observation aircraft. Dropped written messages were effective in adjusting artillery fire on stationary objectives, but that technique proved totally inadequate when directed against moving targets.

At least one important new corps observation tactic was developed during the Meuse-Argonne battle. In what came to be known as "cavalry reconnaissance," observation planes flying at low altitudes conducted close observation of the ground immediately ahead of advancing Allied infantry. After locating strong points, machine gun nests, and other defenses likely to slow the attack, this information, together with the location and strength of enemy reserves, was transmitted quickly to the front line troops by dropped written messages. In this manner the friendly troops were kept informed of developments in the area immediately ahead. Frequently these "cavalry patrols" would machine gun concentrations of enemy soldiers who were delaying the progress of Allied ground units.[24] This type of operation was indeed dangerous work for the fliers.

Pilots and observers were particularly conscientious in carrying out their infantry contact patrol assignments, whatever the weather or aerial opposition. Perhaps the following words set to the tune of Carrie Jacobs Bond's nostalgic and popular song, "When You Come to the End of a Perfect Day," sums up the attitude of most:

> When you sit on the edge of your bunk all day,
>   With a map of France in your hand;
>
> And you search for a spot not so far away,
>   Out there in No Man's Land,

And you know the archies are bursting fine,
And the 50th is on her way,

And you know that our pilots have found the line;
That's the end of a perfect day.[25]

Perhaps the classic example of the dedication of corps observation, as indicated by the song, occurred during the first week of October, when Captain Daniel P. Morse's 50th, the squadron with the "Dutch Girl" insignia, was called upon to locate the "Lost Battalion." On 2 October 1918, the American 77th Division was a part of Pershing's general drive against the German Meuse-Argonne defenses. The division, advancing on the extreme western flank in the wilderness known as the Argonne Forest, ran into stiff resistance in the rugged terrain which was perfectly adapted to defense. The Huns had machine guns hidden in every section of the forest, and those guns were taking heavy toll of the 77th Division attackers. Most of the division was stalled, but six companies of the 308th Infantry Regiment and two machine gun platoons, under the command of Major Charles W. Whittlesey, broke through the enemy's defense and gained the Apremont-Binarville road. However, before the Battalion reached its primary objective, the mill on Charlevaux Creek, it was pinned down in a deep ravine.[26]

The Battalion was not really lost, but by noon of 3 October, it had been completely enveloped by German forces. It could not advance; nor could it retreat. For several days Whittlesey's command was fired on intermittently by Allied artillery because its exact location was not known. Whittlesey managed to send out carrier pigeons with appeals for help, but he was badly oriented and marked his position with the wrong coordinates. The Battalion was short of food and medical supplies and was running low on ammunition. Certainly, their situation was grim.[27]

Despite poor visibility, the 50th Aero Squadron, on the morning of 5 October, attempted to drop supplies to the isolated troops. The fliers had nothing to guide them, as the "lost" infantrymen were reluctant to display marker panels. During the day no less than four observation teams braved terrific rifle and machine gun fire in swooping low over the spot indicated by Whittlesey's last carrier pigeon message to drop their packages. They had no way of knowing that his map coordinates were wrong and that they were risking their lives to supply German troops.*

Later in the day, elements of the 77th Division attempted to rescue the Battalion but were repulsed. Finally an artillery barrage was laid on the Germans' supposed position. Another frantic carrier pigeon message from Whittlesey brought a halt to this operation. The artillery was pounding its own men.

Early on the morning of 6 October, the 50th Squadron was instructed "not merely to drop supplies but find the men who need those supplies." This time the entire squadron participated in the operation. Again the weather was atrocious; nonetheless, team after team took up the search. Perhaps the most audacious effort was made by a team of Lieutenant Harold E. Goettler, pilot, and Lieutenant Erwin R. Bleckley, observer, who made several low-level sweeps over the deep ravines in the Charlevaux Mill area. On the last long pass over the supposed location of Whittlesey's men, Goettler brought his De Havilland down to less than 200 feet. At this level the enemy's fire was murderous. German machine gunners located on the ridges were actually firing down at the American plane. Still, Goettler and Bleckley could see no panel signals or any signs of an American uniform. For their valiant try they picked up at least forty bullet holes in their DH-4.

Several other 50th Squadron fliers were not so lucky on that flaming Sunday afternoon. Lieutenant Francis C. Slater was wounded in the foot and barely succeeded in getting home. Lieutenants George Phillips and Michael Brown flew into a hail of machine gun fire which smashed the pilot's windshield and tore out the instrument panel. A few moments later the Liberty engine died at 300 feet. Barely skimming the trees, Phillips got his plane down in No-Man's Land, and the two men escaped by crawling from shell hole to shell hole back to the Allied lines. Lieutenants Allen Tracy Bird and William Bolt were forced to crash-land their badly damaged plane at Vienne-le-Chateau, just behind the American positions.[29]

Late in the day the squadron suffered its heaviest blow. Goettler and Bleckley, the two who had started the day's work, volunteered for a second mission. After loading up with supplies, the pair again

---

* As it turned out, some of the supplies did actually land in reach of the beleaguered troops; most, however, did not.[28]

climbed off into the murky sky to comb the ravine area south and east of Charlevaux Mill. This time they decided to try to draw fire from the Germans on the floor of the ravine. If they could pinpoint enough of the enemy's positions, they might succeed by the process of elimination to locate the "lost" detachment. In a performance which would have done justice to a modern crop dusting operation, the two roared back and forth at treetop level over the great ravine. Slowly but surely the pair in the De Havilland narrowed down the possibilities. But they paid a terrible price: their plane was riddled from nose to tail. Such a search technique could have only one outcome. Goettler was hit. With his last breath he lifted the battered DH-4 out of the valley of death and crash-landed a few hundred yards in front of the French positions. He was dead when the French found him, and Bleckley was dying. Luckily, the latter had kept his mission notes.[30]

As the sun dropped below the horizon, Lieutenant Maurice Graham, of Monrovia, California, and Lieutenant James McCurdy, of Century, Florida, completed what Goettler and Bleckley had started. McCurdy was shot through the neck, but Graham got him home in time to save his life.[31]

Meanwhile, Whittlesey's men had witnessed the valiant show and guessed what the airmen were trying to do. During the night of 6–7 October, the desperate infantrymen crawled through the darkness to lay out panels marking their position. Lieutenants Robert M. Anderson and W. J. Rogers, flying the 50th Squadron's first mission on the morning of 7 October, spotted these markers and raced full throttle to the 77th Division's dropping ground with the new and accurate coordinates. The "Lost Battalion" had been found! Within a matter of hours the U.S. 25th, 77th, and 82nd Divisions drove to the rescue. For their part in the dramatic episode Goettler and Bleckley were posthumously awarded the nation's highest decoration, the Congressional Medal of Honor. Only two other Air Service men, Lieutenant Frank Luke and Captain Eddie Rickenbacker, received this award in World War I.*

Despite the presence on the Meuse-Argonne front of eight of the best *Jagdstaffeln* in the German Air Force, losses were light in American corps observation squadrons. This, to a large extent, was

---

* Maj. Charles W. Whittlesey also received the Medal of Honor for his efforts with the "Lost Battalion."[32]

due to the effective cover provided by American pursuit units. On the other hand, much of this immunity was bought at the price of many lives in the day bombardment group, whose raids deep behind the enemy lines attracted the German fighters and kept them away from the front lines where the corps observation planes operated.

In the last seven weeks, corps observation units lost a total of twenty-three men killed, ten captured, and twenty-five wounded. Hardest hit was the veteran 1st Aero Squadron which suffered fifteen casualties, seven of whom were killed. Captain James Meredith's DH-4-flying 99th Squadron had ten casualties. The Salmson-equipped 12th, commanded after 25 October by Lieutenant R. C. Paradise, also lost ten fliers, though only two were killed.[33]

During the forty-seven-day campaign, corps observation squadrons more than held their own against aerial opposition. Thirty-six enemy aircraft were shot down by the men in the two-seaters. At the end of the war one corps observation pilot and two observers, all of the 1st Aero Squadron, were listed as aces with five or more victories. The pilot, Lieutenant William P. Erwin, of Chicago, was credited with eight. Lieutenants Byrne V. Baucom, of Milford, Texas, and Arthur Easterbrook, of Fort Flagler, Washington, both observers, scored six and five victories respectively.[34]

Although bad weather conditions hampered corps observation units during the offensive, these conditions were even more of a handicap to the deep ranging army observation squadrons; only a few days of the entire period were suitable for the long-range photography work which constituted a major part of their responsibility. During the long periods of foul weather, photographic missions were sent out to cover only the most important points. Even though required to scout the area from the Moselle on the east (until the organization of the Second Army Observation Group in late October) to Sedan and Mézières on the west, the two day squadrons, the 24th and the 91st, were able to provide the basic information needed by the army commanders. For example, on the morning of 15 October, a 24th Squadron team of Lieutenants George E. Goldthwaite, pilot, and Spessard L. Holland, observer, was sent to locate a large number of German shock troops reported to be moving into the lines. Holland, who later won recognition as governor of Florida and more recently as U.S. senator from that state, described the trials of that sortie:

We crossed the right wing of our First Army, over the 17th French Corps, and then went from east to west about half way along our army front and perhaps about 1 to 3 miles north of same at a very low level because of the heavy clouds. At that point the heavy shift of air blew my goggles and head gear off and we turned out. I readjusted my equipment and we came back in and went almost to the west wing of the First Army where we discovered a large force of German infantry and artillery resting in some fields back of a high hill near or in the Bois de Bantheville. We turned to move out but were immediately hit by many bursts of machine gun fire. Our landing gear was shot away and the gas tank was hit and the gas poured out all over the pilot into his cockpit so that coming down we barely got over our front line and crash-landed about 400 or 500 yards back of the front from which place we made our quick escape while the Germans were trying to get on us with drum fire and also by 77's.[35]

The pair reported their findings, and within minutes Allied artillery was pounding the hiding place of the German reserves.

Army observation squadrons were particularly effective during the last three days of October, when perfect weather permitted the photographing of long-range artillery objectives at Montmédy, Longwy, Spincourt, Dommary-Baroncourt, and Conflans-en-Jernisy.[36]

The 9th Aero Squadron, charged with night reconnaissance, was even more obstructed by the weather than were the day units. Since the most important military movements were made at night, this untried outfit, led by Lieutenant Edward R. Kenneson after 30 September, was desperately needed. In spite of its inexperience, on the nights suitable for observation the squadron did obtain some valuable information and inflicted minor bomb damage on the enemy.*

During the Argonne drive the First Army Observation Group sustained twenty-one casualties—seven killed, five captured, and nine wounded. These losses were comparatively high by observation standards but were not comparable to those suffered by bombardment and pursuit units. In the same period army observation squadrons were credited with twenty-six enemy planes. The veteran 91st Squadron accounted for seventeen of these victories with the squadron commander, Captain Everett R. Cook, scoring five kills. The

* Some machines of the night reconnaissance squadron were equipped to carry small bombs.[37]

91st Squadron's Lieutenant Victor H. Strahm, of Evanston, Illinois, was also credited with five. Two observers in the same outfit, Lieutenants L. C. Hammond and William T. Badham scored six and five victories, respectively.[38]

Target selection for day bombardment during the early stages of the offensive was to a surprising degree influenced by the possibility of using the bombers to engage enemy pursuit deep behind German lines. This tactic was devised to reduce fighter pressure against Allied corps observation squadrons operating in the vicinity of the battle line. In addition, it had the effect of protecting the advancing doughboys from strafing pursuit and battle planes. An example of this use of bombing aircraft occurred late on the opening day of the campaign, when Mitchell spotted a "terrible congestion of motor traffic" a short distance south of Montfaucon. This traffic jam involved practically every wheeled vehicle in the U.S. V Corps. Alarmed about the vulnerability to attack by the dreaded *Schlachtstaffeln* (battle squadrons equipped with armored attack planes), the American Commander* took immediate action by ordering bombing raids against Romagne and Dun-sur-Meuse. This move did much to keep the air fighting in the back areas and away from the stalled vehicles.[39]

Under the command of Major Thomas S. Bowen,† a veteran of the Mexican border crisis of 1916, the 1st Day Bombardment Group showed great improvement in the Meuse-Argonne fight. The early history of the group had been marked by heavy losses, and steps were taken to prevent a recurrence of this. Formation flying and aerial gunnery were practiced and improved greatly. Certainly, tight formation meant safety; an airplane that fell out of formation invited disaster. During the last weeks of the war, objectives were in most cases attacked by the whole group rather than by a single squadron, and these flights were coordinated with pursuit escorts.

---

* Although subordinate to Patrick, Mitchell made most of the operational decisions during the St. Mihiel and Meuse-Argonne campaigns. Gen. Pershing respected the hard-driving and aggressive Wisconsin general and made it known that he wanted him to command the combat squadrons. Patrick, not a flying officer, concerned himself with the administrative duty of keeping the Air Service functioning smoothly. Squadron, group, and wing officers had very little contact with the Chief of Air Service.

† Bowen, who would be promoted to lieutenant colonel on 1 November 1918, replaced the much-disliked Dunsworth early in October.

Such cooperation was relatively easy since the 1st Day Bombardment Group operated under the control of Atkinson's 1st Pursuit Wing.

Early in October, the 166th Aero Squadron, equipped with DH-4's and led by the dashing Captain Victor Parks, was added to the 1st Day Bombardment Group. This squadron, however, was not ready for combat operations until the third week of October. Meanwhile, the short-handed 96th Squadron was able to borrow enough flying teams from the other units to make up a large formation of Breguets. The remaining teams in Heater's 11th and Sellers' 20th Squadrons combined to form one large De Havilland formation. As a result of this pooling of crews and aircraft the normal bombing formation ran as high as fifteen to twenty planes. Certain technical advances were also made when armored seats, detachable fuel tanks, and more reliable machine guns were provided for the Breguets. The combination of larger formations and technical improvements served to reduce casualties, but because of the dangerous mission performed, losses were still higher than in corps observation.[40]

Despite the miserable weather, the 1st Day Bombardment Group undertook at least one raid daily during the first two weeks of the campaign. The mission on 27 September was aborted because of the heavy clouds over the target, but on all other raids bombs were dropped. On 29 September nineteen Breguets attempted to bomb Grandpré on the extreme western flank of the American position. Only thirteen, however, were able to cross the line. Of the twenty DH-4's in the second formation, only six were able to bomb Marq, their objective. In fact, mechanical difficulties with the Liberty engine hampered the 11th and 20th Squadrons throughout the early weeks of the offensive. On 1 October, the group, led by Lieutenant Bruce Hopper, of the 96th Squadron, hammered the crossroads town of Bantheville with 1,240 kilos of bombs* causing much

---

* Bomb production in America was relatively slow to get under way because of numerous difficulties in working up designs of this new weapon. Eventually such companies as Marlin-Rockwell, A. O. Smith, Lycoming Foundry & Machine, and Paige-Detroit Motor Car turned out thousands of demolition, fragmentation, and incendiary bombs. During the first several months, bombs were produced in five different weights: 50 pounds, 100 pounds, 250 pounds, 500 pounds, and finally, 1,000 pounds. Few of these were actually delivered to the combat squadrons. In August, 1918, contracts were let to build the Mark II-B fragmentation bomb. This was an exact copy of the highly successful British Cooper bomb. Since

"damage in the town." During this raid, thirteen of the Breguets reached the target, while only two of the twenty De Havillands in the second flight were able to complete the mission. Only the appearance of the Spad escort prevented the destruction of the trouble-ridden DH-4's.[41]

Late in the afternoon of 4 October, the 1st Day Bombardment Group became involved in one of the largest dogfights of the Meuse-Argonne campaign. Led by Hopper, the Breguets had just completed their bomb run over Landes-St. Georges when they were hit by thirty Fokker and Pfalz fighters. Hopper turned for home and the Boche followed. Within minutes the procession became embroiled near the lines, with the DH-4's on their way to the same target. At the height of the resulting combat, thirty Spads from the American 2nd Pursuit Group dived into the fray. None of the bombers were lost in the fire fight, but each aircraft was damaged by machine gun fire. Crews of the 96th Squadron shot down two of their attackers, and the Spad pilots claimed eleven more. Certainly, the timely arrival of the fighter escort had saved the day.[42]

The nerve-wracking raids continued through the next several days. Landes-St. Georges was visited again on 5 October, and Bantheville, the junction of two major highways, was bombed on the following day. In each of these raids heavy antiaircraft fire was experienced, but no enemy fighters put in an appearance.[43]

The largest single air raid of the Meuse-Argonne campaign occurred on 9 October, when Billy Mitchell assembled more than 200 bombers, 110 fighters, and 50 three-place Caudrons for a strike against a German troop concentration in the Damvillers-Wavrille area. An early morning aerial reconnaissance mission had spotted a considerable force of enemy reserves in the vicinity of Pershing's right flank, and the hard-hitting Mitchell went into action. Without bothering to notify the army commander, he quickly contacted the French Air Division and requested air support. His request was granted, and a few hours later the American doughboys on the ground were treated with a rare sight—over 300 aircraft in two

---

American facilities for loading bombs with high explosive material lagged behind schedule, practically all the bombs used by Air Service fliers in France were of foreign manufacture. The French-built Michelin was the most popular with American day bombardment squadrons. The 20-pound British Cooper bomb was a favorite with the pursuit units.

huge formations droning north to pound the vital German troop build-up. More than thirty tons of bombs were dropped in the face of a vigorous German air attack, and the enemy's impending counterattack on the ground was disrupted. During this engagement a dozen Hun planes were downed, while only one Allied plane failed to return. The British continued the bombing during the night, and within a twenty-four-hour period no less than eighty-one tons of bombs smashed into German positions.[44]

Although no American bombers participated in the big Damvillers raid, elements of the 1st Day Bombardment Group did hit other targets near the front line during the day. Twelve DH-4's of the 20th Squadron, led by Sidney Howard and Lieutenant Samuel C. Hicks, dropped over a ton of bombs on St. Juvin from 12,000 feet. Numerous hits were observed in the town. At approximately the same time, Lieutenants Robert Porter and James Patten led a six-ship formation from the 11th Squadron against Bantheville. Both missions encountered archie but suffered no casualties.[45]

Early on the morning of 10 October, six Breguets and nineteen De Havillands hammered targets in the Dun-sur-Meuse area with nearly six tons of high explosives. The second flight of eleven DH-4's, led by Lieutenants Donald MacWhirter and William Stull Holt,* was particularly effective in destroying the railroad yards in the village of Milly-devant-Dun. As the formations turned for home they were intercepted by twelve light colored Fokkers. In the running fight which followed, Lieutenants W. C. Potter and H. W. Wilmer, of the 20th Squadron, were shot down and killed. Lieutenants E. B. Christian and Sam Hicks, observers in the same outfit, were severely wounded. Once again the arrival of friendly pursuits enabled the hard-pressed two-seaters to escape. The American Spads succeeded in shooting down one Fokker in flames and forced another to crash-land near Clary-le-Petit.[46]

Though casualties in the day bombardment group had been relatively light, the constant strain of operations during the first two weeks of the offensive had taken its toll in both aviators and planes. Nature then provided a much-needed rest. Starting with the morning of 11 October, a week of torrential rains and impossibly low

---

* Holt, who acted as lead observer on the mission, survived the war to become a distinguished American historian. For a short period in the early 1960's he served as editor of the *American Historical Review*.

ceilings kept the air crews on the ground and gave ground personnel an opportunity to repair worn-out equipment.

The weather cleared somewhat on 18 October, and the group mounted its largest effort to that date, an attack on Bayonville, a strategic highway town some twenty miles south of Sedan. All four squadrons made the raid, with fourteen Breguets from the 96th leading the way. Victor Parks's 166th Squadron, flying its first mission of the war, contributed seven DH-4's to the forty-two-plane formation. Five tons of bombs were dropped on Bayonville and the secondary target at Buzancy leaving many buildings in flames. Major Bowen, the new group commander, flew as an observer in one of the lead planes and participated in the air battle, when twenty Fokkers challenged the raiders.[47] Fortunately, the attacking fighters were unable to break the tight bomber formation, and no losses were suffered by the American forces. According to French intelligence sources 250 enemy troops were killed and 700 were wounded on this highly successful mission.[48]

The armada had hardly settled down on the rough sod of Maulan airdrome when the weather turned bad again. For three long days the fliers waited in the rain and mud for another opportunity to "hammer the Hun." American infantrymen had reached the Hindenburg Line at many places along the Meuse-Argonne front, and preparations were being made for the final big effort to push through to Sedan. Impatient at the weather-enforced delays, twenty-six crews from the 96th and 166th Squadrons attempted a bombing mission late on the afternoon of 22 October, but all were forced to return before reaching the target because of "rain and very dense clouds near the lines."[49] Despite poor visibility, De Havillands from the 20th and 11th Squadrons, once again following the steady Sidney Howard, bombed troop concentrations in the Buzancy and Bois-de-Barricourt area on the morning of 23 October. Heavy aerial opposition was encountered. Three of the bombers were forced down on the Allied side of the lines, and one was wrecked. A second raid made up of seven Breguets and thirty DH-4's hit the same targets shortly after noon of the same day. The formation was swarmed by several *Jagdstaffeln* of Fokker, Pfalz, and Albatros fighters, and the machine flown by Lieutenants J. Henry Weimer and H. E. Turner, of the 20th Squadron, was shot down in flames. In addition, the 1st Day Bombardment Group lost three men wounded, and several badly damaged planes were forced to land at the nearest Allied airfield. Four of the attacking pursuit planes were seen to go down out of control.[50]

After another break of four days, imposed by the weather, the 1st Day Bombardment Group attacked Briquenay, a small road junction village five miles north of Grandpré, on the afternoon of 27 October. Nearly four tons of bombs were dumped in the center of the target in such a manner as to disrupt the flow of German troop traffic. The 96th and 11th Squadrons were bounced by a dozen enemy pursuits during the bomb run, and the former had three aviators wounded. In addition, two badly damaged Breguets were forced down on the Allied side of the lines.[51]

With the growing shortage of aircraft, Bowen's little bombing force was forced to return to the small formations which were typical of the St. Mihiel campaign. On 29 October two missions were flown. The first was a raid on Montigny by the 11th and 166th Squadrons, but only seven De Havillands of the latter unit reached the objective. Early in the afternoon all four squadrons sent small formations against Damvillers on the extreme right flank of the American sector. The raiders were attacked by fifteen Fokkers, and two of Captain James Summersett's 96th Squadron fliers were wounded. One of the "Huns was seen spinning toward the earth trailing a long column of smoke."[52]

On 30 October small formations from the DH-4 outfits visited Bayonville. Although strongly pressed by several flights of German fighters, all of the bombers returned to their home airdrome at Maulan. Most of the attacking fighters were Fokker D-7's, but several new Sieman Schuckerts biplanes were noticed.[53]

With only nine pilots available because of recent attrition, the Breguet-flying 96th had been unable to participate in the Bayonville raid. By the next day, however, the squadron was able to contribute ten machines to the group raid on the Tailly-Barricourt area. Once again the bombers were hit by enemy pursuits, some of which seemed to be using the Bayonville-Barricourt road as an airfield, as at least six hangars were spotted along the highway by 11th Squadron fliers. In the battle which took place over the target, the 166th Squadron's Lieutenant S. Pickard was wounded, and his observer, Lieutenaut S. L. Cochrane, was killed.[54]

By 1 November, American ground forces had broken through the Hindenburg Line defenses on all fronts and were advancing rapidly toward the Meuse Valley stronghold of Sedan. Bad weather kept bombardment aviation on the ground until 3 November, when missions were flown against Stenay and Beaumont. On the next day the railroad center at Montmédy was blasted by thirty-nine planes from the 1st Day Bombardment Group. All of the formations encountered severe opposition from aggressive Fokker patrols. Bomber crews claimed seven enemy planes shot down, but they lost two of their own—both from Captain Charles L. Heater's 11th Aero Squadron. Lieutenant Cyrus J. Gatton, one of the squadron's flight leaders, and his observer, Lieutenant George Bures, were shot down by archie and killed. Lieutenants Charles Dana Coates and Loren R. Thrall went down in flames before the guns of a Fokker a little southwest of the target. The popular Gatton was the last survivor of the 11th Squadron's original flight commanders. He, along with Captain Heater, had done much to make the "Mr. Jiggs" outfit an effective fighting unit.[55]

The group's last raid of the war occurred on 5 November, when the DH-4 squadrons, braving rain and heavy clouds, flew down the Meuse River toward Mouzon. Aircraft from the 11th were forced to turn back before reaching the target, and the 166th, with Captain Parks leading, was unable to find Mouzon through the thick overcast. After some search, Parks's aviators dropped their bombs on a secondary target. The 20th, with the ever reliable Sidney Howard leading the way, was lucky enough to spot Mouzon through a small hole in the clouds and bombed with devastating accuracy. Unfortunately, at this point the 20th Aero's luck played out. As Howard began his turn to the south and home, the little eight-ship formation was ambushed by a large number of Fokkers. Pushing their attack with a savagery seldom seen during the war, the German fighter pilots soon had the 20th in real trouble. One of the DH-4's burst into flames, and the rest of the formation watched in horror as the red ball of fire "tumbled to earth, 13,000 feet below." Two other bombers were shot down before the shattered formation could dive into the safety of the clouds farther down. Lieutenants Karl West and William B. Frank, manning the "flamer," were killed. Lieutenant Samuel P. Mandell was killed by German infantrymen after crash-landing his bullet riddled machine in enemy territory. Lieutenants R. W. Fulton, Brooke Edwards, and Karl Payne were taken prisoner.[56]

That bitter battle over Mouzon brought to an end the ordeal of the 1st Day Bombardment Group. The weather closed in for another week and did not lift until the Armistice. During the furious seven weeks of the Argonne campaign, the group lost twenty-four men killed, seventeen men wounded, and seven men captured. In spite of these tragic losses the bombardment forces had fought well. In addition, to carry out their assigned bombing tasks they had attracted enemy pursuits like a magnet and had been credited with the destruction of forty of them. Perhaps the diversion of enemy pursuits from the front lines, an area worked by Allied corps observation aircraft, was day bombardment's greatest contribution to the air war. Because of the small number of bombers involved and the crude bomb sights of the period, American bombardment aviation did relatively little damage to the German war effort. Indeed, really effective bombing, both tactical and strategic, would have to wait until World War II.

The principle of concentration which Billy Mitchell had attempted at St. Mihiel continued to guide his tactics in the Meuse-Argonne. In the latter campaign it was the Americans who occupied the salient and the German Air Force which struck at the flanks, trying, in Mitchell's words, "to make our infantry insist on splitting up our pursuit aviation so as to give local protection everywhere." In his view, the Germans hoped to force the Americans "to spread a thin veneer of airplanes all along the front through which they could break easily at any point with a large group formation." This Mitchell steadfastly refused to do. Instead, he concentrated his forces for single blows at the enemy rather than parceling out his strength to divisions and corps. By incessant attack on the enemy rear, he was able, to a large extent, to forestall German counterattacks.[57]

To cope with German battle squadrons of attack planes, the American Air Commander organized a special force known as "low flying pursuit." Hartney's 1st Pursuit Group was given this task, while the 2nd and 3rd Pursuit Groups worked mainly with bombardment and observation squadrons. The low-flying patrols were made up of five planes each and were assigned six-mile fronts. Flying at very low altitudes, normally under 500 feet, and using friendly antiaircraft fire to spot enemy intruders, these patrols proved successful in breaking up German attacks on ground troops. In addition, the low-flying American planes were in a position to strafe enemy soldiers and knock down enemy observation balloons.[58]

From the very beginning of the campaign, American pursuit was highly successful in eliminating the enemy's observation balloons. Each of the low-flying squadrons picked one or two men to specialize in "balloon busting." The balloon strafers were usually equipped with .45-caliber machine guns, which fired a large flaming bullet.[59] Success in "balloon busting" demanded great luck and almost fanatical daring, for the German "sausages" were always tightly guarded by antiaircraft guns and fighters. The strafing pursuit plane had to run the gauntlet of at least one of these dangers, and sometimes both, several times to knock down one balloon.

Several pilots were eminently successful as "balloon killers." Lieutenant Lansing C. Holden, of the 95th Squadron and New York City, destroyed five "enemy sausages" in running up his score of seven victories during the war. Rickenbacker got four balloons, while Lieutenant Harvey Weir Cook and Captain Hamilton Coolidge, of the 94th Squadron, each burned three on their way to acedom. But the premier "balloon buster" of the American Air Service was the intrepid Frank Luke who flamed fourteen during September, 1918.

In one wild flight late in the afternoon of 18 September, Luke turned in perhaps the greatest single performance by an American during the war. With his flying partner, Joseph Wehner, he left Rembercourt airdrome at 4:00 P.M. to look for enemy balloons. Over St. Mihiel the pair spotted two "sausages" and, while weathering a hail of ground fire, burned both. As the last balloon was going down in flames, a flight of Fokkers pounced on the two Spads. Wehner took the brunt of the attack, for he was higher and off to one side, but Luke climbed full tilt to help him, only to find two red-nosed Fokkers on his own tail. He whipped around and opened fire on the leader in a head-on attack. The Spad and the Fokker flew straight at each other, firing madly, with neither giving way. For a moment it seemed certain that the two would ram each other, but Luke's bullets took effect. The German biplane wavered, then spun straight down into a hillside. After a hard left turn Luke found himself squarely on the tail of the second Fokker. A short burst from the Spad's machine guns sent this German plane crashing a short distance from the first. Luke now anxiously searched the sky for Wehner. There was no sign of his friend. With his fuel running low, Luke reluctantly turned toward Rembercourt. Nearing the lines, he spotted a small concentration of archie and turned to investigate. Almost immediately he observed a Boche reconnaissance plane racing north while being pursued by several French Spads. By banking his Spad over in a vertical turn he was able to wing in between the fleeing German and the pursuers. One long burst sent the two-seater crashing into the trees for his fifth victory in ten minutes. With his gasoline now exhausted, the 27th Squadron's maverick landed near an American artillery battery and waited for his 1st Pursuit Group comrades to find him.[60]

Luke experienced no elation over his almost unbelievable success in the late afternoon duel. Instead, he felt only a deep anxiety over the fate of his flying partner. His feeling of foreboding was justified. Joe Wehner had crashed to his death in a successful attempt to save Luke early in the dogfight over Labeuville.[61]

Sensing that Wehner's death might spur Frank Luke to even rasher deeds, Hartney ordered him to Orly and Paris for a rest leave. This move was not entirely successful, however, for when the combat reports for the opening day of the Meuse-Argonne came in, Hartney was astonished to find one reporting the destruction of an enemy aircraft written by Frank Luke. The restless young man had cut short his leave to return to action.[62]

With fourteen confirmed victories, Luke was now the leading ace of the American Air Service. After Joe Wehner's death he became even more of a loner than before. Lieutenant Ivan A. Roberts, a stocky Massachusetts boy, was assigned to work with him in the role formerly played by Wehner. Roberts' career was short, for on 26 September he was shot down and killed.[63] After that Luke was allowed to continue his one-man war alone. On 28 September he braved a torrent of rifle and machine gun fire to burn a German balloon at Bethenville for his fifteenth victory. His only comment on this victory is contained in his combat report—the last one he ever made:

I flew north to Verdun, crossed the lines at about five hundred meters and found a balloon in its nest in the region of Bethenville. I dove on it firing both guns. After I pulled away it burst into flames. As I could not find any others I returned to the airdrome. One confirmation requested.[64]

The sand was now running very low in Frank Luke's hourglass. Indeed, the savage tempo of his crusade could have only one ending. He was becoming more and more difficult to handle, and his squadron commander, Captain Alfred A. Grant, was at the point of grounding him. Sunday morning 29 September found Luke pleading to be allowed to go on a balloon hunt alone. Finally Hartney, the 1st Pursuit Group commander, gave his permission but ordered him not to "stir off the ground until 5:56 P.M." This late starting time, Hartney believed, would put Luke over the balloon line after the enemy Fokkers had "gone home to roost."

Later in the day Luke flew up to the squadron's advance field near Verdun to get ready for the sortie. A short time after Luke's departure, Major Hartney also flew to Verdun to insure that his order concerning the 5:56 P.M. takeoff was carried out. He found Luke pacing around the Verdun air strip like a caged lion, "almost wild with impatience to get going."[65]

At precisely 5:56 P.M. on that hazy afternoon, Frank Luke's Hispano-Suiza engine roared to life, and within a few moments he was winging away toward the battle lines a dozen miles to the northwest. He had less than ninety minutes to live. Just before sunset he flew low over the American 7th Balloon Company near the front and dropped a note which read: "Watch for burning balloons. Luke."[66]

At 7:05 P.M. Luke exploded the first balloon at Dun-sur-Meuse, then burned a second at Briere Farm. After shooting down two harassing Fokkers, he then continued on to Milly where a third "sausage" fell in flames at 7:12 P.M. Although badly wounded he turned to strafe German troops in the village of Murvaux, killing six and wounding several others. At this point he was forced to land his badly damaged plane beside a small creek in the edge of the town. Here Luke, bleeding from a terrible chest wound, climbed from the cockpit of the Spad and waited beside the fuselage for the German soldiers who were approaching at a run. When they came within range, he drew his .45 automatic and fought until he died.[67]

For gallantry in action and intrepidity beyond the call of duty, Luke was posthumously awarded the Medal of Honor. The three balloons shot down in his final battle ran his confirmed victory total to eighteen, all scored in the final three weeks of his life. Strangely, he never received official confirmation of the two Fokkers downed in the Murvaux area on 29 September. Some victory compilations do list these, along with his 16 August claim, for a total of twenty-one kills.[68] Hartney states that Luke should have been credited with at least ten more.

Fighter pilots can be divided into two classifications, the "hunters" and the "hunted." All great fighter pilots belong to the first classification. In the 1914–1918 war, a few of the "hunters," such as Mannock, Boelcke, Richthofen, and Rickenbacker, were steady enough to be outstanding air combat leaders and teachers. Others, such as Ball, Guynemer, and Charles Nungesser, were brilliant, aggressive lone wolves. The wild, rebellious, and absolutely fearless Frank Luke was one of the lone wolves. Luke Air Force Base near Phoenix, Arizona, is named for him.

In addition to its balloon burning and strafing duties, the 1st Pursuit Group also carried out the more conventional protection patrols with observation planes, which had been provided for under the original plans for the offensive. This work required close cooperation, and during the final stages of the campaign observation planes frequently landed at pursuit airdromes for last-minute coordination before going out on their missions.[69] These briefings were apparently successful, for corps observation losses to enemy fighters were comparatively light during October and November.

As might be expected, the veteran 1st Pursuit Group continued to lead the way in the destruction of enemy aircraft during the seven-week campaign. Captain Rickenbacker, who had shot down six on the Toul front in the late spring and four more over St. Mihiel, pushed his own score to twenty-two planes and four balloons. His last two victories were made on 30 October. No less than eleven new aces were added to the already substantial list of successful pursuit pilots in the period 27 September–11 November. Newcomers to the ace club included such crack pilots as Harold Buckley, Edward P. Curtis, Lansing Holden, Sumner Sewall, and James C. Knowles, of the 95th Squadron; Hamilton Coolidge, Weir Cook, and Reed Chambers, of the 94th; Jerry Vasconcelles, of the

27th; and Wilbert W. White and Francis M. Simonds, of the 147th. In all, 112 victories were credited to the group during the Meuse-Argonne campaign.

Unfortunately, these successes were bought at the cost of some of the finest pilots in the group. On 10 October, Lieutenant Wilbert W. White, tied with Captain Meissner as the top ace of the 147th Squadron, with eight kills, was lost. While leading a patrol over Dun-sur-Meuse, White noticed one of his comrades diving with a Hun on his tail. Without hesitation he plunged to the rescue. To the horror of the onlookers the Spad and the Fokker collided and crashed to the earth. Apparently, White's guns had jammed, and he had rammed the German to save his friend.[70]

A few days later, Captain Hamilton Coolidge, also an eight-victory ace and one of the brightest new stars of the "Hat-in-the-Ring" squadron, was hit by a single archie shell. The Spad exploded into flames and plunged to the ground, carrying Coolidge to his untimely death.[71]

Early in October a fifth squadron was added to the 1st Pursuit Group, the 185th Aero Squadron, commanded by Captain Seth Low. Flying Monosoupape-powered Sopwith Camels, the 185th was the first and only night pursuit outfit to operate with the American Air Service. Although the pilots of this squadron had had little training in night operations and the Camel was tricky for night fighting, the giant German Gothas undertook few raids after the 185th's appearance at the front. It is probable, however, that this decline in bomber activity was due more to bad weather than to harassment by night pursuits.[72]

Night interception work was primitive, to say the least. Listening posts established along the front were connected by telephone and radio with searchlight crews, antiaircraft batteries, and the night pursuit squadron. After dark, planes from the 185th Squadron would climb to 10,000 feet, shut off their engines, and glide, watching for searchlight signals or antiaircraft fire. As one of the big raiders approached, the listening posts reported it to all other agencies. The archie batteries would open up and the searchlights would probe the skies. In theory the searchlights would find the enemy and hold him in the light until the Camel pilot could arrive and shoot him down. In actual practice, however, searchlight crews had great difficulty in pinpointing the intruder or keeping him in focus once he was spotted. On one occasion the lights were focused on the pursuer instead of the pursued, causing the night fighter to make a crash landing near Bar-le-Duc. Fortunately, the pilot was not seriously injured.[73]

Despite the ineptness of the system, Captain Low's squadron (Low was replaced by Jerry Vasconcelles early in November) engaged in several combats and drove a good many bombers back across the lines. One of these engagements involved the 1st Pursuit Group commander, Major Harold Hartney. On the night of 22 October, the tough little major, determined to learn as much as possible about this type of war flying, flew into the inky darkness over Rembercourt. Within a few minutes Hartney reached the assigned altitude and began his patrol. As the German Gothas generally followed the glittering rivers in their raids toward Paris, he orbited his little aircraft high above the Meuse. To assist the listening posts on the ground he shut off the big Monosoupape* engine and glided silently through the darkness. Then, when he had dropped a few hundred feet he started the engine again and climbed back to his original altitude. This whole process was repeated periodically.[74]

As the minutes wore on, the American hunched deeper into his warmly-lined flying suit, as if to shut out not only the bitter cold of the night but also its black loneliness. Suddenly the sky lighted up with exploding antiaircraft shells and probing searchlights. A black-crossed bomber was in the area. Even though the lights failed to focus on the visitor Hartney knew approximately where the intruder must be. Straining his eyes upward, the Camel pilot spotted twin phosphorescent streaks, the telltale blue flames from the exhausts of the enemy ship. Switching on the engine and advancing the throttle, Hartney climbed toward the dark shadow above. As he drew nearer, the enormous wings, spanning seventy-seven feet, and the forty-foot fuselage became faintly visible.

The big Gotha was alone and droned on to the southeast at 85 mph. Hartney decided to make his attack from below and a little behind the German, but good depth perception in the black heavens was difficult. Before he could press the trigger of his twin Vickers he had almost collided with, and overshot, his target. To regain his position behind the big bomber he chopped his engine, thus leading

* The night-flying Camels were equipped with the 165-h.p. Monosoupape instead of the usual LeRhone or Clerget engines.

to other difficulties. The tricky little Camel, sensitive on controls, and still nose high from the climb, stalled and fell into a deadly spin to the right. Before Hartney could get his bearings in the darkness, he had lost several hundred feet.[75]

On recovering from the spin the American again climbed toward the Gotha, whose crew was apparently unaware of the stalking fighter. This time Hartney approached more cautiously and opened fire from close range. The deadly bullets, marked by an occasional tracer, stitched the whale-like belly of the Hun and entered the nacelles of the pusher engines. Strangely, the giant did not catch fire, and as Hartney swung to the side to make a second firing pass his own engine quit. His main fuel tank was empty. The Canadian-born ace quickly turned on the reserve gas supply, but in doing so his heavily gloved hand accidentally knocked the ignition switch to the "Off" position. The flier was unaware of this, and the Mono-soupape remained dead while raw gasoline continued to feed into the cylinders. The crippled bomber was now forgotten as Hartney dived the fighter to start the propeller windmilling. But the engine remained dead, and a forced landing in the impenetrable darkness below was a distinct possibility. Such a landing in the tree-marked terrain was bad enough in daylight, but at night it was suicide. In one last groping cockpit check Hartney discovered his problem and switched on the ignition. He was now greeted with an even greater terror. The engine cowling in front of him erupted into an inferno as the electrical sparks fired the raw fuel which had been draining all the while into the engine. Blinded by the sudden flames, the Major fought sickening panic. He wore no parachute and was faced with a horrible alternative: be burned to a crisp or jump into the blackness. Hartney chose to stay with the ship. For a long minute, which seemed more like an eternity, the flames crackled around the whirling propeller. But here the spinning rotary engine saved the day by literally fanning the flames to extinction. The inferno died as suddenly as it had begun, and the half-blinded pilot eased forward on the stick to avoid a stall. After a short time he was able to orient himself and banked gently toward home. A few minutes later he bounced to a landing at Rembercourt, and with his fuel completely gone had to be pushed to the hangar line. He had, indeed, discovered some of the problems of night pursuit.[76]

Although his machine guns had raked the German bomber from

stem to stern Hartney made no victory claim. This failure probably cost him his seventh kill, for a few days later the advancing Allies discovered a bullet-riddled Gotha in a patch of woods in the exact location of his terrifying encounter.*

Although the 2nd and 3rd Pursuit Groups frequently joined Hartney's 1st Pursuit Group in low-level strafing and bombing missions during the Meuse-Argonne, they were primarily responsible for the protection of the deep-ranging Allied bombardment and army observation aircraft. The atrocious weather was even more of a handicap to the pilots of the fast little single-seaters than for the slower and more stable Salmsons, Breguets, and De Havillands. Nonetheless, the pursuit fliers were in the air every day of the campaign. On the occasional clear days, the two groups flung themselves eagerly at the brightly painted Fokkers of the Goering and von Boenigk Circuses. In a sense, the Meuse-Argonne was for them what Chateau-Thierry had been for the 1st Pursuit Group, and like the 1st Group they had to learn air combat the hard way. Johnson's 2nd Pursuit Group lost twenty-six pilots killed or captured during the offensive, and Thaw's 3rd Pursuit Group lost nineteen. Still others were wounded but managed to struggle back to the Allied lines. Included in the casualty reports were the names of such aces as James D. Beane and Remington de B. Vernam, of the 22nd Squadron, and Karl J. Schoen, of the 139th. By comparison, the seasoned 1st Pursuit Group lost only nine men in the same period.

One of the most successful pursuit-bombardment missions carried out by the 1st Pursuit Wing occurred late on the afternoon of 18 October. Two squadrons from the 2nd Pursuit Group armed with light bombs flew at low altitudes; two squadrons from the 3rd Pursuit Group flew between 6,500 and 10,000 feet; De Havillands and Breguets from the 1st Day Bombardment Group flew at 13,000 feet; and two more squadrons of the 3rd Pursuit Group patrolled at 17,000 feet. All units rendezvoused over the target at Bayonville, and after the bombers dropped their explosives the low flying fighter-bombers applied the finishing touches. The bombardment squadrons were attacked by more than a score of enemy fighters, but the high flying American escort plunged to the rescue, shooting

---

* The 185th Night Pursuit Squadron scored no official victories over enemy aircraft during its short period of operation. Hartney's failure to request confirmation on his Gotha cost the outfit its only real chance of a score.[77]

down at least nine of the gaily colored Fokkers.[78] John Huffer's 93rd Squadron inflicted most of the damage, with Lieutenants Charles D'Olive, Lowell Harding, Chester Wright, and William F. Goulding scoring kills.* Wright shared in the destruction of three of the colorful adversaries to run his score to six. D'Olive's victory was his fifth.[80]

Despite their heavy losses during the campaign, American pursuit units claimed and were credited with over 270 victories. Of these, the battle-hardened 1st Pursuit Group destroyed 112, the 2nd Pursuit Group got 91, and the 3rd Pursuit Group accounted for 68. Pilots in the two latter groups reaching acedom during the period included Martinus Stenseth and Thomas Cassady, of the 28th Squadron; G. deFreest Larner, William T. Ponder, George Furlow, and Frank O'D. Hunter, of the 103rd; Leslie Rummell, Charles D'Olive, and Chester Wright, of the 93rd; Harold George, Wendel Robertson, Edward M. Haight, Karl Schoen, Robert O. Lindsey, and J. Sidney Owens, of the 139th; Frank Hays, Murray K. Guthrie, and Hank Stovall, of the 13th; and Jacques Swaab, Clinton Jones, James Beane, and Remington de B. Vernam, of the 22nd Squadron.

There has been much controversy and confusion over air victories in World War I. In fact in all wars, fighter pilots, no matter what their nationality, have been prone to make dubious claims of success. World War I was no exception. Most of the difficulty seemed to arise from the utter chaos and confusion of dogfights involving large numbers of aircraft. In air-to-air combat a great many things happen very rapidly. One moment the fighter pilot might be quite alone or surrounded by his squadron mates; the next, the sky may become a swirling mass of machines. Hostile and friendly insignia flash and turn before his eyes, and the heavens are torn by angry tracer bullets. The pilot is hard pressed to avoid shooting down his own comrades and is lucky to get off more than a few shots before his target disappears and he himself becomes the target of an unseen foe. Under such circumstances it is almost impossible to ascertain whether an opponent has been shot down. Certainly

---

* According to Lt. Charles R. D'Olive, each pilot screened his own ammunition before it was placed in the machine gun cartridge belt. Most of the ammunition used (whether tracer, armor-piercing, or incendiary) was produced by such American companies as Peters, Remington, and Western Cartridge. Pilots generally loaded the rounds so that each tracer was followed by four "solids."[79]

few pilots have an opportunity to follow a supposed victim down to witness a crash. World War I combat reports are full of claims based upon such observations as "he appeared to fall out of control," "the Hun dove straight down"—or in other words, took normal evasive action. Claims based upon such reports are, to say the least, doubtful. In World War II such claims would more than likely have been listed as "damaged" or, at best, "probable."

According to the Gorrell Reports, only 50 per cent of the American First Army Air Service victories were confirmed by witnesses on the ground or by balloon observers. The remainder were confirmed by "Direction of the Air Service Commander" or by witnesses from Allied aircraft. The same report indicates that American Air Service fliers destroyed 848 enemy planes and balloons while losing 327 of their own.[81] Since most German Air Force records have been destroyed it is impossible to cross-check these statistics from the enemy side. Letters and diaries of individual German pilots and such works as *Jagd in Flanderns Himmel* and Walter Eberhardt's *Unsere Luftseitkrafte, 1914–1918* do not substantiate the American figures. American casualty totals are undoubtedly accurate, but the victory scores seem unrealistic. In the words of one student of this problem, "Considering the experience of the German pilots, their splendid aircraft, and the aggressive enthusiasm of the inexperienced Americans, we are led to the conclusion that we, at best, shot down as many Germans as we lost; but most probably, did not even do that well."[82] After a thorough study of combat records available the author of the present volume would place the actual victories at approximately 425. As might be expected, the leading aces such as Luke, Rickenbacker, Kindley, and Springs had comparatively few of the dubious "out of control" kills. In the case of Luke, practically all of his eighteen victories were witnessed by competent observers.*

---

* In this check such reports as "seen to crash," "down in flames," "his plane broke up," or "he was seen diving straight down at 100 meters" (too low to recover) were considered authentic kills. Also eyewitness accounts by balloon observers or competent ground witnesses have been accepted as legitimate victories. The use of gun cameras in more recent wars have helped the fighter pilot get a more accurate picture of damage rendered. Yet, even in World War II there was a tendency by pilots from both sides to overestimate enemy losses by a factor of three. The greatest offenders in the Second World War, however, were the gunners in large bomber formations. An attacking fighter might draw the fire of a hundred different waist, tail, and turret gunners. Should he be shot down in flames, at least a

Thirteen American and two French balloon companies took part in the Meuse-Argonne campaign. The I Corps Balloon Group, consisting of the 1st, 2nd, and 5th Balloon Companies, operated on the extreme left flank of the American Army. Work on the right flank in the Meuse River Valley north of Verdun was handled by the III Corps Balloon Group, made up of the 3rd, 4th, 9th, and 42nd Companies. The 6th, 7th, 8th, and 12th Companies of the V Corps Balloon Group followed the American divisions driving toward Montfoucon in the center. Assigned to the army artillery command posts were the 11th and 43rd companies and the two French companies.[83]

None of the American balloons were inflated until the night of 26 September, and it was believed that the enemy was not aware of their presence. The rapid advance of the infantry during the first few days of the offensive made work difficult for the balloon companies. Nonetheless, balloon crews moved with the general advance, keeping between five and six miles behind the front lines. This was accomplished even though it was necessary to transport the fully inflated 1,000 cubic meter balloons over open fields strewn with shell holes and barbed wire and along roads which the American artillery had already wrecked.[84] In one day the 8th Balloon Company advanced twenty miles, and during the offensive the balloon units made an aggregate move of nearly 300 miles without a break in communications with division and corps headquarters.

During the Meuse-Argonne effort, twenty-one balloons were lost; fifteen were burned by strafing aircraft, and six more were destroyed by shellfire. One observer made three parachute jumps within twenty-four hours, and two others were gas casualties.[85] On 26 September 1918, the balloon service suffered its first, and only, battle death. Lieutenant C. J. Ross, of the 8th Balloon Company, and a student observer were performing a general surveillance on that hazy Thursday, when their balloon was attacked by enemy planes. The pair remained at their post until the bag burst into flames; Ross, as the senior officer, did not bail out until his companion had jumped and his parachute had opened. The Titusville, Pennsylvania, man then leaped, but it was too late, for the burning balloon

---

dozen gunners might put in a claim for his destruction. Consequently, debriefing officers were frequently misled, with the result that many more requests for confirmation were made than planes destroyed.

dropped on his parachute, setting it on fire. Ross was dashed to the ground from 900 feet and killed instantly.[86]

Balloon company machine gunners became quite expert before the end of the war. The 6th Company shot down two Fokker D-7's behind American lines in a twenty-four hour period early in October. A third was knocked down by the 2nd Balloon Company.

No Air Service organization worked harder than the balloon companies. Balloon observations were made during the daylight hours, and the units advanced during the night. Like the infantry, the officers and men slept in the open, in cold rain and mud, with only primitive shelter. Infantry outfits were relieved periodically, however, while some balloon crews were on the front without relief throughout the Chateau-Thierry, St. Mihiel, and Meuse-Argonne campaigns.[87]

Between 4 October and the end of the month, the American First Army, now numbering over a million men, inched its way through the third German defense line. Casualties mounted as the enemy threw in reserves and stubbornly contested every defensible position. Gains were small but significant as the blazing struggle forced the Germans to transfer units from other parts of the front and commit them to battle. During this grueling period the Argonne Forest was cleared, and the attack was extended east of the Meuse. By 12 October, enough divisions were in action to necessitate the creation of the American Second Army under the command of Major General Robert L. Bullard; Major General Hunter Liggett was given command of the First Army, and General Pershing assumed command of the army group.

Bullard's Second Army was made responsible for that portion of the front extending from Port-sur-Seille, east of the Moselle, to Fresnes-en-Woevre, southeast of Verdun. Preparations were begun immediately for the extension of operations to the northeast in the direction of Briey and Metz, and these operations occupied the last three days of hostilities. Although meeting stiff resistance and possessing a limited number of troops, the Second Army made appreciable gains before the Armistice brought the drive to a halt.

The Second Army Air Service, commanded by Colonel Frank P. Lahm, consisted originally of the IV Corps Observation Group, the IV Corps Balloon Group, the IV Corps Balloon Wing, and one

French Corps Observation Group. The IV Corps Observation Group was made up of the 8th, 135th and 168th Squadrons and was commanded by Major Harry B. Anderson, a veteran of Chateau-Thierry and St. Mihiel. These units were equipped with the American-built DH-4's. The group was later augmented by Captain George H. Hughes's 258th Aero Squadron. That outfit, however, did not begin combat operations before the Armistice. Captain Herbert A. Schaffner's 85th Squadron was assigned to the group on 4 November, and made two flights over the lines before it was reassigned to the Second Army Observation Group.*

In working the area between Verdun and Pont-a-Mousson, the right extremity of the American front, the IV Corps Observation Group demonstrated remarkable versatility. Not only did it carry on regular visual and photographic reconnaissance flights, adjust artillery fire, and accomplish successful infantry contact patrols, but, in the absence of army observation units, it performed long-range army-type missions as well. Also, since no day bombardment squadron was available until 5 November, Anderson's corps observation group made several bombing raids. In addition, group pilots were called upon to drop propaganda leaflets deep behind the German lines. Finally, units of the IV Corps Observation Group engaged in several strafing missions, normally the function of pursuit, and fought some twenty-four combats with enemy aircraft.[89] Five German airplanes and one balloon were shot down by the group, with Captain John Gilbert Winant's 8th and Captain Bradley Saunders' 135th each destroying two planes; Captain Harry A. Miller's inexperienced 168th Squadron knocked down one plane and one balloon.[90] During its four weeks of combat, the group flew some 498 individual sorties and lost one pilot, Lieutenant Perry H. Aldrich, of the 135th, killed, and four other men wounded.[91]

Late in October still another observation group joined the Second Army, when Major Joseph T. McNarney's VI Corps Observation Group was organized. The group was able to put only one new squadron in operation before the Armistice; this was the DH-4-flying 354th, commanded by Captain Frederick J. Luhr, which made its first patrol on 28 October. The nucleus for the VI Corps Observation Group had been formed previously on 23 October, when the

---

* The 8th and 135th Squadrons had seen extensive service in the First Army before joining the Second Army in October of 1918.[88]

veteran 8th Squadron was relieved from the IV Corps Observation Group and transferred to the Saizerais airdrome to build the new group. McNarney's fliers carried out 359 combat sorties, with bombing and propaganda missions added to their usual corps observation duties.[92] Crews from the VI Corps Observation Group fought two air battles and succeeded in bringing down one enemy aircraft.[93]

Although not formally organized until 19 November 1918, the Second Army Observation Group actually began operations one day before the end of the war, when the 85th Squadron flew a reconnaissance mission over the Conflans area. The group's second squadron, Captain Horace N. Heisen's 278th, was at the front but did not see action before the Armistice.[94]

The 2nd Day Bombardment Group, commanded by Major George E. A. Reinburg, was formed in late October, 1918. As of 11 November, the group consisted of two squadrons, both flying De Havillands. The 100th Aero Squadron was led by Captain Belmont F. Beverly, who had been a flight leader in the veteran 96th Squadron; the 163rd was commanded by Lieutenant Charles M. Kinsolving, a former Lafayette Flying Corps pilot who had had a brilliant record with a French bombardment outfit. Kinsolving's squadron flew several familiarization patrols behind its own lines, but neither of the two squadrons actually made a bombing raid against the Germans. Bombing missions had been planned as early as 6 November, but bad weather held the planes on the ground until 11 November. Airmen from the infant 2nd Day Bombardment Group were preparing to take off from Ourches airfield on their first bombing mission when the formation commander was notified that the Armistice had been signed. Needless to say, the eager young fliers were deeply disappointed at not getting "at least one crack at the Huns."[95]

No pursuit squadrons were transferred from the First Army, and it was not until the 141st Aero Squadron began operations from the Toul Airdrome on 23 October that there were any fighters in the Second Army. On 25 October the 4th Pursuit Group, composed of the 141st, 25th, 17th, and 148th Squadrons, was organized. This group, commanded by the veteran Major Charles J. Biddle, had great combat potential. The 17th and 148th Squadrons, two of the top pursuit outfits in the American Air Service, had just been re-

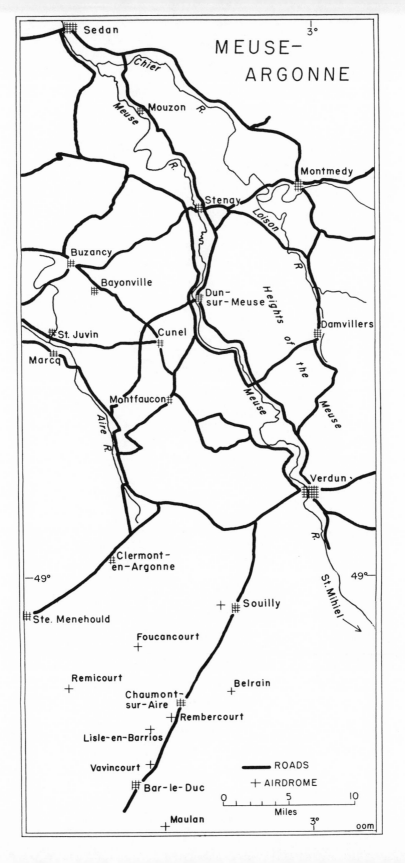

MEUSE-
ARGONNE

Sedan

Chier R.

Mouzon

Meuse R.

Montmedy

Stenay

Loison R.

Buzancy

Bayonville

Dun-
sur-Meuse

Heights

Damvillers

St. Juvin

Cunel

Marcq

of

the

Montfaucon

Aire R.

Meuse

Meuse

Verdun

R.

Clermont-
en-Argonne

—49°

49°

St. Mihiel

Ste. Menehould

Souilly

Foucancourt

Remicourt

Belrain

Chaumont-
sur-Aire

Rembercourt

Lisle-en-Barrios

Vavincourt

ROADS

AIRDROME

Bar-le-Duc

0   5   10

Miles

Maulan

3°

oom

leased by the British and were in the process of converting to the
Spad from the Camel. Their pilots had already accounted for over
120 victories. Although not as experienced, the other two squadrons
also seemed ready for combat. The 25th Squadron, flying British-
built SE-5's, was commanded by a ten-victory ace, Captain Reed
Landis, and numbered in its ranks such crack RAF transfers as
Frederick Luff and Donald Poler. The 141st was superbly trained
and was led by the famous Princeton athlete, Captain Hobart A. H.
Baker.

Of these squadrons only the 141st managed anything more than
token operations on the Second Army front before cessation of hostilities. Some 241 individual sorties were flown, and several air
combats took place.[96] "Hobey" Baker scored the 141st Squadron's
first air kill when, on 28 October, he shot down an enemy aircraft
over the city of Thiaucourt. Eight days later Baker and Lieutenants
Loris V. Cady, Richard D. Shelby, Bryan Hamlin, and Paul R.
Chappell shared in the destruction of a second Hun in the vicinity
of Hageville.[97] The 25th Squadron's first war flight was made on
10 November, when Captain Landis, accompanied by the group
commander, Major Biddle, went on a "hunting expedition" over
the German airdromes in the Metz area. No enemy aircraft were
seen, "but this patrol qualified the Squadron as an actual service
unit operating at the front." A second patrol on the next day had
similar results. Thus, the 25th finished its wartime flying with "no
enemy aircraft seen, no bombs dropped and no rounds fired as a
squadron."[98] The 17th and 148th were still in the process of transition to the Spad when the war ended.

The 5th Pursuit Group, used for training, was not formed until
15 November, four days after the Armistice. This organization was
made up of Captain Dudley L. Hill's 138th,* Captain Edward
Buford's 41st, and Lieutenant Frederick L. Ashworth's 638th
Squadrons. Hill acted as group commander until 1 December, when
he was replaced by Major Maxwell Kirby.

Initially there were only four balloon companies in the Second
Army. All four had been transferred from the American First Army

* Although the 138th Squadron failed to get into combat during the final days of
the war, it did contribute greatly to the completion of this history. J. J. Smith, one
of the squadron's enlisted men, presently of Los Angeles, Calif., has spent years
compiling names and addresses of World War I Air Service personnel. Without his
fine work, present-day students of that war would be greatly handicapped.

and were assigned to a relatively inactive sector. The 10th Balloon Company was located near Dieulouard, the 15th near St. Baussant, the 16th near Limey, and the 69th near Nonsard. At the time of the organization of the Second Army these companies were a part of the IV Corps Balloon Group, commanded by Captain Paul Patterson. Subsequently, the 10th Balloon Company was transferred to the newly created VI Corps Balloon Group, headed by Captain John G. Thornell. It remained at Dieulouard, however, and carried out its usual operations. A third balloon group, the French II Colonial Corps, also operated on the Second Army front. To coordinate the activities of the three groups, the office of Wing Commander, Army Balloons, Second Army was created on 21 October 1918, and Major John A. Jouett was given that post. In spite of the miserable weather during the last four weeks of the war, balloon observers provided the needed artillery and observation service. During the campaign, two balloons were shot down by German fighters, and six observers were forced to jump, two of them twice in the same day.[99]

The last American air victory of the First World War occurred at 10:50 A.M. on 10 November 1918, when Major Maxwell Kirby, flying a 94th Aero Squadron Spad, shot down a Fokker near Maucourt. Kirby, who was scheduled to command the American 5th Pursuit Group then being organized, had been temporarily attached to Rickenbacker's outfit to gain combat experience before taking over his new duties. It had not been easy for him to acquire much real experience since his arrival at Rembercourt a few days before because of the almost constant rain and fog. True, pilots of the American pursuit groups had continued to brave the elements in small patrols, but combats had been few since the opening days of November. Flight after flight had gone out only to return without a glimpse of the enemy. German pilots knowing, undoubtedly, that the end was near simply were not rising to the challenge in their usual aggressive manner. In their view, no amount of last minute fighting and dying would change the outcome.

Kirby had taken off alone on his volunteer patrol nearly an hour before and had been cruising back and forth in the vicinity of the front lines for several minutes. As his eyes searched the cloud-strewn skies he had just about given up the hope of spotting an enemy machine. Suddenly he found himself in a low cloud bank and for a few moments fought to keep his Spad-13 in a straight and level position. On emerging from the clutching white nightmare a few seconds later, he spotted the village of Maucourt. As his straining eyes took in the shell-pocked landscape below, he was startled to find himself practically on top of a Fokker biplane flying in the same direction at 150 feet. Instantly the American pushed the nose of his Spad down and closed to within fifty feet of his unsuspecting opponent and fired a long burst.[100] At that range there could be no missing. As he pulled away from his firing pass he saw the German dive steeply and crash into the side of a small hill. Perhaps it was only fitting that the victor in the last American air battle, like the first combat 210 days before, was to wear the "Hat-in-the-Ring" squadron insignia.

Twenty-four hours and ten minutes after Maxwell Kirby's victim plowed into the battered French landscape the guns on the Western front grew silent. Then, across the shell-torn landscape echoed the cry, *"C'est le finis de la Guerre."*

NOTES

1. Patrick, *Report to Commander-in-Chief,* 234.
2. Air Service, First Army, AEF, G.O. Nos. 10, 12, and 17.
3. G.O. No. 10.
4. Thomas G. Miller, ed., "Casualties of A.E.F. Pursuit Aviation," *Cross and Cockade Journal,* Spring, 1962, 30.
5. *Ibid.,* 35.
6. G.O. No. 13 (amended by G.O. No. 20).
7. G.O. Nos. 13, 15, and 20.
8. "History of the 3rd Pursuit Group, First Pursuit Wing, First Army" (Gorrell Histories, AS AEF, C, XI), 7–9.
9. 1st Day Bombardment Group Operations Report, 26 September 1918, in "History of the 1st Day Bombardment Group" (Gorrell Histories, AS AEF, C, VIII).
10. Recommendation for the DSC (for Sidney C. Howard), "History of the 20th Aero Squadron" (Gorrell Histories, AS AEF, N, XVI).
11. *Ibid.*
12. Miller, "Ordeal of the 1st Day Bombardment Group," *Cross and Cockade Journal,* Spring, 1962, 13.
13. G.O. No. 28.
14. "Casualties in Observation" (Gorrell Histories, AS AEF, M, XXXVIII), 1–3.
15. *Ibid.;* see lists for 9th, 24th, and 91st Squadrons.
16. G.O. No. 17.
17. Patrick, *Report to Commander-in-Chief,* 233.

18. Morse, *50th Aero Squadron*, 37.

19. Mitchell, *Memoirs*, 261; Frank, "Air Service Observation in World War I," unpublished dissertation, University of Florida, 358.

20. Memorandum Number 26, Headquarters, First Army, Chief of Air Service, 9 November 1918 (Gorrell Histories, AS AEF, C, VII), 5.

21. A copy of one of the Air Service information sheets dropped to ground troops is reproduced in Mitchell's *Memoirs*, 262–63.

22. *Ibid.*, 274.

23. Frank, "Air Service Observation in World War I," 358.

24. Director of Air Service, "Brief History," 17; Patrick, *Report to Commander-in-Chief*, 233.

25. Morse, *50th Aero Squadron*, 75.

26. Marshall, *World War I*, 340.

27. William E. Barrett, "The Squadron the World Forgot," *Cavalier*, March, 1961, 54.

28. Morse, *50th Aero Squadron*, 43.

29. *Ibid.*, 45–46.

30. Barrett, "The Squadron the World Forgot," *loc. cit.*, 55.

31. Morse, *50th Aero Squadron*, 46.

32. U.S. Dept. of the Army, *The Medal of Honor of the United States Army*, 261.

33. See corps observation lists in "Victories and Casualties" (Gorrell Histories, AS AEF, M, XXXVIII).

34. *Ibid.*, General Orders.

35. Letter from Spessard L. Holland to author, 13 April 1965.

36. "Tactical History of the Air Service, AEF" (Gorrell Histories, AS AEF, D, I), 81–82.

37. Frank, "Air Service Observation in World War I," 367.

38. See 91st Aero Squadron lists in "Victories and Casualties," *loc. cit.*

39. Mitchell, *Memoirs*, 358. In an article written several months after the war, Gen. Mitchell stated that this action took place on the second day of the offensive, Mitchell, "The Air Service at the Argonne-Meuse," *World's Work*, 19 August 1919, 558. The operations reports of the 1st Day Bombardment indicate that the raid on Dun-sur-Meuse occurred on 26 September, 1918, which would agree with Mitchell's *Memoirs* statement. The only listing for 27 September was a strike against Etain.

40. "Tactical History, Day Bombardment," *loc. cit.*, 133–35.

41. See Operations Reports for 27 September, 29 September, and 1 October 1918, in "1st Day Bombardment Group," *loc. cit.*

42. *Ibid.*, 4 October 1918.

43. *Ibid.*, 5 and 6 October 1918.

44. Mitchell, *Memoirs*, 265–66.

45. Operations Reports for 9 October 1918, "1st Day Bombardment Group," *loc. cit.*

46. *Ibid.*, 10 October 1918.

47. *Ibid.*, 18 October 1918.

48. Bruce C. Hopper, "American Day Bombardment in World War I," *Air Power Historian*, April, 1957, 96; Patrick, *Report to Commander-in-Chief*, 235.

49. Operations Report for 22 October 1918, "1st Day Bombardment Group," *loc. cit.*

50. *Ibid.*, 23 October 1918.

51. *Ibid.*, 27 October 1918.

52. *Ibid.*, 29 October 1918.

53. *Ibid.*, 30 October 1918.

54. *Ibid.*, 31 October 1918.

55. *Ibid.*, 3 and 4 November 1918. See also *History of the 11th Aero Squadron,* 7.

56. *Ibid.*, 5 November 1918; Miller, "Ordeal of Day Bombardment," *loc. cit.; 11th Aero,* 175.

57. Mitchell, "Air Service at the Meuse-Argonne," *loc. cit.,* 558.

58. Director of Air Service, "Brief History," 18.

59. Mitchell, *Memoirs,* 253.

60. Combat Report, 18 September 1918, in "History of the 27th Aero Squadron" (Gorrell Histories, AS AEF, N, V).

61. Hartney, *Up and At 'Em,* 276–78.

62. *Ibid.*, 279.

63. Hartney lists Roberts as being killed on 27 September, but "Victories and Casualties," *loc. cit.,* gives the date as 26 September.

64. Combat Report, 28 September 1918, quoted in Hartney, *Up and At 'Em,* 281.

65. *Ibid.*, 282.

66. Letter from Commander, First Air Depot, to Commanding General, AEF, 23 January 1919, in "History of the 27th Aero Squadron," *loc. cit.* This letter recommending Luke for the Medal of Honor describes the ace's last flight.

67. See Affidavit signed by Mayor Auguste Garre and fourteen other citizens of Murvaux. This document is quoted in Hartney's *Up and At 'Em,* 287. Also see letter from Capt. Chester E. Staten, Graves Registration Officer, to Chief of Air Service, A.P.O., 3 January 1919, cited in the same book.

68. Robertson, *Aces of the 1914–1918 War,* 97; G.O. No. 17 credits Luke with a victory on 30 September. This is in error and very likely refers to his 26 September kill which is not covered by Air Service orders.

69. Frank, "Air Service Observation in World War I," 375.

70. Hartney, *Up and At 'Em,* 203–204.

71. Kenn Rust, "Aces and Hawks," *Air Power Historian,* October, 1962, 220.

72. "Tactical History of American Pursuit Aviation, Meuse-Argonne," *loc. cit.,* 105–12. Frank, "Air Service Observation," 273.

73. "Tactical History," *ibid.*

74. Hartney, *Up and At 'Em,* 234–36; Harry F. Bates, "Colonel Hartney's Night Flight in a Camel," *Air Power Historian,* October, 1964, 119–20.

75. Hartney, *ibid.*

76. *Ibid.*, 236–37.

77. *Ibid.*, 237–39; Bates, "Hartney's Night Flight," *loc. cit.,* 120.

78. "Tactical History of Pursuit Aviation, Meuse-Argonne," *loc. cit.,* 106–10.

79. See letter from Charles R. D'Olive to author, 14 August 1967.

80. G.O. No. 20.

81. "Victories and Casualties," *loc. cit.,* 1–5.

82. Miller, "Last Knighthood," *Cross and Cockade Journal,* Spring, 1962, 30.

83. Director of Air Service, "Brief History," 19.

84. Patrick, *Report to Commander-in-Chief,* 235; Dept. of Air Tactics and Strategy, Air Corps Tactical School, "Tactical History of the Air Service, AEF, 1918," 5. This is an unpublished manuscript in USAF HD Archives.

85. "Balloon Operations in Offensive Combat: Meuse-Argonne" (Gorrell Histories, AS AEF, F, II).

86. Stringer, *Heroes All!* 340. For his action in this affair Lt. Ross was posthumously awarded the American DSC.

87. Frank, "Air Service Observation in World War I," 381.

88. Leo G. Hafferman, "History of the IV Corps Observation Group" (Gorrell Histories, AS AEF, C, XIV), 1–3.

89. Director of Air Service, "Brief History," 20.

90. G.O. Nos. 2, 5, 13, and 17.

91. See lists for the 8th, 135th, and 168th Squadrons in "Victories and Casualties," *loc. cit.*

92. Director of Air Service, "Brief History," 20.

93. G.O. No. 2.

94. Director of Air Service, "Brief History," 20.

95. "History of the 163rd Aero Squadron" (Gorrell Histories, AS AEF, E, XX), 2.

96. Director of Air Service, "Brief History," 20.

97. G.O. Nos. 5 and 7.

98. Excerpts from the 25th Aero Squadron History as quoted in James J. Sloan, "The 25th Aero Squadron, USAS," *American Aviation Historical Society Journal,* Spring, 1962, 22.

99. John A. Jouett, "History of Balloons, Second Army" (Gorrell Histories, AS AEF, F, I), 115–17; Frank, "Air Service Observation in World War I," 385–86.

100. G.O. No. 26; Rust, "Aces and Hawks," *loc. cit.,* 220.

Epilogue

FROM that misty Sunday morning on 14 April 1918, when Douglas Campbell and Alan Winslow sent two German fighters crashing into the wet sod of Gengault airdrome, until the Armistice a little less than seven months later, American fliers were credited with the destruction of 776 enemy planes and 72 enemy balloons.[1] American squadrons staged 150 separate air raids, dropped 275,000 pounds of bombs, and penetrated as far as 160 miles behind enemy lines. They flew 35,000 hours over the lines and took some 18,000 photographs of German positions, from which over a half million prints were made by the photographic sections attached to observation units. In addition, the young warriors spent innumerable hours regulating artillery fire, keeping track of Allied infantry movements, and machine-gunning enemy batteries, convoys, and troops on the ground.[2]

In the performance of these duties, 290 American planes and 37 balloons were lost to enemy action.[3] Of the 569 battle casualties in France, 164 fliers were killed in action, 102 were captured, 103 were wounded, and another 200 were labeled "missing in action." In addition to these losses, 319 were killed in accidents, and 335 died of other causes. Certainly, many of the aviators who were killed might have been saved had they been equipped with parachutes, as were the Germans in the last few months of the war. Most Air Service records indicate that American fliers could have been supplied with these safety devices "but they were turned down as useless until after the Armistice—not by the War Department, but by the flying officers themselves."[4]

When the war ended on 11 November 1918, the total Air Service strength stood at approximately 20,000 officers and 175,000 enlisted men, of which 6,861 officers and 51,229 men were in Europe. Forty-five American air squadrons and 23 balloon companies saw actual combat service. Yet, the 740 planes assigned to those squadrons constituted only 10 per cent of the total Allied air strength in November of 1918. Few of the assigned planes had been built in America; most had been borrowed or purchased from the Allies. American factories produced nearly 12,000 planes during the war but only 3,500 were of combat type. Of these only 1,200, mostly DH-4's, were in France at the time of the Armistice, and scarcely a third of that number were actually assigned to combat squadrons.[5] This figure was indeed a far cry from the skies darkened with "regiments and brigades of winged cavalry mounted on gas driven flying horses" foreseen during the late spring of 1917. Nevertheless, in the fall of 1918, American industry had reached a high state of efficiency, and six more months of war might have seen an Air Service such as was promised in the opening days of the conflict.

As a combat force the American Air Service had come a long way from its cautious beginning in April, 1918, when a single observation squadron equipped with obsolescent aircraft and two pursuit outfits flying unarmed Nieuports ventured into the skies over Toul. The three-month stay in the "quiet" Toul sector had been all too short. In the savage battle around Chateau-Thierry in July and August, the little American force, then numbering seven squadrons, was thrown against some of the best *Jagdstaffeln* in the German Air Force. The experience was bloody but the Americans learned their lessons well. It was around the survivors of the Marne inferno that the Air Service built for the autumn campaigns coming up. At St. Mihiel, American units fighting alongside their French, British, and Italian Allies began to look like an effective force. Several of the twenty-six American squadrons involved were still raw and inexperienced, but the presence of the veterans of the Toul and Marne fighting gave the First Army Air Service stability. In the rain and mud of the Meuse-Argonne offensive the Americans proved worthy of their opponents in every way. Had the war lasted a few more months, the Air Service would, without a doubt, have reached the awesome fighting potential so optimistically predicted in June, 1917.

Certainly lessons, most of them grim, had been learned. In daylight bombing it was discovered that the Breguets and DH-4's simply did not have the range necessary for deep penetration. Nor did they have the bomb carrying capacity adequate for true strategic bombing. The Trenchard-Mitchell thesis of diverting enemy pursuit aircraft from the battle front to protect rear area targets did prove a success but at a bloody cost to the day bombardment crews. Night bombardment was possible but not technologically sound. American fliers were never equipped with the Handley-Page, and they wisely decided against the smaller single-engine bombers for night operations.

The United States actually had little to do with the development of over-all air doctrine during the first world war. In fact, her own air war policies were determined, to a large extent, by the circumstances of the moment. When she entered the war against the Central Powers in 1917, the conflicting points of view between ground and air officers were carried from the field of theory to the field of battle. Unfortunately for the air advocates, this transfer tended to strengthen the ground leaders "because the war had to be fought with the available, not potential weapons, and because the battle on the Western front had already become frozen in a complex pattern of ground operations." American forces simply had to fit into the pattern already established. The war was a struggle of infantry, trenches, and artillery, "of attack and counterattack, of attrition and reinforcement." As one authority on this problem has written, "It is no wonder that the high command regarded air operations as an adjunct to the mighty ground forces which had been committed to the mortal and decisive combat."[6]

Many American aviators saw the possibility of a different type of war and a more effective use of the airplane.* The great majority of them, however, were junior officers in the Army and had little voice in the ultimate decision. As long as the air arm was under the control of ground officers there was little likelihood that the airplane would be used for anything other than direct ground support.

---

* As early as 28 November 1917, a group of air officers headed by Lt. Col. Edgar S. Gorrell, officer-in-charge of Strategic Aviation, Zone of Advance, AEF, submitted a proposal for around-the-clock strategic bombardment of German objectives. Under the proposal, four specific industrial areas were defined as within bombing range. The four target centers were: the Dusseldorf Group, the Cologne Group, and Mannheim Group, and the Saar Valley Group. In addition to target selection, the Gorrell Committee worked out the details on methods of attack, possible difficulties, air routes, weather, etc.

In the words of General Pershing, aviation should be used to "drive off hostile airplanes and procure for the infantry and artillery information concerning the enemy's movements."[7] Observation and "close-in" pursuit work would, of course, fit this policy perfectly; such was not the case with bombardment or offensive pursuit.

When certain strategic-minded air officers advanced the view that the true objective of war might be the enemy's national will and industrial capacity they were sharply corrected by their army superiors. Even cooperation with Trenchard's Independent Air Force was viewed with some suspicion. Approval was finally given but with the proviso that American bombardment units remain an integral part of the AEF. In a letter to Patrick in June, 1918, Major General J. W. McAndrews, Pershing's chief of staff, emphasized that it was extremely important that the higher officers in bombardment be impressed with the necessity for coordination of all effort toward a common tactical end. According to McAndrews, these bombardment advocates must be warned against any idea of independence, and they should be taught from the beginning that their efforts must be closely linked with the operations of the ground army. When land operations reached a crucial point, Pershing's headquarters would designate the region to be bombed. Selection of targets during these critical periods would depend solely upon their importance to actual and projected ground operations.[8]

As a result of these restrictions American bombardment aviation was in a large measure limited to work in the battlefield area. On occasions such as the big air raid on German troop concentrations in the Damvillers-Wavrille area on 9 October 1918, bombardment was able to render valuable service. Despite the limitations imposed by ground generals, Mitchell had, by the end of the war, made some progress in selling the idea of strategic bombardment. Pershing, who had great respect for his hard-driving air officer, apparently had given his approval for night raids against German industrial centers, to begin early in 1919. According to Mitchell's diary, the AEF Commander had even given his approval to a Mitchell proposal to use parachute troops against the enemy.*

* According to this plan sixty squadrons of Handley-Page bombers were to be used as troop carriers. Each bomber would carry ten men, not counting the two-man crew. These airborne soldiers were to be dropped behind enemy lines; attack planes were to make diversionary strikes ahead of the troop carriers, while fighters were to provide immediate support and protection.[9]

In still another area of air doctrine there was controversy. Air officers who were convinced of the need to employ air units as a concentrated force opposed the permanent assignment of squadrons to the various ground commands as desired by many army leaders. These aviators, such as Mitchell, Foulois, and Brereton, favored the greatest possible concentration of air striking forces under the direct command of an air officer for whatever missions might be needed by the high command. The Germans had already demonstrated the effectiveness of this approach during their great offensive of March, 1918. They had quickly gained control of the air and were able to harass Allied troop movements with virtually no interference. It was not until the Allies adopted the same doctrine of concentration that the tide was turned.[10] Billy Mitchell, as the Air Service First Brigade commander in the Chateau-Thierry campaign, ran into considerable difficulty with army corps commanders over control of air squadrons. He eventually won at least partial support from the American Expeditionary Force Commander, and in the St. Mihiel and Meuse-Argonne offensives he was able to concentrate air units from various ground commands into a powerful unified force. Although Mitchell, as First Army Air Service commander, was still required to report directly to Pershing's headquarters, he was for all practical purposes in full control of all air units assigned to the sector.

Owing to its late entry into the conflict, the American Air Service did relatively little pioneering in the art of air combat. The Germans had introduced the first true fighter when Anthony Fokker developed a fixed machine gun synchronized to fire through the propeller of one of the early models of Fokker scouts. Also, the Germans had led the way in the use of large pursuit formations for air combat. The French and British had quickly caught up, and the British had developed an effective night fighter to contest night raids on London by enemy Zeppelins and Gotha bombers. Both the French and the British had made unique contributions in observation work, and the British, along with the Italians, had made some real advances in the area of strategic bombardment. For the most part, the infant American force followed the pattern of its more experienced allies. In the area of "balloon busting," low-level pursuit, and "cavalry reconnaissance" the Americans made valuable innovations.

Viewed in retrospect, World War I was merely a transitional phase in the development of the air weapon. The war expanded the frontiers of air tactics from mere reconnaissance and observation to the more complex field of operations in support of land and sea forces. The experience of the 1914–1918 war, limited as it was, forecast some of the awesome potentialities of large-scale bombing raids of more recent conflicts. In the words of one authority on air power, "Air raids on both sides caused interruptions to production and transportation out of all proportions to the weight of bombs dropped. They led to the withdrawal of interceptor planes from the fighting fronts and required an enormous diversion of effort to anti-aircraft measures and to widespread passive defenses which subsequently were called air raid precautions."[11] The first air war gave great impetus to the improvement of aircraft* and to the training of fliers. These factors, plus the glamour of the air heroes, served to produce a new generation of air-minded youth. Certainly, air power did not win the first world war; in fact, it played a relatively small role, but its lessons were not lost on the military and political leaders of the second great conflict which started in 1939.

Aerial combat in World War I produced more than a new pattern of warfare and improved aircraft; a race of gallant men emerged from the flaming conflict. With such individuals as Frank Luke, Kenneth Littauer, Eddie Rickenbacker, Sidney Coe Howard, Leland Carver, Harold Goettler, and Field Kindley, America contributed her fair share of those men of valor who fought in Europe's hostile skies.

* Some aviation authorities argue with considerable logic that the American success in mass-producing the heavy Liberty engine actually held back the advancement of pursuit aviation in the 1920's. Certainly, there was a tendency to hang on to the Liberty, one of America's few production triumphs in World War I, long after it had become obsolete.

NOTES

1. "Victories and Casualties" (Gorrell Histories, AS AEF, M, XXXVIII), 3. According to Bruce Robertson, ed., *Aces of the 1914–1918 War,* eighty-two American fliers became aces with at least five victories.

2. Patrick, *Report to Commander-in-Chief,* 225.

3. "Victories and Casualties," *loc. cit.,* 3. Gen. Patrick places American losses at 357 planes and 35 balloons. See Patrick, *ibid.*

4. Arnold, *Global Mission,* 49. Recent interviews of several World War I aviators by the author reveal a somewhat different story.

5. Sweetser, *Air Service,* 247–48.

6. Thomas M. Greer, *Development of Air Doctrine in the Army Air Arm, 1917–1941* (USAF Historical Study No. 89), 3.

7. Pershing, *My Experiences in the World War,* II, 337.

8. Memorandum, Chief of Staff, GHQ, AEF to Chief of Staff, Air Service, 18 June 1918" (Gorrell Histories, AS AEF, B, VI).

9. Levine, *Mitchell,* 247–48.

10. Greer, *Development of Air Doctrine,* 5.

11. Edward Mead Earle, "The Influence of Air Power," *Yale Review,* Summer, 1946, quoted in Eugene M. Emme, *The Impact of Air Power,* 107–108.

TABLES

TABLE I

PLANES DESTROYED BY AIR SERVICE PURSUIT SQUADRONS AND
CONFIRMED VICTORIES OF INDIVIDUAL PILOTS

Squadron	Squadron Victories	Victories by Individual Pilots
94th	70	84
148th	64	70
27th	54	79
95th	48	70
22nd	42	57
17th	39*	43
139th	34	74
103rd	32	43
93rd	32	43
147th	31	63
13th	28	59
49th	25	36
28th	14	30
213th	12	20
141st	2	6
	526	777

* Does not include fourteen enemy aircraft destroyed on the ground in the Varssenaere raid on 13 August 1918.

TABLE II

RECORDS OF U.S. AIR SERVICE ACES IN WORLD WAR I

Name	Organization	Airplanes Destroyed	Balloons Destroyed	Total	Home Town
Capt. Edward V. Rickenbacker[1]	94th	22	4	26	Columbus, Ohio
2nd Lt. Frank Luke, Jr.*	27th	4	14	18	Phoenix, Ariz.
Maj. Raoul G. Lufbery*[2]	94th	17	0	17	Wallingford, Conn.
1st Lt. George A. Vaughn	17th	12	1	13	Brooklyn, N.Y.
Capt. Field E. Kindley	148th	12	0	12	Gravette, Ark.
1st Lt. David E. Putnam*[3]	139th	12	0	12	Brookline, Mass.
Capt. Elliott White Springs	148th	12	0	12	Lancaster, S.C.
Capt. Reed G. Landis[4]	25th	9	1	10	Chicago, Ill.
Capt. Jacques M. Swaab	22nd	10	0	10	New York, N.Y.
1st Lt. Paul F. Baer[5]	103rd	9	0	9	Fort Wayne, Ind.
Capt. Thomas G. Cassady[6]	28th	9	0	9	Spencer, Ind.
1st Lt. Chester E. Wright	93rd	8	1	9	Cambridge, Mass.
1st Lt. Lloyd A. Hamilton*[7]	17th	6	3	9	Burlington, Vt.
1st Lt. James D. Beane*	22nd	6	2	8	Concord, Mass.
1st Lt. Howard Burdick	17th	8	0	8	Brooklyn, N.Y.
1st Lt. Henry R. Clay	148th	8	0	8	Fort Worth, Tex.
Capt. Hamilton Coolidge*	94th	5	3	8	Boston, Mass.
1st Lt. Jesse O. Creech	148th	8	0	8	Washington, D.C.
1st Lt. William P. Erwin (observation pilot)	1st	8	0	8	Chicago, Ill.
1st Lt. Frank O'D. Hunter	103rd	7	1	8	Savannah, Ga.
2nd Lt. Clinton Jones	22nd	8	0	8	San Francisco, Calif.
1st Lt. Gorman de Freest Larner[8]	103rd	8	0	8	Washington, D.C.
Capt. James A. Meissner	147th	7	1	8	Brooklyn, N.Y.
1st Lt. Joseph Fritz Wehner*	27th	2	6	8	Boston, Mass.

1st Lt. Wilbert Wallace White*	147th	7	1	8	New York, N.Y.
Maj. Charles J. Biddle	13th	7	0	7	Andalusia, Pa.
Capt. Reed M. Chambers	94th	6	1	7	Memphis, Tenn.
1st Lt. Harvey Weir Cook	94th	4	3	7	Toledo, Ohio
1st Lt. Lansing C. Holden	95th	2	5	7	New York, N.Y.
Maj. John Huffer⁹	93rd	7	0	7	Paris, France
1st Lt. Wendel A. Robertson	139th	7	0	7	Fort Smith, Ark.
1st Lt. Leslie J. Rummell	93rd	7	0	7	Newark, N.J.
1st Lt. Karl J. Schoen*	139th	7	0	7	Indianapolis, Ind.
1st Lt. Sumner Sewall	95th	5	2	7	Bath, Me.
1st Lt. Martinus Stenseth	28th	7	0	7	Twin Valley, Minn.
1st Lt. William H. Stovall	13th	7	0	7	Stovall, Miss.
1st Lt. Byrne V. Baucom (observer)	1st	6	0	6	Milford, Texas
Capt. Arthur R. Brooks	22nd	6	0	6	Framingham, Mass.

* Killed in Combat.

[1] Rickenbacker's 26th victory was not officially confirmed by the U.S. Air Force until 20 January 1960. Consequently, many official lists credit him with only twenty-five kills.

[2] Lufbery scored all seventeen of his victories while flying with the Lafayette Escadrille. He had been assigned to the 94th Pursuit Squadron for several weeks when he was killed in combat.

[3] Putnam scored at least eight of his official kills while flying with the Lafayette Flying Corps. He was killed while leading the 139th Aero Squadron on the first day of the St. Mihiel Campaign.

[4] Landis scored all of his victories with 40 Squadron, RAF, before his assignment as commander of the U.S. 25th Squadron.

[5] Baer scored most of his successes while assigned to the Lafayette Flying Corps.

[6] Of the nine planes destroyed by Cassady, five were knocked down while he was assigned to French squadrons.

[7] Hamilton's total include at least four kills scored while attached to the RAF.

[8] Three of Larner's eight victories were scored with French Escadrille SPA 86.

[9] Served with French Escadrille SPA 62 before transferring to the American Air Service. While flying with the French, Huffer scored four of his seven victories.

TABLE II (continued)

Name	Organization	Airplanes Destroyed	Balloons Destroyed	Total	Home Town
1st Lt. Douglas Campbell	94th	6	0	6	Mt. Hamilton, Calif.
1st Lt. Edward P. Curtis	95th	6	0	6	Rochester, N.Y.
1st Lt. Murray K. Guthrie	13th	6	0	6	Mobile, Ala.
Capt. James Norman Hall[10]	94th	6	0	6	Colfax, Iowa
Capt. Leonard C. Hammond (observer)	91st	6	0	6	San Francisco, Calif.
Lt. Col. Harold E. Hartney[11]	27th	6	0	6	Saskatoon, Canada
1st Lt. Frank K. Hays	13th	6	0	6	Chicago, Ill.
1st Lt. Donald Hudson	27th	6	0	6	Washington, D.C.
Maj. James A. Keating	49 Squadron RAF	6	0	6	Unknown
2nd Lt. Howard C. Knotts	17th	6	0	6	Carlinsville, Ill.
1st Lt. Robert O. Lindsey	139th	6	0	6	Maderson, N.C.
2nd Lt. John K. MacArthur	27th	6	0	6	Buffalo, N.Y.
1st Lt. Ralph A. O'Neill	147th	6	0	6	Nogales, Ariz.
1st Lt. William T. Ponder[12]	103rd	6	0	6	Mangum, Okla.
2nd Lt. Kenneth L. Porter	147th	6	0	6	Dowagiac, Mich.
1st Lt. Edgar G. Tobin	103rd	6	0	6	San Antonio, Tex.
1st Lt. Remington de B. Vernam*	22nd	3	3	6	New York, N.Y.
1st Lt. William T. Badham (observer)	91st	5	0	5	Birmingham, Ala.
1st Lt. Hilbert L. Bair[13]	24 Squadron RAF	5	0	5	Fort Wayne, Ind.
Capt. Clayton L. Bissell	148th	5	0	5	Kane, Pa.
1st Lt. Harold R. Buckley	95th	4	1	5	Agawam, Mass.
1st Lt. Laurence K. Callahan[14]	148th	5	0	5	Chicago, Ill.
Capt. Everett R. Cook (observation pilot)	91st	5	0	5	San Francisco, Calif.
1st Lt. Charles R. D'Olive[15]	93rd	5	0	5	Suggsville, Ala.

1st Lt. Arthur E. Easterbrook (observer)	1st	5	0	Fort Flagler, Wash.
1st Lt. George W. Furlow	103rd	5	0	Rochester, Minn.
1st Lt. Harold H. George	139th	5	0	Niagara Falls, N.Y.
Capt. Charles G. Grey	213th	4	1	Chicago, Ill.
1st Lt. Edward M. Haight	139th	5	0	Astoria, N.Y.
1st Lt. James A. Healy	147th	5	0	Jersey City, N.J.
1st Lt. James Knowles	95th	5	0	Cambridge, Mass.
1st Lt. Frederick E. Luff[16]	25th	3	2	Cleveland, Ohio
2nd Lt. J. Sidney Owens	139th	5	0	Baltimore, Md.
Capt. David McK. Peterson[17]	95th	5	0	Honesdale, Pa.
1st Lt. Orville A. Ralston	148th	5	0	Lincoln, Neb.
1st Lt. John J. Seerley	13th	5	0	Chicago, Ill.
Maj. Victor H. Strahm (observation pilot)	91st	5	0	Evanston, Ill.
1st Lt. Francis M. Simonds	147th	5	0	New York, N.Y.
Lt. Col. William Thaw[18]	103rd	4	1	Pittsburgh, Pa.
1st Lt. Robert M. Todd	17th	5	0	Cincinnati, Ohio
Capt. Jerry C. Vasconcelles	27th	4	1	Denver, Colo.
1st Lt. Rodney D. Williams	17th	4	1	Waukesha, Wis.

[10] Hall scored several of his victories while flying with the Lafayette Escadrille. Some victory lists credit him with only three kills.

[11] Hartney gained five of his six victories while flying with the British. He commanded the 27th Aero Squadron at Toul and during the Chateau-Thierry campaign in August took command of the 1st Pursuit Group.

[12] Before joining the 103rd Aero Squadron, Ponder served with French Escadrille SPA 67, where he scored three of his six victories.

[13] Bair scored all of his victories while attached to the RAF.

[14] Three of Callahan's victories were scored while he was attached to RAF squadrons.

[15] D'Olive was added to the ace list in 1963, when he received official confirmation for a plane shot down on 13 September 1918.

[16] Luff scored all five of his kills while serving with the British.

[17] Peterson gained one of his five victories while flying with the French.

[18] Thaw's victories were scored while serving with the Lafayette Escadrille.

TABLE III

OFFICERS WHO SERVED AS CHIEFS OF AIR SERVICE OF THE
VARIOUS ARMY CORPS IN THE AEF

First Army Air Service[1]

Chief, Air Service, I Corps	Col. William Mitchell	1 June–1 July 1918
	Maj. Ralph Royce	1 July–10 Aug. 1918
	Maj. Melvin A. Hall	11 Aug.–24 Oct. 1918
	Capt. Oliver P. Echols	25 Oct.–11 Nov. 1918
Chief, Air Service, III Corps	Maj. Ralph Royce	19 July–26 July 1918[2]
	Maj. Joseph T. McNarney	26 July–8 Aug. 1918
	Maj. Melvin A. Hall	8 Aug.–25 Aug. 1918
	Capt. Kenneth P. Littauer (acting)	31 Aug.–10 Sept. 1918
	Lt. Col. Joseph C. Morrow	15 Sept.–22 Oct. 1918
	Capt. Kenneth P. Littauer	22 Oct.–11 Nov. 1918
Chief, Air Service, V Corps	Lt. Col. A. R. Christie	27 July—8 Oct. 1918

Second Army Air Service

Chief, Air Service, IV Corps	Maj. Harry B. Anderson	Sept.–11 Nov. 1918
Chief, Air Service, VI Corps	Maj. Joseph T. McNarney	23 Oct.–11 Nov. 1918

[1] Although the First Army was not officially created until 10 August 1918, the I, III, and V Corps were already in existence.

[2] Note that an officer might, in certain emergencies, serve as Chief of Air Service in two corps at the same time.

BIBLIOGRAPHY

The unpublished documents consulted during the preparation of this book can be found in several collections including those of the United States Air Force Historical Division Archives, the Air University Archives, the Air Force Museum, Aeronautical Chart and Information Center, National Air Museum (Smithsonian Institution), Library of Congress, New York Public Library, National Archives, and various individuals. The most important of these collections are described below.

The USAF Historical Division Archives at the Air University, Maxwell Air Force Base, Alabama, is the official repository of unit histories and supporting documents for the Air Force and its predecessor organizations such as the Aviation Section of the Signal Corps, the Air Service, the Air Corps, and the Army Air Force. Although a large part of the more than a million documents are concerned with World War II and Korea, a considerable number pertain to the Air Service record in World War I. Of significant value to the student of the World War I air effort are the Foulois, Jones, Salsman, Lahm, and Caproni collections. In addition, the Archives contain many of the studies developed between the two world wars by the Department of Air Tactics and Strategy of the Air Corps Tactical School.

Still another gold mine of Air Force material is the Air University Library, also located at Maxwell Air Force Base. This library collection contains approximately one million items, including extensive unpublished official matter, military regulations, technical manuals and pamphlets, and U.S. government publications relating to the Air Force, as well as books and many files of newspapers, journals, and magazines.

In addition to its fine collection of historical military aircraft, the Air Force Museum, in Dayton, Ohio, maintains a Reference and Research Division of one-half million documents, films, and books portraying the history of the United States Air Force. Of special interest to the student of the Air Service combat efforts in the first world war is the collection of diaries, letters, and papers of many of the combatants. This valuable collection is growing rapidly as more and more of the war birds are turning over their private papers to the Museum.

The Library of Congress, in Washington, D.C., not only houses one of the world's finest collections of aeronautical books and journals, but it also holds the papers of such men as Henry H. Arnold, Carl Spaatz, Billy Mitchell, and

Glenn L. Martin. These papers, in the Manuscript Division of the Library, include personal mementos, correspondence, diaries, journals, notes, reports, and a host of miscellaneous items. The papers of Generals Arnold and Mitchell were especially helpful in the preparation of this book.

The New York Public Library contains one of the most complete collections of published Air Force unit histories. A bibliography of items in this collection, known as the C. E. Dornbusch Collection, was published in 1958 as the *Unit Histories of the United States Air Force: Including Privately Printed Personal Narratives*.

Without a doubt, the richest source of material on World War I military aviation is the National Archives, which houses a whole series of pertinent record collections. These collections fall into two different official classifications. Records Group Number 18 contains material pertaining to the Air Service and the Bureau of Aircraft Production in the United States, while Records Group Number 120 contains material on the Air Service in the AEF. Records Group Number 18 includes such important items as (1) The Bureau of Aircraft Production Historical File; (2) The Bureau of Aircraft Production, Executive Office Files; (3) The Bureau of Aircraft Production, Miscellaneous Historical File; (4) The Files of the Administrative Division of the Division of Military Aeronautics; (5) Office of Chief, Air Service, Files; (6) The Finance Advisory Board File; and (7) AEF Cable File.

Of even greater value is the material classified under Records Group Number 120. This group is split into the broad categories of (1) World War I Organization Records, Air Service Historical Records and (2) Air Service, AEF, History. Since the material in this group was collected under the general supervision of Colonel E. S. Gorrell, the group is usually called the Gorrell Histories. Although this author has seen the originals, the footnotes of the present work refer to the microfilm organization of the records. Because this collection is so important, a more detailed breakdown of its contents follows:

Series A–Early History and General Organization of the Air Service (27 vols.)

Series B–Foreign Relations (14 vols.)

Series C–Tactical Units (14 vols.)

Series D–Air Service Tactical History of the War (2 vols.)

Series E–Squadron Histories (26 vols.)

Series F–Balloon Section, Service of Supply, and Zone of Advance (7 vols.)

Series G–Photographic Section, Service of Supply, and Zone of Advance (4 vols.)

Series H–Mechanics Regiments, Construction Companies, and Air Parks (5 vols.)

Series I–Paris Headquarters and Supply Section, Service of Supply, and Zone of Advance (28 vols.)

Series J–Training Section and Schools (12 vols.)

Series K–Technical Section (2 vols.)

Series L–Personnel, Information, Radio and Cable Sections, and Medical Service (14 vols.)

Series M–Miscellaneous (48 vols.)

Series N–Duplicates of all First Army Material (23 vols.)

Series O–Weekly Reports on Programs of the Air Service Activities, Victory and Casualty Lists, etc. (30 vols.)

Series P–History of Headquarters, Air Service, Third Army of Occupation (2 vols.)

Series Q–Air Service Liquidation (5 vols.)

Series R–Results of Air Service Efforts (4 vols.)

DOCUMENTS AND UNPUBLISHED MATERIAL

"Air Service Activities in Italy." Caproni Collection, USAF HD Archives, Maxwell AFB, Ala.

Air Service Bulletin, VII, No. 302 (31 October 1918).

Alford, Maj. James S. "The History of the First Fighter Group." Unpublished manuscript in USAF HD Archives, 1959.

Arnold, Henry H. "History of the Aviation Section (Signal Corps) and Division of Military Aeronautics, From April 1917 to October 1918." Unpublished manuscript in Arnold Papers, Manuscript Division, Library of Congress, Washington, D.C.

Avery, Walter R. "World War I Story." Unpublished manuscript in Avery Collection, Boca Raton, Fla.

Barnett, A. J. "Air Operations in the St. Mihiel Offensive." Unpublished thesis, Air Corps Tactical School, 1934.

Bissell, Clayton L. *Brief History of the Air Corps and Its Late Development*. Langley Field, Va.: Air Corps Tactical School, 1927.

Campbell, Douglas. "Interview by Ken Leish, June, 1960." Unpublished transcript in USAF HD Archives, Maxwell AFB, Ala.

"The Cross License Agreement." Bureau of Aircraft Production File, Box 11, National Archives, Washington, D.C.

Deickman, Gen. der Flieger A. D. Paul. "German Air Force Operations in Support of the Army." (USAF Historical Study No. 163.) Ed. by Dr. Littleton B. Atkinson, Brig. Gen. Noel F. Parrish, and Dr. Albert F. Simpson. USAF HD Archives, Maxwell AFB, Ala., 1962.

Department of Air Tactics and Strategy, Air Corps Tactical School. "Tactical History of the Air Service, AEF, 1918." Unpublished manuscript in USAF HD Archives.

Foulois, Benjamin D. "Air Service, American Expeditionary Forces, 1917–1919." Unpublished manuscript in Foulois Collection, USAF HD Archives, Maxwell AFB, Ala.

Frank, Sam H. "American Air Service Observation in World War I." Unpublished Ph.D. dissertation, University of Florida, 1961.

Hartney, Maj. Harold E. "Observation on Night Pursuit." Unpublished document in Lahm Collection. USAF HD Archives, Maxwell AFB, Ala.

Hennessy, Juliette A. "The United States Air Arm in World War I." Unpublished manuscript in USAF HD Archives, Maxwell AFB, Ala.

Hopper, Bruce C. "When the Air Was Young: American Day Bombardment, A.E.F., France, 1917–1918." Unpublished manuscript in Library of Congress, Washington, D.C.

Layman, Walter G. "Meuse-Argonne." Unpublished thesis, Air Corps Tactical School, 1933, Maxwell AFB, Ala.

McFarland, Russell M. "The Foreign Missions to the United States." Unpublished manuscript in National Archives, Washington, D.C.

Mitchell, William. "Before Pershing in Europe." Unpublished manuscript in Mitchell Papers, Manuscript Division, Library of Congress, Washington, D.C. This is the uncorrected draft of Mitchell's wartime diary.

———. "Biographical Note." Mitchell Papers, Manuscript Division, Library of Congress, Washington, D.C.

Neumann, George P. (compiler). *The German Air Force in the Great War.* From the records and with the assistance of twenty-nine officers and officials of the naval and military air services. Translated by J. E. Gurdon. Manuscript in USAF HD Archives, Maxwell AFB, Ala.

Paegelow, Maj. John A. "Operations of Allied Balloons in the Saint Mihiel Offensive." Unpublished manuscript in Lahm Collection, USAF HD Archives, Maxwell AFB, Ala.

Patrick, Mason M. *Final Report of Chief of Air Service, A.E.F.* (Air Service Information Circular II, No. 180.) Washington, D.C.: Government Printing Office, 1921.

Powel, Harford W. H. "Brief History of the Army Air Forces." Unpublished manuscript in USAF HD Archives, Maxwell AFB, Ala.

"Preliminary Inventory of the Records of the Army Air Forces." Unpublished manuscript in National Archives, Washington, D.C.

Rickenbacker, Capt. E. V. "Interview by Donald Shaughnessy, 20 February 1960." Unpublished transcript in USAF HD Archives, Maxwell AFB, Ala.

U.S. Army, American Expeditionary Forces. *Final Report of General John J. Pershing, Commander-in-Chief, American Expeditionary Forces.* Washington, D.C.: Government Printing Office, 1919.

U.S. Army War College. *Order of Battle of the United States Land Forces in the World War, American Expeditionary Forces,* 2 vols. Washington, D.C.: Government Printing Office, 1931–37.

U.S. Department of the Army, Historical Division. *United States Army in the World War, 1917–1919,* 17 vols. Washington, D.C.: Government Printing Office, 1948.

U.S. Department of Justice. *Report of the Aircraft Inquiry.* Washington, D.C.: Government Printing Office, 1918.

U.S. War Industries Board. *American Industry in the War.* Washington, D.C.: Government Printing Office, 1921.

War Department, Office of Director of Air Service. "Brief History of Air

Service, A.E.F." Unpublished manuscript in USAF HD Archives, Maxwell AFB, Ala.

Weyerhaeuser, F. K. "War Experiences, 1917–1918." Unpublished manuscript in Weyerhaeuser Collection, St. Paul, Minn.

BOOKS

Archibald, Norman. *Heaven High, Hell Deep, 1914–1918*. New York: A. & C. Boni, 1935.

Arnold, Henry H. *Global Mission*. New York: Harper & Bros., 1949.

Arnold, Henry H., and Eaker, Ira C. *Winged Warfare*. New York: Harper & Bros., 1941.

Baldwin, Hanson W. *World War I: An Outline History*. New York: Harper & Row, 1962.

Barrett, William E. *The First War Planes*. Greenwich, Conn.: Fawcett Publications, 1960.

Barth, Clarence G. *History of the Twentieth Aero*. Winona, Minn.: Winona Labor News, 1919.

Biddle, Charles J. *The Way of the Eagle*. New York: Charles Scribner's Sons, 1919.

Bingham, Hiram. *An Explorer in the Air Service*. New Haven: Yale University Press, 1920.

Bishop, William A. *Winged Warfare*. New York: George H. Doran Co., 1934.

Boyle, Andrew. *Trenchard*. London: Collins, 1962.

Brewer, Leighton. *Riders of the Sky*. Boston: Houghton Mifflin Co., 1934.

Buchan, John. *A History of the Great War*, 4 vols. New York: Houghton Mifflin Co., 1922.

Buckley, Harold. *Squadron 95*. Paris: Obelisk Press, 1933.

Carver, Leland M., *et al. The Ninetieth Aero Squadron, American Expeditionary Forces*. Hinsdale, Ill.: E. Harold Greist, 1920.

Chandler, Charles de Forrest, and Lahm, Frank P. *How Our Army Grew Wings*. New York: Ronald Press, 1943.

Chapman, Victor. *Victor Chapman's Letters from France*. Memoir by John Jay Chapman. New York: Macmillan Co., 1917.

Clapp, Frederick M. *A History of the 17th Aero Squadron*. Garden City, N.Y.: Country Life Press, 1918.

Coolidge, Hamilton. *Letters of an American Airman, Being the War Record of Capt. Hamilton Coolidge, U.S.A., 1917–1918*. Boston: privately printed by Norwood, Plimpton Press, 1919.

Craven, Wesley F., and Cate, James L. (eds.). *The Army Air Forces in World War II*, 6 vols. Chicago: University of Chicago Press, 1948–55.

Crowell, Benedict, and Wilson, Robert F. *How America Went to War*, Vol. V, *The Armies of Industry*. New Haven: Yale University Press, 1921.

Cruttwell, C. R. M. F. *A History of the Great War, 1914–1918*. Oxford: Clarendon Press, 1936.

318 ↱ ↱ BIBLIOGRAPHY

Cuneo, John R. *Winged Mars,* Vol. I, *The German Air Weapon,* 1870–1914, Vol. II, *The Air Weapon, 1914–1916.* Harrisburg, Pa.: Military Service Publishing Co., 1942, 1945.

Department of the Army. *The Medal of Honor of the United States Army.* Washington, D.C.: Government Printing Office, 1948.

Dornbusch, C. E. *Unit Histories of the United States Air Forces: Including Privately Printed Personal Narratives.* Hampton Bays, N.Y.: Hampton Books, 1958.

Douhet, Gen. Giulio. *The Command of the Air.* New York: Coward-McCann, 1942.

Eliot, George F. *Bombs Bursting in Air: The Influence of Air Power on International Relations.* New York: Reynal & Hitchcock, 1939.

Emme, Eugene. *The Impact of Air Power.* Princeton, N.J.: D. Van Nostrand Co., 1959.

Fitch, Willis. *Wings in the Night.* Boston: Marshall Jones Co., 1938.

Fuller, Gen. J. F. C. *Armament and History.* New York: Charles Scribner's Sons, 1945.

Gauvreau, Emile, and Cohen, Lester. *Billy Mitchell.* New York: E. P. Dutton & Co., 1930.

Gibbons, Floyd. *The Red Knight of Germany.* New York: Doubleday, Page & Co., 1927.

Goldberg, Alfred (ed.). *A History of the United States Air Force 1907–1957.* Princeton, N.J.: D. Van Nostrand Co., 1957.

Gorrell, E. S. *The Measure of America's War Aeronautical Effort.* Northfield, Vt.: Norwich University, 1940.

Goss, Milton P. *Civilian Morale Under Aerial Bombardment, 1914–1939,* 2 vols. Maxwell AFB, Ala.: Air University, 1948.

Greer, Thomas. *Development of Air Doctrine in the Army Air Arm, 1917–1941* (USAF Historical Study No. 89). Montgomery, Ala.: Air University, 1953.

[Grider, John MacGavock]. *War Birds: Diary of an Unknown Aviator.* New York: George H. Doran Co., 1926.

Gurney, Gene. *The War in the Air.* New York: Crown Publishers, 1962.

Haddow, G. W., and Grosz, Peter M. *The German Giants: The Story of the R-Planes, 1914–1919.* London: Putnam, 1962.

Hall, Bert, and Niles, J. J. *One Man's War: The Story of the Lafayette Escadrille.* New York: Holt, 1929.

Hall, James Norman. *High Adventure.* New York: Houghton Mifflin Co., 1918.

Hall, James Norman, and Nordhoff, Charles B. (eds.). *The Lafayette Flying Corps,* 2 vols. Boston: Houghton Mifflin Co., 1920. Reissued by Kennikat Press, Port Washington, N.Y., 1965.

Harbord, James Guthrie. *The American Expeditionary Forces: Its Organization and Accomplishments.* Evanston, Ill., 1929.

———. *The American Army in France, 1917–1919.* Boston: Brown & Co., 1936.

Hart, B. H. Liddell. *Strategy.* New York: Frederick A. Praeger, 1954.

Hart, Percival G. *History of the 135th Squadron.* Chicago, 1939.

Hartney, Harold E. *Up and At 'Em.* Harrisburg, Pa.: Stackpole Sons, 1940.

Haslett, Elmer. *Luck on the Wing.* New York: E. P. Dutton & Co., 1920.

History of the 11th Aero Squadron. Privately published by members of the squadron, 1922.

Holley, I. B., Jr. *Ideas and Weapons.* New Haven: Yale University Press, 1953.

Kenney, George C. *History of the 91st Aero Squadron, Air Service, U.S.A.* Koblenz: Gebruder Breuer, 1919.

Knappen, Theodore M. *Wings of War.* New York: G. P. Putnam's Sons, 1920.

La Guardia, Fiorello H. *The Making of an Insurgent: An Autobiography: 1882–1919.* Philadelphia: J. B. Lippincott Co., 1948.

Levine, Isaac D. *Mitchell, Pioneer of Air Power.* New York: Duell, Sloan & Pearce, 1943.

Lewis, Cecil. *Sagittarius Rising.* New York: Harcourt, Brace & Co., 1936.

Lewis, Peter M. *Squadron Histories: R.F.C., R.N.A.F., and R.A.F., 1912–1959.* London: Putnam, 1959.

McConnell, James R. *Flying for France.* Garden City, N.Y.: Doubleday, Page & Co., 1917.

Mann, Arthur. *La Guardia, a Fighter Against His Times,* 2 vols. New York: J. B. Lippincott, 1959.

Marshall, S. L. A. (narrator). *American Heritage History of World War I.* New York: American Heritage Publishing Co., 1964.

Mason, Herbert Malloy. *The Lafayette Escadrille.* New York: Random House, 1964.

Mitchell, William. *Memoirs of World War I.* New York: Random House, 1960.

Mixter, G. W., and Emmons, H. H. *United States Army Aircraft Production Facts.* Washington, D.C.: Government Printing Office, 1919.

Morse, Daniel P. *The History of the 50th Aero Squadron.* New York: Blanchard Press, 1920.

Musciano, Walter A. *Eagles of the Black Cross.* New York: Obolensky, 1965.

Nordhoff, Charles B., and Hall, James Norman. *Falcons of France.* Boston: Little, Brown & Co., 1929.

Nowarra, H. J., and Brown, Kimbrough. *Von Richthofen and the "Flying Circus."* Letchworth, Herts, England: Harleyford Publications, Ltd., 1958.

Oughton, Frederick. *The Aces.* New York: G. P. Putnam's Sons, 1960.

Ovitt, Spalding West. *Balloon Section of the American Expeditionary Forces.* New Haven: Tuttle, Morehouse & Taylor Co., 1919.

Palmer, Frederick. *Newton D. Baker: America At War,* 2 vols. New York: Dodd, Mead & Co., 1931.

Parsons, Edwin C. *I Flew With the Lafayette Escadrille.* Indianapolis: E. C. Seale & Co., 1963.

Patrick, Mason M. *The United States in the Air*. Garden City, N.Y.: Doubleday, Doran, 1928.

Pershing, John Joseph. *My Experiences in the World War*, 2 vols. New York: Frederick A. Stokes Co., 1931.

Poolman, Kenneth. *Zeppelins Over England*. London: Evans Bros., 1960.

Raleigh, Walter, and Jones, H. A. *The War in the Air*, 6 vols. Oxford: Clarendon Press, 1922–37.

Reynolds, Quentin. *They Fought for the Sky*. New York: Rinehart & Co., 1957.

Richards, George B. (compiler). *War Diary and Letters of John Francisco Richards II, 1917–1918*. Kansas City, Mo.: Lechtman Printing Co., 1925.

Rickenbacker, Edward V. *Fighting the Flying Circus*. New York: Frederick A. Stokes Co., 1919.

Roberts, E. M. *A Flying Fighter: An American Above the Lines in France*. New York: Harper, 1918.

Robertson, Bruce (ed.). *Air Aces of the 1914–1918 War*. Letchfield, Herts, England: Harleyford Publications, Ltd., 1959.

Roosevelt, Quentin. *Quentin Roosevelt: A Sketch with Letters*. New York: Charles Scribner's Sons, 1921.

Russell, William Muir. *An American Aviator in the Great War, 1917–1918*. Detroit, Mich.: Saturday Night Press, 1919.

Stringer, Henry R. (ed.). *Heroes All!* Washington, D.C.: Fassett Publishing Co., 1919.

Sweetser, Arthur W. *The American Air Service*. New York: D. Appleton, 1919.

Taylor, John W. R. *C.F.S. Birthplace of Air Power*. London: Putnam, 1958.

Taylor, W. P., and Irvin, F. L. (compilers). *History of the 148th Aero Squadron*. Lancaster, S.C.: Tri-County Publishing Co., 1957.

Toulmin, H. A. *Air Service, American Expeditionary Force, 1918*. New York: D. Van Nostrand Co., 1927.

Turnbull, Archibald D., and Lord, Clifford L. *History of United States Naval Aviation*. New Haven: Yale University Press, 1949.

Whitehouse, Arch. *Legion of the Lafayette*. Garden City, N.Y.: Doubleday & Co., 1962.

————. *Decisive Air Battles of the First World War*. New York: Duell, Sloan & Pearce, 1963.

————. *Years of the War Birds*. Garden City, N.Y.: Doubleday & Co., 1960.

Wintringham, Tom. *The Story of Weapons and Tactics from Troy to Stalingrad*. Boston: Houghton Mifflin Co., 1943.

Woodhouse, Henry. *Textbook of Military Aeronautics*. New York: Century Co., 1918.

ARTICLES

"Air Service, A.E.F. and the Air War in France," *Air Force Magazine*, August, 1957, 101–107.

Atkinson, J. L. Boone. "Italian Influence on the Origins of the American Concept of Strategic Bombardment," *Air Power Historian,* IV (July, 1957), 141–49.

Barrett, William E. "The Squadron the World Forgot," *Cavalier,* XI (March, 1961), 22–26, 54–57.

————. "The War Bird Who'll Never Die," *ibid.,* X (March, 1960), 30–36.

Bates, Harry F. "Colonel Hartney's Night Flight in a Camel," *Air Power Historian,* XI (October, 1964), 119–20.

Bingham, Hiram. "Building America's Air Army," *National Geographic Magazine,* XXXIII (January, 1918), 48–86.

Bourjaily, Vance. "Memoirs of an Ace," *Esquire,* LXII (August, 1964), 29–32.

Brewer, Leighton. "How It Was," *Cross and Cockade Journal,* III (Spring, 1962), 69.

Brooks, Arthur Raymond. "22nd Aero Squadron," *ibid.,* IV (Summer, 1963), 109–12.

Contact. "Making a Pilot," *Blackwood's Magazine,* CCIII (March, 1918), 289–301.

Earle, Edward Mead. "The Influence of Air Power," *Yale Review,* XXXV (Summer, 1946), 577–93.

Flammer, Philip M. "Lufbery: Ace of the Lafayette Escadrille," *Air Power Historian,* VIII (January, 1961), 13–22.

Foulois, Benjamin D. "Early Flying Experiences," *Air Power Historian,* II (April, 1955), 17–35.

Frank, Sam H. "Organizing the U.S. Air Service—Developments in the United States," *Cross and Cockade Journal,* VI (Summer, 1965), 135–47.

————. "Organizing the U.S. Air Service. Part Two—Developments in Europe," *ibid.,* Autumn, 1965, 258–71.

Hart, Percival G. "Observations from a DH-4," *Cross and Cockade Journal,* II (Winter, 1961), 230–44.

Hauprich, N. H., *et al.* "German Jagdstaffeln and Jagdgeschwader Commanding Officers, 1916–1918," *Cross and Cockade Journal,* II (Autumn, 1961), 265–78.

Hennessy, Juliette A. "The Lafayette Escadrille—Past and Present," *Air Power Historian,* IV (July, 1957), 150–61.

Hood, R. T. "An Interview with Horace P. Wells," *Cross and Cockade Journal,* I (Winter, 1960), 86.

Hopper, Bruce C. "American Day Bombardment in World War I," *Air Power Historian,* IV (April, 1957), 87–97.

Hudson, James J. "Air Knight of the Ozarks: Captain Field E. Kindley," *American Aviation Historical Society Journal,* IV (Winter, 1959), 233–53.

————. "Captain Field E. Kindley: Arkansas' Air Ace of the First World War," *Arkansas Historical Quarterly,* XVIII (Summer, 1959), 3–31.

Kirschner, Frederic P. "Aerial Armament of WW I," *Cross and Cockade Journal,* V (Spring, 1964), 69–73.

————. "A Thumbnail Sketch of the 24th," *ibid.,* 53–68.

Lahm, Frank P. "Early Flying Experiences," *Air Power Historian,* II (January, 1955), 1–10.

Lynch, A. J. "Interview with Leftenant Richmond Viall, 46 Squadron, RAF, 25 August 1961," *Cross and Cockade Journal,* II (Fall, 1961), 243–44.

McClendon, R. Earl. "The Rise of Air Power," *Current History,* XXVI (May, 1954), 276–83.

McGuire, Capt. Frank R. "Who Killed Von Richthofen?" *Cross and Cockade Journal,* IV (Summer, 1963), 159–66.

"Making Aviators to Man Uncle Sam's Big Air-Fleet," *The Literary Digest,* XXII (January, 1918), 56–60.

Maurer, Maurer. "Another Victory for Rickenbacker," *Air Power Historian,* VII (April, 1960), 117–24.

————. "Flying with Fiorello: The U.S. Air Service in Italy," *ibid.,* XI (October, 1964), 113–18.

"The Men and the Machines, Part IV—World War I, Early Phases," *Air Power Historian,* IV (October, 1957), 192–206.

"The Men and the Machines, Part V—Air Operations in World War I," *ibid.,* V (January, 1958), 37–53.

Miller, Thomas G. (ed.). "Air Service Combat Organization," *Cross and Cockade Journal,* III (Spring, 1962), 1–6.

————. "Balloon Section, AEF," *ibid.,* 89–91.

————. "Casualties of A.E.F. Pursuit Aviation," *ibid.,* 34–36.

————. "Confirmed Victories of A.E.F. Pursuit Groups, 1918," *ibid.,* 43–60.

————. "Eyes of the Army: The Observation Corps," *ibid.,* 71–87.

————. "The Last Knighthood," *ibid.,* 24–33.

————. "Ordeal of the 1st Day Bombardment Group," *ibid.,* 6–12.

Mitchell, William. "The Air Service at St. Mihiel," *World's Work,* XXXVIII (August, 1919), 360–70.

————. "The Air Service at the Meuse-Argonne," *ibid.,* September, 1919, 552–60.

Moreira, George A. "Clifford Allsopp and the 11th Aero Squadron," *Cross and Cockade Journal,* II (Autumn, 1961), 179–93.

Oliver, Bennett. "Words from a Warbird: An Interview with 1st Lt. Bennett Oliver Conducted by Paul E. Parker, Jr.," *Cross and Cockade Journal,* II (Winter, 1961), 316–23.

Puglisi, William R. (ed.). "German Army Air Aces," *Cross and Cockade Journal,* III (Autumn, 1962), 216–27.

————. "The 27th Squadron's Black Day," *ibid.,* 229–39.

Ransom, Harry H. "Lord Trenchard, Architect of Air Power," *Air University Quarterly Review,* VIII (Summer, 1956), 59–67.

"Report of Aeronautical Commission, 15 August 1917," reproduced in *Air Power Historian,* VII (October, 1960), 223–32.

Rogge, Robert E. "A History of the 148th Aero Squadron," *Air Power Historian,* IX (July, 1962), 151–65.

Rust, Kenn. " 'Aces and Hawks,' History of the First Fighter Wing," *Air Power Historian,* IX (October, 1962), 213–24.

Sloan, James J. "The 148th American," *American Aviation Historical Society Journal,* IV (Winter, 1959), 253–64.

———. "The 12th Aero Squadron, Observation—Part I," *ibid.,* IX (Fall, 1964), 179–88.

———. "The 12th Aero Observation Squadron—Part II," *ibid.,* X (Spring, 1965), 45–51.

Sloan, John, and Hocutt, George. "The Real Italian Detachment—Transcription of a Tape Recorded Interview with Brigadier General Claude E. Duncan, U.S.A.F. (retired)," *Cross and Cockade Journal,* I (Summer, 1960), 43–52.

Tegler, John H. "The Humble Balloon: Brief History—Balloon Service, AEF," *Cross and Cockade Journal,* VI (Spring, 1965), 1–29.

"Two Boche Planes Felled by Yankees," *Stars and Stripes,* 19 April 1918, quoted in *Cross and Cockade Journal,* I (Spring, 1960), 54–55.

Tynan, John E. "U.S. Air Service Emerging from its Cradle," *Air Power Historian,* X (July, 1963), 85–89.

Whitehouse, Arch. "The Beginning of Tactical Aviation," *Air Power Historian,* V (April, 1958), 89–101.

Wills, Kelly, Jr. "History of the 213th," *Cross and Cockade Journal,* VI (Summer, 1965), 121–34.

———. "Richardson's Remembrances," *ibid.,* 103–20.

Winans, David R. "World War I Aircraft Fuels and Lubricating Oils," *Cross and Cockade Journal,* II (Autumn, 1961), 225–39.

Wynne, H. Hugh. "Escadrille Lafayette," *Cross and Cockade Journal,* II (Spring, 1961), 1–84.

———. "A Brief History of the 27th Aero Squadron—First Pursuit Group, AEF," *ibid.,* Summer, 1960. 13–15.

INDEX

325